Sociology for Social Workers

Second Edition

ANNE LLEWELLYN, LORRAINE AGU AND
DAVID MERCER

polity

The right of Anne Llewellyn, Lorraine Agu and David Mercer to be identified as Authors of this
Work has been asserted in accordance with the UK Copyright, Designs and Patents Act 1988.

First edition published in 2008 by Polity Press
This second edition first published in 2015 by Polity Press

Polity Press
65 Bridge Street
Cambridge CB2 1UR, UK

Polity Press
350 Main Street
Malden, MA 02148, USA

ISBN-13: 978-0-7456-6032-5
ISBN-13: 978-0-7456-6033-2 (pb)

A catalogue record for this book is available from the British Library.

Library of Congress Cataloging-in-Publication Data
Llewellyn, Anne.
  Sociology for social workers / Anne Llewellyn, Lorraine Agu, David
Mercer. -- 2nd edition.
     pages cm
  ISBN 978-0-7456-6032-5 (hardcover) -- ISBN 978-0-7456-6033-2
(papercover) 1. Sociology. 2. Social case work. I. Agu, Lorraine. II.
Mercer, David, 1957- III. Title.
  HM585.L58 2014
  361.3'2--dc23
                                            2014016836

Typeset in 9.5 on 12 pt Utopia
by Servis Filmsetting Ltd, Stockport, Cheshire
Printed and bound in Great Britain by Clays Ltd, St. Ives PLC

For further information on Polity, visit our website: politybooks.com

Contents

Acknowledgements

We would like to thank the anonymous reviewers for their helpful and constructive feedback at various stages in the development of this book, and Jonathan Skerrett for his enduring support, patience and advice. We also thank various cohorts of social work students whom we have tried various exercises out on and colleagues who have helped us to formulate ideas. Above all, we extend our gratitude to our respective partners, children and close friends for their love and support.

Introduction

Our own experiences are shaped by dominant political and institutional practices and discourses. However, we need to find ways that allow us to look outside our own experience in order to see how the people we work with view their circumstances. Sociology offers some important social theories which help us to do this and provides explanations and critiques of human behaviour, social action and interaction and the institutions and structures of society (Oak, 2009). The fact that social workers are concerned with social change and problem solving is precisely why sociological theories are so important to social workers (Thompson, 2005). An exploration of the riots in Britain in 2011 can help us to see some of the key issues that sociological theories are concerned with.

A scene of the 2011 London riots, Woolwich Powis Street. (© Greg Brummel/Flickr)

In Hackney, a multi-ethnic area in east London, close to the site of next year's Olympic Games, hooded youths set fire to rubbish bins and pushed them down a street toward police, while hurling bottles and bricks.

Many laughed as they ran back when police charged them.

In a street thick with smoke, looters smashed their way into a local shop, stealing whisky and beer. One man grabbed a packet of cereal, another ran off laughing with four bottles of whisky. (Ambrogi and Abbas, 2011)

These riots of August 2011 were seen as the worst outbreak of mass violence for a generation (*Guardian* and London School of Economics, 2011), and many, including academics, journalists and politicians, have sought to understand and analyse what caused them, how they expanded across the UK, how the police responded to them and what lessons can be learned (Clarke, 2011; *Guardian* and London School of Economics, 2011; Nwabuzo, 2012). Sociologists have also contributed to this debate (Bristow, 2013), arguing that the role of sociology is to 'seek to explain – not explain away – these events' (Brewer and Wollman, 2011). They look to key sociological issues such as social inequality, poverty and deprivation, racism and ethnic conflict, youth unemployment, and social institutions such as the police and criminal justice systems and the education system, to find explanations for the riots and to inform evidence-based solutions. Sociology does not provide solutions to social problems per se, but sociological theories provide explanations that can inform practitioners and policy makers. The purpose of this book is therefore to introduce you to a range of theories that can help you to understand the social context of social work practice and service user experiences. This social context is complex as social workers work with a vast range of service user groups, whose lives are affected by a myriad of social factors. For ease of reading, we have divided the book into chapters that address different social factors or service user groups, but in reality these will often overlap.

This book is intended as a foundational text, introducing social work students to sociology and the ways that sociological theories and perspectives can contribute to our understanding of the history, role and purpose of social work within contemporary British society. Social work does not operate in a vacuum, but is a 'socially constructed phenomenon . . . defined by the economic, social and cultural conditions in which it takes place' (Payne, 2005: 7). It is therefore important that social workers understand the social conditions and processes within which they operate, and sociology offers theories to understand these processes and the nature of the social world that we inhabit. It can help us to understand the world that we are part of through the exploration of how institutions are structured, how power is distributed and impacts on individuals, and how individuals interact and make sense of social situations.

Is sociology common sense?

One prevalent view of sociology is that it is just common sense and that you do not need theories in order to explain the social world. However, the examples above demonstrate that a greater understanding and analysis can be developed through sociological inquiry, and the theories that will be developed throughout this book will show how the world can be explained from different perspectives, to help to develop a richer understanding of our lives and those of the individuals with whom we come into contact in practice. Howe (1992) stresses the importance of understanding theory to inform social work practice and explores the inter-relationships between different theories that can help to explain human activity and experiences.

Sociology therefore is not a single discipline offering one set of theories, but a complex range of theories offering explanations and understandings from different perspectives. No one theory is more valid than others, but all can contribute to our

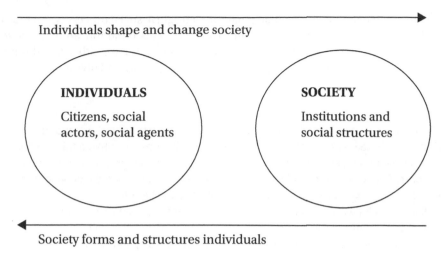

Individuals shape and change society

Society forms and structures individuals

Figure i.1 Diagrammatic representation of the relationship between individuals and social structures.

understanding of the social world. In its simplest form, we can say that sociology can help us to understand individuals through the ways in which the structures of society shape individual experiences and through exploring individual experiences based on interactions with others (e.g. patriarchy – see Chapter 3; race and ethnicity – see Chapter 4; Figure i.1). Sociology therefore helps us to explain social relationships and the interpretations of social situations.

In their day-to-day work, social workers encounter some of the most vulnerable and marginalized people and groups in society, and sociology helps us to explore and explain the nature of inequality in society and the construction of disadvantage and advantage and helps to inform 'anti-oppressive practice' and 'anti-discriminatory practice' (Oak, 2009). It follows that, if we are concerned with the relationship between the individual and society, then helping people to problem-solve will also involve structures, institutions and systems within society.

Thompson (2005) has argued that social work is sometimes viewed by society as a profession that mops up society's problems and deals with the failings of social policies in the areas of education, crime, health, housing and income maintenance. This relates to work with a variety of user groups who experience social policy changes and trends: for example, work with the unemployed, the poor, the homeless, the mentally ill or the disabled. This can be seen to reflect the early origins of social work, where philanthropy was concerned with the 'fallout' from nineteenth-century economic and political conditions (Horner, 2013). Although this may be viewed as a little simplistic for the complexities of contemporary social work, in that it does not necessarily reflect the whole range of roles of the social worker, it is a useful starting point for a discussion of the fact that social workers are often engaged with individuals, groups and communities who suffer some form of social disadvantage.

The fact that the title 'social worker' starts with 'social' is not coincidental (Thompson, 2005). The nature of social work is fundamentally located in and influenced by social factors, processes and ideas in the following ways:

- Many problems and disadvantages have their origin in social processes. For example, poverty and disadvantage result from processes of stratification. Societies are not just divided into two opposing parts, where you are either one thing or another, but are made up of a plurality of different groups and divisions.

Case study

Alison, aged 26, has been diagnosed with an autistic spectrum disorder and finds it difficult to socialize and communicate with others. She has never had a full-time job, and is reliant on benefits. Until recently, she lived with her parents, but now lives in supported living accommodation. Although she enjoys having some independence, she does get upset when local youths taunt her and call her names.

If we unpick this case study, we can see a number of social processes and factors that impact on Alison's life. Her lack of employment and reliance on benefits will place her at the lower end of the income stratification scale, and is likely to lead to poverty and material disadvantage (see Chapter 2). Her gender may influence her social position, in a society that is structured around a male breadwinner model and male power (see Chapter 3), and her disability will impact within a society that is structured around able-bodiedness (see Chapter 5). There are other social factors that may also be relevant for determining Alison's experiences, such as sexuality (see Chapter 6) and ethnicity (see Chapter 4).

- The solutions to individual problems may lie within wider social and community processes. Using the case study above, we can see that Alison's material disadvantage is not of her own making, but is related to wider social processes within the labour market. Similarly, her feelings of distress are a result of practices within the wider community, which may be related to a culture of disablism. Thus, rather than just helping Alison to cope with the taunts, a longer-term solution would be to challenge these disablist attitudes and practices.
- Individual behaviours and experiences do not operate in a vacuum, but are located within wider social contexts. Social and structural processes influence individual decisions and behaviours. Thus Alison may feel disempowered in applying for a job, as she has been influenced rough her experiences of the education system, the labour market and social attitudes to her. Furthermore, individual actions and experiences may be related to processes of interaction. Identity is an important concept in sociology and is shaped through our interactions with others (see below).
- Social work itself does not operate within a vacuum, but is located within the wider social organization and is impacted on by social, economic and political factors and sets of dominant ideas. An exploration of the history of social work demonstrates how it has changed in relation to changing ideas about the way in which societies manage the welfare of vulnerable citizens (see, e.g., Blewett et al., 2007; White, 2008).

Social work is a contested area and has changed and evolved in relation to the wider political, economic, policy and social context. There have been specific times in history where different theoretical perspectives have dominated the construction of social work knowledge (see chapters throughout the book). However, the significance of a sociological understanding for social work is reflected by the QAA Benchmarks, which, alongside Health Care Professions Council (HCPC) and The College of Social Work (TCSW) requirements, offer a prescribed curriculum for social work education and training. The importance of sociology for social workers can be seen in the following HCPC statements about the knowledge base of social work, which require social workers to have an understanding of:

- the impact of injustice, social inequalities, policies and other issues which affect the demand for social work services;
- the relevance of sociological perspectives to understanding societal and structural influences on human behaviour.

(Health Care Professions Council, 2012)

Sociology can also help social workers to think critically, reflecting on the context of practice and challenging the processes that lead to disadvantage and oppression. Social work and the social context within which it operates are dynamic activities and processes, and therefore are constantly changing. A good understanding of sociology can help social workers to understand this changing context as well as helping to develop critical reflective skills to facilitate problem solving and decision-making in practice (Wilkins and Boahen, 2013). The policies and case studies that are used as illustrations throughout this book demonstrate how sociology can help us to understand the social context of social work practice and the individual and structural influence on and impact of social change.

Sociological theory is not static, but is constantly adapting and developing in order to explain social change and individuals' responses to it, as well as offering different interpretations of the social world. Contemporary theories of sociology are often grouped under the term 'critical sociology' and explore key concepts such as social disadvantage, discrimination and prejudice, power and control, and citizenship and identity, which correspond to important social work values of social justice, empowerment and anti-oppressive practice (Oak, 2009). In summary, sociological perspectives in social work are useful for understanding the role of social work in society by helping us to understand:

- how and why social work developed as a profession
- the purpose of social work in society and the role and function of social work
- the nature of social problems that social workers may encounter
- social divisions, inequality and discrimination and the contribution of sociological perspectives in the development of anti-oppressive practice.

These key sociological areas will be explored in more depth throughout the book in relation to specific service user groups, social institutions and processes that social workers will encounter in their professional practice. The book is divided into twelve chapters, although many of the areas overlap, and you will see that issues are cross-referenced throughout the book. Chapter 1 will provide a more in-depth overview of key sociological theories, which will be developed in context in the subsequent chapters. Each chapter will be structured to explore the following sociological perspectives:

- structural theories
- social action theories

- critical sociology
- global sociology.

You will also find a number of exercises and case studies that will help you to understand the theories and perspectives, but will also help you to apply these theories and perspectives to different areas of social work practice. Links will be provided throughout the chapters for you to develop your understanding beyond foundational level, and questions for discussion can be found at the end of each chapter to summarize the debates and to help with your further exploration of sociology. In addition, you will find annotated bibliographies to guide your reading and help you to explore some of the key theories in more depth.

1 What Is Sociology?

Introduction

This opening chapter outlines some of the key sociological themes which permeate the rest of the book. Key issues and themes in this chapter help us explore the nature of sociology and understand, analyse and critically reflect on the nature of social work practice.

> **The key issues that will be explored in this chapter are:**
>
> - the nature of sociology, identifying broad perspectives within the discipline
> - structural theories, including consensus and conflict theories
> - social action theories, including social interactionism
> - an introduction to critical sociology, including feminist and anti-racist perspectives
> - issues in relation to social identity, the body and consumerism.

> **By the end of this chapter, you should be able to:**
>
> - discuss some key sociological theories
> - distinguish between structural theories and social action theories
> - understand the changing nature of sociology and explain how critical sociology can help us understand a plurality of viewpoints
> - explain the importance of identity to individuals and groups.

Sociology offers a view of the world that we live in and helps us to explain and predict social situations, behaviours and actions. Mills (1959) used the term 'the sociological imagination' to demonstrate how sociological theories help us to see familiar situations in new ways or give us insights into unfamiliar situations and social worlds.

Exercise: the social world

- In small groups, discuss what you mean by the social world.
- How does this differ from the natural world? (See Table 1.1.)
- Compare your list with other groups. Are there common elements? Is the social world made up of individuals and institutions? What is the relationship between these different elements?

Table 1.1 *Differences between the natural and social world*

	Natural sciences (natural world)	Social sciences (social world)
Focus	The world of nature	Human behaviours; social divisions and social constructions; social interactions
Purpose	To explain and predict events in the natural world	To explain and understand the social world and human behaviours
Examples	Biology Physics Geology Chemistry	Sociology Psychology Politics Economics Anthropology

Source: Adapted from Henslin (2010)

Sociology helps us to explain social relationships and individual interpretations of social situations. However, there are also clear inter-relations between sociological theories and some psychological theories that explain human growth and development from *micro* and *macro* perspectives. In particular there are similarities between sociological perspectives and ecological theories. For example, Bronfenbrenner's (1979) ecological perspective on human development discusses the influence of the immediate micro world of the family and local community and the macro world of the national picture – policies, approaches and laws. This links to sociology, and the theories are complementary rather than repetitive.

Micro the immediate influences that impact on an individual.

Macro larger-scale influences such as politics, structures of society.

Political theory is also related to sociological perspectives. The 'macro' world that Bronfenbrenner describes impacts on society through the 'top-down' effect of national policies, which are driven by political ideologies in a given period. Giddens (2013) discusses how political actions and behaviours have been of interest to sociologists in terms of how they shape people's lives and experiences. However, political trends are both 'top-down' and 'bottom-up'. For example, the student demonstrations in London against education cuts and the introduction of tuition fees were an attempt to influence politicians to change these policies. The interaction between politics and society is therefore fundamental to sociological understanding.

The discipline of sociology is important for understanding people's social location and how this impacts on their experiences. Social location refers to people's position in society and is influenced by important factors such as occupation, income, health, education, gender, age, race and ethnicity, and sexuality (Macionis and Plummer, 2012). These provide important social contexts which shape people's experiences and how they relate to others. The sets of ideas in society that contextualize experiences

Student protests in Parliament Square, London, 2010. (© Bob Bob/Flickr)

are derived from structures of power and dominance. For example, the patriarchal organization of society impacts on the nature of women's experiences, both within the home and within the paid labour market (Andersen, 2008; see also Chapter 3), whilst institutional racism within the criminal justice system has impacted on the experiences of black people in their encounters with the police, the judiciary and the prison system (Bowling and Phillips, 2002; see also Chapter 4).

Thus social contexts are not random, but are structured and patterned. This also means that they are not independent and static, but are constantly modified by human interactions and actions, a process referred to as structuration.

Historical development of the discipline of sociology

The discipline of sociology can be traced back to a historical period known as the *Enlightenment*, which signalled a shift in thinking and the way in which society was understood. Prior to the Enlightenment, religious teachings were the dominant set of ideas which helped people to make sense of their worlds. During the Enlightenment, religious doctrine was increasingly replaced with critical and rational thinking. Human behaviour and society came to be understood in a more *objective* and systematic way and the discipline of sociology grew within this overall context (Macionis and Plummer, 2012).

Auguste Comte (1798–1857) was the first person to use the term 'sociology' and is viewed as the founding father of the discipline. Comte was concerned to explain the impact of rapid *industrialization* and *urbanization*, as well as the French

Enlightenment a philosophical period of the eighteenth century based on notions of progress, reason and rationality, leading to an emphasis on human control and a decrease in religious dogma as a way of understanding the social world.

Objective a way of seeing the world based on facts rather than feelings or perceptions.

Industrialization methods of production within manufacturing and agriculture. A region, nation or culture becomes more economically dependent on manufacturing than on traditional methods of farming.

Urbanization growth of towns and cities. This particularly relates to economic changes in industry from the nineteenth century onwards. This has led to a vast growth in cities within modern societies. In the nineteenth century, manufacturing and production moved to large-scale factories in urban environments.

Positivism the science of sociology, where only observable and measurable behaviours should be studied.

Empiricism a view of research which emphasizes factual inquiry through the collection of data based on facts and observation as opposed to reflection and theoretical inquiry.

Functionalism dominated sociological thinking until the 1960s and stresses the importance of the 'functional fit' of the institutions that make up society and the importance of socialization of society's norms and values in order to promote a consensus.

Collective consciousness associated with Durkheim to mean shared moral values derived from religion or from the education system.

Revolution, on individual lives. However, he took a particular perspective: that is, that the rules and functioning of the social world could be explained objectively by observation of known facts in the same way that the natural sciences explained the physical world. This approach has been termed *positivism*. Comte observed society and drew conclusions, seeing this as the key to social reform. He believed that if society and social processes can be understood through application of scientific methods of experimentation and observation (*empiricism*), then people are able to objectively observe the social context and make changes (Giddens, 2013).

Theoretical perspectives in sociology

Comte's contribution is important, as a number of perspectives have developed from his original observations which help to inform social work practice. These can be broadly defined as:

- functionalism, which explains society as a set of systems with functions that complement each other – roles and functions are important for equilibrium and the maintenance of the status quo within this theory
- conflict theory, which explains the social world in terms of the conflicts and tensions between certain groups
- social action theories, which are a set of theories that explain the social world from the subjective perspective of individual perceptions and experiences.

Functionalism

Émile Durkheim (1858-1917) was heavily influenced by Comte's views, and saw society as being made up of a set of inter-related components that could be objectively studied. This is known as the *functionalist* perspective, where society is not just about the interests and actions of individuals but is the sum of these inter-dependent parts. As a functionalist, Durkheim believed that in order for societies to maintain cohesion and stability, these components should operate in conjunction with each other (O'Byrne, 2011). Durkheim was influenced by the French Revolution, and, as such, was particularly interested in how social solidarity was achieved. He further argued that individuals are influenced by the structures and institutions of society to develop a *collective consciousness*. This collective consciousness is based on collective norms of society; it promotes expectations for acceptable behaviour and places restraints on deviant behaviour (O'Byrne, 2011).

Durkheim believed that societies were consensual, with shared belief and value systems and a moral cohesion. However, for him, this cohesion did not denote a static society, but one that is able to collectively adapt to change in order to maintain equilibrium. Equilibrium and the maintenance of the status quo are important concepts within the functionalist perspective, with individuals performing roles and functions in order to contribute to the collective whole (Macionis and Plummer, 2012).

Durkheim's theories were influential in 1960s sociology, but still have some resonance in understanding today's social processes and problems. The functionalist perspective of role differentiation remains central to the organization of the labour market and is reflected in hierarchies of status and income levels (Edgell, 2006; see Chapter 2). Education, training and accreditation are important elements of this differentiation, and this can be seen in social work developments which have established the roles of social workers. For example, in England and Wales, the Central Council for Education and Training in Social Work (CCETSW) was established in the Health Visiting and Social Work (Training) Act (1962). This body, which was formed in 1971, unified the profession and established a centralized regulatory framework for the education and practice of social work with a key role for higher education institutions in the development and delivery of knowledge and skills for practice (Sheldon and MacDonald, 2009). In 2003, social work became an all-graduate profession, with further reforms following the report of the Social Work Taskforce in 2010. The knowledge, skills and competencies for social work practice are now clearly set out in the Health Care Professions Council's (2012) Standards for Occupational Proficiency for Social Workers and The College of Social Work's (2012a) Professional Capabilities Framework, firmly establishing the key functions of social workers within contemporary society. These are further established in the 2014 guidance on the roles and functions of social workers, produced by The College of Social Work (College of Social Work, 2014).

Welfare professionals such as social workers are seen as important players in the maintenance of social equilibrium. The activity of early social work was characterized by individual intervention based on the principles of *normalization* and *moralization*. The first principle centred on the belief that vulnerable people should be encouraged to live a life that was as near to normal as was possible. Moralization was based on the belief that Christian values and morals of self-reliance, hard work and clean living should be promoted, and from this emerged concepts of the deserving and undeserving poor. The deserving poor were those who were seen to be helping themselves or who were experiencing difficulties through no fault of their own, whilst the undeserving poor were seen as morally deficient (Fraser, 1984). These principles can be seen today in interventions such as the Troubled Families agenda, where social workers have a key role to play in reversing processes of social disadvantage and promoting the norms of society (Churchill, 2013; see also Chapter 8).

> **Normalization** process by which groups of people can be integrated into the usual and typical life of the majority of the community.
>
> **Moralization** process by which governing rules or behaviours are promoted as the common standards, in the interests of society.

Like Comte, Durkheim believed that social facts can be studied in a scientific and objective way and that this objectivity transcends individual behaviour. Some social facts he saw as normal and necessary for a healthy society, whereas others he saw as unhealthy and pathological, creating disharmony and disequilibrium. A good example of his views can be seen in his study of suicide (1952, originally published in 1897). Durkheim studied rates of suicide and concluded that individuals were more likely to commit suicide if they were dislocated from the collective. This he termed *anomie*, a state of not belonging to the collective organization.

Anomie   term used by Durkheim to describe a state of disorganization in modern society that leaves individuals without structure or norms to follow. Durkheim used this term to describe the feelings of despair and helplessness that can lead to suicidal thoughts and tendencies.

Although the causes of suicide in contemporary society are multiple and complex, research demonstrates that Durkheim's views of anomie still have some relevance. A UK government report on preventing suicide in England emphasizes the importance of people having a sense of belonging within society, stating that: 'Suicides are not inevitable. An inclusive society that avoids marginalising individuals and which supports people at times of personal crisis will help prevent suicides' (HM Government, 2014: 9).

Talcott Parsons (1902–79) further contributed to the theory of structural functionalism through his theory of the social system. Parsons' contribution to sociological thinking is concerned with how the elements of society interlock to form a network of systems with shared values, thus providing a stable and coherent society. Within his theory, there are clearly defined roles and role expectations which govern institutions and individuals (Giddens, 2013). Parsons identifies four sub-systems (or institutions) which contribute to the maintenance of the whole and represent different structural elements of society:

1   the economic system, providing and distributing economic resources to individuals and institutions
2   the political system, governing individuals and forming collective goals
3   kinship institutions, providing an important environment for socialization into a shared value system of accepted norms and behaviours
4   community and cultural institutions (e.g. religious, education and mass media), integrating various elements of society as well as preventing social isolation and contributing to a collective consciousness.

The following statements from The College of Social Work's Professional Capabilities Framework demonstrate the relevance of these sub-systems for social work practice.

- Understand how an individual's identity is informed by factors such as culture, economic status, family composition, life experiences and characteristics, and take account of these to understand their experiences, questioning assumptions where necessary

- Recognise how the development of community resources, groups and networks enhance outcomes for individuals

- Recognise that social work operates within, and responds to, changing economic, social, political and organizational contexts.

(College of Social Work, 2012a)

Social stratification   term used to describe and discuss the structure of groups within societies. It is normally applied to inequalities within society. In modern societies, this is based on wealth, power and opportunities.

Functionalists also see *social stratification* as an important element of society, and in societies such as the industrialized West, where stratification is an important aspect of a complex division of labour, the stratified system is seen as a set of inter-dependent and cooperative groups (Macionis and Plummer, 2012). Power is derived from the fact that society places particular value on certain traits/attributes, and therefore individuals who possess those traits are seen to have greater status. Thus, social inequality and relative disadvantage are necessary elements for the functioning of society. Whilst Parsons acknowledges that there may be some conflict between those who are advantaged and those who are relatively disadvantaged, this is kept in check by the pursuit of collective goals. An example of this is the fordist approach to labour production, where the task of building a car, for example, is broken down into different parts, with each individual in the process having a specific role related to a set of skills (Thompson, 1989). A similar process is argued to operate in social work, where the social work task is broken down into component parts and distributed within hierarchies of skill, knowledge and status (Harris, 1998). For example, Samuel (2011) argued that non-qualified staff are carrying out an increasing percentage of social work tasks, such as initial assessments, so that social workers can concentrate on more complex cases, such as safeguarding. Although we may debate the desirability of this, this does demonstrate the differentiation of tasks and the nature of the skill mix in the pursuit of collective goals.

Within functionalism, **social rituals** play a significant role in promoting a sense of communal cohesion. Durkheim saw religion as an important social institution in this respect. He studied traditional, small-scale societies and argued that religious symbols represent the shared values and ideals of the community (Callinicos, 1999). Thus the collective rituals of religious worship help reaffirm social cohesion and solidarity. For Durkheim, collective social rituals also feature as an essential part of social responses to life transitions: births, marriages and deaths. According to Van Gennep, social rites and rituals are important for the smooth running of society, as they offer a process by which individuals may make the transition into their new social role, and thus may maintain the equilibrium of society.

Exercise: transitions and social rituals

Think about the social rituals that people may engage with in contemporary society in order to symbolize the transition into a particular group (such as starting school, getting married).

Conflict theory

In contrast to the functionalist theories of equilibrium and collective goals, conflict theories see society as characterized by inherent tensions and conflicts between different groups within the hierarchies. The earliest conflict theories are associated with **Karl Marx (1818–83)**, whose theories explore the changing nature of industrial capitalism in the nineteenth century – a period in which there was a shift in the nature of economic and social relations, from a society based on feudal principles, to one that was based on the notion of waged labour.

Marx saw society as being based on a social division into two classes, the first of which he defines as the *bourgeoisie*, a relatively small group who own the means of production

Bourgeoisie the name Marx gave to the dominant class who own the means of production in capitalism and have an invested interest in preserving the capitalist status quo.

Proletariat the term used by Marxist theorists to describe the working class in capitalist societies.

Surplus value a Marxist term referring to the extraction of profit, as wages are below the price at which one sells goods. Thus there is a gap between what the individual receives in wages and the production and sale of goods in capitalist society.

(traditionally, factories, raw materials, tools) and who have control over the process of production. The second group is the *proletariat*, who are a much larger group of workers, who do not own anything except their own labour power, which they sell to gain wages. Within capitalist society, Marx argues that the bourgeoisie are motivated by profit accumulation, and therefore workers produce more than is actually required in order to create a *surplus value* (O'Byrne, 2011). The bourgeoisie can make enough money to cover capital and labour costs from the sale of a percentage of the goods, and the remaining percentage is sold for profit. This relationship is based on exploitation of the workers, which is necessary for the accumulation of profit. For Marx, power was concentrated in the hands of the bourgeoisie, and social disadvantage resulted from the relations of economic production and the exploitation of the proletariat. In addition, Marx believed the proletariat became alienated from the processes of production through the fragmentation of tasks (O'Byrne, 2011).

Like Durkheim, Marx believed that religion was an important institution of society, promoting social values and morals. The values and morals of society were created by human beings, but then projected onto the gods, and thus came to be seen as alien from human beings. Marx viewed religion as the 'opium of the masses', as people accepted the sufferings and hardships of life as they pursued the promises and values of the afterlife, which were an important element of Protestantism. Thus, the social injustices and oppressions that were created through the capitalist organization of society were justified by the social control of religion via doctrines such as 'the meek shall inherit the earth'.

The Marxist vision was that the relationship between the proletariat and the bourgeoisie was based on conflict, and that once the proletariat realized that the bourgeoisie would only ever make concessions to them within the existing capitalist structure, they would rise up and revolt against the system of production, regaining control for themselves. Thus Marx believed that societal change would occur through proletariat revolution rather than through the evolution of social processes. Within this theory the notion of *class consciousness* is an important concept, whereby the different classes develop their own ideology (or set of ideas) which is collectively shared throughout the class. Thus Marx believed that the proletariat would develop their own ideologies and overthrow the ruling bourgeoisie in order to create a socialist society based on a fairer distribution of power and resources (O'Byrne, 2011).

Class consciousness Marxist theory relating to an awareness of one's own class position. This assumes shared values and common interests within classes, which can result in division and conflict between classes.

Since Marx developed his theory, other writers have built upon this in order to explain the increasing social divisions of modern society (Bidet and Kouvelakis, 2009). It can be argued that, throughout the twentieth century and continuing into the present, a society made up of two opposing classes has been replaced by a much more complex set of groups, although it remains dominated by a ruling elite. In particular, attention has been addressed to the development of an intermediary group of workers, known as welfare professionals, heralded by developments in the welfare state (these include social workers, teachers, doctors and nurses). Writers such as Navarro (1976) have argued that these welfare professionals serve the ruling elite by ameliorating the *diswelfares* created by the capitalist organization, in order to protect the dominance of the establishment (ruling elite) (Titmuss, 1967). Welfare is therefore used as a concession to individuals, so that they believe that the state is providing for them, in order to divert attention from the structural factors which create the social divisions and exploitations. Thus the status quo of capitalist organization is maintained.

> **Diswelfares** Titmuss used the term to demonstrate that welfare provisions may only partially compensate for the social inequalities and disservices created in society

Although some have argued that Marxism has not stood the test of time, as the predicted revolution has not occurred, Wright (1997) would argue that the theory retains contemporary relevance, in that society remains based on social divisions and continued exploitation. A good example of this is the use of sweatshop labour, particularly within the Global South by multinationals, who pay minimal wages to workers in the pursuit of greater profits (Engler, 2006). (See below for discussion of the impact of globalization.) Income and conditions can be seen as comparable here to those of Western industrialized countries in the mid to late nineteenth century.

If we return to an exploration of the riots in parts of Britain in the summer of 2011, we can see that some explanations focus on the social disadvantage of many of those who were involved. As stated in the BBC News, 'The most comprehensive statistics published so far on people charged over the August riots in England reveal they were poorer, younger and of lower educational achievement than average' (BBC News, 2011). A Marxist analysis would see this as the product of the disservices created by capitalist organization, which has led to the social disadvantage of many of those who were charged. For example, more than a third of the young people who were charged in the courts had been excluded from school in the previous year and just over 10% had been permanently excluded (Home Office, 2011). A further indicator of poverty and disadvantage can be seen in the fact that 42% of those school-aged people who were charged were in receipt of free school meals, compared to a national average of 16% of pupils in maintained secondary schools (Home Office, 2011). Thus, one explanation for young people's involvement in the riots can be based on the social disadvantage that they experience and the fact that they do not feel that they have a stake in the future of the society.

Marxist theory may therefore be useful for social workers to critically reflect on the social divisions and sources of oppression and alienation for the vulnerable groups that they often come into contact with and is a theory that has influenced the radical social work movement (Ferguson and Woodward, 2009). Social work has always had a dichotomous relationship with care and control, but the radical social work movement, influenced by Marxist sociological critiques of class relations, power and professionalism, challenged the profession's contradictory relationship with the state. Radical critiques challenged social work's concern with individualistic and psychological explanations of social problems and demanded social workers work collectively with service users rather than being used as agents of state control (Dominelli, 2010).

Social action theories

An opposing set of sociological theories have developed which argue that the key to a true understanding of society must be derived not from objective measures, from institutions and structures, but from an understanding of individuals and their actions. These theories are collectively referred to as social action theories (Macionis and Plummer, 2012).

In social action theory, the meaning and interpretations of individuals are important in determining our understanding of the social world. By simply observing someone's behaviour or interactions, we put our own interpretations on the meaning behind the behaviour or interaction. However, if we ask people about their subjective interpretation of events, interactions and behaviours, we may get a different picture. Meanings and interpretations are based on *subjectivity*, and social interactions are important within this tradition. Thus social actions theories are much more concerned with how individuals make sense of their social world within the broader structures and systems of society (Jones, 2003).

Subjectivity an emotional or interpretative way of looking at things. This is contrasted with objective, fact-based and scientific approaches.

Max Weber (1864–1920) was one of the early theorists within the social action tradition. Weber agreed with structuralists that institutions, classes and groups were important elements of society, but he was also interested in the way in which individuals influenced and created the structural elements of society. Weber's fundamental view was that sociologists should seek to understand those whom they study and not place their own interpretations on behaviours and interactions. In Weber's view, ideas and values have as much impact on social change as economic conditions do (Giddens and Sutton, 2013).

Weber saw religion as being instrumental in the process of social change. Whereas both Durkheim and Marx viewed religion as an essentially conservative institution, Weber, from his study of worldwide religions, believed that religious affiliations and movements often produced radical social transformations. For example, the development of industrial capitalism was driven by Protestantism, and in particular by Calvinists. These Christians believed that human beings were carrying out God's work, and that material rewards gained through one's vocation were a sign of divine favour (Giddens and Sutton, 2013). Weber thought that religion provided moral guidance, and thus had a social control function. Therefore, sin and the concept of being rescued from sinfulness are important in terms of salvation and moralization.

Weber's notions of social action were more systematically developed through **symbolic interactionism**, which relates to a set of theories often attributed to the work of **George Herbert Mead (1863–1931)**. Mead argued that the thing that sets humans apart from other forms of life is our ability to use language and to develop meaning through the use of language. 'It is through the acquisition of language that we become human and social beings: the words we speak situate us in our gender and our class. Through language, we come to "know" who we are' (Sarup, 1996: 46). Language is a symbol which allows us to express individuality and to see ourselves as others see us. Mead distinguished between the *I* and the *Me* of self, whereby the I refers to the individual who thinks and acts, and the Me refers to the self as an object viewed by others. So, for example, if you are sitting in a meeting that you cannot see the relevance of, the I of self may feel like walking out and getting on with some other work, but the Me of self may decide to stay as you have been asked to attend by your practice educator and do not want to be seen as disobedient or conflictual.

Putting oneself in the place of the other is an important concept within symbolic interactionism. Goffman (1982) explained the concept in the sense that the social world is like a stage play, with different actors playing out different roles. These roles influence our relationships with others as behaviour is constructed and modified through our interactions. The social work role emphasizes the importance of a person-centred approach, hearing the views of the service user and understanding needs from their perspective (Sheldon and MacDonald, 2009). Thus, theories of symbolic interactionism are particularly relevant to social workers in enhancing their understanding of the behaviour of individuals, based on the way that they see the world and the competing interpretations of meanings (Jones, 2003).

Case study

Joshua, aged 15, has a history of arrests for anti-social behaviour, truancy and short-term exclusions from school. When you speak to him, he avoids eye contact, uses aggressive language and appears disinterested in any help that you are trying to offer.

If we interpret this objectively, we may conclude that Joshua is disaffected and disinterested, leading us to try to find solutions that we think may engage him. However, from Joshua's point of view, he may have few positive role models, and he may see himself in a negative light as he is constantly getting negative feedback from others. All his dealings with people in authority are based on punishment and have contributed to his negative self-perceptions. An understanding of the way that Joshua interprets his world can help us to engage him and collaborate in finding solutions and strategies (Boeck and Fleming, 2011). (See also the discussion of social capital in Chapter 8.)

The concept of **social identity** has developed from the symbolic interactionist school of thought and is fundamental to an understanding of people as individuals and how they construct their identities within their social context. Identity is about a sense of belonging to a social group, about the location of oneself within social relationships, and about a complex set of interactions with others. Identity can either signify sameness or can differentiate individuals in groups from other groups. But what do we mean by identity, and why is an understanding of identity important for social work practice?

Exercise: exploring your identity

- Answer the question, who am I?
- Write down the first 20 answers that come into your head.
- Answer as though you are answering the question for yourself rather than for someone else.
- Within your answer, you may have identified a number of factors and influences that have shaped your identity. Roles, attitudes, influences and physical appearance may all be factors that shape our identity as well as our location within society or a social context.

Figure 1.1 Overlapping identities in social work.

It could be argued that individuals do not have a singular and static identity, but have overlapping identities that are socially constructed within specific contexts. If we use social work as an example, we can see that an individual's personal identity will overlap with their professional identity and their identity within the organizational culture and structures where they work (Figure 1.1).

Professional identity may incorporate specific traits related to social work claims of uniqueness (see Chapter 12 for further discussion of professions and professionalism) and can be related to occupational standards and codes of professional practice. In addition the public perception of professional identity is constructed through media portrayals as well as individual experiences of social work practice. A literature review of media representations of social work and social workers found that the majority of media coverage was negative (Galilee, 2005), thus constructing a negative image and identity.

Language and the use and meaning of language are important within symbolic interactionism, and theorists within this tradition often focus on face-to-face interactions and the lived meaning of people's experiences. Language may also be an important symbolic identifier of identity, where the use of words and mannerisms denotes a sense of identity within a social group. Bernstein's theory of socio-linguistics (1975) explores the relationship that individuals have to language, and how this is linked to social structures of society, in particular the class structure (see Chapter 2). He argued that the working classes are much more likely to use language in a way which signifies solidarity with their contemporaries, and that language is used in a prescriptive, rather than an expressive, way. Thus, he argued, children from working-class backgrounds learn to use language in a format that reinforces cultural norms and differences. Children from middle-class families, however, have a different relationship with language, and are more likely to be encouraged to use language expressively, as a way of explaining and exploring individual actions. Thus Bernstein argued that there is a restricted and elaborated code used in language (the elaborated code tends to be used more by the middle classes and has greater universalistic meaning and understanding attached to it). The way that language is

Table 1.2 *Comparison of theoretical perspectives in sociology*

Perspective	Level of analysis (usual)	Focus of analysis	Key terms
Functionalism (or structured functionalism)	Macro – focuses on large-scale patterns of society	Relationships between different parts of society Degree to which these are functional (beneficial for society) or dysfunctional (detrimental to society)	Structure Functions Dysfunctions Equilibrium (or status quo)
Conflict theory	Macro – focuses on large-scale patterns of society	Struggle for resources by different groups Structures of power	Inequality Power Conflict Competition Exploitation
Social action theory	Micro – usually focuses on small-scale interactions	Face-to-face interactions How people use symbols to create meanings and social worlds	Symbols Interaction Meanings Definitions

developed is an important cultural signifier and may contribute towards social stratification and one's perception of others.

Table 1.2 provides a comparison of the three theoretical perspectives we have been discussing here: functionalism, conflict theory and social action theories. We will now turn to consider critiques of these views.

Critique of classical theories

Whilst these classical sociological theories are important for developing ways of exploring and understanding the social world, they have recently been subjected to a number of criticisms:

- Theories have largely been developed by white heterosexual males, and therefore have limited value for explaining and understanding other viewpoints.
- The views and understanding of other significant groups in society have been overlooked and under-represented (e.g. women, minority ethnic groups, lesbians and gays, people with disabilities).
- On occasions when different perspectives have been included, they have often been distorted by the white male heterosexual *hegemony*.

(Macionis and Plummer, 2012)

Hegemony concept associated with Antonio Gramsci to explain how the upper class maintains power through the subtle use of ideas to win the consent of subordinated groups. Ordinary people are led to believe that the prevailing existing order is somehow natural and normal.

Feminist critiques of sociology

Feminist theories arose out of the invisibility of women and gender issues within sociology. Oppression and inequalities in the patriarchal society led to the exclusion, marginalization and invisibility of women in society, and this too was reflected in early sociological analyses (Millett, 1977). The dominance of 'male-stream' sociology meant that women were ignored, both in terms of the subject of sociological study and analysis, and in developing and constructing sociological theory. Abbott et al. (2005:4) offer the following critique of 'male-stream' sociology:

> **Male-stream** a term coined within sociology to refer to the dominance of the male viewpoint and male interests.

- Sociology has been mainly concerned with research on men and, by implication, with theories for man.
- Research based on male subjects is generalized to the whole population.
- Areas of concern for women are often overlooked and seen as unimportant.
- When women are included in research, they are presented in a distorted and sexist way.
- Sex and gender are seldom seen as important explanatory variables.

Feminist sociology emerged out of the women's movement, and, in providing a brief overview of the development of the movement, it could be said to have developed along a number of specific periods or 'waves' (Abbott et al., 2005). The first-wave feminists were active in the nineteenth and twentieth centuries and fought for equal rights concerning property, voting and education; they were typified by the suffragette movement in Britain. The 'second wave' of feminism began after the Second World War and tended to focus upon the analysis of the family as a site of women's oppression. Third-wave feminism refers to the body of feminist understandings which emerged in the 1980s following the apparent weaknesses of former feminist perspectives; it challenges essentialist notions of womanhood with their bias towards white middle-class women (Abbott et al., 2005). (See Chapter 3 for further discussion of feminism and key feminist writers.)

Anti-racist theory/black perspectives

Traditional and more recent perspectives within sociology have tended to ignore or minimize the significance of race, ethnicity and oppression within society. Sociological interest in race emerged with significance in the 1960s following the aftermath of global changes in relation to race (Gilroy, 1997). The end of empire, mass migration to Britain and the civil rights movement in the USA resulted in major social economic and political changes, which had significant global impact but which also transformed the lives of black and white communities (Mason, 1995). Sociologists began to recognize that an analysis of race and ethnicity was central to an understanding of contemporary societies (Gilroy, 1997; Hall, 1992; Pilkington, 2003).

Mason (1995) describes the sociology of race as being concerned with social relations and the observation of actions at an individual and a group level. This usually involves:

- explaining what is meant by concepts of 'race' and ethnicity
- understanding racial and ethnic differences between people in terms of, for example, employment, housing
- explaining racism and discrimination
- understanding the interconnectedness of racism with other forms of discrimination and oppression.

Black perspectives in sociology have challenged traditions within the social sciences, which have centred on European nations and people (*Eurocentric* perspective) and distorted and misrepresented black people's experiences. (See Chapter 4 for further discussion of race and ethnicity.)

> **Eurocentrism** the domination of white Western European values and norms over other cultural perspectives.

Modernity and post-modernity

In seeking to explain the social world and human behaviours, the discipline of sociology has developed to account for the social changes that are occurring. Giddens (1991) has argued that Western industrialized countries witnessed a period of massive social and economic change in the twentieth century, which he called high modernity or late modernity, although in wider sociological writings the period has been described as post-modernity, to distinguish it from the period of modernity.

The period of *modernity* was characterized by a process of modernization through industrialization, capitalism and urbanization and the decline of traditional communities. This process of modernization began in the 1890s and 1900s and was a time of massive technological development and change. The term 'grand narratives' was used to tell the story of the impact of this change on institutions and individuals.

> **Modernity** historical period from the end of the eighteenth century that saw great industrial and political change.

Toennies' work on communities is useful for helping us to understand the impact of these changes on people's lives. In attempting to make sense of the changes associated with processes of modernity, Toennies (1963) used the terms *Gemeinschaft* and *Gesellschaft* to demonstrate the change in society. *Gemeinschaft* refers to the sense of community based on kinship networks, neighbourhoods and a shared purpose based on honour and virtue, whereas *Gesellschaft* refers to the impersonal urban communities associated with modernity and urbanization, with a much greater emphasis on individualism and self-interest. He argued that modernity undermined the strong social fabric of society and the family unit by its focus on individualism and the pursuit of efficiency for profit maximization in a capitalist society. Lee and Newby (1983: 52) characterize this contrast as follows:

> **Gemeinschaft** a term used by Toennies to describe a community based on kinship networks, neighbourhoods and a shared purpose based on honour and virtue.

> **Gesellschaft** a term used by Toennies to describe the urban communities associated with modernity and urbanization, which are seen as individualist and impersonal.

> There is an implied antithesis between the past, when, so it is believed, the individual was integrated into a stable and harmonious community of kin, friends and neighbours, and the less palatable present when all too often it is possible to feel like a piece of human flotsam, cast adrift in a sea of apparently bewildering social changes and buffeted by impersonal and alien social forces.

The concept of post-modernity denotes a society which is in some way different from this period of modernity. Society has become increasingly fragmented and there is a plurality of perspectives and meanings. **Ralf Dahrendorf (1929–2009)** has developed conflict theory, arguing that societies are made up of many different groups (*pluralism*) with different interests, and these groups are often in conflict, not just in economic terms, as Marx stated, but also through power and authority. Dahrendorf sees the conflict as one between the ruled and the unruled, those who have authority and those who do not.

Pluralism a variety of different views and perspectives make up and contribute to a society or culture.

Lyotard (1984) has argued that the grand narratives of modernity, which use all-encompassing theory to try to explain the whole of society, are reductionist and no longer relevant. Instead, we need to understand the social world from local perspectives to fully understand the range of experiences, and within these perspectives individual narratives are important sources of explanation. In *post-modernity*, it has been argued that there has been a decline of locality as a basis for community. People live in impersonal urban environments, therefore trust is difficult as populations become increasingly mobile and there is a pursuit of self-interest.

Post-modernity the view that society is in a different era from that of modernity. Generally dated from the 1960s.

Fragmentation of communities results from an increase in transient populations, loss of stable employment and incomes, rising house prices and a consequent weakening of social cohesion (Macionis and Plummer, 2012). The result is the social exclusion of individuals and a breakdown of community cohesion, which places increasing strain on the family unit. Urban environments have been divested of community, as large supermarkets have moved to out-of-town sites, leading to competition and the decline in local and locally sourced shops in many areas. In addition, many people have moved into the leafy suburbs of societies, leading to the marginalization and residualization of inner-city dwellings.

Secularism the process whereby religious beliefs and practices no longer dominate in contemporary societies. This has been a gradual development, with religious institutions losing social significance over time.

Post-modern society is seen to be an increasingly *secular* society. Although there is a lack of agreement amongst sociologists about the precise definition of secularization (Giddens and Sutton, 2013), it is generally agreed that organized religion is less significant than it was in modernity. Whilst organized religion still plays a significant role in many people's lives, this may be in particular times of celebration or crisis. Hockey (1997) has identified the continuing role of the clergy and religion in many funeral ceremonies, whilst Davies (2000) has identified the importance of religious organizations and institutions during disasters such as the shooting of 16 children and a teacher in Dunblane or the death of 95 football fans at Hillsborough. In addition, there has been an increase in 'new religious movements' (Giddens and Sutton, 2013).

Within new perspectives of critical sociology, there is an emphasis on hearing the multiple views and voices within society, including those of women, minority ethnic groups, older people, lesbians and gays, people with disabilities, children and youths. Critical sociology therefore rejects the use of grand narratives as there can be no single 'big story' to tell with this plurality of meanings, but instead there is a need for many different stories to explain the features of contemporary capitalist societies.

In addition, whereas modernity focused on continuity and order, post-modernity is characterized by disorder and a constant state of change. Giddens (1991) used the term 'runaway society' to denote this changing society and the process of rapid social change that distinguishes the post-modern period from the modern period. Giddens also argues that as society has become increasingly fragmented with the rejection of grand narratives, individuals now construct meanings about their social world through constant self-reflection on actions and interactions within the social world – he terms this *self-reflexivity*. There are no universal truths; instead there is an ever-changing set of truths and individual interpretations.

> **Self-reflexivity** people make sense of the social world through constant reflection on their experiences and the knowledge of those personal experiences.

Thus sociology has to adapt in order to explain this rapid social change and individuals' responses to it as well as offering different interpretations of the social world. As discussed above, social identity is an important sociological concept, and the ways in which social identities are constructed and experienced remains a key area of contemporary sociology. Within this understanding we can see how social constructions can influence individual interpretations, thus exploring social phenomena from the perspective of both structure and agency.

Social constructionism

Social constructionist theory is built on the observation that many aspects of our lives are not objective realities, but are shared understandings that are constructed through social interactions, institutional practices or collective social actions (Burr, 2003). As such, they only exist in the context of those implicit agreements and therefore change between social, historical and cultural contexts. The system of money and exchange that we use is an example of this. Although it is an integral part of our daily lives, it is a system that exists in the shared understandings of a capitalist society, with the emphasis on waged labour and consumerism. Another good example is the way that illness is treated. In Western societies, the dominant model of illness diagnosis and treatment is based on biological understandings through the medical model of care (see Chapter 11). However, in other societies, health understandings may be based on a spiritual model of care, where illness is seen to be the product of invasion of spirits in the body, which need to be driven out by a local practitioner (Turner, 1992). Thus our social realities and what we understand are largely based on social constructions, as we can see in the discussion of risk below.

Risk

In social work the concept of risk is a familiar one and it could be said that all social work practice either implicitly or explicitly involves elements of risk (Stalker, 2003). Risk is also inextricably linked to the blame culture that exists within social work, and recent child deaths and murders or attacks by people who have mental health conditions have focused many aspects of professional practice on the assessment and management of risk (Calder, 2011).

Giddens (1991) and Beck (1992) have argued that we live in a risk society, where risk is ubiquitous – every day we make decisions related to risk taking and risk avoidance. Although the concept of risk is not a new one, there is a social context to risk and risk behaviours, related to social practices and processes and social constructions. Contemporary risks are related to:

- environmental change and degradation
- population growth and migration (see Chapter 10)
- new patterns of social consumption and lifestyle practices (see Chapter 2)
- threats of terrorism and illicit criminal activity, such as human trafficking and the drugs trade (see Chapter 7).

Risks are manufactured through lifestyle practices, practices of social organization and the important role of the media. People take risks all the time, weighing likely potential dangers against likely potential gains. But risk and consumerism are related to patterns of social organization and social disadvantage, and, as such, risks and threats are not equally distributed throughout societies (Dominelli, 2010). (See subsequent chapters for further discussion of risk in relation to specific social groups.)

Post-modernity and identity

A key feature of post-modernity is the change in consumption practices and how these relate to culture and identity. Contemporary sociologists are increasingly interested in how we consume and how identities interact with these consumption practices (Macionis and Plummer, 2012). As Malpas (2005: 122) argues: 'The circulation, purchase, sale, appropriation of differentiated goods and signs/objects today constitute our language, our code, the code by which the entire society communicates and converses.'

Boden (2006) explores the influence of popular culture on young people's identities and the influence of commercial sports, fashion and celebrity cultural icons. This popular culture helps to shape young people's identities, with the UK branded clothing market estimated to be worth £6 billion.

Thus clothing and bodily adornments may be consumed as a way of demonstrating identity and identifying with a certain group of individuals. Throughout history, there have been numerous examples of the use of clothing, hairstyle and fashions as a way of identifying with a particular group: teddy boys, mods, rockers, skinheads and punk rockers, and, more recently, the chav, who wears 'Burberry' and bling. Fashion styles serve an important function of identifying a group's boundaries 'in relation both to its members and all outsiders, a function which has particular consequences for the group's continued existence' (Hall and Jefferson, 1976: 53).

A sense of belonging and identification with other people is therefore achieved through the cultural signifiers of fashion and appearance. However, these can also lead to processes of labelling by people outside the group, with the way someone presents themselves being used as a judgement of character and purpose. Savage and Warde (1993: 184) have argued that 'judges, the police and social workers will use stereotypes based on appearance and dress to label groups and link them with certain characteristic kinds of behaviour'.

Understanding symbols and meanings is particularly relevant for social workers. Failure to understand the symbolic value of language, actions and behaviours from the individual's own standpoint can lead to labelling and stereotyping and is incompatible with core social work principles of anti-oppressive practice and a respect for diversity.

The body

Contemporary sociological theory has also focused on the body as a symbolic bearer of value and identity. For theorists such as Shilling (1993) and Williams (2000), the body is not just a physical entity, but is also a way of portraying social identity or cultural belonging/heritage (Bourdieu, 1986). The body is shaped, constrained and invented by society, with ideas about the body corresponding to dominant social agendas (see Chapters 3 and 5). Shilling (1993) argues that in post-modernity, the body is a project, in a constant process of becoming, a canvas to be worked upon in order to constitute identity. The recent fashion trends of tattooing and body piercing are indicative of this phenomenon, where the practices are used as a way of portraying identity or belonging, or marking transitions in the life-course.

Constructions of the body are important, with parameters of normality and abnormality being constructed through dominant social norms and mediated through professional ideologies. Thus the body becomes an important site of power and control. From a phenomenological point of view, the body is seen as the site for lived experience (Shilling, 1993). From a symbolic interactionist perspective, body image is important as it impacts on the sense of self-identity or self-esteem, as well as social interactions with others (Shilling, 1993). For example, someone who is seen as obese may be stigmatized by society, leading to social judgements by others, with consequences in terms of, for example, employment, self-esteem and social interactions (Puhl and Heuer, 2009).

The body and meanings about the body are thus shaped by the society within which we live. However, the body is not just the result of industrial production, but also the site for the marketing of products. Thus the body has become commodified in industrial capitalism, through, for example, the dieting and leisure industries. Consumerism and practices of consumption are important elements of advanced capitalist society, and the marketing and merchandising of products has become big business (Macionis and Plummer, 2012). This commodification process can be linked to developments in the global economy and how these reflect the priorities of the more powerful nations and exacerbate social divisions and differentials (Cohen and Kennedy, 2000)

Globalization

As social work evolves in the twenty-first century, the processes of change continue to affect the context and content of practice and continue to be affected by social, economic and political factors at local, national and global level. Just as the processes of industrialization and urbanization were instrumental in the developments of nineteenth-century social work practice (Horner, 2013), changes in the global economy and the information and technology age have created new processes of social disadvantage and inequality (Cohen and Kennedy, 2000) and create new contexts for the practice of social work on an international basis (Dominelli, 2010).

Similarly, changes in global structure and the globalization of society have had an important impact on changing social contexts and conditions and the context in which social work operates. Globalization is defined as the process of increasing global interconnectedness, whereby goods and services, capital flows and workers increasingly move around the world, encouraged by trade and revolutions in communications and technology (Martell, 2010). Viewing our own society within the context of the wider world helps us to realize that the perspective we may have about the way it operates is only one of many that are possible, and other societies may see things quite differently (Dominelli, 2007a).

As we have seen from the discussion above, sociology is concerned with understanding patterns of behaviour, which are influenced by historical patterns of social organization. Thus sociology is not a static discipline and the ideas that interest sociologists reflect the changing nature of societies (Cohen and Kennedy, 2000). Early sociologists tended to focus on the concerns of the Western industrialized world, but there has been an increased focus on globalization and globalism since the 1990s. Globalization refers to the inter-connectedness of societies across the world, as nation states become increasingly linked through material and economic, political and symbolic or cultural exchanges (Martell, 2010).

This is particularly related to technological advancements, with the increase in global tourism and travel through advances in the aviation industry and in global informational technology (Martell, 2010). Thus multinational corporations have benefited through increased markets for profiteering. This global capitalism has produced new social divisions, inequalities and exploitations, as the new network and informational society can result in social polarization, social inequality and social exclusion.

Although globalization can lead to positive trade arrangements and inter-connectedness, it can also have deleterious consequences, exacerbating existing social divisions and perpetuating inequalities. The process reflects existing power relationships and dominant discourses, and economic inter-dependency can create a ripple effect where an economic crisis in one area of the world has far-reaching implications in distant localities and countries (Martell, 2010). Globalization has led to new areas of social oppression and exclusion generated by the displacement of people through immigration and emigration and increased vulnerability as a result of lifestyle and consumer practices (Harrison and Melville, 2010). For example, if we look at world poverty and life chances, there are gross disparities across the world, with many people in developing nations experiencing absolute poverty rather than relative deprivation. (See Chapter 2 for a more detailed discussion of the definitions of poverty.)

- Almost half the world (over 3 billion people) lives on less than $2.50 per day.
- At the turn of the twenty-first century, nearly 1 billion people were unable to write their name or read a book.
- One in two children throughout the world live in poverty (1 billion children).
- 640 million children live without adequate shelter.
- 400 million children do not have access to clean and safe water.
- In 2003 roughly 29,000 children per day died before they reached the age of 5.

(Adapted from Shah, 2010)

Globalization has also shaped the context of social work practice, and social work curricula have developed to address new social problems resulting from this process, with an emerging international research agenda that informs social work practice (Harrison and Melville, 2010). Although, as discussed above, the concept of risk is not a new one, there is a new social context to risk and risk behaviours related to global social practices and processes which impact on social work. These risks are related to environmental change and degradation, population growth and migration, new patterns of social consumption and lifestyle practices, and threats of terrorism and criminal activity (Titterton, 2011).

As social work is a profession that is ostensibly preoccupied with risk and risk management, this new context of risk has fundamentally altered its curriculum and practice agenda and accelerated the pace of change in social work education (Dominelli, 2007b). There is little time for consolidation and evaluation, leading to constant change and a preoccupation with bureaucratic processes both in social work practice and in social work education.

Adopting a global perspective therefore helps us to see our own society within the context of the wider world and can help us to reflect on the world-view that we have and how this has been shaped by particular historical contexts and social processes, related to colonialism and our social and economic position in international trade (Cohen and Kennedy, 2000). (See Chapter 4 for further discussion of the impact of colonialism and post-colonial processes.)

Case study

Li arrived in the UK six months ago, with his pregnant wife. He is seeking asylum from a politically oppressive regime, under which he was persecuted and tortured. He worked with IT in his host country, but because of legal restrictions on employment, he now takes on a number of menial jobs in order to earn a meagre income. Some groups of people in the local community have called him names, attacked him and made it clear that they do not welcome him. He is frightened and upset by the hostility that he has experienced.

- How do you think global economics and politics impact upon this situation?
- How does this also relate to issues of social disadvantage and power?
- How can sociological perspectives help you to understand Li's experiences so that you can provide effective support?

This case study raises important issues that social workers face when working with vulnerable people, whether they are children, people from different ethnic and/or cultural backgrounds, people with mental or physical health problems or disabilities, older people or those who are seen as criminal offenders. There are common concepts that sociology can help us to understand and explain so that social work can be practised according to the values of social justice, empowerment and anti-oppressive practice:

- social disadvantage, discrimination and prejudice
- power and control
- citizenship and identity.

Conclusion

Sociology is not a single discipline offering one set of theories, but is a complex range of theories offering explanations and understandings from different perspectives. No one theory is more valid than others, but all can contribute to our understanding of the social world.

It is important for social workers to have a broad knowledge of these different theories in order to help them explain and understand the social world that they and the people with whom they work inhabit.

Exercise: sociology and professional competencies

- Look at the Health Care Professions Council (2012) Standards of Occupational Proficiency and The College of Social Work's (2012a) Professional Capabilities Framework for End of Last Placement.
- Reflect on your learning from this chapter and how knowledge of sociological theories can inform your practice with service users.

Summary points

- The discipline of sociology is made up of a range of theoretical perspectives which help us to explain and analyse the social world.
- The founding fathers of sociology can be divided into two broad camps: structuralists, who emphasize the importance of institutions and structures in shaping people's lives; and social action theorists, who explore the social world through the eyes of individuals.
- Sociologists define the period of modernity as one of rapid social change associated with industrialization and urbanization, where grand narratives were used to explain collective social experiences.
- According to sociologists, we are now experiencing a period of post-modernity, characterized by fragmentation and a plurality of perspectives.
- A critical sociology has developed which helps us to understand the many experiences of diverse groups and individuals in contemporary societies.

Questions for discussion

- Do you think stable structures are necessary for society to function?
- Reflect on the discussion of identity and social constructionism. What have been the major influences on the construction of your own identity?
- Can you identify sources of conflict and consensus in your social work role?

Further reading

Dominelli, L. (2010) *Social Work in a Globalizing World.* Cambridge: Polity
This is a very readable book which focuses on key social inequalities and how processes of globalization raise new agendas for social work practice.

Giddens, A. and Sutton, P.W. (2013) *Sociology.* **7th edition. Cambridge: Polity**
Giddens is one of the key contemporary writers in the discipline of sociology, and this revised edition provides a comprehensive exploration of contemporary debates in sociology. There is a very useful glossary of terms.

Macionis, J. and Plummer, K. (2012) *Sociology: A Global Introduction.* **5th edition. Harlow: Prentice Hall**
This is a very readable book which, as the name suggests, explores key sociological perspectives and areas of sociological inquiry in a global context.

Oak, E. (2009) *Social Work and Social Perspectives.* **Basingstoke: Palgrave Macmillan**
Oak provides a comprehensive discussion of the relationship between social theories and social work practice, exploring how different sociological theories can help social workers to understand their practice with a range of service user groups.

2 Social Class, Poverty and Social Exclusion

Introduction

Throughout its history it could be argued that social work has remained a class-specific activity (Jones, 2002), as poverty, social exclusion and inequality are key factors that face the majority of users of social work. Therefore exploration of these concepts is crucial for social workers to understand the nature of the social problems that are faced by the recipients of social work interventions. Categories of domination and subordination are not static, but are dynamic processes, with movement over time, as groups may use their collective experience to resist the position of subordination. It is important for social workers to understand key theories of social stratification and processes of oppression and subordination, as the majority of the individuals and groups with whom they work will be some of the most vulnerable and marginalized groups.

This chapter will explore these issues, principally in relation to the class system and income inequalities in contemporary Britain, discussing different theories that help us to understand both the structural context of inequality and the impact on individuals and their actions.

The key issues that will be explored in this chapter are:

- different perspectives on how society is divided according to occupation and income
- definitions of poverty (including absolute poverty and relative deprivation)
- explanations for the existence and persistence of poverty and disadvantage
- the impact of these inequalities on individuals within Britain and globally
- the implications for social work of working within a stratified society.

By the end of this chapter, you should be able to:

- explain the nature of social divisions and social stratification in contemporary society
- identify the nature of poverty and discuss some of the causal explanations for its persistence
- distinguish between poverty and social exclusion
- identify the relationship between social disadvantage and ability to participate in the consumer society
- explain the nature of oppression and the impact on the lives of service users.

Social divisions

Modern societies are structured along a number of social divisions. One does not have to look very far to see that society is divided and differentiated. So what do we mean when we talk about social divisions? A simple definition would look at the division between the haves and the have-nots. Whilst this provides a useful starting point, it does not really help us to understand why some people have more than others and why some people struggle to make ends meet and satisfy even the most basic of human needs such as food, shelter and clothing.

Social stratification

Social stratification refers to processes within society, where individuals are classed in the *hierarchical* system, and incorporates ideas of power, inequality and difference. Social division and stratification often refer to a hierarchy of positions of inferiority and superiority in society, with a ranking of different

> **Hierarchy** a system of ranking based upon superiority and subordination.

individuals according to certain traits, criteria or subjective interpretation. Thus value judgements may be associated with positions in the hierarchy. Differences may be biological/natural or they may be social and cultural (Garrett, 2002). Social divisions can be described in terms of differences between groups and diversity within populations, derived from shared language, regional origin, nationality and national identity, physical condition or marital status. Difference therefore may be seen in positive terms, acknowledging the richness and diversity of experiences, social positions and beliefs and contributing to a pluralist and varied society. Diversity refers to a 'difference claimed upon a shared collective experience which is specific and not necessarily associated with a subordinated or unequal subject position' (Williams, 1996: 70). Divisions, however, are based on notions of power and oppression and can be defined as the 'translation of the expression of a shared experience into a form of domination' (Williams, 1996: 70).

Social class

Social class is an important concept in the exploration of social stratification, and is widely used. In everyday conversations, we hear people talking about working class, middle class and upper class as a way of identifying broad groups within society. But what do we mean by these different terms? Are they subjective definitions, representing our perception of where we sit vis-à-vis others, or do they reflect a more objective category of a system of stratification? Are 'working class', 'middle class' and 'upper class' descriptive terms, based on assumptions about shared position and broadly similar lifestyles?

If we look at the classic comedy sketch by Ronnie Corbett, Ronnie Barker and John Cleese, three comedians of varying heights, they suggest class is associated with relative positions in a hierarchy of value and status (Figure 2.1). Is this then what class is about? Is it about our location within a hierarchical system of social organization, where people occupy a particular position relative to other groups? How, then, do we explain how people come to be part of a certain class, and how do we explain how

Figure 2.1 Comedy sketch about social class.

they come to be seen as superior or inferior to others, or indeed how they may come to see themselves as superior or inferior? Is it about birth and heritage – for example, members of a royal family who are born into a system of privilege, or marry into such a system? This seems to reflect a fairly static view of society and a rather negative view that you are born into a particular group and there is little room for movement within the hierarchy. It also tells us little about the social construction of notions of value and privilege and social identity, and the way that structural processes and institutional practices may group individuals.

Exercise: social class

- How would you define your own class position?
- What are your reasons for defining yourself in this way?
- Do you think there is a consensus about the definition of social class?

A more common way of exploring class divisions in society is based on the notion of work segregation and occupational grouping. A feature of modernity and post-modernity has been the increase in labour specificity, with greater specialization of tasks and division of labour. Labour market segregation has its roots in the industrialization process and shift to market capitalism of the late eighteenth century and has been a feature of labour market organization ever since. With the drive towards efficiency and profit accumulation, the labour market has become increasingly segregated and specialized. *Fordist* and post-fordist methods of work

Fordism a form of industrial economy within advanced capitalist societies based on mass production associated with Henry Ford's techniques and processes in the manufacture of cars.

organization saw production tasks being broken down into a number of component parts for the pursuit of increased efficiency (Thompson, 1989).

The labour market of contemporary industrialized societies is one that is based on horizontal and vertical segregations, reflecting differences in class, gender (Chapter 3), ethnicity (Chapter 4), age (Chapter 10) and disability (Chapter 5). The social division of labour is related to other social divisions, with access to benefits and patterns of consumption being dependent on a person's position within the social division of labour. Le Grand (1982) has shown how people higher up the social ladder have better access to health and educational welfare benefits, whilst classic studies by Titmuss (1958) and Sinfield (1978) have shown the relationship between labour market position and the benefit system, with those in secure and well-paid employment having access to better levels of occupational and fiscal benefits in terms of, for example, pension provision and sickness and disability pay schemes. (See also Rose, 1981, for a feminist perspective on these theories.)

Although there are some disagreements amongst sociologists about the definition of class, there is some consensus that class is based on economic divisions and that people can be categorized on the basis of how they make their living or derive their income. Thus class is often associated with occupational status. However, class is not just about differential income levels, but also about ways of living associated with those incomes and shared value systems. (There may be conscious and unconscious mediators of attitudes, lifestyles and behaviours.)

It could be argued that the concept of class has three dimensions:

- economic: wealth, income, occupation
- political: status and power
- cultural: values, beliefs and norms, and lifestyles.

Measuring social class

The concept of social class may be either an objective or a subjective one, and has focused on the differentiation of either individuals or broader groupings within society. There have been several attempts to produce criteria for the objective measurement of social class, many of which use occupational categorization to classify people. One of the earliest approaches to differentiating people according to class was the Registrar General's Classification (RGC) in 1911, which divided people according to occupational position, and made broad assumptions about similarities within these groupings in terms of income, status and lifestyle. The Registrar General's Classification has been used for the compilation of statistical information, to help to develop policy. (See, for example, the Acheson Report, 1998, which explores the relationship between health status and wealth status.)

Within the Registrar General's Classification, approximately 20,000 different occupations are grouped into five categories (see Table 2.1). Although this classification is widely used, sociologists have been very critical of it for a number of reasons. Assumptions are made about shared status, identity and lifestyle, which may be misleading. The classification tends to be descriptive and normative rather than theoretical and critical. People between different occupational groupings may have shared income levels, aspirations and lifestyles or the occupational groupings may

Table 2.1 *Registrar General's Classification of Social Class*

Social class		Examples
I	Professional and higher managerial	Lawyers, doctors, bank managers
II	Intermediate managerial	Social workers, teachers, nurses
IIInm	Administrative professional	Secretaries, technicians
IIIm	Skilled non-manual	Electricians, bus-drivers
IV	Semi-skilled	Postal workers, agricultural workers
V	Unskilled	Window cleaners, labourers

Source: Standard Occupational Classification, 2010. Office for National Statistics. Crown Copyright.

hide differences. In addition, the degree of objectivity is questionable, as it seems to be a scale of relative standing in the community, based on subjective criteria of value, and makes assumptions about status and shared value systems. In the 1980s, the Conservative Government adopted the Standard Occupational Classification (SOC) for official statistical purposes. This system uses a nine-category occupational scale for dividing the population. Whilst this system of classification may not address all the criticisms that have been levelled at the RGC, it does provide slightly less conflated categories of occupation. It does, however, still make assumptions about shared characteristics, lifestyle and income levels, and fails to explore the construction of differences and oppressions between the different classes.

Structural theories of class

Functionalism

The founding fathers of sociology viewed social class in terms of the relationship between different economic groups in society. For functionalists such as Parsons, stratification is both functional and necessary for the smooth running of society (see Chapter 1). They argue that not everyone can occupy an equal status and lifestyle, and that society is made up of a number of different roles and positions, which contribute to the overall functioning of the whole system. In any society there are tasks or jobs that need to be undertaken, some of which require training and expertise. For example, a surgeon requires a protracted period of training and education, whereas the role of a hospital cleaner is deemed more straightforward. From this viewpoint it is argued that those who perform the difficult tasks are entitled to more power, prestige and financial reward. Such an unequal distribution of society's rewards is necessary to encourage people to take on the more complicated roles, and the rewards attached to a particular job reflect their functional importance to society. These arguments have been used by some to justify the huge salaries and bonuses awarded to roles such as bankers and chief executives of major corporations.

Functionalists such as Davis and Moore (Levine, 2006) believe in a system of stratification in which high status or position in society is achieved through individual ability and effort, as opposed to, for example, inheritance. As such, occupation is allocated on the basis of ability and merit, as opposed to ascribed factors such as gender, race and class, or privilege or family connections. This is known as meritocracy, and the extent to which Britain is a meritocratic society is an important aspect of sociological inquiry, particularly in relation to the analysis of the education system, the labour market and the distribution of income and wealth in society. An education-based meritocracy is founded on the premise that the system rewards children according to their educational attainment, rather than their social background, ethnicity or gender. Notions of meritocracy incorporate ideals of social efficiency, social mobility and social justice, which do not necessarily lead to equality of opportunity as differences in levels of ability and achievement are intended to keep people in their place (Young, 1962). The concept of meritocracy has been used in Britain and the USA to justify differential outcomes based upon assumed differential abilities.

There is considerable evidence (e.g. Halsey et al., 1980; Runnymede Trust, 1985) to support the assertion that ascribed factors significantly influence educational attainment at compulsory and post-compulsory levels, which later impact on an individual's life chances: 'While systems of distinction and discrimination have evolved, they continue to underpin and reproduce inequality, dramatically shaping the lives and opportunities of those they position' (Gillies, 2005: 836).

Tumin (1953) argued that if societies operate in the ways that functionalists suggest, then all societies would be meritocracies. Instead he found that gender and the income of an individual's family were more important predictors of life chances than was ability or what type of work an individual did.

Education has become an increasingly important factor in determining which jobs people enter and in determining their social class position. Within Britain, educational achievement is overwhelmingly linked to parental occupation, income and qualifications. Children from a higher social class have greater chance of gaining higher-level qualifications than those from less advantaged classes (Perry and Francis, 2010), which in turn influences their future employment. Hobcraft's (1998) findings suggest that educational test scores during compulsory schooling are 'the most frequent and effective childhood predictor of adult outcomes', and that lack of educational attainment is strongly linked to unemployment and social exclusion. It is accepted that whilst educational standards are rising, there is persistent inequality in levels of attainment between children from higher social class groups and those from manual and unskilled backgrounds (Department for Education and Skills, 2004). Factors that influence educational achievement include poverty, parental interest and support (driven by parental experience of education), neighbourhood, and the quality of schooling (Department for Education, 2003).

Whilst class remains an overwhelming predictor of attainment, it does intersect with other factors, such as gender and ethnicity. There has, however, been a significant improvement in the performance of girls compared with boys (Department for Children, Schools and Family, 2009a), though this does not translate to higher education or income (Office for National Statistics, 2006). In relation to post-16 schooling, there has been significant emphasis via government policy on increasing the proportion of young people from lower social classes entering higher education. As a result, the number of people in higher education rose from 0.6 million in 1970/1 to 2.4 million in 2003/4 (Office for National Statistics, 2006). Yet participation rates for young people from manual social classes remain low compared to those from non-manual social classes, and to students from minority ethnic groups (particularly those from students of Indian origin). Moreover, despite Government reassurances, there has been a negative impact on higher education participation rates for students from low socio-economic backgrounds as a result of the changes in tuition fee policy (IOE, 2012).

The emerging interest amongst welfare agencies concerning the position of young people who are not in education, employment or training, otherwise known as NEETs, reflects an awareness of the risks associated with a lack of qualifications and skills. A report by the Prince's Trust (2007) identifies the personal, social and economic costs of educational underachievement and unemployment during a time of growing national prosperity.

Case study

Despite being described by teachers as 'bright', Rochelle left school with no qualifications. Her father left her mother when she was born and her mother experienced difficulties with alcohol and drugs, resulting in Rochelle's removal from home at the age of 8 owing to neglect. From the age of 13, Rochelle became bored and disillusioned with school and started to truant at regular intervals.

During her final year she attended a maximum of 36 days. Rochelle is now 20, lives in a flat with her boyfriend, and has ambitions to train as a beauty therapist. She hopes that a local salon will employ her as a trainee, although she has had no success to date. She is ambivalent about going back to college as she does not have the required GCSEs to start her chosen course, but realizes that this is the only way to achieve her ambition.

- How can sociological theories help to explain Rochelle's underachievement, despite the fact that her teachers described her as 'bright'?
- What do you understand by Young's comments regarding meritocracy, and how do they relate to this case study?

Conflict theories

Most sociologists would agree that conflict theories offer the most plausible explanations for social stratification and that inequalities are explained in terms of the relative power that different groups have. Tumin (2010: 114), for example, claims that:

> Social stratification systems function to provide the elite with the political power necessary to procure acceptance and dominance of an ideology which rationalizes the status quo, whatever it may be, as 'logical', 'natural', and 'morally right'. In this manner social stratification systems function as essentially conservative influences in the societies in which they are found.

For Marxists, class is defined in terms of the relationship to the means of production (see Chapter 1). Marxists view class as a relationship between two polar opposites, based on oppression and subordination and underpinned by conflict. Social status and position in society are related to economic position (Wright, 1978).

Marx referred to the group who were outside the class system of the bourgeoisie and the proletariat as the 'lumpenproletariat, the surplus or relatively stagnant population group' characterized by individuals who were largely excluded from the labour market and society in general. Marx's description of the 'lumpenproletariat' as the 'passive putrefaction of the lowest strata' (cited in Bovenkerk, 1984: 16) demonstrates the disregard that he had for this residual group, and the generally pejorative way in which they were classified.

The concept of power is central to Marxist perspectives and is important when exploring social divisions. Power is differentially distributed in society and may derive from one's position within the hierarchy of the social system. Related to the notion of power is ideology, which is defined as the set of ideas which shape the structures and relationships of society. Gramsci (1971) refers to 'ideological hegemony', where there is a dominance of one set of beliefs over another, deriving from the power of the ruling elite. For example, in a capitalist society there is a dominant ideology of waged labour and capitalist modes of production. Those with power are able to perpetuate these sets of dominant beliefs. A single mother living in poverty on a marginalized council estate in an area of urban deprivation may not agree with the dominant set of values and beliefs which contribute to her disadvantaged situation, but she lacks the resources to challenge the ideology or change her situation. In contrast, dominant groups use their different status as a way of protecting their privileged position within society.

Social action theories

Social action perspectives on class draw upon Weberian theory and see class in terms of economic resources, whereby class is related to market position, with the role of the labour market being crucial (Evans and Mills, 1998). However, they distinguish class from status, seeing status as being derived from more than just economic position, although this is clearly important. Neo-Weberians continue to use economic position and occupational role to explain social groupings, based on the assumption of a shared value system and lifestyle amongst people who have similar occupations and income levels. The Hope–Goldthorpe Scale, for example, acknowledges that people may be located within a stratification system based on their market position as well as the job they do. Thus class is associated with market situation as well as work situation. Hutton (1995) uses the concept of the 30:30:40 society to explain the fundamental changes in the class composition in modern Britain as a result of processes of global capitalism. The selected criteria which he uses to explore the different groups have parallels with the dual labour market model of employment, which sees the labour market being divided into two sectors, primary and secondary (see Chapter 3).

Bourdieu (1988) draws upon both Marxist and Weberian theories to provide an analysis of power. He explores notions of cultural reproduction in relation to the continuation of privilege: different actors and groups in society have power through their access to resources, which he terms capital. However, power is derived not just from economic capital, but also from social, cultural and symbolic capital. Social capital refers to the social networks and group membership that people may be able to utilize in their struggle for privilege; cultural capital refers to educational credentials and cultural goods (the value of which is constructed through social processes); and symbolic capital relates to the perceived legitimacy of all forms of capital. Through the possession of capital, Bourdieu argues, those who hold privileged positions are able to perpetuate that privilege, as they are better placed to be able to mobilize their capital resources.

Parkin (1979) explores exclusionary practices that groups employ in order to limit membership of the group and therefore protect their position within society. For example, many occupational groups use a system of regulation to control entry of individuals into their training or educational programmes, based on academic achievement and the ability to present oneself in a particular way at interview. Thus, the occupational group may become a fairly homogeneous group of shared backgrounds and similar cultural and social viewpoints. This may be perpetuated through promotion processes, which are influenced by implicit assumptions, such as the old school tie network.

The underclass theory

Underclass a group of highly deprived people who are regarded as being at the bottom of the class divisions. They are seen as constituting a class in their own right. Commentators relate this to factors such as race and economic and political power.

The term the *underclass*, as it is used today, emerged towards the end of the twentieth century as a way of referring to those who are located right at the bottom of the class structure, seeing them as a class that is distinct from the *respectable* working class. The term largely emanates from Charles Murray's (1994) work in the USA, in which he identified a group of marginalized and excluded individuals and groups, whose living standards were significantly lower than those of the rest of society. Similar to Marx's lumpenproletariat, the groups within the underclass reflect a culture and behaviour that are seen as anti-social and deemed dangerous. It could be argued that the underclass can be traced back to Victorian Britain, with distinctions being drawn between the deserving and undeserving poor, the idle and the feckless.

For Murray (1994), there were three factors that united members of the underclass: illegitimacy, violent crime and drop-out from the labour market, related to an over-reliance on the welfare and benefits system. He primarily focused on members of minority ethnic groups, identifying a high rate of illegitimate births among young black females, a high rate of crime and long-term unemployment. The benefits system is crucial to Murray's analysis, as he argues that benefits that are too easily accessible reduce incentives to work and create a class of individuals who are disaffected and dislocated. Other commentators have argued that similar patterns of social organization can be identified amongst black or immigrant groups throughout Europe who have limited access to secure employment, housing, and so on, and who may operate on the fringes of society within a black economy (see, e.g., Giddens, 2013).

Commentators relate this to factors such as race and economic and political power from the labour market and the rest of society. From this perspective, the rise in teenage pregnancy is seen as being related to young girls getting pregnant in order to get council or social housing, and being reliant on the state benefit system for their income maintenance. The underclass represents a form of social disintegration, and the term has been used in the sense of a moral panic about the breakdown of society.

Graffiti and defaced property, which may be a feature of areas of urban deprivation. (© Galina Barskaya/iStock)

Society is viewed as spatially segregated, with pockets of urban deprivation based on the existence of the underclass. Ghettoes and sink estates are seen as representative of this underclass and social disintegration with weak infrastructures, leading to poor educational and health care facilities, reflecting the notion of the Inverse Care Law, where those with the greatest need are least well served by statutory sector services. These areas are also associated with run-down and marginalized housing and a lack of local opportunities for meaningful employment. Crime may be a significant feature, with drugs, gangs and violent crime using guns, knives and other weapons being a concern for many (see Chapter 7).

Murray (1994) has argued that there is an emerging underclass in Britain, with significant minorities being long-term unemployed, living in poor-quality accommodation or having no permanent residency, and being dependent on state benefits for long periods. Although not exclusively related to ethnicity, there are a disproportionate number of blacks and Asians located within the underclass in Britain (see Chapter 4).

Other groups within white working-class communities, particularly those defined as chavs and NEETs, are viewed as part of the new late twentieth- and early twenty-first-century underclass. Since 2010 has come to represent the emergence of the category of NEET, a further discourse in which the personal consequences associated with being young, unemployed and not engaged in any form of education and training are set against the wider risks to society.

Within this analysis there is little recognition of the post-industrial changes in the labour market that have led to a decline in traditional manufacturing, low pay and the casualization of jobs, which have disproportionately affected the young and working class. The global recession has also had a disproportionate impact on young people. Unemployment amongst 16- to 24-year olds for the past few years has been around 20%, and a report by IMPETUS-PEF (2014) suggests that of children born in this millennium, there is a strong risk that one in five will become NEETs. Research by Britton et al. (2011) discusses the importance of GCSE attainment as a good indicator for determining whether young people re-enter education or training. They identify that whilst NEETs tend to come from lower socio-economic backgrounds, there is an increasing incidence of young people from affluent families with poor GCSE results joining this category.

Yet successive government policies have contributed to the demonization of young people, based on the ideology of the deserving and under-serving poor, and welfare-to-work policies seek to help people to help themselves in the labour market, thus reducing dependence on the benefit system (Prideaux, 2005). The Citizens' Inquiry into the Tottenham riots (Citizens UK, 2012), which spread to other parts of the UK in 2011, identified, alongside a hatred of the police, high youth unemployment as a major contributor to a lack of hope and civil unrest.

Hayward and Yar (2006: 16) note that the marginalization of working-class youth is not new:

> The latest articulation involves groups of young people, clad predominantly in sports apparel, who engage in minor forms of unruly behaviour in and around town centres, entertainment zones and certain fast-food outlets. Indeed, during the 1990s a plethora of (highly derogatory) terms emerged in various parts of the United Kingdom that sought to overtly label such behaviour and its associated conventions of meaning, symbolism, and style. These names include but are not limited to: 'Scallies' (Merseyside), 'Neds' (Glasgow), 'Townies' (Oxford/Cambridge and most university towns), 'Rarfies', 'Charvers' (Newcastle/North East), 'Kevs' (London/Bristol), 'Janners' (Plymouth), 'Spides' (Belfast), 'Hood Rats', 'Rat Boys', 'Bazzas', 'Kappa Slappas', 'Skangers', 'Scutters', 'Stigs', 'Sengas' and 'Yarcos'.

They recognize the economic and political processes that result in marginalization and exclusion but also discuss the ways in which culture, media and patterns of consumption have helped to sustain the phenomenon of the 'chav'. Jones's work *Chavs* (2012) provides a further useful and accessible discussion on the subject.

Discourses surrounding chavs reflect the way in which it has become socially acceptable for the middle classes to mock working-class young people. We can see how these discourses resonate with those of Murray's analysis of the underclass in the 1980s and provide a legitimacy for government welfare reforms which are targeted at reducing welfare to the most economically disadvantaged within our society (see Chapter 8).

Beresford (2012) is critical of constructs of an underclass theory which demonizes working-class culture and values, and instead he suggests that there is evidence of the existence of an 'overclass' which seeks to threaten traditional work ethics and values and poses more of a threat to society. The overclass is 'tied in with some of the most damaging developments in our society: the extreme risk taking of the banking industry, unaccountable and overpowerful media proprietors, rising inequality and disadvantage, declining social mobility and a careless approach to vulnerable people'.

Exercise: measuring social class

- Looking at the theories and scales above, how useful do you think it is to have a measure of social class?
- Is class still a useful concept for understanding people's position in society?

Critical theories

Critical theories of social class challenge constructions of class as an objective reality with fixed boundaries, but acknowledge the subjective reality of class in terms of differing meanings and individual constructions. They suggest that changes in the labour market, the effects of globalization and patterns of consumption mean that it is more difficult to identify people with specific social class groupings and it is harder to attribute particular lifestyles and activities to individual classes. The example of football is an interesting one. The commercial consequences of this global sport, once identified as working class, have changed the demographics of participation within it. Many match-attending fans now struggle to pay for the price of a ticket to watch their beloved team and there is evidence to suggest that football has become a more popular sport for both boys and girls who attend independent schools (*Independent School Parent* Magazine, n.d.).

Post-modern theories on class claim that advanced capitalist societies have moved away from a command economy model, based on class stratification, to become status societies, characterized by cultural stratification. As such, post-modern societies, identity and stratification arise from individual tastes, patterns of consumption and lifestyle (Pakulski and Waters, 1996).

Patterns of consumption and risk

Because of the difficulties of measuring and determining social class, some sociologists have argued that class is no longer a useful concept for explaining the divisions of society, and that social stratification needs to be explored within the context of multiple variables such as age, gender, ethnicity, disability and sexuality, as well as economic status (Crompton, 1998). Since the Second World War, there have been changes in forms of production, with a decline in heavy manufacturing industries and an increase in service industries. In addition, there has been a fragmentation into part-time work and short-term contracts and a loss of emphasis on a job for life. There has also been a decline in class politics, with a focus upon new social movements where individuals group together according to shared characteristics other than occupation (Crompton, 1998). Thus patterns of consumption are seen as important indicators of social groupings and collective identities.

In advanced capitalist societies, there is an emphasis on consumerism. This has led to banks and credit companies offering growing numbers of people greater access to lifestyle and consumer durables via loans and credit and hire-purchase arrangements. Thus it is increasingly difficult to differentiate lifestyles on the basis of occupational group. Consumerism is important when exploring the nature of divisions within contemporary Britain, yet ability to participate in the consumer market

Consumption cleavages divisions in society are based on the ability to pay for goods rather than being derived from occupational income.

is related to income levels. Dunleavy (1986) coined the term *consumption cleavages* to explain people's positions within society. Divisions are based on the ability to participate in the consumer market, and identity is increasingly being constructed through the consumption choices that we are able to make. In relation to needs and wants, preferences are revealed when people make choices in a consumer market.

The market is dominated by big brand names in the fields of clothing, foodstuffs, consumer durables and leisure. Identities become constructed through choice of clothing, music, cultural and leisure pursuits. According to *Social Trends* (Office for National Statistics, 2000), shopping is the second most popular leisure activity in Britain (watching television being the first). Shopping is no longer a purely functional activity, but is a leisure pursuit, with the growth of more and more retail outlets in competition with each other (including home shopping, internet shopping and TV channels which are purely devoted to shopping).

Associated with this rise in consumption has been a concomitant rise in the credit industry, with a dramatic increase in the use of credit cards. Between 1991 and 2004, credit card transactions increased from £1 billion to £5.5 billion (Office for National Statistics, 2006).

Managing consumption patterns and participation in the consumer market has led to a huge problem of debt in contemporary Britain, though the rise in use of credit cards has subsided as consumers have opted for debit cards as a way of managing personal debt (UK Cards Association, 2011).

Not surprisingly, the problem of debt affects those lower down the socio-economic scale disproportionately, although credit card spending, mortgages and borrowing are a wider feature of contemporary society. The economic risks associated with personal debt and national debt have been heavily debated and reflect the present-day Coalition Government policy in relation to austerity and spending cuts. The Morgan Report (2011), which resulted from the alarmingly entitled Armageddon Project, highlights the risks associated with the Government's failure to tackle the debt crisis. Whilst the Report assesses the reliability of the Government's efforts to move out of recession, Morgan also refers to an out-of-control consumerist ethos, which has plagued Britain and which he sees as one of the causes of the UK riots of 2011: 'We conclude that the rioting reflects a deeply flawed economic and social ethos ... recklessly borrowed consumption, the breakdown both of top-end accountability and of trust in institutions, and severe failings by governments over more than two decades' (cited in Hawkes, 2011).

Whilst the effects of a consumerist culture cannot be ignored, sociologists provide a contrasting analysis of the causes of the riots in 2011, pointing to a complex myriad of factors which include: the status of young people within society; unemployment and income-based inequality; relationships with the police; a sense of increasing alienation from politics and power; and the dynamics of group behaviour (Morrell et al., 2011). In the words of one young person from Birmingham quoted by Morrell et al. (2011: 48):

> The majority of people my age, like, resort to street life because you know you can earn money and you make a lot of close friends and it is easier to live that sort of life-

style and you get what you want really . . . but if there were more opportunities out there, then I think it would attract a lot more people my age to brighten up and look to the future and see the opportunities that are there for them, instead of resorting to the streets.

Whether we choose to define social divisions according to class, or other scales of difference, the concept of social stratification is important, as it explores the divided society and the differences in power, status and income that different individuals and groups have. These differences also reflect different life chances and the ability to make lifestyle choices. Thus sociologists are interested in patterns of advantage and disadvantage and the processes that contribute to disadvantage and discrimination in society and the growth of the number of consumer durables that are available within the market.

Global perspectives and social class

Sociologists discuss how the globalization of production can be seen through labour migration, whereby production has shifted or been outsourced from higher-waged economies in the North to low-wage economies in the South. As global corporations seek opportunities in countries which are investment-friendly, sociologists have explored the effects of this for people and communities within the *Global North* and *Global South*. These include changes in patterns of migration and employment for men and women, the depression of wages, deregulation and the pervasive insecurity of employment.

> **Global North** and **Global South** refers to the ways in which those countries north of the Equator tend to be rich and economically developed whereas those countries south of the Equator tend to be underdeveloped and poorer.

Some sociologists claim that processes of globalization promote the individualization of labour and class decomposition (e.g. Beck, 1999). They assert that global processes have left all classes at risk of unemployment and job insecurity, and, as such, the concept of class is no longer relevant as a way of understanding life chances and inequality. However, whilst middle-class communities are not immune from the effects of the global recession, this chapter has highlighted how UK societies continue to be stratified by income and inequality. Indeed, Bernardi (2009), in his study of inequality within European countries, recognizes the relative importance of gender and ethnicity and argues how inequality based upon social class remains relevant in determining life chances.

Globalization has resulted in greater inequality and what Robinson and Harris (2000: 11) refer to as the creation of a new élite global ruling class.

> It is a ruling class because it controls the levers of an emergent trans-national state apparatus and of global decision making. . . . A new hegemonic bloc consisting of various economic and political forces that have become the dominant sector of the ruling class throughout the world, among the developed countries of the North as well as the countries of the South.

Forced labour and human trafficking have become forms of modern-day slave trade and they represent two of the most harrowing features of a globalized labour market and organized crime. The UNODC Global Report on Trafficking in Persons (United Nations Office on Drugs and Crime, 2012) suggests that whilst over 20 million people are subject to forced labour, it is difficult to estimate how many of these have been the result of trafficking. The overwhelming majority of trafficked persons are women and children who are trafficked for sexual exploitation, and some of those experiences are discussed in Chapter 7. Forced labour is the next most common reason, though this may be under-represented as it tends to be less frequently detected. Governments globally can be accused of ignoring or underestimating the extent of human trafficking.

Poverty and inequality

Inequality is an important concept in relation to social stratification. Inequality may be both material and symbolic, where individuals have differential access to material resources as well as to power and control. Thus within a socially stratified system, a group becomes superior or inferior to other groups. Disadvantage and vulnerability are often associated with poverty and social exclusion. For social workers, poverty and social exclusion are important concepts, as the people they work with may often suffer from the multiple disadvantages associated with processes of differentiation. Thus poverty, social exclusion and the underclass are concepts which have sociological relevance in the understanding of the position and experiences of the most disadvantaged within society.

Islam (2005) discusses how the study of poverty was central to sociology particularly between the 1940s and the 1960s. This area has been largely taken over by economists and social policy makers, yet sociology is useful in helping us to understand the causes of poverty and its effects on the lives of individuals and communities. Sociology can help explain what we mean by poverty, measure the extent of its existence, and analyse how it is defined and measured. It is important to have an understanding of different concepts of poverty, as the way that we define poverty is likely to have an impact on perceptions, measurement, identification, causes, attitudes and solutions. Different measurement scales are likely to reflect the values that we hold about acceptance of poverty. Sociologists have distinguished between what is known as absolute poverty and relative deprivation.

Absolute poverty

Rowntree's study of poverty in York in 1899 set the pattern for other studies of poverty and established an important concept of the poverty line, a level of income below which one is deemed to be in poverty. Rowntree defined poverty as the situation in which total earnings are insufficient to maintain the minimum necessities for the maintenance of physical efficiency (e.g. food, clothing, housing, heating, lighting, cooking utensils) – all of which should be purchased at the lowest prices and in quantities only necessary for maintenance of physical subsistence. A notion of deserving/undeserving underpins this theory, with moral undertones.

It was argued in the 1960s that poverty had largely disappeared from industrialized societies, based on the definition of absolute poverty (Abel-Smith and Townsend, 1965). There was a widespread view that a safety net of welfare provision, providing a subsistence level of provision for those who could not contribute to the social security insurance system, had eliminated poverty. However, the concept of relative deprivation was developed to explore the relationship between different individuals and groups in terms of their access to resources and consumption patterns.

Relative deprivation

As the name suggests, within this concept, poverty is viewed in relative terms, where needs are not just physiologically determined, but also have a social and cultural dimension (Townsend, 1979). This is not fixed in terms of time or historical period, but is a dynamic process associated with the changing nature of societies and patterns of consumption. From this perspective, poverty is relative to the living standards and income of the rest of the population. In addition, poverty is not just about income and money, but must include non-material items like the ability to participate in society. People are seen to be poor if they are excluded from normal living standards.

Exercise: understanding deprivation

- What would you say are needs?
- Draw up a list of your ten most important needs.
- Do some needs have greater priority than others?
- Might someone in a different culture and environment have quite different ideas about what needs are?

This concept broadens the notion of necessities of life and recognizes that people have social roles as well as physical needs. One becomes an outsider if one lacks resources for participation and is deprived of certain rights. Relative deprivation explores the whole issue of what we understand by resources. Inequality is not just related to money and material possessions, but is also about the ability to participate fully within a society.

There are also differences between what we need and what we want. For example, if the rest of your social group has the latest mobile phone technology, even though you may not need a new mobile phone, you may feel excluded from full participation in the group if everybody else is exchanging messages, games and music. Needs are therefore more basic or essential than wants – we may need things we do not necessarily want, such as immunizations to prevent the spread of infectious diseases. Needs and wants are also not necessarily objective categories, but classification of need may be based on the interests of dominant groups who are better able to articulate those needs.

Although the concept of relative deprivation is seen as more inclusive and explanatory than the concept of absolute poverty, it has been subjected to a number of criticisms, in that it is difficult to make comparisons over time, the indices that are used may be quite selective, and there is a failure to analyse the structural factors created by capitalist organization and modes of production as explanations for positions of relative advantage and disadvantage (Alcock, 2008).

Exercise: the deserving and the undeserving

- How far would you agree that a deserving/undeserving category of the poor exists within contemporary society?
- Are there groups of poor who are seen as more deserving than other groups?
- How is this reflected in public attitudes and charitable activity?

A food bank in Newcastle-under-Lyme. In 2013, over 700,000 people received three-day emergency food aid from the Trussell Trust, which organizes a national network of food banks in the UK (*http://www.trusselltrust.org/*). (© Staffs Live/Flickr)

Exercise: the disadvantaged

Look at the statistics for low income in Social Trends 41 (Office for National Statistics, 2010a).

- What can you deduce about the sources of disadvantage from these statistics?
- In what ways does societal structure contribute to social disadvantage and social division?

Explanations of poverty

Individual or Social Darwinian theory of poverty

This is one of four main sociological theories which seek to explain the causes of poverty (Kerbo, 1996). It sees poverty as the result of one's own personal deficiencies and is known as the social pathological model (MacNicol, 1987). Various theories are subsumed under this umbrella term, the most common of which is the genetic theory, which sees behaviour and social activity as directly attributed to genetic make-up.

Within this theory there is a belief that poverty can be linked with inheritance, intelligence and social class. Inherent within this definition is the notion that natural processes are at the root of disadvantage, as it is passed between the generations. The eugenics movement of the late nineteenth and early twentieth centuries reflected this social pathological view of poverty, with selective programmes operating throughout Europe and the USA to breed out undesirable and deviant characteristics such as poverty. This theory fails to account for factors that are extrinsic to the individual which shape intelligence, access to labour market position and economic and wealth status.

Cultural theory of poverty

The cultural theory of poverty causation focuses on the roles of families and family sub-culture. Within this theory, it is argued that families who are poor have a certain belief system, totally different from the rest of society, and therefore children are socialized into poverty (O. Lewis, 1998). In the 1970s, the Secretary of State for Health and Social Services, Sir Keith Joseph, argued that there was a cycle of deprivation where deprivation is transmitted from one generation to the next. This is a good example of how poverty becomes viewed within the context of family behavioural patterns. Within this perspective the solution rests on changing attitudes to break this cycle of deprivation (Figure 2.2). Some evidence of this approach can be seen to underpin some of the policies that were introduced to tackle child poverty under the New Labour Government elected in 1997. Initiatives such as Sure Start,

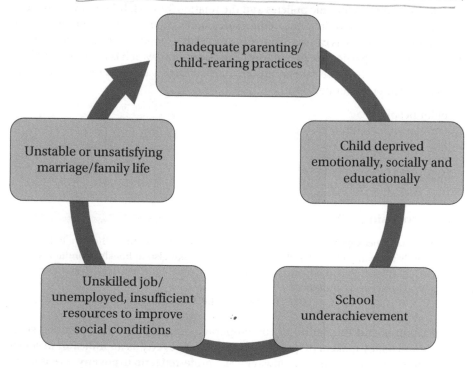

Figure 2.2   The cycle of deprivation.

pre-school education for 3- and 4-year-olds and parent preparatory classes can all be seen within the context of this approach. In addition, social casework with families living in multiple deprivation are aimed at changing the values of parents. While Sir Keith Joseph and Pierre Bourdieu may not be the most natural of bedfellows, there are some parallels here in the notion of intergenerational reproduction. However, the cycle of deprivation tends to *pathologize* individuals and families and ignores wider processes of structural disadvantage, which contribute to persistent and intergenerational poverty. (See Holman, 1978, for a critique of this theory.)

> **Pathologize** to attribute causes/symptoms to a breakdown of the body or to disease. Can be applied medically or socially.

Situational theory of poverty

This recognizes the structural conditions that give rise to poverty but suggests that the poor behave differently to others in that experiences can be explained by their behaviour and how they respond to the situation in which they find themselves. For example, a person may recognize that further education and training may help to improve their situation but they choose not to adopt those values and that behaviour. It does not become a priority for them.

Structural theory of poverty

The structures of society lead to poverty and the persistence of poverty. Inequalities in the labour market, economic policies and the relationship to labour market policies, unemployment, early retirement, redundancy and under-employment, as well as low wages, are all seen as causes of poverty and relative deprivation. This then affects people's ability to participate in patterns of consumption, which is an important part of advanced capitalism. Certain groups are particularly susceptible to poverty owing to socially created dependencies:

- older people
- families with children
- low-paid wage earners
- the unemployed
- the sick or disabled.

Social exclusion

> Exclusion processes are dynamic and multidimensional in nature. They are linked not only to unemployment and/or to low incomes, but also to housing conditions, levels of education and opportunities, health, discrimination, citizenship and integration in the local community.
>
> (Commission of the European Communities, 1994: 37)

Social changes and the nature of contemporary capitalist societies have led sociologists and policy makers to question the utility of poverty as an indicator of social disadvantage. Social exclusion is now seen as a preferred term to poverty, as it is more encompassing.

Social exclusion can encompass a range of factors that limit one's ability to participate fully in society. Economic exclusion is one aspect, where an individual's ability to participate in the normal consumption patterns of society is inhibited, as discussed above. Levitas (1998) has argued that policy responses have often focused on integration through employment, reflecting a Durkheimian notion of integration. However, people may also be socially excluded through:

- exclusion from access to the law, exclusion from voting or being able to participate in the democratic processes of the criminal justice system: jury service, right to a fair trial, and so on
- failure of supply of social goods or services to individuals or a group of individuals. For example, failure to supply an adequate education system or health service will lead to social exclusion, or a child who sees the education system as irrelevant to their needs may voluntarily exclude themselves from school, through truancy, leading to patterns of exclusion in other areas of life.

Social exclusion has become a significant feature of advanced capitalist society and is related to economic changes associated with global capitalism and concomitant changes of welfare regimes, with a greater emphasis on selectivity and targeting of statutory support services. There have also been demographic changes, with a higher level of unemployment and a greater longevity, leading to many more people living in retirement (see Chapter 10), which have contributed to a social differentiation of incomes, as well as social judgements and social values being based on ability to participate in the labour market. Thus unemployment and old age may be stigmatized in a society that values economic participation. Spatial processes of segregation and separation (ghettoization; travelling communities; refugees and asylum seekers; homeless and transient populations) have also led to patterns of social, legal and cultural inclusion. In a speech on 15 January 2007, Oliver Heald, Conservative Shadow Secretary of State for Constitutional Affairs at the time, said:

> We clearly have problems of social exclusion; the proportion of children in workless households is the highest in Europe, more than half the children in inner London are still living below the poverty line, more than 1.2 million young people are not in work or full-time education despite a growing economy, and 2.7 million people of working age are claiming incapacity benefits – three times more than the number who claim jobseeker's allowance. (Heald, 2007)

Social exclusion and social inclusion are useful terms for understanding processes of social differentiation in societies, as they are related to the notion of rights. Human rights can be categorized as follows:

- civil rights – basic freedoms under the law
- political rights – the right to vote, to join and participate in political parties and to hold government accountable
- social rights – rights to education, social welfare, social security, and so on.

Citizenship is related to notions of freedom to participate within society, through political and civil processes as well as through social and economic processes. Thus the rights of citizenship are affected by inequalities in provision and quality of education, health care, housing, transport and other social amenities, as well

Isolated and displaced individuals on the streets of major towns and cities are an increasing reminder of the numbers of people who are socially excluded. (© Dan Eckert/iStock)

as by inequalities in ability to participate in economic life. In addition, as argued above, citizenship is related to the ability to participate in the consumer market. Furthermore, the rights of citizenship are related to freedom from victimization and abuse (Bochel et al., 2009). Thus racial victimization, domestic violence, elder abuse and child abuse can all limit people's freedoms. Justice is related to freedom and citizenship within a democratic society.

Exercise: excluded groups

- Think of a group who are excluded from society. What are the characteristics that define them as excluded?
- Compare your list with that of someone who has identified a different excluded group. What are the common features of these groups?

Poverty and social work

The number of people living in poverty is rising, and in Britain income inequality is rising faster than in any other OECD country. Poverty is a key factor for many users of social work. Bebbington and Miles' research (1989) into looked after children suggest that children living in poverty are 700 times more likely to come into local authority care. There is a persistent and widening gap between health and wealth. Those with the least economic resources in society have higher incidences of premature mortality and self-reported morbidity, limiting their activities of living. There is also a strong class gradient in terms of lifestyle behaviours. For example, there is a strong social class gradient in the prevalence of obesity, particularly amongst women, and there is a higher incidence of obesity in manual groups. Poverty and material and social disadvantage and social exclusion remain important issues within the stratified society of contemporary Western societies. However, policy responses and professional ideologies have largely failed to tackle the structural processes that contribute to these inequalities. The social pathological model has dominated policy decisions over time, and in many ways social work has failed to challenge the assumptions underpinning this approach. From the Poor Law to the notion of social problem groups, which has dominated social work practice since the 1960s, there has been an underlying assumption of the deserving/undeserving distinction, notions of individual moral deficiency and a pathologization of the behavioural traits of individuals and groups. Thus social work has historically focused on tackling poverty at an individual level and neglected the sources of the inequalities (Jones, 2002).

Emancipatory social work needs to acknowledge the structural and ideological factors that affect the continuation of poverty (and in recent years, the widening gaps between the haves and have-nots, with a greater number of individuals experiencing poverty). We would argue that the persistence of poverty cannot solely be attributed to family traits. External factors that can limit people's opportunities and prevent people from climbing out of poverty must also change. Poverty must be located within the context of society in order to find the cause(s), which result from the inequalities within society. It has previously been suggested that social workers have a good understanding of the impact of poverty on people's lives; however, Holman (1978: 75) argues that while some workers understand how years on low income can impact on parenting, 'there is evidence that social work does not have a good record in understanding or combating family poverty'. Though social workers are required to take into account wider environmental factors, an understanding of poverty and social exclusion is not seen as central to assessment approaches in children's and family work and other areas of practice. Increasing bureaucracy and managerialism within social work leave practitioners as gatekeepers to resources as service users are expected to fit into more closely defined eligibility criteria. The role of social workers within the social exclusion agenda has been marginalized. Rather than tackling poverty, they are expected to monitor, maintain and supervise those most damaged by it (Jones, 2002). Mantle and Backwith (2010) discuss the possibilities of social workers learning from professionals in other countries, such as Australia, in adopting the principles and practices associated with community social work in order to effectively challenge the effects of poverty amongst service users.

As the Government's welfare reforms continue to hit the poorest users of social work, it is important that social workers demonstrate their commitment to addressing the effects of poverty and inequality. The College of Social Work's Professional Capabilities Framework (College of Social Work, 2012a) requires the profession to address economic well-being. Currently the PCF is not mandatory beyond newly qualified social workers; however, the expectation is that strategic leaders within social care will 'develop strategies (including regarding resources and commissioning) to promote social inclusion and access to opportunities which may enhance people's economic status' (College of Social Work, 2012b).

Case study: a lost generation trapped on our forgotten estates

A five-year-old boy in a ripped coat and dirty trousers hammered on the front door of his council estate flat at 11 p.m. last Wednesday. 'Come on, you smack heads,' he shouted to his parents inside. 'I know what you're doing.' By the boy's feet sat a plastic bag with bread and milk. The only shop open at that time is on the opposite side of a busy motorway, a fifteen-minute walk away. According to neighbours, it is a journey the child regularly makes on his own. 'Unless someone rescues that wee kiddie and gives him a second chance, he's doomed', said Jean, who has lived on the Clyde Court housing estate in Leeds for seventeen years. She is too scared of her neighbours to give her full name. On an estate where deprivation and violence are commonplace, the boy's bleak, hopeless life is the norm and, if he takes his ambitions from those around him, his life chances are near to zero. In a few years he could seek to emulate Steven Gedge, a twelve-year-old local boy recently arrested for the fifty-fifth time. He has already been given up for lost by his mother, his school and the local council. Steven in turn has little to model his life on except the family living around the corner, three of whose four children are heroin addicts including the youngest, who had an abortion two years ago when she was eleven. The only child in this family not using heroin is a sixteen-year-old girl who had a child last year with a local lad. The baby has never seen its father: he was arrested for drug dealing before his son's birth. Two weeks ago, the local newsagent was robbed by a fourteen-year-old boy, high on drugs, wielding a butcher's knife and a plank of wood spiked with nails. The local church has barricaded its windows and surrounded itself with razor wire. Looming at the heart of the estate is the residents' apex of fear: the sixteen-floor Clyde Court tower block where bloodied tissues lie in pools of urine and tinfoil stained with crack drifts around the stairwell like autumn leaves. The block is a favourite with local youths, who have stripped it of every piece of metal down to the lift call buttons. They attach used syringes with their needles exposed to the underside of the banisters, and throw shopping trollies from the roof heedless of anyone walking below.

Amelia Hill (2003) *The Observer*, Sunday 30 November 2003 © Guardian News and Media Limited 2003. Reprinted with permission.

- How could individual, cultural and structural explanations of poverty explain this boy's situation?
- What factors contribute to social exclusion on this estate?
- How can knowledge of these theories be useful in informing social work practice with people who experience widespread disadvantage?

Conclusion

In order to promote anti-oppressive and anti-discriminatory practice, social workers must engage with the key theories and debates about social division and social differentiation. Social workers need to understand not only the experiences and impact of divisions and oppression, but also the structural and institutional context. Social work can only be truly empowering if these structural contexts are challenged, otherwise the focus remains on individual adaptation within existing structures: '. . . an understanding of these issues can aid the social work profession in its dual commitment . . . to social justice, understood as the need for the redistribution of resources for the benefit of those who have been deprived and to individual well-being' (Weiss, 2005: 108).

Summary points

- Society is divided according to occupation and income levels, with a hierarchy of positions.
- Social divisions in society lead to inequalities and are reproduced through systems of privilege, which favour the dominant classes of society.
- Poverty and social exclusion are related to systems of stratification, and ability to buy goods in the consumer market is related to economic position.
- Processes of inclusion and exclusion reflect power and economic ability.
- Inequalities are experienced in many areas of life, including health status, access to housing and access to education.
- Social workers often work with people who are economically disadvantaged or socially excluded, but in the past there has been a tendency to focus efforts at an individual level.
- Understanding the structural and social causes of inequality and social exclusion can help social workers to work in a more empowering way.

Questions for discussion

- Think of your local area. What indicators are there of deprivation? Is there an identifiable gap between communities that you perceive as advantaged or disadvantaged?
- Is social class still a useful concept for understanding the divisions in society? How do sociological perspectives of social class differ from concepts of social exclusion?
- What do you think Jones (2002) means when he talks about social work being a class-specific activity?
- What can social workers do to help to alleviate the problems of social disadvantage?

Further reading

Gordon, D., Levitas, R. and Pantazis, C. (eds) (2006) *Poverty and Social Exclusion in Britain: The Millennium Survey* (Studies in Poverty, Inequality & Social Exclusion Series. Bristol: Policy Press
This book provides a comprehensive study of poverty and social exclusion within twenty-first-century Britain.

Jones, O. (2012) *Chavs: The Demonization of the Working Class.* 2nd edition. London: Verso

Whilst not an academic text, this revised version contains an interesting discussion about the 2011 riots and explores how working-class people and culture have become the focus of ridicule and contempt.

Parrott, L. (2014) *Social Work and Poverty: A Critical Approach.* **Bristol: Policy Press**
This is a valuable book that discusses some important topics, including the impact of welfare reforms and the experiences of poverty for service users.

Payne, G. (ed.) (2006) *Social Divisions.* **2nd edition. Basingstoke: Palgrave Macmillan**
This book provides a comprehensive discussion of the nature of division, class and stratification in Britain. There are chapters exploring the relationship between social categorizations and social divisions (gender, ethnicity, national identity, age and old age, childhood, sexuality, disability, health and community).

Roberts, K. (2001) *Class in Modern Britain.* **Basingstoke: Palgrave**
This book is an accessible introduction to theories and measurement of social class.

3 Gender

Introduction

Social work is a feminized activity, in that women as qualified or unqualified workers perform the majority of social work and the majority of service users are women. Sociological insights into gender have been successful in developing feminist analyses of social work as a profession, and campaigns against particular issues have had a major impact on social work practice undertaken with women (e.g. violence directed towards women and children). The International Federation of Social Work (2012) recognizes the extent of social work with women and girls across the world and identifies its ethical responsibility and special commitment to enhancing their well-being. This is not to say that gender is not an unproblematic concept for social work, as there are many areas of practice that would benefit from a gendered analysis, particularly in the area of working with men and boys.

The key issues that will be explored in this chapter are:

- the contributions made by specific sociological theories regarding sex and gender in working with women, men and children within social work
- the relationship between public and private spheres and roles
- the employment of women and men within social work and social care
- globalization, work and sexual exploitation
- constructions of masculinity and femininity.

By the end of this chapter, you should be able to:

- distinguish between the concepts of sex and gender
- explain the role of socialization in the development of gender roles
- discuss the relationship between the public and private domains of home and work in relation to gendered roles
- discuss the gendered nature of the labour market
- describe the evidence in relation to changing gendered identities.

What is gender?

What do we mean when we talk about *gender*? What is the difference between sex and gender? Oakley (1974) has argued that there is an important distinction between sex and gender:

> **Gender** a cultural term reflecting social attributes associated with being male or female.

sex refers to basic biological differences between men and women, such as genitalia and reproductive systems; gender, on the other hand, refers to the socially and culturally specific traits and behaviours of men and women. These may be actual differences, or they may be *normative* differences – the way in which men and women are expected to behave. Thus, when we talk about sexual differences, we are distinguishing between males and females, whilst when we discuss gender differences, we distinguish between notions of masculinity and femininity. Much sociological debate has focused on whether these gender differences are the product of nature or nurture (biologically determined or the product of socialization). Other feminist sociologists, meanwhile, such as Butler (1990) and Delphy (1993), go further in arguing that the binary categories associated with sex and gender (i.e. male and female; masculinity and femininity) are permanently contested.

> **Normative** a system of rules or expectations, which are common to the majority and become the expected ways of behaving.

Butler (1990) suggests that just because one may possess a particular physical form, it does not follow that one should be categorized as either male or female; indeed, both concepts of sex and gender are socially constructed. Gender can be viewed as not something that we 'are' but something that we 'become' – 'One is not born, but rather becomes, a woman' (de Beauvoir, 1997: 295).

Biological explanations of gender difference

Many popular conceptions of behavioural traits of men and women (and girls and boys) have been based on notions of innate difference related to genetic composition and biological make-up. Beliefs about boys being more naturally aggressive and girls being more naturally caring have a surprisingly long history. The Greek philosopher Aristotle (384–322 BC) wrote that women are 'more compassionate . . . more envious, more querulous, more slanderous, and more contentious', whereas men are 'more disposed to give assistance in danger' and 'more courageous' (cited in Miles, 1989: 700).

Can we really say that there are objective and observable differences between males and females based on biological differences, or do the different behavioural traits represent a socialization process related to social and cultural norms, environments and the differential nurturing of boys and girls? Psychologists have argued that there are variations in ability between boys and girls, such as the claim that boys have superior spatial ability (the ability to see how objects would appear at different angles and how they would relate to each other in a given space) and superior mathematical ability. However, the findings from the psychological tests of the 1960s and 1970s that produced these conclusions have been the subject of much debate and criticism.

Exercise: gender traits

- List the traits that you think are most associated with males and females.
- Is there a clear distinction?

The socialization of gender

Sociologists have drawn attention to the role of nurture and *socialization* in the construction of masculinity and femininity, leading to a social construction of gendered characteristics. The family and education systems serve as institutions for the primary socialization of children, providing the environmental and social context for the development of normative gendered traits. Thus boys may be encouraged not to display emotion (big boys don't cry), to develop practical skills and to stand up for themselves.

> **Socialization** the process of learning how to behave in a way that is appropriate for an individual's particular culture. This process is governed by certain standards and values about behaviour and roles within society.

Girls, on the other hand, may be encouraged to be more emotionally expressive, to be involved in cooking and cleaning and to be more passive. This socialization may either be a deliberate manipulation of behaviour, or may be done unconsciously, the stereotypical behaviours being so firmly entrenched in society.

Exercise: gender roles

- Look at ways in which children may learn about gendered roles.
- Watch the adverts that frequently appear between children's television programmes.
- How do they reflect social constructions of difference between boys' and girls' play patterns and behaviours?

'If you make me clean my room, won't it encourage the stereotype of the female as subservient housemaid?' (© 2003 by Randy Glasbergen. www.glasbergen.com)

Structural theories of gender

Functionalist theories of gender tend to focus upon the construction of gender roles as being necessary for family and societal functioning. They provide an analysis of the family and the different roles that are ascribed to men and women. This is explored more fully in Chapter 8. Conflict perspectives suggest that the subordination of women benefits not only men but the wider capitalist system. Gender inequality is maintained through the ideology of sexism, which results in gender-based discrimination.

Social action theories of gender

Social action or interactionist theories of gender enable us to understand how gender is socially constructed. Gender is not intrinsically related to sex, but the physical, biological differences associated with sex come to be regarded as symbols that differentiate rights and rewards in society. As humans have agency to influence the society around them, sociologists use the concept of 'doing gender' to describe the way in which men and women routinely perform gender-specific roles (West and Zimmerman, 1987). This may appear unconscious, but they would argue that gender is not what we are but something we do in our everyday lives and interactions with others when we choose to wear trousers or skirts, use make-up or have short hair.

Feminist theories and gender

Alsop et al. (2002) argue that feminist analyses of the social construction of gender can be broadly divided into two strands: materialist theories and discursive theories. Materialist approaches emphasize objective categories and the nature of *macro* power in constructing women's disadvantaged position. Discursive theories, on the other hand, emphasize subjective experience and how women attach meaning to social labels. Language and culture are important in understanding experiences, whilst power is seen to operate at the micro level, rather than through the structures of society. Thus discursive theories emphasize women's different experiences and how roles may be contradictory, complex and fluid.

Materialist theories

Materialist theories emerged in the 1970s and 1980s and stress the importance of structural processes and how they impact on men's and women's lives. From this perspective, men and women are fitted into different roles and pathways, and the social relations of family, work and sexuality are important for understanding the systems of power, exploitation and oppression that frame women's experiences. There are two different strands to material theories: Marxist theories, which stress the importance of capitalist relations of production in the construction of gender divisions (Barrett and McIntosh, 1982); and *patriarchy*, which explores the nature of power and oppressive gendered practices, which may or may not be related to processes of capitalist production (Millett, 1977).

Patriarchy male domination of a system or network, leading to the oppression of women.

Patriarchy is a useful concept in understanding the different political strands of feminism. Meade et al. (1988) have argued from a social anthropological perspective that the patriarchal society is not just associated with industrial capitalism, but also with agrarian and hunter-gatherer societies. Although there are examples of matriarchal societies, patriarchy is the dominant form of social organization globally. Patriarchy is a system that controls women and constitutes their inferiority and inequality within society and becomes embedded in the institutional practices of the society.

It is not possible here to do justice to the broad range of feminist thought, but it is useful to provide an overview of a number of key perspectives which have been influential within sociology. The categories below could represent ideal types, but ideal types rarely exist, and as women have multiple identities, sociologists may not always fit neatly into a single category of being, for example, a black feminist, but may also share Marxist or radical ways of thinking (Dominelli, 1997).

Liberal feminism

Liberal approaches to feminism tend to focus upon issues of discrimination against women in society and view equality of opportunity as a way of addressing inequality. Hence the sources of women's inequality are seen to reside with the law and policies and differences in the socialization of males and females. Consequently, changes to the law, via equal opportunity legislation such as the Equal Pay Act or the Sex Discrimination Act, and changes to the socialization of boys and girls and the expectations placed upon them, would serve to reduce the inequalities between men and women. Liberal feminists hence see an end to women's inequality within the existing social frameworks and without significant structural change, and thus reflect a functionalist view of society.

Marxist feminism

Marxist feminists recognize the inadequacy of Marxist theory in explaining the exploitation and subordination of women through capitalist relations of production. Marxist feminists argue that traditional Marxist theory was gender-blind and failed to recognize the specificity of women's oppression (Abbott et al., 2005). They wish to retain aspects of Marxist theory, but seek to offer an explanation of the centrality of women's experiences in the labour market, in either low-paid or unpaid work (as housewives), for the benefit and maintenance of capitalism. They see the domination of class relations as central to the definition of women's oppression.

Radical feminism

Radical feminists view the dominance of patriarchy or the rule of men as being responsible for women's oppression. Patriarchal relations are seen as permeating all forms of oppression and men are seen as the main enemy in this respect. Some radical feminists view men and women as separate sex classes, which causes antagonism and friction (Firestone, 1971), and assert that only by overthrowing patriarchy can women and children become truly emancipated. Some radical feminists would argue that separatism (either by the avoidance of heterosexual relationships or by artificial insemination) is the only way that women can be removed from the oppressive relationships associated with childbearing (Dominelli, 1997). Radical feminists have been particularly influential in developing an understanding of women's sexual exploitation and campaigning against male violence towards women and the pornographic exploitation of women (Dworkin, 1981).

Socialist feminism

Socialist feminism recognizes the inter-relationship between patriarchy and capitalism in oppressing both men and women. This is sometimes referred to as *dual systems theory*, as it seeks to provide an explanation of women's oppression by retaining the materialist aspects of a Marxist analysis, whilst incorporating a radical feminist emphasis on patriarchy (Abbott et al., 2005). Socialist feminists hence seek to engage men in feminist struggles either through reform in housework or childcare or by promoting anti-sexist social relations in tackling male violence towards women (see Dominelli, 1997). They seek to appreciate the diversity and commonality of women's experiences.

Dual systems theory a feminist theory that recognizes that both the public world and the domestic world impact on the oppression of women.

While there are different political strands of materialist approaches, they share the common view that gendered relations operate within and are influenced by the structures of society, such as paid work, the private domain of the household, and sexuality and sexual relations (Walby, 1990).

Discursive theories

More recent feminist theories have challenged the notion of a common notion of sisterhood and a common experience for women. Giddens' (1991) concept of the runaway society is useful here (see Chapter 2), arguing that the world is rapidly changing, and people's experiences within this changing society are dynamic and varied. Post-modernist feminists (e.g. Nicholson, 1990) are concerned therefore with women's diverse and changing experiences, and how the meanings that women attach to their experiences are shaped by structures and ideologies. Black feminists have also challenged the concept of sisterhood and questioned the term of womanhood as a uniting concept (Mohanty, 1992). Similarly, feminists within the disability movement have critiqued mainstream feminism for failing to account for disabled women's experiences (Lonsdale, 1990), whilst gerontologists have been critical of feminism's neglect of older women's experiences (Arber and Ginn, 1995).

Black feminism

Although black feminism is defined here under a single umbrella, it is important to recognize the range of black feminist thought that exists and appreciate that black feminists may also align themselves with radical, Marxist or other forms of feminist thought. The roots of modern black feminist thought arose out of the civil rights movement in the United States in the 1960s and the women's movement in the 1970s, and gained particular momentum in the 1980s. Black feminists have challenged the assumed sisterhood that exists between black and white feminists and the assumed universality of women's experiences, and argue that much white feminist thought has tended to minimize the experiences of black women (Collins, 2000). bell hooks (1991) also challenges forms of racism within the construction of feminist knowledge, which expects black women to write from the heart about their experiences and white women to write from the head.

Black feminists argue that racism and sexism are inextricably linked in causing women's oppression and do not see men as necessarily the main enemy, but recognize the oppression of black men in particular and suggest that black women and men should work together to fight racism (Lorde, 1984). Black feminists have also challenged white feminists' critique of family as the location of patriarchal power, and instead recognize the significance of familial relations as a potential haven of support in a hostile and racist society (Collins, 2000). The pressure that is sometimes placed on black and minority ethnic women to leave violent relationships without consideration of the significance of a move outside their neighbourhood on wider family and community support systems highlights an example of ethnocentric social work practice (hooks, 1991). An understanding of the intersectionality of identity helps to explain black women's position in society, and black feminists argue that elimination of oppression on the basis of race, sex and class would lead to freedom for all women (Collins, 2000; Crenshaw 1991).

Post-modern feminism
Feminism is a political activity and could be said to be at odds with post-modernism, which has often been described as apolitical. However, there has recently emerged a body of thought which is described as post-modern feminism. Some of the tensions between feminism and post-modernism concern the challenges that post-modernism makes to feminism in challenging the grand theories (e.g. patriarchy, race and class) which seek to explain women's oppression. It also questions unitary concepts such as woman and femininity, emphasizing multiple identities that individuals possess.

This raises the question that if individuals can no longer be defined as being women, are they able to unify around common concerns which are central to the varying strands of feminist thought? 'This approach runs the risk of encouraging fragmentation of social entities through collective action or the isolation of the self' (Dominelli, 1997: 39). Nevertheless, post-modernist perspectives focus on women's subjective accounts of meaning, and the analysis of ideology and discourses is important in these subjective experiences. The ideology of gendered roles is based on a set of ideas which reflect the interests of those who are dominant economically. These ideas then become a framework to guide the actions of others, and thus shape the experiences of men and women. The ideology of gendered roles can be seen in societal attitudes to women who do not want to have children, or who leave the marital home and their children. Furthermore, women who commit crimes against children are viewed as particularly deviant and invoke a hostile reaction from the public, as well as achieving notoriety for their crimes. For example, the public reaction to Rosemary West or Maxine Carr reflects this outrage that women should harm children. (This is not to say that men who commit crimes against children are not also seen as deviant and invoke feelings of horror, but that the hostility directed towards women who do so is disproportionate.) The notion of the female nurturing role is also reflected in child settlement policies following divorce, with the woman often being favoured.

Feminists argue that these gendered differences are a specific outcome of power relations and the patriarchal oppression of women, which is derived from the distinction between the public and private spheres of society (the public sphere being the labour market, political and economic systems, whilst the private sphere is the home and the ideologically structured notion of the family – see Chapter 8). Thus roles become socially constructed to provide resources within these separate spheres of society, reflecting the construction of a male breadwinner society under industrial capitalism. The skills and attributes associated with masculinity become more highly valued, with greater status and wealth being associated with masculine roles.

Sociological perspectives on masculinity

A gendered analysis of sociological theory and perspectives has focused upon women's experiences and the causes of women's subordination. However, more recent theory on gender has begun to incorporate theories on masculinity and male experiences (e.g. Mac an Ghaill, 1996). Sociological perspectives on the construction of maleness and masculinity are particularly relevant for a social work practice, which has often struggled to engage with men and boys. The influence of the women's movement has been partly responsible for the rise of the men's movement in Britain since the late 1970s. The early movement was pro-feminist as men aligned themselves with women in challenging women's oppression, articulated and supported by academic sociological knowledge (Hearn, 1996).

The 1990s witnessed a growth in the sociology of masculinity, and some perspectives, rather than being pro-feminist, blamed feminism for the *demasculinization* of men as traditional roles for men have been challenged (Cree, 1996).

There are four themes that are central to the theories about masculinities:

1   Masculine identities are historically and culturally situated.
2   Multiple masculinities exist.
3   There are dominant hegemonic and subordinate forms of masculinities.
4   Masculinities are actively constructed in social settings.

Functionalist perspectives on masculinity regard male roles in terms of the benefits for the individual and society. Gilmore (1990), for example, identifies three features of masculinity:

1   Man as impregnator who takes the initiative in courtship and relationships.
2   Man as provider, which relates to the concept of male breadwinner.
3   Man as protector, from other men.

Men who conform to societal expectations of masculinity tend to be rewarded with high status whilst non-conformers may receive ridicule or negative sanctions. Such fixed notions of masculinity are problematic, as many women work hard as contributors to or sole providers of the family income (see Chapter 8), and male violence towards women challenges notions of men as protectors. Men who enter social work or other caring professions may find themselves having to justify their motivation for their career of choice or apparent lack of ambition if they do not wish to attain management positions (Parker and Crabtree, 2012).

Sociological insights into sex and gender explore ways in which cultural differences between men and women interact with biological ones. Connell (1995)

This image of Barack Obama as Superman from the 2008 US Presidential election campaign challenges notions of hegemonic masculinity. (© Liam d'Noit/Flickr)

emphasizes the plurality of masculinity and recognizes the emergence and decline of different masculinities. Hegemonic masculinity represents the dominant forms of masculinity which exist within society. In British society this may be represented by white, heterosexual, able-bodied forms of masculinity and is subject to challenge by women or black and gay men. Sexuality is integral to constructions of masculinity, and while men may benefit from dominant forms of masculinity in society, masculinity is not fixed and contradictions exist.

The body and gender

Ideas of appropriate femininity and masculinity are constructed through normative perspectives of the ideal body. The body is not only a physical entity, but also a socially constructed phenomenon, depicting symbolic value, based on notions of the good and bad body type. Foucault (1979a) argued that constructions of the body are developed through discourses representing dominant ideologies and constituting processes of social control. There is a long history of the relationship between the female body and constructions of identity, value and social control (Ehrenreich and English, 1978), and Showalter (1987) has demonstrated how the institution of psychiatry has been instrumental in controlling perceived female 'deviance'.

In the contemporary Western world, slenderness is seen as the attractive ideal, and is the standard against which ideas of normality and social worth are constructed (Williams and Germov, 1999). The second wave of feminism of the 1960s saw this thin ideal being more firmly embraced, and the super-fit, slender female was seen as indicative of women's strength and control – a woman who could control her eating habits had personal control, and was thus valued in a society of plenty. Related to this, Orbach (1985: 87) has argued that 'the self-starvation in anorexia represents a struggle for autonomy, competence, control and self-respect'. She has further argued that anorexia has been feminized as women's power lies in their aesthetic beauty and eating disorders represent an attempt to conform to the ideal and the judgements of society (see also Frith and Gleeson, 2006).

Since the 1970s, we have seen a commodification of the female body image, with the fashion, cosmetic and dietary industries promoting the slender body as the norm of attractiveness and beauty.

A number of studies have explored the link between female body image and media images and argued that an unobtainable ideal of the slender female is promoted through the media and the diet industry and this can lead to body dissatisfaction (Ferguson et al., 2011). In a more recent study, however, Ferguson (2013) has argued that this link may not be as significant as previously argued, and that there are other social variables, such as stress, anxiety and parental influence, that are also relevant.

Exercise: body image and the media

When watching commercial TV or looking at a popular magazine, note how many adverts link food to body image and gender.

For some individuals the social construction of the idealized body and construction of self can have negative consequences for psychological and physical health. A number of studies have linked body dissatisfaction to increased dieting and disordered eating (Espeset et al., 2011; Stice, 2002). Although there is a growing incidence of eating disorders among boys and men, with the number of inpatient admissions for men with eating disorders more than doubling in the UK between 2000/1 and 2010/11 (Duffin, 2012), these are still disorders that disproportionately affect women.

Anorexia is most likely to manifest in the teenage years, with approximately 1 in 150 15-year-old females and 1 in 1,000 15-year-old males in the UK being affected (Micali et al., 2013). About 40% of people with anorexia recover completely, but a further 30% will experience long-term problems.

Some individuals may use exercise rather than diet to try to control or manipulate their appearance, and there is a growing body of sociological research exploring the pursuit of the ideal body through physical activity (Homan, 2010). This in turn can lead to negative consequences, where, in a kind of reverse anorexia, people believe they are undersized and may adopt unhealthy approaches in an attempt to get the toned and muscular body that they strive for. The use of protein shakes to build muscle tissue has become a regular part of young men's diet. There are concerns about the rise in the number of people who are using anabolic steroids, a synthetic and illegal drug, related to male sex hormones, which can increase muscle mass, but also have side-effects, including abscesses, heart problems and increased aggression and violence. It is difficult to get exact figures on the number of people who are using steroids, but the Advisory Council on the Misuse of Drugs (2010) noted an exponential increase in the numbers of people misusing them.

Gender and inequality: the domestic division of labour and the paid labour market

The notion of the division between work in the home and work in the paid labour market is relatively new. During the rise of industrial capitalism, there were relatively good opportunities for paid employment outside the home for women, although the jobs tended to be of lower status and less well paid, reflecting constructions of masculinity and femininity. However, the rise of industrial capitalism led to an emerging division of labour, with men working outside of the home and women providing unpaid work within the home, with responsibility for the maintenance of a future healthy working and fighting force (the national efficiency argument: children are the future, and therefore need to be provided for and maintained in order to safeguard the nation's economic position and national security). Ironically, middle-class women tended to employ single women to do the household chores, leaving them free to participate in other forms of unpaid work, namely charitable activity and voluntary work. Nevertheless, the model of the male breadwinner/female homemaker society became well established by the beginning of the twentieth century. The homemaker role came to be known as the housewife role, and the scientific discipline of domestic science emerged to give it some credence. Female employment in the UK remained relatively steady at approximately 33% between 1901 and 1951, compared with 84–91% for men (Hakim, 1996).

The unpaid domestic work model for women has become fairly well embedded in kinship and community relationships, as well as being perpetuated through social policies. For example, the Beveridge blueprint for social security, which formed the basis for post-Second World War income protection policies, was based on assumptions about male full-time working patterns and female dependence within a marriage. Feminists such as Callender (1992) have demonstrated how women have been disadvantaged with respect to unemployment policy, both in terms of public provision through contributory benefits and in the sphere of work-related fringe benefits. The male breadwinner model of social security also fails to take account of the unequal distribution of resources within the household (Pascall, 1997).

The second wave of feminism succeeded in identifying unpaid work as a concept, and this has resulted in campaigns to identify domestic work within public accounting systems (Himmelweit, 1995). Some feminists and policy makers, with the aim of acknowledging the contribution of women's domestic role to the functioning of the capitalist economy, promoted the notion of the family wage (Barrett and McIntosh, 1982). However, other feminists have been critical of this, arguing that it reinforces women's subordinate position within the division of labour.

A significant shift has occurred in the labour market in the post-Second World War period, with increasing numbers of women taking on paid employment outside the private sphere of the home. Between 1971 and 2008, changes in employment patterns for both men and women saw a decrease in the gender pay gap as more women became economically active. Changes in equality legislation and reproductive technologies have also enabled women to participate on a long-term basis within the labour market, with women occupying managerial positions particularly within the public sector (Perrons, 2009). There have been numerous cases in which female workers have used the legal system to successfully challenge inequalities in pay. Local authorities have been required to compensate female workers, such as dinner ladies, who have for decades been paid significantly less than their male counterparts, and such workers are now deemed to require similar levels of knowledge and skills as, say, refuse collectors.

However, gendered inequalities within the labour market reflect social constructions of stereotypical gendered roles. Dex (1985) explored the value and sex-role stereotypes in relation to labour market employment, and concluded that work roles reflecting traditional male stereotypical traits were more highly valued than those that reflected femininity and therefore attracted higher status and remuneration. Logical thought and rationality, strength, drive, focus and aggression typify gendered roles associated with masculinity, whilst the skills of nurturing and caring are seen as inherently feminine qualities and thus are less valued.

The labour market

Horizontal segregation the division of the employment market into 'men's work' and 'women's work'. The origins are usually historical, but even today there is usually a pay and status differential between jobs done primarily by men and jobs done primarily by women.

Vertical segregation the division of the workplace into top and bottom jobs divided by a 'glass ceiling'. Such segregation keeps women at the bottom or lower levels of organizations.

Dual labour market theory theory associated with Barron and Norris that sees the labour market divided between secure well-paid jobs in the primary sector and insecure low-paid jobs in the secondary sector.

The domestic division of labour and socialization of gendered roles is transposed to the paid division of labour. Rose (1981) argues that the domestic division of labour and the contribution that it makes to the creation of sexual divisions within the labour market and in welfare provision can be attributed to the patriarchal ideology on which it is premised. This is further reflected in the division of labour by gender, which is segregated both vertically and horizontally. *Horizontal segregation* occurs when men and women are generally employed in separate spheres of the labour market, while *vertical segregation* occurs within the same occupation, with men predominantly occupying the higher-grade posts, whilst women are concentrated in the lower grades. Gender segregation is significant, with over 50% of the female workforce employed in 10 out of 77 occupations. Alongside teaching, the five Cs – cleaning, catering, clerical, caring and cashiering – tend to represent women's work (Equality and Human Rights Commission, 2009). This accounts for the disparities between men's and women's pay.

The *dual labour market* theory of Barron and Norris (1976) argues that the labour market can be divided into two related but separate sectors. The primary sector is characterized by high pay, job security and promotional opportunities, whilst the secondary sector is characterized by semi- or unskilled work, relatively low pay and job security and lack of a career path. Barron and Norris argue that men are usually employed in both sectors, whereas women tend to be largely employed in the secondary sector. This theory describes the situation facing many women, who, owing to the combined responsibilities of caring and working outside of the home, are more likely than men to gain part-time and more flexible employment.

Beechey's *reserve army of labour* thesis (1982) provides a Marxist feminist explanation of disadvantage in the workplace, where the cyclical nature of production under capitalist economies results in periods of boom and bust. At times of boom, more workers are required and women represent a flexible source of labour. In this instance women represent a reserve army of labour and their concentration in low-paid, less organized and unionized employment is an attractive source of employment for employers.

> **Reserve army of labour** a Marxist and a feminist term used to describe sections of the society who are employed when the economy is buoyant or doing well.

There are many professional women, however, who are employed by the state, as in social work, and though they may have been subject to public expenditure cuts, traditionally they were generally protected from cycles of boom and bust. However, the policy of government austerity towards public expenditure has had a disproportionate impact on women as women have been hardest hit by the cuts to jobs, wages and pensions (Fawcett Society, 2012).

The concept of women as workers is characterized through motherhood and caring responsibilities and reflected in the concentration of women within particular sectors of employment which are under-valued, leaving them more vulnerable to the effects of recession. A Fawcett Society report (2009) claims that unemployment is not a reliable indicator with regard to the impact of the recession on women. It highlights how women who live with partners are less likely to register as unemployed, tend to change their jobs more regularly and experience maternity discrimination. Since 2000, the UK has dropped from 13th to 18th on five key indicators of female economic empowerment. These include the equality pay gap, women's employment in absolute terms and relative to men, female unemployment and the proportion of women in full-time employment (PwC, 2013). Single mothers, black and minority ethnic women, disabled and older women have been disproportionately affected.

Men have a particular place within social work, and feminine occupations like social work construct and maintain particular forms of masculinity (Hearn, 1996). Hegemonic forms of masculinity are replaced by more liberal forms, which allow men to accelerate in terms of management and leadership positions within social work. Christie (2006) employs the concept of 'rehabilitated masculinities' to describe men's involvement in feminist social work practice. Male social workers may be depicted as heroes – or heroic men of action – who are used as protectors against hostile or violent service users, whereas gentle men may be seen as soft and effeminate – a form of subordinated masculinity.

There may be different representations of masculinity depending upon the location and position of men within social work. In some areas of social work, men are significantly under-represented (e.g. childcare and work with older people), while in other areas, the proportion of men increases (e.g. probation and mental health), and in management positions men proliferate. These different positions may impact upon the way in which masculinities are represented. Considering the impact of managerialism within social work, it may be hard to relate liberal forms of masculinity to contemporary social work.

There are some groups of women who are particularly disadvantaged in the sexual division of labour. The combination of sexist and ageist assumptions and practices

Table 3.1 *Average time per day spent on household chores (excluding shopping and childcare)*

Women	Men
Nearly 3 hours	1 hour and 40 minutes

Note: Women spend more time than men looking after children (4 hours 20 minutes per day compared to 2 hours 30 minutes per day on average) and men spend more time than women at work or studying.

Source: UK Time Use Survey, Office for National Statistics (2003)

means that older women may come up against the 'glass ceiling', whereby promotion prospects are denied to them (either consciously or unconsciously) (Arber and Ginn, 1995).

The increase in female employment in the paid labour market has led sociologists to question whether the male breadwinner/female homemaker role is still relevant for contemporary industrialized societies. Young and Wilmott's (1973) classic study in the East End of London looked at the changing nature of the family and gendered roles within the family. They used the term

Symmetrical family a family where there is a more equitable division of domestic labour between men and women.

the *symmetrical family* to explain the family where both parents worked in the paid labour market and shared household duties and tasks. However, despite changes in labour market participation, many argue that women continue to perform a disproportionate number of household duties, and where men participate, this too is selective, based on gendered assumptions of masculinity and femininity (see Table 3.1).

Despite some women having the resources to challenge traditional gendered roles in the domestic division of labour (Benjamin and Sullivan, 1999), the reality for many is that they take on roles in the paid labour market in addition to their roles in the home. Finch and Groves (1983) identified a triple burden of the housewife role: paid work, unpaid work and contributing to men's paid work, by acting as a receptionist or book-keeper. Castells (1997) elaborated on this, stating that women may do a quadruple shift of paid work, homemaking, child-rearing and the night shift for the husband.

Exercise: horizontal and vertical segregation

Examine the data shown in Figure 3.1.

- What evidence is there of vertical and horizontal segregation?
- How useful are theories of gender and socialization to explain this data?

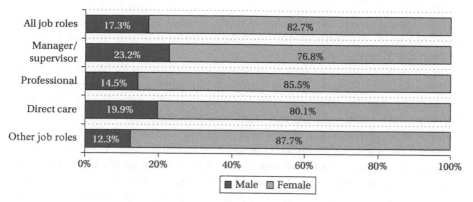

Figure 3.1 Gender distribution of workers in children's local authority services by job group.

Source: The Local Authority Children's Social Care Services Workforce Report, December 2012, England, p. 10.

Gender and caring

Since the 1960s, the social care agenda has been dominated by the concept of community care, and Finch and Groves (1983) have argued that community care has come to be seen as care by women owing to the gendered division of labour. Underpinning the notions of community care are assumptions that people within a locality or local social system will provide care for each other in times of hardship. The notion of a locality as a community (Lee and Newby, 1983) is flawed as a premise for community care, as it assumes that people will care for each other by virtue of being in the same locality. Equally, the idea that community is defined by a set of social relationships is inadequate as a premise for community care, as notions of care are constructed through particular ideologies. Sex role stereotyping and construction of gendered roles are significant in an analysis of caring. Cree (2000) makes a useful distinction between care and caring. Care generally refers to support provided by agencies in a domiciliary or institutional setting. Caring refers to a support role fulfilled by a relative or friend, which is generally unpaid. Someone who lives with the person may provide caring or there may be a varying amount of support provided by a number of people. Graham (1983) argues that in order to understand the ideas which underpin caring and the gendered nature of caring, we need to distinguish between caring about and caring for. Caring for is concerned with tending to someone's needs. Caring about is concerned with emotional attachment. Both men and women are capable of both types of care, but Dalley (1988) argues that caring about and caring for coalesce in motherhood, which is seen as an integral part of women's nature and role. Caring is seen as part of the essentially passive nature of women – an innate or socialized characteristic, as discussed above.

Feminists such as Pascall (1997) have been critical of the assumptions underlying the ideology of caring, arguing that there are consequences for women such as their subordination in the domestic sphere, which is bound up with the assumptions about their caring function. At the basis of assumptions about family care and the domestic division of labour is the notion of the nuclear family, although family units are structured around many different forms, with the nuclear family only accounting for just over one quarter of all family types (see Chapter 8). As Dalley (1988: 16) puts this, 'The nuclear, individualistic family is the reality for relatively few, but the model for the many' (Dalley, 1988: 16).

The premise of family care (either for dependent children or for other family members in need of care) is based around normative expectations of gendered roles within the domestic division of labour. This is an ideological construct which becomes translated into social policies and may be internalized by women themselves. Women invest large amounts of time in maintaining the family, but also invest more emotional energy in the family unit (Duncombe and Marsden, 1993). This is not to suggest that men are not involved with caring. Indeed, there are ideological assumptions in relation to male caring. Men may be expected to take responsibility for care, but not to provide the care themselves necessarily (a man who provides care is seen as untypical). In spite of government support to enable men to participate in the care of their newborn or adopted children, a recent study (Williams, 2013) suggests that over 40% of men do not take their entitled paternity leave. Spousal caring is becoming more common, but daughters and daughters-in-law are far more likely than sons and sons-in-law to give up paid employment or reduce working hours to provide informal care. Thus the ideological constructs are translated into social policies – male carers are seen as heroically coping and tend to be offered more support from statutory care providers than female carers, who often remain invisible (Blaxter, 1976).

Women may have feelings of duty and obligation to care, even though caring is context- and relationship-bound. There may also be feelings of burden and frustration or resentment, and the increased acknowledgement of practices such as domiciliary elder abuse (see Chapter 10) fundamentally challenges the assumptions underpinning the ideology of caring.

In the 1970s, feminists began to critique the issue that caring was 'private' and part of the family. Rather it was argued that women fulfilled caring responsibilities in the family which benefited the public arena of paid employment. This reflects the sexual division of labour, which was postulated by feminist theorists in the 1970s (Oakley, 1974). Women traditionally have been employed in low-paid and unskilled jobs and caring reflects this, as a low-status and low-paid activity. This feminist critique of caring is exemplified in the work of Finch and Groves (1983), who discussed how women were keeping the new community care policies going. As women support the family, and community care relies on the family, then they are most likely to be in a caring role. Caring is often an isolated and stressful activity, which can lead to carers themselves developing physical and mental health problems (McKinlay, 1995), as well as encountering financial difficulties.

Case study

The duty team refers 58-year-old Joan to you, who lives with her 80-year-old mother, who has Alzheimer's. Joan has rung social services 'in desperation', saying she has not slept properly for months. She says she does not really see anyone else, apart from the neighbours, as her mother 'is an embarrassment'. She used to work as a teacher, but now cannot leave her mother on her own. She is also worried about finances, as she has used most of her savings to keep her and her mother afloat.

- What are the principal stresses for Joan?
- How could sociological theory help you to understand Joan's situation?

Feminist perspectives on caring have been criticized for a number of reasons. Abrams (1978) discusses the positives of caring for both individuals and society, where caring is seen as a reciprocal activity. In return for support in childhood, family members repay a 'debt of gratitude'. Caring is not necessarily a burden, but experiences vary and are linked to a range of psychological, sociological and environmental factors. Finch and Mason (1993) discuss how there is an element of obligation to caring, but that this is by no means universal. People from working-class communities may be more likely to take on a caring role than their middle-class counterparts, for example.

The feminist critique of caring also loses sight of other groups who provide care. The 2001 Census showed that while the majority of carers were still women, 42% were men. This is particularly the case among carers who are 70 years or over.

The commodification of care

Although informal care has always been important, policy changes in health and social care since the 1980s have strengthened the role of informal care within a mixed economy of welfare (Evers et al., 1994). In the UK, payments such as Invalid Care Allowance (1975) were introduced to support carers, and carers have become central providers of care.

Rather than being the expert providers of care, health and social care professionals are increasingly working in partnership with carers. There have even been calls for a ban on the term 'informal care' as it fails to give sufficient credit to the work that carers do.

Care is increasingly being commodified, with a policy shift from payments to carers to payments to care users. The social model of disability and the disability movement have been particularly influential here (see Chapter 5). Thus individuals become empowered to pay for their own packages of care, which fundamentally shifts the relationship between the family, the market and the state and challenges processes of medicalization, professionalization and bureaucratization. In terms of caring, there is a breakdown of the boundaries between the gift relationship (Cheal, 1988), where care is provided within the context of a personal relationship, and the market economy, where care becomes a commodity. However, whilst the nature of caring in the informal sector may be changing, it still remains a gendered activity, with women providing much of the care within the mixed economy of welfare (Ungerson, 1997).

In conclusion, there is now a body of literature and research on caring and the needs of carers. While feminist perspectives have been criticized, there appears to be a correlation between caring and women. Interestingly, there are issues about caring tasks. Clarke (2001) discusses how women are likely to carry out more personal care tasks than men. Certainly, caring represents a significant issue for women, and the roots of this can clearly be seen in sociological debates around gender and gendered roles.

Exercise: recruitment and social care

More than 1 million people are employed in the care workforce in Britain – over 750,000 in social care and nearly 350,000 in childcare. They are mostly women (88 per cent), especially in childcare, and, apart from social workers, they have below-average levels of qualifications. With the increase in the levels of qualifications of school leavers, the pool of young women with low levels of qualifications is likely to shrink, implying more competition between those occupations which draw on this pool of recruits. As the qualification requirements within the sector rise, new competition for recruitment is introduced, particularly with the health and education sectors. (Simon et al., 2003)

- What are the implications of this for the future of social care provision in Britain?
- What impact might the commodification of care have on women's paid employment and the value that is attached to caring?

Critical theories on masculinity and femininity

Critical perspectives are useful for deconstructing concepts such as masculinity and femininity. They challenge the ways in which constructions of gender, masculinity and femininity are linked to biological sex identity, and how they are constructed as binary opposites, within a hierarchical relationship in which masculinity is seen as dominant and femininity is seen as subordinate.

There have been changes in roles and behaviours, with traditional female and male identities being questioned. Annandale (2008) identifies a shift in lifestyle, with females adopting more of the health-damaging behaviour that has traditionally been associated with males. For example, in terms of alcohol consumption, there has been a narrowing of the gap between teenage boys and girls (Alcohol Concern, 2010).

This change in female behaviour and lifestyle practices has led some commentators to suggest that there is a moral panic about the nature of femininity and the role of girls in society. Barron and Lacombe (2005), for example, have suggested that there has been a rise in aggressive and anti-social behaviour in girls, while an OECD Survey (2009) claims that in the UK, the proportion of teenage girls binge drinking has risen from 17 to 27%, the highest in Europe. Other studies point to a rise in mortality and morbidity from cirrhosis and other alcohol-related disorders amongst women as a result of changed drinking practices (Alcohol Concern, 2010). Whilst the proportion of girls and boys drinking has fallen, prevalence amongst boys and girls is at similar levels (National Centre for Social Research, 2012).

Exercise: girls and alcohol

What period would you guess that the following headlines are from?

> . . . she doesn't really care whether she gets married or not, so long as she can earn a comfortable living and have a good time . . . [she] crawls home at three or four in the morning, a haggard, weary-eyed creature.

These quotes are actually taken from the 1920s (*Girls' Weekly*, cited in Jackson and Tinkler, 2007: 3).

- How far do these concerns reflect changing gender roles or the nature of adolescent transition?

Jackson and Tinkler (2007) have argued that the moral panic of ladette culture has been exaggerated, and the changes in lifestyle behaviours have a rather longer history than many commentators suggest. It has also been suggested that there is a crisis in masculinity as a result of changes in the economy, social structures and household composition. According to Cleaver (2001):

> The 'demasculinising' effects of poverty and of economic and social change may be eroding men's traditional roles as providers and limiting the availability of alternative, meaningful roles for men in families and communities. Men may consequently seek affirmation of their masculinity in other ways; through irresponsible sexual behaviour or domestic violence for example.

This crisis is not universal but confined to particular groups of men.

The decline of manufacturing has primarily hit working-class men, with unemployed, unskilled and unmarried men having higher mortality and illness rates than other groups of men. In non-traditional employment areas such as social work, men may not necessarily conform to constructions of hegemonic masculinity, though they do benefit from being located in a female-dominated profession (Hearn and Parkin, 2001). A study carried out by the Joseph Rowntree Foundation in 2001 explored 'the "laddish" attributes commonly associated with white working-class masculinity and whether they have become a disadvantage in the new labour markets'. It found that young men's views of masculinity in some ways conformed to the notion of a 'lad', but also emphasized domestic conformity. Attitudes, behaviours and definitions of masculinity were varied, changing and complex, but the 'traditional' notions of masculinity dominated as opposed to a 'new version of masculinity which might be more in tune with the requirements of a service-based economy' (Joseph Rowntree Foundation, 2001).

Links have been made to masculinity and young men's perception of themselves, and this may have effects on their mental well-being. Suicide is the most common form of death for men aged 35 and under in England, having doubled in the last 20 years. Males in lower socio-economic groups and gay and bisexual men are more likely to commit suicide than are heterosexual and middle-class men. Conversely, new roles and expectations of young men in society may lead to loss of self-esteem if they are unable to live up to these. They may then be vulnerable to suicide if they lack appropriate supportive social networks or are not able to communicate their concerns (McClure, 2001: 471).

In his study of this area, McClure (2001) concluded that those young men who held stereotyped perceptions of masculinity were less likely to express their feelings and seek help with their problems. This was reinforced by agencies' responses to them; they felt that there was little point in targeting this group. Rather than a preference to see male workers, the study identified that men did not want to be viewed as weak or vulnerable by other men, challenging notions of 'role modelling' as promoted by some texts. Instead of talking through their difficulties with a professional, men preferred to escape the stress through the use of alcohol, use 'inner strength' to protect themselves or 'talk it out with a friend'. Differences in emotional expression were mostly related to the significant differences between gay and straight men (see also Chapter 11).

Marked gender differences have been noted in the way in which men respond to loss and bereavement. Thompson (1998) has argued that models of grief and bereavement have been constructed around normative constructions of femininity and masculinity, with men being expected to be strong and supportive of others. Thus men may be disenfranchised through societal expectations that they will not be emotionally expressive (Martin and Doka, 2000). There are numerous examples of how the media invigilate these societal expectations, with men being portrayed as strong and in control (Walter et al., 1995).

Working with men as service users

Cree (1996) challenges what she views as a reluctance by feminist social workers to address working with men, as they have given priority to working with women. It is argued that 'men blindness' in feminist social work runs the risk of reinforcing traditional stereotypes about women's roles and behaviour as well as leaving men to challenge male power and masculinity in areas such as violence towards women and children.

Social work has been criticized for failing to engage with men, either as service users in their own right or as fathers of children and other relatives. A conference by the Family Rights Group in 2005 highlighted the systematic failure of health and social care services to engage fathers and father-figures through failing to listen to fathers' concerns, negating the role of fathers in assessments and inadequate provision of support. A Social Care Institute for Excellence research briefing (2005a) discusses the specific issues raised for fathers who are caring for disabled children.

There are some understandable reasons why social workers are reluctant to engage with men. Female service users may be perceived as less threatening and intimidating than male service users, as men carry the threat of violence even when it is not transferred into action (Cree, 2000). However, engaging and working effectively with fathers and other men who affect the well-being of children and families is now firmly emphasized in policy frameworks as a strategic requirement for all children's services, and a number of projects have been set up in social work with such a remit.

Hearn and Parkin's (2001) research on male violence towards women is significant in terms of the minimal contact the men had with social service departments and other agencies. When contact is made, the focus is not directed at stopping the violent behaviour as other problems are addressed. Hearn recommends that agencies, including the police, probation services, health and social services, address men's power and their oppression of others through development of specific policies and practices. In addition, agencies should address men's experiences of their personal problems and their avoidance of agency contact. Hearn further suggests that the challenge for those male-dominated agencies is how to renounce violence and not collude with it. Cree (1996) has developed a useful code of practice for females working with men in social work, while Pease and Pringle (2001) provide a model for anti-sexist practice for male social workers.

Exercise: working with men

- What are the issues for female social workers in engaging with men?
- What role can male workers play in working with men?
- How we do influence future attitudes of boys to fatherhood and working with children?
- How would sociological theories explain this?

Risk and exploitation

There are risks associated with gendered roles and societal expectations, and feminists have argued that patriarchal oppression causes risks for women in terms of economic and sexual exploitation. The economic relations of society and the sexual division of labour have led to a feminization of poverty (Scott, 1984), whilst oppressive practices within the domestic sphere may lead to domestic violence, which is a risk for a significant number of women within the institutions of marriage and the family.

A central feature of the risk society is an increase in individualization as traditional supportive forms such as the family, community and fixed gender roles are reconstructed via new forms of socialization (Beck, 1992). As men and women break free from traditional roles regarding constructions of masculinity and femininity, they are faced with not only new opportunities but also new risks. Women are no longer dependent upon men for economic support, but for many women economic freedom may also bring about financial hardship (Office of the Deputy Prime Minister, 2004). Women may also be disempowered and denied the rights of citizenship through domestic violence. The Home Office *Crime Survey for England and Wales* (2012a) records some sobering statistics here:

- One in three women worldwide will be subject to intimate partner abuse.
- In the UK one in four women and one in six men will be a victim of domestic violence in their lifetime.
- In 2010/11 21 men and 93 women were killed by a partner, ex-partner or lover.
- There are more repeat victims than in any other crime.
- Domestic violence is the largest cause of morbidity worldwide for women aged 19–44.

Most feminist theories of domestic violence emphasize patriarchal power relations that exist within society and heterosexual relationships and reject individualistic explanations that highlight the pathological behaviour of the aggressor. There has been a significant shift in the law (Children Act, 2004) and social work practice which recognizes the risks posed to children where domestic violence persists. While a shift in policy and practice is a welcome aspect of child protection, these changes are born out of a concern for the welfare of children as opposed to a concern for women. In recognition of a growing understanding of power and control in young people's relationships and the use of sexual violence by males in gangs, Government extended the definition of domestic violence to include coercive control of those over 16 (Home Office, 2013b; see also Chapter 7).

Domestic violence is often hidden, but this staged picture demonstrates some of the psychological effects on women. (© Marcel Pelletier/iStock)

The notion of patriarchal violence has led to questions about men's position in social work, which faces several contradictions in relation to men's roles as workers in a 'caring' profession and men as service users. Following a series of abuses by social workers, significantly in residential care homes for children, the role of men in caring professions has come under scrutiny. Feminist social workers have challenged the failure of many public inquiries to consider the gendered nature of the abuse. However, some have argued that men should not be employed in childcare work because of the risk posed by male abusers. Pease and Pringle (2001) recognize that women may also act as perpetrators of violence towards children, but conclude that men perpetrate the overwhelming majority of sexual abuse. Explanations of male sexual violence towards children draw upon psychological as well as sociological theories, and social psychologists discuss the role of the peer group in rape-supportive cultures in which such violence is accepted and socially endorsed.

Theories of socialization may also explain male violence in terms of power and subordination in personal and social relations. Connell's (1995) concept of hegemonic masculinities, in which masculinity is in part expressed through sexual desire, may explain why men are more likely than women to engage in abusive sexual relations. Pringle (1995: 179) similarly claims that 'imperious sexual desire plays an important role and is strongly linked to a sense of personal adequacy and success; numerous conflicts and uncertainties over dependency and personal adequacy remain that may be resolved by satisfaction of sexual desire.' They do remind us, however, that the majority of men and boys do not commit sexual violence towards children.

Male violence and men's role in the caring professions challenge personal, interpersonal and structural gendered relations within social work and wider society.

Globalization, work and sexual exploitation

Sociologists are interested in how the economic and social changes associated with globalization affect the lives of men and women. Whilst globalization has undoubtedly created more employment opportunities for women within the manufacturing and services sectors, providing greater economic freedom, there are concerns about the negative consequences of a globalized labour production as female workers tend to be concentrated in the labour-intensive, export industries in developing countries and dominate the international migration of care services workers (Barrientos et al., 2004): 'The jobs that women are moving into in the financial, information and communications industries, for example, have been characterized as work within "electronic sweatshops"; low paid and highly stressful. Whilst those highly paid jobs within these industries remain male dominated' (Elias, 2003). Flexibilization is associated with deregulated work practices, which offer little protection for workers, and has been linked to feminization of employment.

The migration of female care workers is of direct relevance to social work. The UK has a history of recruiting migrant workers, particularly to work in the National Health Service, but less so in social care. However, the situation has changed since the early 2000s. According to the most recent Labour Force Survey estimates, 135,000 foreign-born care workers were working in the UK in the last quarter of 2008, though this is likely to be an underestimate owing to the unreliability of data collection methods (Cangiona et al., 2009). Migrants account for 18% of all care workers, approximately 23% in health care and 14% in social work. The effects of an ageing society, the commodification of care and the personalization agenda have influenced the demand for migrant workers. Cangiona et al. (2009) consider the impact of this on the migrant workers themselves, the quality of care for older people and the future provision of social care. They identify a reliance on migrant workers to provide sufficient care within the UK and identify a number of recommendations in order to improve the consistency and quality of care provided whilst safeguarding the rights of workers.

Case study

Louisa arrived in the UK in August 2008, her migration being fuelled by her need to support her three children as a lone parent. She was a nurse attendant in the Philippines, doing work similar to her current occupation as a carer in a domiciliary care company. Yet she finds the jobs difficult because she has been subject to numerous experiences of exploitation. She has been exploited by her recruitment agency in the Philippines, because they didn't give her sufficient information about the job, by the UK recruitment agency, because of coercion and financial exploitation, by the training agency (more financial exploitation) and finally by her current employer (financial exploitation, emotional abuse). The employer has made it clear to Louisa that she owes them because they 'paid' for her and that she must withstand exploitative circumstances or face punishment if she protests. They even told her that she could not leave the company. Louisa discovered that this was wrong after contacting an agency (through the researcher), which advised her that she could indeed leave and that they could intervene on her behalf if she wanted. Scrutinizing the visa renewal policy, and thinking she needed to be working in a nursing home to get her visa renewed, she has found another job with staff who have promised her more support. She is encouraged by her contact with this agency that she can be supported on a student visa and is hopeful about working for her new employer.

Source: Cuban (2010)

- What support should social care employers provide for migrant social care workers?
- How can staff raise matters of concern about working conditions and their treatment by service users?
- What strategies are in place to ensure that migrant workers are not exploited and that aspects of quality of care include relationships?
- What should social workers consider in drawing up support plans with individuals, and how can they raise issues regarding fair employment conditions so that neither party is exploited?

(Adapted from Manthorpe, 2009)

Prostitution and trafficking

The regulation and exploitation of women's sexual behaviour is seen as a key feature of the patriarchal domination of women. The word 'prostitute' generally refers to a woman over the age of consent who willingly exchanges sexual services for money. While prostitution is legal in Britain, many activities associated with it remain illegal. Prostitution is heavily stigmatized and prostitutes continue to receive harassment from the police and the wider community. Prostitution is illegal in some countries, including much of the USA. In Iraq, dozens of women suspected of prostitution have been beheaded (*Matter of the Inquiry*, 2002). Criminalization does not put an end to prostitution, however, and leaves women vulnerable and at risk of further victimization and exploitation.

Feminists have long debated whether prostitution represents a form of control and subordination or whether it is a legitimate form of work in a wider sex industry, which requires state regulation and protection. The term 'sex worker' emphasizes the employment aspect of the role and places prostitutes alongside other women who experience low pay and poor status in a segregated labour market. Dworkin (1981: 144–5) claims:

> When men use women in prostitution, they are expressing a pure hatred for the female body. It is as pure as anything on this earth ever is or ever has been. It is contempt so deep, so deep, that a whole human life is reduced to a few sexual orifices, and he can do anything he wants.

Some feminists argue for the redefining of prostitution as sex work, emphasizing the need for the empowerment and protection of women through better rights and police protection. They object to 'the designation of prostitution as a special human rights issue, a violation in itself', as this

> emphasises the distinction between prostitution and other forms of female or low-status labour . . . however exploitative they are. It thus reinforces the marginal, and

therefore vulnerable, position of the women and men involved in prostitution. By dismissing the entire sex industry as abusive, it also obscures the particular problems and violations of international norms within the industry, which are of concern to sex workers. (Bindman and Doezema, 1997: 3)

Some feminists view globalization as an opportunity for women in providing a global platform from which to articulate women's political agenda through increased communication and the presence of global institutions such as the EU and UN.

Global feminism can provide an analysis of

> the intersection of gender with race, class, and issues related to the colonization and exploitation of women in the developing world. Global feminism is a movement of people working for change across national boundaries. The world is interdependent and becoming more so. Global feminism contends that no woman is free until the conditions that oppress women worldwide are eliminated. (Bunch cited in Lindsey, 2013: 249)

Biemann (2002), however, argues that globalization through an expanding global sex trade and the migration of women into low-paid domestic service has led to the feminization of migration. Human trafficking, a form of globalized slavery, is a gendered activity and is closely linked with sexual exploitation. Reports estimate that between 2 million and 5 million men, women and children are trafficked each year (International Labour Organization, 2005), and approximately 80% of those trafficked are women and children and up to 50% are minors (US Department of State, 2007). The majority of trafficked people come from the poorest parts of the world, including Africa, Asia and Eastern Europe. Following arms and drugs trafficking, human trafficking is the third largest source of income for organized crime, generating approximately $9.5 billion (US Department of State, 2007). Until recently, there was no specific law or penalty in Britain that dealt with trafficking, and other laws tended to be used to prosecute offenders. In 2005, two Albanian men became the first people to be prosecuted for human trafficking under the Sexual Offences Act (2003). Now under the Asylum and Immigration Act (2004) traffickers can face up to 14 years in prison for trafficking for forced labour or organ removal. However, the Centre for Social Justice (2013) is critical of current practice in dealing with cases of human trafficking. They call for a Modern Slavery Act to bring together forms of trafficking and slavery and the creation of an Anti-Slavery Commissioner (based upon the Children's Commissioner model) to provide a multi-agency coordinated response to the growing problem. The safeguarding of trafficked children is discussed in Chapter 9.

Exercise: what's wrong with prostitution?

During the 2006 football World Cup Final in Germany, it was estimated that over 40,000 women would be trafficked for prostitution. Germany legalized prostitution in 2002 and Berlin has over 8,000 registered prostitutes.

- What is the difference between someone who has chosen to be a prostitute and someone who is forced into it?
- What difference does it make to the man who pays a woman for sex whether the prostitute he has sex with is there by choice or force? Should it make a difference?

- What is your reaction to all of this? Is prostitution fair?
- What bearing does sex trafficking have on the nature of the protection of the victims of trafficking?

Towards a feminist social work practice

Dominelli (1997: 86) uses the phrase 'feminist sociological social work' to refer to 'the sociological insights into women's condition provided by both black and white feminists'. This is an attempt to recognize the diversity of thought that exists within feminist sociology and also to firmly locate feminist social work practice as concerned with challenging and eradicating racism as well as other forms of oppression which women experience. 'Feminist social work is a form of social work practice which takes gendered inequality and its elimination as the starting point for working, whether as individuals, or within organizations, and seeks to promote women's well-being as women define it' (Dominelli, 2002: 27).

Insights from sociological perspectives on gender relations within society are not only valuable in developing feminist social work practice with women, but are particularly relevant in developing an understanding of gender relations in working with all men, women, girls and boys in all areas of social work practice.

Summary points

- Social work is a feminized activity.
- Feminism is not a single theory, but a range of theoretical perspectives which help us to understand the position of women in society.
- Sex and gender are differentiated. Whilst sex tends to refer to fixed biological entities and gender relates to social processes and experiences that influence men and women's lives, it could be suggested that both are socially constructed.
- Feminist theories have traditionally focused on women's oppressions. More recently, there has been a growing body of theory exploring the nature of masculinity, which has helped to inform contemporary debates in social work about working with men and boys.

Questions for discussion

- How can theories of gender relations contribute to your understanding of social work practice?
- What evidence is there that the differences between the genders are narrowing?
- Think about the roles in your household. Who does what? Are there distinctive gendered roles?
- What are the dominant ways that men and women are depicted in society?
- On your next placement, look at the gendered roles in the department. How far do these reflect segregated roles in the workforce?

Further reading

Abbott, P., Wallace, C. and Tyler, M. (2005) *An Introduction to Sociology: Feminist Perspectives.* **London: Routledge**
This is a useful book for exploring a range of feminist perspectives and their contribution within the sociological debate.

Dalley, G. (1988) *Ideologies of Caring: Rethinking Community and Collectivism.* **Basingstoke: Macmillan**
Although rather old now, this is a classic text in the analysis of the construction of caring and the relationship to gendered roles and expectations that underpin the politics of care.

Dominelli, L. (2002) *Feminist Social Work: Theory and Practice.* **Basingstoke: Palgrave Macmillan**
One of the few books that explore a range of feminist theories in relation to social work practice.

4 Race and Ethnicity

Introduction

Within sociology, race is a problematic concept. The inequality and exploitation that exist as a result of racial categorization are real and enduring; however, it is largely accepted that the scientific basis for such categorizing has been discredited.

Race is sometimes described by sociologists as having been invented to justify the exploitation and enslavement of less powerful groups by more dominant groups within a society. Hence the sociology of race is concerned with the causes and consequences of the socially constructed division of social groups according to their so-called 'racial' origins.

The history of race and racism means that race and ethnicity have become highly sensitive and controversial issues within British society, and this is particularly true within the professional arena of social work. Social workers have a responsibility to work with all sections of the community and in particular with disadvantaged and marginalized groups.

The key issues that will be explored in this chapter are:

- definitions of race and ethnicity and the legacy of scientific racism
- explanations of discrimination on the basis of racial and ethnic categorization
- social work's relationship with race and ethnicity
- contemporary issues within the context of social work practice with BME service users. *

By the end of this chapter, you should be able to:

- explain the differences between the terms 'race' and 'ethnicity'
- discuss issues of discrimination, disadvantage and oppression related to ethnic categorization
- explain what is meant by the terms 'institutionalized racism' and 'internalized oppression'
- understand the impact of immigration on social and psychological well-being
- discuss the role of social workers in working with BME service users.

---

* Within this chapter we will be using the term black and minority ethnic (BME) to refer to the experiences of black and other minority groups. It is recognized that notions of majority and minority are contested and are subject to challenge and change.

Social work and race

Social work's relationship with race and racism has an uncomfortable history. Social work practice has at best been accused of being ethnocentric and at worst of being racist. Social work has been criticized from within and outside of the profession for constructing a knowledge base that has heavily drawn on white, middle-class European perspectives, which consequently fail to adequately explain BME groups' lived experiences. Social work was also accused of racist practices in pathologizing black culture, lifestyles and practices. For example, Asian households were stereotyped by constructing notions of family life based upon the control and oppression of women and children, whereas African Caribbean families were regarded as fatherless, punitive and lacking warmth (Dominelli, 2008).

Owusu-Bempah (1993) suggests that the differentiation between Asian and African Caribbean families could be construed as an attempt to respond to cultural difference, though it could also reflect the dominant discourses regarding race and ethnicity within social work. Social control within social work could be seen in relation to mental health provision, in which specific experiences of black people within mental health and psychiatry led to accusations of insensitive and racist practice by social workers and other professionals.

> The pathologization of the black community, and of cultural differences in particular, is taken a step further by the racialization of schizophrenia that British psychiatry has achieved in its institutional practice. This only leads to psychiatry being used, once again, as a powerful medium for articulating ideas about race rather than about mental illness. (Sashidharan, cited in Taylor, 1989: 119)

What was emerging in social work was practice in which BME service users found themselves over-represented in the more controlling aspects of welfare such as child protection and school exclusions and in the compulsory use of mental health legislation, and under-represented in the more supportive, non-compulsory aspects of welfare such as family support, family therapy and counselling (Dominelli, 2008). Some of the issues concerning race, ethnicity and social work practice will be developed later in the chapter, but first we will explore how sociology contributes to our understanding of race.

The myth of scientific racism

> Race and ethnicity are not 'natural' categories, even though both concepts are often represented as if they were. Their boundaries are not fixed, nor is their membership uncontested. Race and ethnic groups, like nations, are imagined communities. People are socially defined as belonging to particular ethnic or racial groups, either in terms of definitions employed by others, or definitions which members of particular ethnic groups develop for them. They are ideological entities, made and changed in struggle. They are discursive formations, signalling a language through which differences accorded social significance may be named and explained. But what is of importance to us as social researchers studying race and ethnicity is that such ideas also carry with them material consequences for those who are included within, or excluded from, them.
>
> (Bulmer and Solomos, 1998: 822)

The idea of a scientific basis to race emerged in the mid-1700s with the view that human beings could be separated into distinct racial groups based upon biological and phenotypical characteristics (the expression of genes – skin/eye colour, hair type). The races which were identified included Caucasian, African and Mongoloid, and within those groups emerged a hierarchy with white European males being placed at the top and others placed below on a scale of differences marked by skin colour and skull size and shape.

This period in history, known as 'the Enlightenment', reflected a time of a growing interest in rationalization whereby differences in people could be articulated and measured (see Chapter1). Differences in behaviour, intelligence, morality and godliness were attributed to physiological differences, and Africans were viewed as amoral and less intelligent and human than Caucasians. There were similar comparisons being drawn in the area of criminality and prostitution, and differences in skin, eyes, ears and skull size were seen as a causal link for any behaviours that were defined as immoral (Nott and Gliddon, 1854, cited in Haralambos and Holborn, 2004).

It is widely believed that racism as an ideology developed at the end of the sixteenth century and was used to justify the slave trade between Africa, Europe and America. The racism that was associated with notions of Britishness and superiority was used to promulgate colonial expansion into Africa and Asia. The ideology epitomized by Rudyard Kipling's 1899 poem 'White Man's Burden' was used to justify European domination and control in colonized countries, whereby civilized white people, under the guise of paternalism, could take responsibility for the economic and legal governance of uncivilized communities that were unable to rule themselves. Ideologies of racial superiority were extended beyond colour to include all immigrants to Britain in the nineteenth century. There is evidence of Irish settlement in Britain as early as the twelfth century, though mass immigration did not occur until prior to, during and after the Great Famine of 1846, when approximately 1.5 million people emigrated. In terms of scientific racism, Irish people were viewed as being only marginally superior to Africans (Irish people were sometimes referred to as White Negroes) and concerns were raised regarding the over-breeding of the Irish and the threat to Anglo-Saxon community and culture (Douglas, 2002).

Scientific racism validated the aspirations of the eugenics movement in Western Europe and the USA in the early twentieth century. It promoted the use of science to control breeding in order to increase desirable characteristics and remove inferior ones, with the primary aim of creating a pure race. This pure race consisted of white, able-bodied, heterosexual human beings. The scientific basis of race differences has been refuted, and any differences in genetic make-up between people do not reflect the so-called 'racial' groups. Jones (1993) states that modern genetics shows that there are no separate groups within humans and that genetic differences between people are individual as opposed to being based upon any ideas of nationality or 'race'. However, despite this discrediting of the scientific basis of race, the debates concerning the so-called 'biological' differences between people continue. A controversy has been in the area of intelligence differences between racial groups. This first arose in the 1950s (Eysenck, 1971) and later through the work of Herrnstein and Murray (1994), in which it was claimed that black people score consistently lower on IQ tests than whites. In 2006, a university lecturer, Frank Ellis, wrote a controversial article claiming that black students were intellectually inferior to their white counterparts (see BBC News, 2006). This article, which appeared in a university student union publication, again fuelled a debate concerning the scientific basis of race and demonstrates the continued power and significance of discourses surrounding race within contemporary British society. So whilst there is no biological basis for the concept of race, the social and political aspects of racial categorization persist and the area of race and ethnicity has emerged to be a significant aspect of sociological inquiry.

Critical race theory (CRT), which originated from the USA in the 1970s, focuses upon the social construction of race and racism, recognizing how racism is embedded within society through social structures, relationships and practices (Delgado and Stefancic, 2012). In recognition of this, most sociologists now prefer to use the term 'race' to mean a socially constructed way of categorizing people.

Explaining ethnicity

The legacy of scientific racism has meant that in common usage the term 'race' is used to refer to physical or visible differences between people, and 'ethnicity' and 'ethnic group' are associated with cultural differences (Fenton, 1999). Though they are conceptually different, there are times when the terms 'race' and 'ethnicity' tend to be used interchangeably, particularly in relation to research and social work practice. Some sociologists prefer to employ the concept of ethnicity as opposed to race, in an attempt to dismiss notions of biological determinism and recognize the centrality of social constructionism (see Chapter 1).

Theories of ethnicity and ethnic relations have re-emerged in sociology following ethnic conflicts in Europe and Africa. Ethnicity can be described as the identification of individuals with particular ethnic groups. An ethnic group can be defined as 'a group whose members identify with each other, usually on the basis of a presumed common genealogy or ancestry' (Smith, 1986: 21). Ethnic groups are also usually united by common cultural, behavioural, linguistic or religious practices, which may or may not be associated with common descent. The 2001 UK Census changed its classifications of ethnicity to include the category 'mixed' instead of 'other', representing the significant growth in numbers of people from mixed ethnic backgrounds. Mixed race, like other terms such as mixed heritage or mixed parentage, is a generic concept. The idea that ethnicities can be mixed is a problematic one and is rooted in the biological construction of race and ethnicity. Bulmer and Solomos (1998), quoted earlier in the chapter, assert that ethnicity is both fluid and unboundaried, and it can be argued that terminology such as 'mixed race' or 'mixed ethnicity' implies that pure races or ethnic groups exist. Some sociologists may use the term 'mixed origins', whilst others view this as ambiguous, lacking any specific reference to ethnicity (Aspinall, 2009).

Identification of membership of a particular ethnic group is based upon an understanding (by self or others) of a sense of shared history or belonging, real or imagined. Pilkington (2003) identifies processes of ethnic group formation in his discussion of a black or African American ethnic identity, which unified culturally and nationally diverse groups of people from West Africa through the processes of enslavement and *diaspora*.

> **Diaspora** a term used to describe the dispersion of people from their homeland. It is usually used to mean a forced dispersion of a religious or ethnic group, but, recognizing the flawed origins of the term, it can refer to the situation of any group dispersed, forcibly or voluntarily, throughout the world on the basis of assumed biological differences.

The idea of groups can imply a static category, with the risk that cultural distinctiveness can be exaggerated (Pilkington, 2003), whereas viewing ethnicity as social classifications within relationships avoids *essentialism* and recognizes the fluidity that exists between ethnicities. Ethnicity can thus be understood as a relative or relational social process, involving the shifting of boundaries and identity which people draw around themselves in their social lives (Fenton, 1999). From a static category perspective, by contrast, whiteness and majorities are assumed to be natural and the norm, whereas blackness and minorities reflect difference and diversity. White people can therefore operate from a position where their way of being is seen as the norm, while other ways of being are, at best, exotic and, at worst, dysfunctional. This can lead to a danger of ethnocentrism, whereby one judges other groups or societies by the standards that apply in one's own society. These issues are explored by Mohanty's (1992) critique of Western feminist discourse, which, she argued, overgeneralizes the concept of woman and fails to see the diversity of women's experiences within the developing world.

Essentialism the way in which groups become defined as homogeneous on the basis of predefined characteristics or dispositions.

Certain forms of 'Englishness' have been associated with national identity at football matches, and at times have been seen as perpetuating racist attitudes. (© Simon Askham/iStock)

Ethnocentrism can also refer to the way that the lifestyles, experiences, values and norms of one group in a society are assumed to be common to everyone. This has been one of the criticisms of social work practice with black users, which will be explored later in this chapter.

Sociologists have fallen into the trap of assuming white homogeneity, and it is only recently that the construction of whiteness has become a focus of exploration within sociology. In particular, sociology has been accused of ignoring the racialization of Irish people and the experiences of Irish communities as a minority ethnic group (Hickman, 1995). Discourses regarding ethnicity usually involve constructions of ethnic majority and ethnic minority, a form of dualism in which differences are exaggerated. Within discussions of ethnicity it is often assumed that reference is being made to ethnic minority groups. There is an assumption of homogeneity within the so-called 'ethnic majority' and that it is not worthy of analysis.

> Perhaps one reason that conversations about race are so often doomed to frustration is that the notion of whiteness as 'race' is almost never implicated. . . . Exnomination permits whites to entertain the notion that race lives 'over there' on the other side of the tracks, in black bodies and inner city neighbourhoods, in a dark netherworld where whites are not involved. (Williams, 1996: 4)

The provision of accurate information on the ethnic composition of the UK can be problematic as much data collection relies upon self-identification; however, it is useful to note trends in migration. For the period 2002-9, the Office for National Statistics (2010b) estimated that for England and Wales the majority category of White British people remained fairly static, whilst the number for other ethnic groups rose from 2.5 million to 9.1 million over the same period (Office for National Statistics, 2013a). Whilst there has been an increase in the White Non-British categories, reflecting an increase in populations from Australia, Canada and South Africa, populations from White Irish backgrounds have declined.

The data reflect a complex picture of migration patterns, global political conflict and regional variations, as well as differences in birth rates for specific ethnic groups – information which is necessary for agencies such as the National Health Service and local authorities planning the delivery of services.

Exercise: identifying ethnicity

Some of the difficulties associated with self-identification can be highlighted through this group activity. Look at Figure 4.1.

- How would you describe your ethnicity?
- Do you belong to an ethnic group?
- How is your ethnicity characterized?

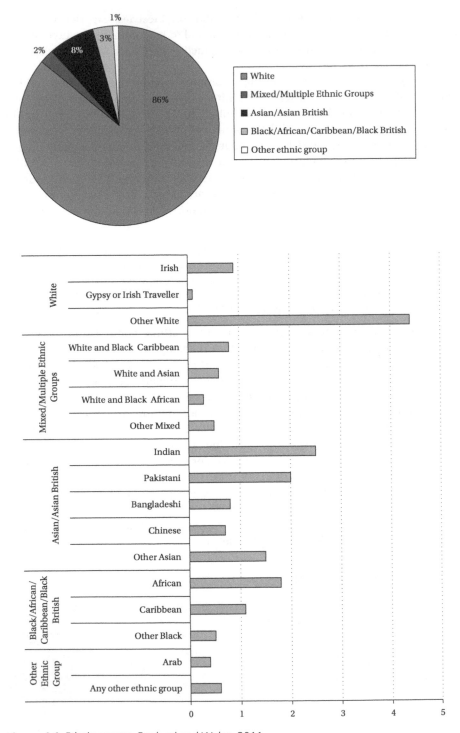

Figure 4.1 Ethnic groups, England and Wales, 2011.

Source: Office for National Statistics, 2012b.

Structural approaches to understanding race and ethnicity ▬▬▬

Functionalism

Integrationist approaches to race focus upon black people and immigration and point to the problems of immigration in terms of securing employment, gaining appropriate education and training and obtaining housing. Once people have adjusted to living in Britain and have assimilated within British society, problems of unemployment and exclusion and differences between groups should disappear.

Functionalist perspectives on race have tended to explain racism and discrimination in relation to integration and *assimilation* by the migrant communities into the host society (Best, 2005). In his analysis of American society in the 1950s and 1960s, Parsons viewed the discrimination faced by black Americans as based upon shared values which viewed black skin colour as inferior – a belief that was used as justification for

> **Assimilation** the process whereby minorities adopt and blend into the dominant culture of the host nation. This was a feature of 1960s race relations policies.

the uniform treatment of black American people. He saw the existence of such racism as failure by black American communities and white American society to successfully include black people in the dominant culture and value system (Best, 2005).

In order to successfully integrate into the host community, migrants are required to adopt the dominant cultural value systems. Since resistance to inclusion can take place on both sides, Parsons favoured state intervention in the form of anti-discriminatory legislation to assist this process.

Merton (1938) also saw the common value system as important in understanding racism. He developed a theory regarding prejudice and discrimination which suggested that there are four main types of relationship between prejudice and discrimination (Table 4.1). Merton concluded that prejudice does not necessarily lead to discrimination and that people may discriminate for a variety of reasons, for example material gain.

- The bigot is a racist person who is prejudiced and does discriminate.
- The timid bigot is also a racist, in that this person is prejudiced but does not discriminate, possibly because s/he believes it to be wrong or fears the consequences of discrimination.
- The fair-weather liberal is a person who is not prejudiced but who does discriminate, possibly owing to the advantages of indirect forms of discrimination.
- The all-weather liberal is not a racist, is not prejudiced and does not discriminate.

Table 4.1 *Merton's typology of personalities*

Personality type	Prejudice	Discrimination
Bigot	+	+
Timid bigot	+	–
Fair-weather liberal	–	+
All-weather liberal	–	–

Source: 'Merton's typology of personalities', in *Understanding Social Divisions* by Shaun Best (London: Sage Publications, 2005): 155. Reprinted with permission.

Some of the main criticisms of functionalist theories focus upon the premise that racism and discrimination will disappear as communities become more integrated within society and its failure to explain the persistence of racism and inequality in almost all aspects of social and economic life. Functionalism also assumes a consensus within the host society and ignores the differences and hostilities that exist within white communities. It assumes that there is a consensus of the superiority of white English or American culture, and blames BME communities for the inequality they experience and their apparent failure to integrate successfully into host communities and gain full citizenship.

Singh (1992) provides a discussion of social work's recent history of working with BME communities, acknowledging the significant strides made within the profession in recognizing and meeting the needs of BME individuals and groups. The book does not necessarily represent a successful progression of social work in recent decades. Instead, it discusses the at times uncomfortable and controversial history of social work with regard to race and ethnicity, and recognizes that at any one time poor and ineffective practice can be found alongside creative and empowering practice with black service users. Social work values, centred on notions of equality and treating people the same, have led to accusations of colour blindness, where social workers, not wanting to discriminate or recognize difference, have found themselves ignoring specific cultural and religious needs of black service users and instead provided inappropriate services or no services at all. The emphasis within social work and other welfare agencies was one of assimilationist and integrationist practices, in which particular cultural needs were ignored or minimized – a one-size-fits-all approach. It was assumed that if immigrant communities learned the language and adopted the customs and norms of the majority society, then they would be integrated into the host community and would overcome some of the specific issues faced with regard to education, housing and employment. A colour-blind approach could be seen in relation to the placement needs of black children in the public care system (see section on 'Race, Adoption and Practice' below). A critical attack on social work practice with black children was provided by the *Black and in Care* Report (1985). The report identified over-representation of black children in care, the lack of recognition of children's religious, cultural and linguistic needs, the proportionally longer time spent in care compared to white counterparts, and the placement of black children with white foster carers. The overwhelming message was that black children were being denied their blackness and were being failed by the state as corporate parents. The position today presents a similar picture of the over-representation of non-white children within the looked after children population (Owen and Statham, 2009).

Integrationist approaches remain popular, and can be illustrated by the UK Government Citizenship Test. Introduced in 2005, the controversial 'Life in the UK' Citizenship Test is designed to assist with integration within British society and covers questions such as the UK Constitution, life in the UK and entitlements. The test has received widespread criticism for providing a racially and class-biased view as to what constitutes 'Britishness', whilst some reports state that over 70% of current UK citizens would fail the test (Ipsos MORI, 2012).

In 2013 the test was revised (*http://lifeintheuktest.ukba.homeoffice.gov.uk/*) and now emphasizes British history and achievements, though this may not serve to provide a consensus as to what constitutes British identity within the twenty-first century.

Exercise: citizenship test

Complete a sample citizenship test. (There are a number of practice citizenship tests available via the web, for example *http://www.citizenshiptest.org.uk/*.)

- Do you think that the test 'focuses on values and principles at the heart of being British'?
- Did you achieve the 75% necessary to pass? If not, what does your score suggest about your identity or nationality?

Marxist and neo-Marxist perspectives

Traditional Marxist approaches to understanding race and ethnicity tend to regard race as being largely irrelevant and assert that discrimination and oppression experienced by BME groups are a product of capitalism. The bourgeoisie generate racism to justify exploitation and the underdevelopment of the Third World. Hence the eradication of capitalism will lead to the removal of racism. Traditional Marxists explain working-class racism as the product of false consciousness, which draws divisions between black and white workers.

The Birmingham Centre for Contemporary Cultural Studies (CCCS), which included in its ranks notable writers such as Solomos, Findlay, Jones and Gilroy, produced a collection of essays in 1982 entitled *The Empire Strikes Back* which provide a neo-Marxist critique on race. They regarded traditional theories as being too simplistic and economically reductionist, in which everything is explained by the capitalist economic system. There is also some evidence to suggest that racism predates capitalism (CCCS, 1982). The CCCS therefore regarded race and racism not in evolutionary terms, but as a series of different events – 'struggles, breaks and discontinuities' – in which black people do not simply submit to racism, but resist and challenge it. Solomos et al. in the CCCS (1982) recognized what they described as the concept of New Racism, which expressed superiority and inferiority through cultural differences rather than biological ones. Cultural superiority emphasized difference in which black culture, values and beliefs were regarded as inferior to those of white British communities. Rather than focusing purely on capitalism as creating racism, neo-Marxist sociologists such as Miles (1989) consider the ways in which class and race interact in some form of causal dependency to create racialized factions within classes.

Miles (1989) regards race as a social construct, and argues that racialization occurs in any situation where racial meanings are attached. He separates out the concept of race from the ideas associated with it, describing it as a 'socially imagined', arbitrary term which singles out only particular physical features. However, while Miles recognizes the significance of race as a social construct, racism tends to be subsumed under class exploitation.

Social action approaches to race and ethnicity

Race relations the term used to describe how different cultural groups interact within society.

Within Weberian theories of race and racism, race is regarded as a separate class. The term *race relations* is used in an attempt to construct a theoretical framework for the analysis of race and racism. For Weber, inequality in power and advantage takes three forms: class, status and party. Class inequality relates to inequality produced as a result of the capitalist economy, where black people tend to be concentrated in low-paid, low-skilled, non-unionized work, as well as having a disproportionate presence among the unemployed. Status reflects the different amounts of social standing that groups possess within society. In this instance, BME groups tend to have lower status within society, possessing a form of status inequality. Finally, in relation to party, ethnic groups tend to be politically marginalized. For Weberians, BME groups occupy a weak market position, and in their combination of class, party and status, they constitute a separate class or *underclass* (Rex and Tomlinson, 1970). The underclass thesis was initially coined by Weberians (and later hijacked by New Right ideology) and is characterized by groups' inability to improve their situation owing to discriminatory employment laws and practices (see Chapter 2). It explains how exclusionary practices (by employers, trade unions, colleagues, etc.) result in situations whereby BME communities are given differential rewards on the basis of their race and ethnicity, and hence people of BME backgrounds tend to be located in the secondary market. Similar processes operate in relation to access to

Social closure employed by Weber to describe the action of social groups who restrict entry and exclude benefit to those outside the group in order to maximize their own advantage. This exclusion denies other social groups positive life chances.

health, welfare and housing. The concept of *social closure* is used to explain the exclusionary practices within occupations whereby BME workers face exclusion from or restricted entry to certain occupations or professions. Carter (2003) suggests that the concentration of BME groups in particular areas of employment is associated with boundary markers such as gender and ethnicity, as opposed to the more objective elements of skill and qualification. Interviews in Hackney conducted by Koutrolikou (2005) highlight aspects of the Weberian concept of social closure as poor minority groups compete over limited resources and often shifting boundaries as groups redefine their identities. The underclass thesis does not account for the social mobility that exists within some black communities and assumes consensus and homogeneity within class and occupational groupings. The concept of race is used in an uncritical way, minimizing the significance of race as a social construct. These perspectives have been questioned for their tendency to focus upon individual or personal racism and as such reduce racism to the individual actions of those who exclude or discriminate: for example, employers in the labour market or teachers in education.

Critical theories: post-modernist perspectives

Post-modern critiques of traditional approaches to the understanding of race, ethnicity and racism tend to suggest that discourses around race arise out of the need to see the world in terms of binary opposites (black/white, majority/minority). They view concepts such as race and black ethnicity as totalizing; they are seen as too rigid

The reasons behind choosing to wear a veil may be many and varied, reflecting the multiple nature of a person's identity. (© Hasan Shaheed/iStock)

and inflexible, seeking to emphasize sameness and commonality within complex and diverse peoples (Anthias and Yuval-Davies, 1998; Hall, 1992; Rattansi, 1992). They regard such concepts as linguistic categorizations and challenge the essentialist notions that are expressed by other theories. Essentialism is used to refer to the 'essential essence' of people and the ways in which complex and multiple identities are reduced to a single attribute such as race or ethnicity. Hall (1996) employs the term '*new ethnicities*' to challenge notions of blackness or black identity as a fixed category, recognizing instead the plurality of ethnic identities that exist within non-white communities. All groups are ethnically differentiated (white and non-white), thus weakening the emphasis on difference between black and white. As discussed earlier in the chapter, ethnicity is not an absolute concept and new ethnicities emerge, as reflected by state recognition through inclusion of the category of 'mixed' in the 2001 UK Census. There is a shift

> **New ethnicities** a post-modern term used to refer to changing ethnic identities (see Stuart Hall).

away from the concept of black to represent all non-white groups, as there are no essential black subjects who share common histories, interests and lifestyles. Totalizing labels such as Black or Asian tend to suppress the diversity and difference that exist within BME communities, as some minority groups struggle to represent themselves (Rattansi, 1992).

An example of this within popular culture could be seen as British-born, second-generation Muslim women choosing to wear the veil as an expression of their religious and cultural identity. Anthias and Yuval-Davis (1998) argue that multiple identities based upon gender, race and class should be understood in terms of the context in which they are constructed. Different social processes, based upon the social divisions of race, class and gender, inter-relate to create specific social outcomes for people, thus resulting in situations in which people with multiple and contradictory identities are located in positions of subordination in different social and economic contexts. For example, BME women occupy spaces of subordination within the family, work and sexuality, and although white working-class men may be subordinate through class, they still may be seen as dominant (Best, 2005).

The particular experiences of Irish discrimination in Britain provide an illustration of the construction of racial categories and the visibility/invisibility of particular ethnic groups. Assumptions regarding white homogeneity have meant that Irish people are often classified with the native population or with other white minorities, and as a result Irish people often remain invisible.

The ethnic category of 'Irish' was only added to the Census in 2001, although there is much evidence to indicate that Irish people as an ethnic group experience systematic discrimination and exclusion throughout society. However, the absence of census data results in a lack of research evidence to support claims for services to meet specific needs and furthers the denial or minimization of the individual and cultural needs of Irish people. The Commission for Racial Equality Report *The Irish in Britain* (1997) indicates that Irish people are discriminated against and disadvantaged in employment, housing, education and the criminal justice system, and in access to health and social care services. Irish people are twice as likely to be unemployed and more likely to be involved in manual, unskilled and personal service employment. High proportions of Irish men are unskilled workers and are employed in the building industry, where employment patterns are often erratic (Commission for Racial Equality, 1997). The report *Room to Roam* (Power, 2004) provides comprehensive research into the experiences of Irish travellers and identifies the specific needs of traveller children and their difficulties concerning access to education. Irish people make up the largest single group sleeping rough in Britain's cities, and are more than twice as likely to be admitted to hospital with a diagnosis of mental illness as the indigenous population. Since the troubles in the North of Ireland, Irish people have been subject to police harassment, and it is considered that stop and search has gone far beyond the powers under the Prevention of Terrorism Act and reflects widespread anti-Irish attitudes in the British police force.

Explanations of the racialization of specific ethnic groups are complex and are illustrated by the experiences of Irish people and more recent economic migrants to Britain. However, the hostility that is directed towards migrants from Eastern Europe contrasts sharply with that directed towards migrants from Australia or the USA. Hence post-modern perspectives within sociology, in rejecting totalizing constructions of black identity, recognize difference and diversity within BME communities. However, the representation of difference may in fact promote nationalism and fundamentalism, as people may feel threatened with losing their cultural distinctiveness. This can be seen among some groups who wish to assert Englishness following devolution in the UK. Malik (1996) is critical of these perspectives, suggesting that post-modernism is apolitical and defeatist in its approach to promoting strategies to eradicate racism, and that it is associated with an acceptance of the status quo in a fragmented and disunited world. The relevance of post-modern perspectives has also been challenged in terms of their effectiveness for social work practice.

> Without wishing to minimize the importance of ideas such as those of Foucault, I think it is wise to bear in mind these were not developed in social work or even in a field akin to social work but in the context of purely academic disciplines whose practitioners are not required to make decisions about how to respond to problems in the real world. (Beckett, 2006: 79)

There are, however, some writers within social work education, such as Fook (2002) and Healy (2005), who are successfully combining aspects of post-modern ideas and concepts in their understanding of social work theory and practice.

Race, racism and social work

The changing context of race in Britain was characterized by marked civil unrest in a number of English cities in the 1980s, leading to policy initiatives challenging racial inequality. The subsequent Scarman Report (1982) highlighted that racial discrimination existed in the police force on individual levels (a few bad apples) as opposed to at an institutional level. Lord Scarman said that 'the direction and policies of the Metropolitan Police are not racist'. He recognized that the actions of some officers were 'ill considered, immature and racially prejudiced', but made it clear that institutionalized racism itself was not a problem. The solution, therefore, was centred on more recruitment of black officers and what was known at the time as Race Awareness Training. Anti-racist initiatives were also reflected in social work education and practice. Many social work organizations engaged with RAT for their staff. This was intended to educate white staff about the nature of multiculturalism in society and to challenge conscious and unconscious racist beliefs and attitudes. This training received mixed responses and was sometimes referred to as tokenistic 'steel bands, saris and samosas'. Donald and Rattansi (1992: 2) argue that, 'by focusing on the superficial manifestations of culture, multiculturalism failed to address the continuing hierarchies of power and legitimacy that existed among different centres of cultural authority'.

Such approaches were criticized for focusing upon individual workers' personal prejudices, attitudes and beliefs rather than on the institutional practices and structural inequality that led to differential treatment for BME communities. Some organizations took on a more radical approach to addressing racism within service delivery and replaced RAT with Anti-Racist Training (ART), which was intended to go beyond consciousness-raising. Instead it attempted to identify ways of working and engaging with BME communities and service users to address specific areas of inclusion and exclusion.

The response of some black communities to the lack or denial of appropriate services was via self-help with the organization and provision of their own services. The growth of the black voluntary and community sector was particularly evident in the area of mental heath and childcare. Though voluntary organizations have often struggled to maintain their independence and funding, organizations such as the Muslim Women's Helpline (*http://www.mwnuk.co.uk*) reflect the awareness of needs within black communities as well as an understanding of the processes of discrimination (Chouhan and Lusane, 2004).

The appointment of black staff under Section 11 of the 1966 Local Government Act to work specifically with BME communities was common not only in social work but also in other areas of the welfare state. Gilroy (1997) suggests that black workers' position in state institutions leads to contradictions in terms of both class and race. As a part of a middle-class profession, black workers found themselves performing local state functions with the poor and powerless. The stress of managing competing and contradictory identities resulted in black social workers espousing 'a black cultural nationalism', particularly in relation to the placement needs of black children (Gilroy, 1997). The demand for same-race placements, whereby black children would be placed only with black carers as opposed to being trans-racially placed in foster or adoptive families, was seen as an understandable response to poor practice within childcare. However, this was criticized by Gilroy for being misplaced, as the black community was too small and fragmented to respond in that way. The assumption that the inclusion of more black people in positions of power would lead to an end to racism within social work fails to consider the role of organizational structures and systems in maintaining the status quo and therefore in perpetuating systems of discrimination. Anti-racist initiatives targeted social work education as well as service delivery. The Central Council for the Education and Training of Social Work (CCETSW) implemented an anti-racist policy, a Black Perspectives Committee and a steering group, which looked at specific ways of educating students and qualified practitioners regarding anti-racist practice. The Diploma in Social Work (DIPSW), which was introduced in 1991, required qualifying students to specifically demonstrate knowledge of race and racism and evidence of their ability to combat racism in their practice (Central Council for the Education and Training of Social Work, 1991). The promotion of anti-discriminatory practice was seen as a key part of social practice, but race and racism were the only specific form of discrimination identified, representing a victory for the anti-racist campaign within social work. The General Social Care Council became the regulator of social work education and training and was responsible for the introduction of the degree in social work in 2003. Its Code of Conduct stated that social care workers must not discriminate against service users, and was seen by some as watering down of social work's commitment to actively combating racism (General Social Care Council, 2002). In 2012 the regulation of social work was taken over by the Health and Care Professions Council (HCPC) with The College of Social Work (TCSW). The HCPC standards for social work subsume race under the other categories such as equality and discrimination, whereas TCSW is more specific in identifying race and racism. The Professional Capabilities Framework requires that social workers recognize the multi-dimensional context of diversity and the need to challenge forms of discrimination (College of Social Work, 2012a).

The concept of internalized oppression or epidermilization (Fanon, 1952) is a useful one for understanding some of the impact on black service users of racism and domination within social work and society. Internalized oppression refers to ways in which oppressed groups through processes of domination and learning accept and articulate some of the values and attitudes of the oppressor. Internalized oppression can be expressed (consciously or unconsciously) in a number of ways and can include hatred, self-loathing and wishing to be white. The personal impact of this is brought home powerfully by the *Black and In Care* video, which includes footage of black children scrubbing themselves with bleach to rid themselves of their black skin. Skin lightening creams have been on sale in Western countries since the 1950s. Rather than seeing this as a part of black pathology, it should be understood as a normal aspect of how people may respond to processes of oppression and discrimination (Lipsky, 1987). Freire (1972: 54) discusses how oppressed groups need to unlearn the dominant ideologies in order to achieve liberation: 'Only as they discover themselves to be "hosts" to the oppressor can they contribute to the midwifery of their liberating pedagogy. As long as they live in the duality where *to be* is *to be like*, and *to be like* is *to be like the oppressor*, this contribution is impossible.'

Race, adoption and practice

Sociological understandings concerning race and ethnicity provide a framework for analysing discourses that exist within social work practice, yet the complexities and contradictions involved in providing social work are highlighted through the example of child placement. A study by the National Children's Home (Selwyn et al., 2004) summarized some of the issues concerning the recruitment of BME adoptive families and highlighted a number of practice issues, including a shortage of all minority ethnic adopters and, in particular, a need for black, black mixed-parentage and mixed-relationship adopters. The impact of racism, though, has affected people's willingness to approach agencies.

While minority ethnic children comprise 18% of all the children looked after in the UK and 22% of children on the National Adoption Register, they represent only 13% of those adopted. Black children take on average over 50% longer to be placed for adoption than children from other ethnic groups. Some minority ethnic groups have very young age structures. There may be few minority ethnic adults living in the community and thus a very limited pool of potential adopters. There is a need for agencies to understand the demographics of their areas. The National Children's Home report suggests that social workers need to give greater consideration to how adopters would help a child understand their heritage and culture and form a positive sense of self, and asks whether a black or a white family is a perfect match for a black mixed-parentage child. Minority ethnic communities tend to be characterized by large family sizes, poverty and poor housing, and myths and stereotypes around adoption are still prevalent in minority ethnic communities, despite all the advertising and publicity. The recruitment of more minority ethnic social work staff is a factor in gaining more applicants from BME communities (Selwyn et al., 2004).

Yet social work has, since the late 1990s, witnessed a backlash from politicians and other commentators (particularly in the media) against anti-racist and other equality initiatives. Successive government ministers from different political backgrounds have been highly critical of social work practice concerning the placement of BME children for adoption, leading to accusations of dogmatism and political correctness.

There are far-reaching benefits for children by making concerted efforts to recruit more black adoptive families. (© Kevin Russ/iStock)

Speaking in 1998, the Labour minister Paul Boateng stated: 'It is unacceptable for a child to be deprived of loving parents solely on the grounds that the child and adoptive parents do not share the same racial and cultural background. We must not let dogma get in the way. We have to put children first' (BBC interview, 18 November 1998). The then Coalition Secretary of State for Education, Michael Gove, echoed these views more recently: 'Edicts which say children have to be adopted by families with the same ethnic background, and which prevent other families adopting because they don't fit left wing prescriptions, are denying children the love they need' (Hill, 2011). Such statements, though populist in nature, have made little impact upon social work policy and practice in considering the ethnic and religious needs of children. However, the present government, through the Children and Families Bill (Department for Education, 2013), has announced reforms to adoption practice with proposals to remove the need to pay due consideration to a child's cultural and religious back ground. This has again fuelled accusations of colour blindness and colonialism within adoption practice.

In its submission to the House of Commons Select Committee, the Association of Black Social Workers and Allied Professionals responded: 'The most valuable resource of any ethnic group is its children. Nevertheless, black children are being taken from black families by the process of the law and being placed in white families. It is, in essence, "internal colonialism" and a new form of the slave trade, but only black children are used' (Sissay, 2012).

Although the views above may appear overstated, there are concerns within the profession that genuine efforts to recruit more BME adoptive families may be undermined by the Government's efforts to fast-track the adoption of black children by white adopters. Such proposals fail to acknowledge the importance of ethnicity, culture and religion in developing identity and fail to answer the critical questions as to why BME children are over-represented within the public care system.

Case study

Joel is a healthy 5-year-old of mixed Irish and African background. Joel had a difficult start to life, experiencing physical abuse and neglect. He is an active boy who enjoys all sports. He needs to build his trust with adults and benefits from having clear behavioural boundaries. Joel needs one or two parents, preferably with no other children or with children much older than him.

- As a social worker, what sort of family do you consider suitable for Joel?
- List the advantages and disadvantages of 'same-race' and trans-racial placements.
- Does it matter if the prospective carers are black or white and wish to adopt from a different ethnic background? What other factors affect 'matching', such as class and background?
- How can sociological theories regarding 'essentialism' and race and ethnicity inform adoption practice?

Global perspectives

Sivandanan (2004) locates racism within the context of globalization, as globalizing processes associated with trade and political changes seek to promote imperialist or racist ideologies. He argues that changes in racist discourse have created a new type of racism: one that is not so much associated with skin colour but originates from being identified formally or informally as an asylum seeker. As in any discourse, the language associated within this 'new racism' is significant. People who fled Nazi Germany during and after the Second World War and Idi Amin's Uganda in the 1970s were described as refugees, affording people the status of having to seek refuge. Contemporary discourses use the term 'asylum seekers', which could indicate that they are either genuine or fake; more commonly, asylum seekers may be described as 'real' or 'bogus'. The majority of people seeking refuge in 2001, according to the Refugee Council, came from Iraq, Zimbabwe, Afghanistan and Somalia, areas which have witnessed brutal wars and oppressive regimes, though this seems to have had little effect on the anti-immigration argument. The very nature of this form of racism has been successfully deployed by the British National Party (BNP), who gained a number of seats in the local elections of May 2006. Whilst many of those seats were lost in subsequent elections, the English Defence League (EDL) and more moderate parties such as Ukip continue to promote an anti-immigration agenda reflecting attitudes and values within British society.

Debates concerning asylum have become a significant feature of discourses regarding race, ethnicity and nationality in Britain and Europe in the 1990s and early twenty-first century. Social workers have unwittingly found themselves working with and against the state in order to meet the needs of families and individuals who are seeking a place of safety. In spite of demands for social workers to refuse to engage in what have sometimes been described as racist asylum policies and practices, they increasingly find themselves involved in work with refugees and asylum seekers, particularly in the area of work with children (Humphries, 2004).

The relationship between social work and asylum is an uncomfortable one and one which produces tensions and dilemmas within the profession's own ranks. Social workers may find themselves working with unaccompanied children in need and disabled people who require assessments under community care legislation, or with people who present with the effects of trauma and mental distress. Workers often feel unprepared for such work, with little attention being paid to the issues faced by asylum seekers on qualifying and post-qualifying programmes of education. Humphries discusses the implications for contemporary social work of the emphasis on regulation and identification and assessment, and she calls for a resistance to collusion with oppressive and dehumanizing immigration controls. She also remarks that: 'Talk of anti-racist and anti-oppressive practice in social work is nonsense, a self-deception and hypocrisy. White social workers continue to accept without a murmur of protest their allocated role in the hounding and harassment and the impoverishment of some of the most vulnerable people in the planet' (Humphries, 2004: 39).

This could be harsh criticism, which may also implicate black and other minority workers. Such accusations are not new for social workers, whose humanist values appear to be at odds with the care and control functions they perform on behalf of the local and national state. The dichotomous role of social work is apparent in areas such as asylum, mental health and child protection, and social work has struggled to engage in anti-oppressive practices in what appear to be oppressive situations.

Racism, Islamophobia and inter-ethnic conflict

The roots of anti-Muslim attitudes can be traced to Christian writers prior to the Crusades of medieval Europe. Said (1997) discusses the origins of Islamophobia in his analysis of discourses regarding Orientals which emerged in the nineteenth century. Orientalism, for Said, represents the Western world's relationship with and representation of the Orient, which is characterized by racist images of and attitudes and beliefs towards people from the Eastern world. With Muslims representing 4.8% of the population, Islam is now this country's second largest faith after Christianity (Office for National Statistics, 2001). Muslims and Islam have been seen as a particular threat to the values of Christianity and Britishness, and this was further amplified by events such as 9/11 in the USA in 2001, the international war on terror and the 7/7 bombings in Britain in 2005. Islamophobia has now become a recognized form of racism in Britain and in other parts of the world. The Pew Research Centre (2006), in an examination of Muslim attitudes across 13 countries, stated that 'Muslim opinions about the West and its people have worsened over the past year and by overwhelming margins.' The Parekh Report on the future of multi-ethnic Britain stated that: 'Recently Muslims have emerged as the principal focus of racist antagonisms based on cultural differences' (Parekh, 2000: 31). The report entitled *Islamophobia: A Challenge for Us All*, by the Runnymede Trust (1997), is an illustration of the extent of the racism towards Muslims in Britain (*http://www.runnymedetrust.org*).

The report discusses the history of Muslims in Britain, current issues faced by

Muslims of all generations, and the role and responsibility of the media in reinforcing Islamophobia. It also highlights violence and racial harassment towards those perceived as Muslim and systematic social exclusion in all areas of life from employment to politics. Polarizing attitudes regarding this issue can be seen in an ICM/*Observer* opinion poll in Britain in which 71% of those polled felt 'That immigrants should embrace the British way of life'; this had been 59% before the attacks of 9/11. The numerous recommendations made within this report incorporate the three central concepts of cohesion, equality and difference to be addressed by services such as education, the police and health and social care.

Malik (2005) expresses some caution regarding recent discourses of racism resulting in the concept of Islamophobia being used widely and in an uncritical manner. On one hand, Islamophobia may be referred to as the fear and hatred of Muslims, and, on the other hand, it may be used to describe legitimate acts such as criticism of Islam. Malik discusses underachievement and poverty among Pakistani and Bangladeshi communities, and while acknowledging the pervasiveness of anti-Muslim attitudes amongst individuals and in organizational practices, he cites the causes of long-term disadvantage among specific ethnic minority populations as being due to a myriad of factors, including class, race and religion.

There is some evidence to suggest that hostilities exist within BME communities. The tensions that existed were highlighted in Birmingham in 2006 with the death of an African Caribbean man by Asian men following allegations of an assault against an African Caribbean girl. One local resident said: 'You'd have to walk miles to find a black-run business in Lozells, even some of the businesses selling Caribbean food like yam, they've been taken over by Asians, forcing African Caribbeans to spend their money with Asian businesses' (John, 2006).

In challenging attitudes and assumptions regarding race, Milner's research (1975)

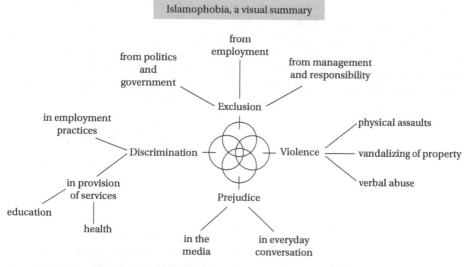

Figure 4.2   Islamophobia: a visual summary.

Source: Runnymede Trust, 1997: 11.

into the development of racial attitudes in young children is useful. It identified that in many children an appreciation of racial differences starts from around the age of 3 years old, and that by 5 years old children reproduce versions of the stereotypical social roles of black and white people.

Race and child protection

Discourses concerning child protection with BME families in Britain have concentrated on a number of issues, including the possible over-representation of black children in care populations. Professionals have been accused of misunderstanding and having stereotypical views of practices concerning BME families, resulting in an apparent failure of the child protection system to prevent and protect BME children from harm.

Questions as to whether BME children are over-represented in the public care system are difficult to assess as there is a paucity of research in this area and there are no general statistics about how many BME families are referred to Social Services Departments in any year.

A study by Owen and Statham (2009) identified that children of mixed ethnic background are over-represented in the three categories of children in need, children on the child protection register and children who are looked after. Asian children are under-represented in each category, and black children, although they are over-represented in the children in need and children looked after categories, are not significantly represented on the child protection register. The reasons for this are varied, and studies point to the effects of poverty, lack of preventive/early intervention services, cultural barriers, anxiety amongst professionals and institutional racism (Owen and Statham, 2009). This may leave black children under-protected.

The death of Victoria Climbié and the subsequent inquiry has been one of the defining features of British childcare practice in recent years, and followed a number of controversial child deaths concerning BME children in the 1980s (notably Jasmine Beckford and Kimberly Carlisle). While Lord Laming, who headed the inquiry, never accused the local authority of racist practice, the fact that Victoria was an African child had a racializing impact on the case, and Part 5 of the Report addresses issues of working with diversity (Department of Health and Home Office, 2003). Victoria's counsel suggested that: 'Race can affect the way people conduct themselves in other ways. Fear of being accused of racism can stop people acting when otherwise they would. Fear of being thought unsympathetic to someone of the same race can change responses' (Part 5, paragraph 16.7). The Report stressed that, while cultural factors must be considered, the overall objective is one of child safety and that Victoria should have been treated like any other child and her needs and rights should have been recognized.

> There is some evidence to suggest that one of the consequences of an exclusive focus on 'culture' in work with black children and families is [that] it leaves black and ethnic minority children in potentially dangerous situations, because the assessment has failed to address a child's fundamental care and protection needs. (Part 5, paragraph 16)

Lord Laming states:

> Several times during this Inquiry I found myself wondering whether a failure by a particular professional to take action to protect Victoria may have been partly due to that professional losing sight of the fact that her needs were the same as those of any other seven-year-old girl, from whatever cultural background. (Part 5, paragraph 16.2)

The above quotes from the Laming Report indicate that, while the professionals involved were not accused of racist practice, professional ideologies regarding the construction of Victoria as a black African child permeated the case.

The response of health and social care to cases of female genital mutilation, honour-based murders and witchcraft-related child abuse are further examples of how professionals struggle to recognize their safeguarding responsibilities to BME children in the midst of cultural sensitivity. Instead church-based group and charitable organizations such as AFRUCA (*http://www.afruca.org/*) have highlighted the lack of knowledge and understanding amongst professionals.

Case study

On Christmas Day, 2010, Kristy Bamu, age 15, died after experiencing months of torture at the hands of his sister Magalie Bamu, and her partner Eric Bilkubi. They accused him of being a witch and deprived him of food and water, beat him with iron bars and tortured him with pliers. The case was horrific and received widespread attention. There are on average eight reported incidents a year in Greater London where children have been abused using witchcraft-based exorcisms.

(Press Association, 2012)

The creation of a *National Action Plan to Tackle Child Abuse Linked to Faith or Belief* (Department for Education, 2012a) was in part a response to Kristy's death and reflects an attempt by national government, The College of Social Work and local agencies to develop a coordinated approach to a range of safeguarding issues which affect BME children. Drawing upon recommendations from the Munro Report (Department for Education, 2011a), the action plan focuses upon strategies which will engage with communities to build trust and effective working relationships, empower practitioners through focused education and training, and support victims and their families by listening to children and providing supportive interventions.

Social workers are required to be more culturally competent, though Chand and Keay's research (2003) also suggests that monitoring referral rates to social care departments based upon ethnic composition are challenging practices that involve control measures rather than supportive ones. There is also a need to challenge myths, stereotypes and workers' values and work in partnership with voluntary organizations, which may have a more successful history in working with BME families. Social workers have to recognize and balance the fears of being accused of over-intervention in black families with the risks of failing to protect children from abuse and harm.

Professionals need to develop the capacity to challenge unacceptable behaviour – even if it's associated with particular cultural or religious customs – and interrogate information in a fair and objective manner. This requires an understanding of how to interpret information about race and ethnicity; how to interrogate and question whilst protecting people's human rights; and how and when to challenge and take action against behavior which threatens the enjoyment of basic rights. (Social Care Institute for Excellence, 2011a)

Conclusion

The majority of social workers enter the profession with the intention of enabling service users to improve the quality of their lives. Yet the effects of racial and ethnic categorization have resulted in a social work profession which has struggled to find effective ways of working to address the inequality experienced by many BME communities. While some minority ethnic communities have responded through the provision of their own services and forms of support, such provision is uncertain, and it is only through a consistent commitment to understand and challenge the systems that perpetuate individual and organizational forms of discrimination that racial discrimination and oppression will be eradicated. The understanding and application of sociological theories regarding race and ethnicity allow social workers to understand the shifting nature of racism within society and provide a framework within which to provide a challenge to professional and institutional practices which marginalize the shifting population of minority ethnic groups.

Summary points

- While race and ethnicity are social constructs, the effects of categorization for BME communities are real.
- Constructions regarding race are complex and extend beyond a simple black/white dichotomy.
- Changing sociological perspectives in understanding racial and ethnic categorizations help explain the emergence of 'new ethnicities' and multiple identities.
- Sociological theories can enable social workers to understand the differential experiences of some BME communities within social work practice.

Questions for discussion

- Explain why sociologists prefer to use the term 'ethnicity' as opposed to 'race' to refer to people's experiences.
- What evidence is there to suggest that institutions like the police or social services are institutionally racist?
- How can social workers challenge racist practice?
- How can sociological explanations enable you to understand discourses concerning asylum and immigration?

Further reading

Despite the significance of race and ethnic categorization, there are few accessible texts within sociology, and particularly within social work, which focus exclusively on understanding race and ethnicity and which discuss the implications for practice.

Back, L. and Solomos, J. (eds) (2008) *Theories of Race and Racism: A Reader.* **2nd edition. London: Routledge**
This is a useful reader for students as it brings together comprehensive discussion of articles regarding the sociology of race.

Bhatti Sinclair, K. (2011) *Anti-Racist Practice in Social Work (Reshaping Social Work).* **Basingstoke: Palgrave Macmillan**
An accessible book that incorporates some useful exercises to consider the potential for anti-racist social work practice.

Lavette, M. and Penketh, L. (2013) *Racism and Social Work: Contemporary Issues and Debate.* **Bristol: Policy Press**
A welcome book that addresses contemporary issues of racism within Britain and the impact for social work practice.

5 Disability

Introduction

Historically, mainstream sociology has largely ignored disability, with sociological perspectives focusing on health and chronic illness. However, more recently sociological perspectives have been influenced by the emergence of disability studies, which have informed the development of 'medical' and 'social' models of disability and have influenced contemporary health and social care policies in this area. This is particularly the case in relation to the social model of disability, which has been the focus of critical sociological discussion. Throughout this chapter, debates and discussions about these perspectives will be explored. This chapter is concerned with looking at people with a range of disabling conditions, whether these are congenital (present from birth) or acquired (through illness or accident). References and examples will be made to people with physical, learning and sensory (hearing/vision) disabilities.

> ## The key issues that will be explored in this chapter are:
>
> - the historical and structural context of disability and social welfare – institutionalism, disability and social exclusion
> - the emergence of the social model of disability and the disability movement
> - disability, social action theories and the lived experience
> - critical sociological perspectives and the development of disability studies
> - global perspectives relating to disability, human rights and citizenship
> - contemporary issues for social work practice.

> ## By the end of this chapter, you should be able to:
>
> - demonstrate an understanding of the institutional and structural context of disability and social welfare services
> - discuss the nature of social disadvantage and disempowerment experienced by people with disabilities
> - understand a range of perspectives relating to the development of critical sociological thought concerning disability
> - have an awareness of how sociological thought on disability relates to contemporary issues in social work practice.

Disability and sociological discourse

In helping us to understand the historical and structural context, the language used relating to disability is important. Language has been used to classify disabled people as part of professional roles within health and social care. This relates to sociological debate concerning discourse. Health and social care professionals use different language to talk about people with disabilities, which to a degree reflects different theoretical perspectives. Social services and social care academics talk about people with disabilities and adult social care services. Health services and health academics talk about people with chronic illnesses and/or long-term conditions. The sociology of disability, the sociology of the body and the sociology of health and illness are all sub-disciplines of sociology which are relevant to an understanding of health and disability. There is considerable debate between these sociological perspectives and how they relate to biomedical and social models of health, illness and disability. There has been a tendency to present these models as polarized and juxtaposed, but the two models can be complementary, using different aspects of expertise appropriately to provide *holistic* care.

> **Holism** the idea that a system can be explained or determined not by its component parts but through an understanding of how the system operates in total or as a whole

Oliver and Barnes (2012b) identify significant problems with terminology and definitions relating to disability, including using a holistic approach within health and social care assessments. They argue that definitions lead to generalized approaches by professionals in their work with disabled people, reinforcing stereotypes and professional power. This serves to reinforce oppressive practice towards disabled people within the provision of social welfare and accompanying social policies.

Defining disability

Historically, the following World Health Organization (1980) definition has been widely used:

International classifications of impairments, disabilities and handicaps

Impairments (I) Abnormalities of the body structure and appearance and of organ system function, resulting from any cause; in principle 'impairments' means impairments at the organ level

Disabilities (D) The consequences of impairment in terms of the functional performance and activity of the individual; disabilities thus represent disturbances at the level of the person

Handicaps (H) The disadvantages experienced by the individual as a result of impairments and disabilities; handicaps reflect interaction with and adaptation to the individual's surroundings

(Wood, 1980: 14)

According to this definition, disability is very much concerned with how the body functions and can be treated, and this has been the subject of criticism from the disability rights movement. It is argued that this definition reinforces an individual or tragedy model of disability. As a result, the World Health Organization amended the above definition in 2002 to include the impact of personal and environmental factors.

The *first World Report on Disability* in 2011, however, continued to define disability in terms of interaction between medical and social model perspectives (World Health Organization, 2011).

The usefulness of the World Health Organization's redefinition of disability in 2002 is contested. Sociologists such as Bury (1997) have argued that the redefined ICIDH classification of disability helped assess the needs of disabled people within both a biomedical and a social model framework. In his view, it does take account of social and environmental issues which impact upon people with disabilities. These needs are supported by functional assessment (what people can/cannot do without support), rehabilitation and counselling. However, Oliver and Sapey (2006) see the above classification as focusing predominantly on the functional aspects of the individual's impairment, rather than the reaction of society to impairment, and it is still viewed as too closely connected with medical model perspectives. The principal focus of this model is on rehabilitative assessment, with social and environmental factors being seen as secondary. Services for disabled people are therefore provided on the basis of professional expertise using contested definitions. This is important in terms of meeting support requirements, as the number of disabled people in the UK has risen in the first of the twenty-first part/century (see Table 5.1).

Table 5.1 *Numbers of disabled people in Great Britain (figures in millions)*

	Adults of working age[a]	Adults of state pension age[b]	All adults	Children	All ages
2002/3	5.0	4.7	9.7	0.7	10.4
2003/4	4.9	4.6	9.5	0.7	10.1
2004/5	4.8	4.6	9.5	0.7	10.1
2005/6	5.2	4.9	10.1	0.7	10.8
2006/7	4.9	4.9	9.8	0.7	10.4
2007/8	4.8	5.0	9.8	0.8	10.6
2008/9	5.0	5.1	10.1	0.7	10.9
2009/10	5.1	5.1	10.2	0.8	11.0
2010/11	5.3	5.2	10.4	0.8	11.2
2011/12	5.7	5.1	10.8	0.8	11.6

[a] Working age: men aged 16–64 and women aged 16–59.

[b] State pension age: men aged 65 and over and women aged 60 and over. (State pension age changed from 2010/11 and so the definition of state pension age and working age is not consistent over time. The state pension age for men is 65 for men born before 6 April 1959. For women born on or before 6 April 1950, the state pension age is 60. From 6 April 2010, state pension age for women born on or before 6 April 1950 started to increase gradually between April 2010 and November 2018. For the purpose of these data, women are defined to be of state pension age based on their date of birth and the date of the interview.)

Source: Disability prevalence estimates 2011/12 available at *http://odi.dwp.gov.uk/docs/res/factsheets/disability-prevalence.pdf.*

Functionalism

From a functionalist perspective, professionals 'manage' illness and health problems, supporting a stable society (see Chapter 1). Definitions support this process by creating systems within health and social care for the assessment and care planning process. Parsons (1951) was one of the first sociologists to look at health and illness. He developed the idea of a 'sick role' for people with disabilities. His emphasis was on people taking responsibility for their sickness/treatment and getting better, as illness prevented them from carrying out the 'normal' functions in society (e.g. employment, contributing to their community). Hence, their role was to get well and commit to this process. This process was very much seen as medically orientated, requiring ongoing treatment from health professionals. This continual process of assessment and revision can be seen within contemporary social policies relating to disability: for example, in assessment for eligibility for incapacity benefit (Burchardt, 2000). This would seem to echo the view that illness or disability is related to work ability and societal obligations and responsibilities (Nettleton, 2013).

A number of criticisms have been levelled at a functional analysis of disability. Many disabled people would not see themselves as sick, and such an analysis does not take account of impairment as opposed to sickness (Oliver, 1993). Many disabled people are not sick, but have ongoing impairments that do not present as daily health problems. For example, a person who is blind or deaf is probably not going to need or be in receipt of ongoing treatment. Also, some people are not going to recover from long-term health problems or disabilities. How would their role in society fit into Parsons' model of the sick role?

Another major concern is that by focusing on the 'sick' role, much of the solution is in the hands of health professionals to help people get well. This creates a label and a stigma associated with sickness, and reinforces a strong power dynamic between doctor and patient. Stigma serves to compound the structural oppression that disabled people experience in relation to societal institutions, and professional power is therefore disempowering rather than enabling. From an interactionist perspective, the work of theorists such as Goffman shows how labelling can be used to distinguish between individuals or groups within society who are 'normal' and 'abnormal' (Goffman, 1968).

Additionally, the sick role does not seem to take account of other ways in which people obtain help and support. Bilton et al. (2002) discuss how there is an assumption that individuals will seek the support of their doctor. In fact, studies show that other avenues of support are explored prior going to the doctor (Scambler, 1997). Increasingly, people are turning to new alternative and complementary methods of support with illness. Parsons' analysis does, therefore, seem simplistic, although Radley (1993) has argued that the sick role may still have relevance for people with chronic conditions, who may have periods of exacerbation of symptoms where they require acute medical care. However, the key issue here is that a focus on disability and the sick role focuses on a biomedical model of disability.

The impact of a medical approach on disabled people

Biomedical model the theory that the basis of disease, including mental illness, is physical in origin. Illness can be identified objectively through signs and symptoms and treated scientifically with technology, e.g. drugs and surgical interventions. The body can be likened to a machine that can be broken down into its component parts.

The *biomedical model* has historically heavily influenced studies of health, illness and disability. Within this perspective, the organization of health and illness has been seen to be very much concerned with treatment and improving function, and this is examined further in Chapter 11. The biomedical model does seem to often ignore the nature of many disabling conditions and sidesteps a debate about how society *reinforces* barriers for disabled people in society. The debates about whether biomedical and social constructionist perspectives on health and disability can be coterminous or are separate continue. There is therefore a debate between those who are seen to focus on impairment and those who reject impairment as the key issue for disabled people (Thomas, 2004). It is this debate which has led to the emergence of critical sociological thought concerning the social model of disability. There has been some discussion about whether the social model is a theory or an approach (Oliver, 2004; Thomas, 2004), but it has offered an alternative discourse to the biomedical model.

The central premise of this challenge was that the focus should be on social, political and economic constructs and not on the individual and their illness. From this perspective, it is society and its structures that are seen as a more significant problem than the illness or disability itself. From a structuralist perspective, disabled people are excluded from key political and economic organizations and are not generally visible within the media or popular culture. They are excluded in areas such as housing, employment and transport, predominantly because of access issues. It is these barriers to participation in society that are the problem rather than impairment or illness.

For social model theorists such as Oliver, professional expertise has been focused on medicalized assessment rather than overcoming the social and attitudinal barriers relating to disability. Many writers have been critical of the medical model because it implies some kind of 'personal tragedy' (Oliver, 1990), contributing to assumptions about the 'tragedy' of illness and disability by non-disabled people. Disabled writers have also been critical of the voluntary as well as the state sector, which they saw as reinforcing dependency and the 'personal tragedy' model. By the 1960s a plethora of charitable groups and organizations were in existence. Disabled writers saw them as being very much tied to the medical model, and being preoccupied with research, cure and treatments. These writers also saw such organizations as being concerned with fundraising and 'doing for' people. They were critical of charities for not campaigning on social care, transport and other environmental barriers. As such, charities were part of the structures that segregated and isolated disabled people. Community care and social welfare services for disabled people can therefore be seen to have developed in relation to an individual or 'medical' model of disability.

The historical context of community care

The development of social policy and social welfare services needs to be related to a historical context where the institutions of the state served to segregate disabled people from wider society. Barnes (1991) discusses how the fear of the abnormal contributed towards the enforced dependency, institutionalization and segregation of disabled people. Capitalist modes of production led to changes in societal structures and systems, and disabled people struggled to compete in a mechanized and industrialized economy (Oliver, 1993). As a result, disabled people became marginalized economically and therefore a social problem, leading to increased segregation (Goble, 2004). Whilst disabled people were not necessarily independent in pre-industrialized society, industrialization can be seen to have exacerbated exclusion and social disadvantage.

Industrialization also led to the study and classification of 'normal' and 'abnormal' bodies, in a similar way to sexual behaviour. This has led to divisions between medical professionals and sociologists that are apparent today, and the focus on illness can be seen in the language of law and policy until very recently. This relates to the discussion about discourse at the start of the chapter. 'Handicapped', 'spastic' and 'retarded' are all terms that can be seen within policy and medical procedures throughout the nineteenth and twentieth centuries. Barton (1996) discusses how the terms themselves imply lack of function and therefore lack of worth, illustrating the power of discourse.

Historically, there also appears to have been a difference between the treatment of those with intellectual and those with physical difficulties. Race (2002) discusses the way in which people with learning disabilities were colonized and shut away from society. At the end of the nineteenth century, there was a real concern that people with learning disabilities would impact upon birth demographics. This was part of a wider concern about population growth and the growth of poverty, and at the beginning of the twentieth century there was much support for the theory of eugenics. Eugenics theory can certainly be seen to have contributed towards 'shutting disabled people away', leading to asylum or colony care that continued until the 1960s. People with disabilities lived in self-contained communities, where opportunities for independence and empowerment were virtually non-existent and standards of care and support were variable. The eugenics debate about 'imperfect genes' is still relevant today. As science advances, there are possibilities to clone certain characteristics, and 'abnormalities' can be more accurately detected earlier in pregnancy. There is therefore still a debate about the 'value' of people with learning (and other) disabilities. This is reflected in current debates about citizenship and rights for disabled people, explored later in the chapter.

The segregation of disabled people within large-scale institutions and asylums gradually gave way to social welfare services within the community by the 1960s. Notions of community care were first introduced in the 1959 Mental Health Act with the argument that it was better to care for people with enduring mental illness outside institutions. Arguments for the de-institutionalization of a number of care groups (older people, people with mental illnesses, people with disabilities) gathered momentum through the 1970s and 1980s, culminating in the 1988 Griffiths Report, advocating care in the community to maximize independence and to increase service user choice. However, it can also be argued that community care was cheaper than care within institutions, and it was this economic imperative that shaped developments (A. McDonald, 2006). Griffiths had recommended a more coordinated approach to care services and assessing needs, which was made the responsibility of the local authority. The White Paper that followed Griffiths also introduced the mixed economy of care, with the establishment of an internal market within health and social care and both public and private provision (Department of Health, 1989).

Ideologically, the increased attention to care in the community in the late 1980s also reflects the Thatcherite notion of rolling back the frontiers of the 'nanny' state. This reflects the rise of neo-liberalist thought in relation to social welfare services. Institutional care was seen as creating dependency as well as being costly. The ideal of community care is viewed as providing maximum independence to individuals and choice over the range of services that they may access. The question of choice relates to the normalization debate, and the work of theorists such as Wolfensberger (1972) was key to the idea that people with learning disabilities should lead 'normal' and valued lives in the community. Institutional care was seen to limit choices. Oliver and Sapey (2006) discuss the lack of choice and the care regime in homes for physically disabled people in the 1970s.

The advent of the 1990 National Health Service and Community Care Act was therefore intended to reduce dependency and reduce segregation within society. Under this legislation, clients were allocated a 'care manager' (generally a social worker) who assessed them and organized 'packages of care' from a variety of statutory, private and voluntary organizations. It was also envisaged that the 'care manager' would have an overview of the disabled person's needs and would work within a 'needs-led' rather than a 'resource-led' framework (Sharkey, 2007). This principle of community care has continued under successive governments.

However, community care policies have been heavily criticized by the disability rights movement. One of the key issues here is the development of the care management role within the community care framework. Priestley (1999) sees care management as oppressive in the way that it defines the needs of disabled people. The links with gate-keeping resources, assessing needs and providing support within eligibility criteria are seen as reinforcing exclusion and oppression for disabled people. Community care has continued to classify disabled people on the basis of eligibility and controlled access to services.

So community care does not necessarily provide choices. The mixed economy of care does not provide the 'consumer' with choices as there is a limited range of 'products' for disabled people to choose from. Sharkey (2007) discusses the notion that community care is perceived as 'picking' your product off the supermarket shelf. This is not the case, with resource constraints leading to restricted choices. Therefore the availability of choice is dependent on wider issues relating to social policy and social welfare, which vary according to the social, political and economic context. It is this critique of community care which has led to a call for services based on rights rather than needs.

The disability rights movement

Throughout the book, we examine issues of individual, group and state power in relation to a range of user groups. Certainly, hierarchies of power exist in relation to gender and sexuality (Connell, 1987, 1995). Disabled people have also lacked power in comparison to other groups in society. French and Swain (2012) discuss the lack of power disabled people have over their lives, particularly in childhood. This concerns professional power in relation to access to services and the historical segregation of disabled people. It is only relatively recently that some change has occurred in this area.

Unlike lesbians and gay men (see Chapter 6), people with disabilities have been more visible throughout history. However, this did not initially lead to disabled people challenging structural inequalities and their lack of power. The impact of stigma and labelling throughout society can be seen individually and collectively. For example, derogatory language to describe disabled people has been used for many centuries and has passed into common parlance. Disabled people were seen as 'freaks', exhibited in circus shows and in lunatic asylums, and were seen as a threat to the social norms of the day owing to societal fear of the unknown and abnormal (Barnes, 1991). This was at the root of segregation. Barnes (1992) argues that the media have been a significant force in shaping social attitudes towards disabled people. He argues that disabled people have been portrayed in the media as the passive recipients of charity in need of extensive help and support or as objects of pity/fear. Williams-Findlay (2014) discusses how stereotypes of disabled people indeed continue to dominant news media.

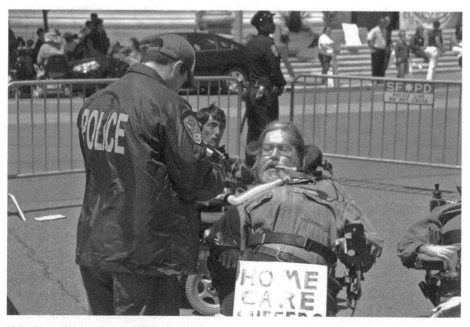

This photo shows how disabled people have increasingly campaigned against disabling barriers within society. (© Steve Rhodes/Flickr)

Disabled people themselves began to challenge structural oppression and attitudinal barriers. In the 1960s the disability rights movement began to emerge, partly as a response to criticisms of asylum care (Goffman, 1961). An inquiry into poor patient care at Ely Hospital in the 1960s received widespread publicity (Race, 2002). In this same period, disabled people themselves were beginning to question models of colony and asylum care. There has been a move away from institutional and community care services to models of independent living. Here the focus is on the disabled person being in control of their own care and support needs (Morris, 2004). This challenges a professional model of care and presents new challenges for professionals in terms of an inclusive approach to support and care. Academically, there also arose a questioning of the way in which disabled people were being treated.

Exercise: asylum care and disability

Find out where your local learning disabilities hospital/asylum was sited. Some of the buildings may be associated with learning disabilities to this day. It may also be possible to view archive photos of the hospital through your local town or city photographic records.

- From a sociological perspective, think about how disabled people might be controlled and disempowered by asylum care.
- What lessons can we learn about poor institutional practice, and how could this be applied to current 'scandals' concerning poor care?

Weeks (2010) discusses the role of social movements at times of flux in society. The disability rights movement has had a similar impact on society to the development of the lesbian and gay movement or the feminist movement. Since the 1960s, there have been significant changes to how disabled people are viewed in society and to how disabled people are living. This can be related to the way in which disabled people themselves have shaped the social context of disability:

- There have been significant changes to the law about how disabled people should be treated at work and should have access to all public buildings (e.g. the Disability Discrimination Act, 2005 – *http://www.legislation.gov.uk/ukpga/2005/13/contents*).
- The Community Care (Direct Payments) Act (1996) helped disabled people to control and organize their own personal care (*http://www.opsi.gov.uk/acts/acts1996/1996030.htm*).
- The emphasis on individual choice and control has continued with the development of personalization, self-assessment and individual budgets (Department of Health, 2007a).
- Disabled people have become politicized and have campaigned for change. For example, the Disability Rights Commission advocates for a right to independent living.

These are a few examples of how a social movement has impacted upon how disabled people are perceived in society and also reflects the impact of new theories and ideas from disabled writers. Changes in societal structures and social welfare have necessitated professionals engaging and communicating with disabled people in different ways. This can particularly be seen in relation to a rights-based approach to independent living

Independent living and citizenship ███████████████

As discussed, community care has been seen as reinforcing dependency and limiting choices for disabled people (Oliver and Sapey, 2006). Social workers have also been seen as part of the problem here rather than part of the solution (Oliver et al., 2012). The developments within independent living can be seen to be rooted within a rights-based approach to individual empowerment. Here disabled people are in control of their own lives through personal choice and freedom. Disabled people are citizens rather than recipients of social care and social welfare services. Duffy (2010) sees this as disabled people being in control of all aspects of their lives. He argues that this requires service providers to rethink relationships with disabled people. Social workers should be supporting disabled people in becoming active citizens. On this view, social work could be seen as transformatory, particularly in relation to personalized services.

Direct payments were the first significant step in relation to personalized services, arising from the campaigning work of disabled people themselves. In the 1990s, direct payments were widely seen by the disabled people's movement as a means by which disabled people could control and manage their own care packages. By controlling the money for their care, disabled people are in control of what Morris (2004) calls their 'additional care requirements'. For example, a disabled person can employ their own carers so as to have their personal choices accommodated. Research has indicated that direct payments give control to disabled people themselves and are empowering (Stainton and Boyce, 2004). However, there have been issues about the take-up of direct payments for some groups. For example, the 2001 White Paper *Valuing People* (Department of Health, 2001b), on services for people with learning disabilities, highlighted how few people with learning disabilities were in receipt of direct payments. A review of the above White Paper discussed how significant progress still needed to be made in this area (Department of Health, 2009a). Direct payments themselves may be subject to resource constraints, and Fruin (2000) points to the variations between local authorities in implementing direct payments. The issues surrounding resources have continued as personalized services have developed.

Direct payments are now one of a number of ways in which disabled people can be in control of their own lives. The development of individual budgets (also known as personal budgets) enables a greater degree of control by bringing together funding from a number of agencies and income streams (Department of Health, 2007b; Prime Minister's Strategy Unit, 2005). Individual budgets are part of personalized services involving self-assessment and person-centred planning. Carr (2008) sees personalization as having developed from service user and disability movements and a result of social action. Personalization has also led to changes within professional roles and necessitates partnership working with service users. French and Swain (2012) discuss how personalization presents an opportunity for social workers to develop more positive and empowering relationships with service users.

However, resourcing personalization has been raised as a significant issue in a time of recession. Williams (2009) discusses concerns that personalization has been developed as an opportunity to dismantle care services on the basis of creating cheaper individual personalized services, and this will be explored later in the chapter. There is also concern that professionals may be fearful that personalization is a threat to their professional autonomy and power (Glasby and Littlechild, 2009). Lymbery (2012) has reported that the early promise that social workers would be actively involved in enabling personalized services appears to have given way to a concern about marginalization. Roulstone (2012) argues that enabling social work practice with disabled people generally needs further exploration within social work education and training. This can be seen to commence with listening to the voices of disabled people themselves.

Narrative and the lived experience

Social workers engage with disabled service users in a problematic and contradictory context. Engagement has generally been characterized by use of professional processes and systems that relate to our previous discussion about a biomedical model. Within social work, for example, core communication with disabled people has centred on the assessment process. Professionals have generally decided what 'effective' communication is. French (1993a), however, outlines how professional language can confuse or mystify service users and in itself does not facilitate listening to the direct experience of disabled people. She argues for inclusive communication as a means of supporting change for disabled people.

Yet what do we actually know about what disabled people want? Writers such as Atkinson have focused on the use of narrative to explore the 'lost' history of people with learning disabilities. This has particularly focused on autobiographical accounts (Atkinson and Warmsley, 1999) associated with structural oppression through institutional care. However, the use of narrative and storytelling approaches can also be seen to have developed the identity of disabled people. Atkinson (2005) claims that narrative approaches promote inclusive research and thus the empowerment of people with learning disabilities. Corker (1998) argues that disabled people for whom communication is a particular issue have often been excluded from social model accounts. Responding to individual accounts can therefore support greater understanding of the lived experience of disabled people.

Life story work has been used across social work practice as a way of engaging with service users' experience (Campbell, 2009). Williams (2009) refers to life history review as a method of hearing the individual's voice in relation to learning disability – perhaps in circumstances where this has not been the case previously. Within disability research, the term 'narrative' is used to describe the process by which researchers compile individual experiences. Focusing specifically on the experiences of the individual can have a number of significant benefits. Firstly, the use of techniques such as life story work can provide a rich amount of qualitative data. This can be transformatory for the individual, but also in terms of providing evidence of the need for change on a range of social, economic and political issues. Secondly, engaging with the individual experience may enable the person to make changes within their life. The experience of being heard (perhaps for the first time) can be seen as emancipatory. In terms of working with disabled people, narrative can also be a tool for building a partnership approach by focusing on and listening to the service users' experience. A good example of this would be a community organization that highlights a particular issue by publicizing individuals' stories or experiences. Scott-Hill (2004) discusses how narrative provides a social history about the context of disabled people's lives. Personal stories connect and shape experience, and this is particularly true where groups have been oppressed or excluded.

Rather than professionals controlling the agenda, people with disabilities should feel that their voice is being heard and is the primary focus of interaction with professionals. Using narrative could facilitate this process. Campbell (2009) discusses how life story work is a frequently used technique with children and young people in their encounters with social workers. It can also be seen to be beneficial for disabled people. Warren (2007) argues that user and carer participation can have an individual as well as a collective benefit. This is where narrative can be important. Being actively listened to and 'heard' can have therapeutic value for the individual as well as potential collective benefits. Social workers need to employ a number of skills in 'hearing' the voice of service users, as explored in the next section.

Empowering practice: working with the social model of disability

Empowerment can be defined as: 'A process in which individuals, groups or communities become able to take control of their circumstances and achieve their own goals, thereby being able to work towards maximizing the quality of their lives' (Adams, 1990: 43). This is further developed by Braye and Preston-Shoot (1995), who identify the following features of empowerment:

- extending one's ability to take effective decisions
- individuals, groups and/or communities taking control of their circumstances and achieving their own goals, thereby being able to work towards maximizing the quality of their lives
- enabling people who are disempowered to have more control over their lives and to have a greater voice in the institutions, services and situations which affect them.

Central to this is the notion of power, where people have the power to make decisions and are not just the recipients of exercised power. Brager and Sprecht (1973) use the concept of a ladder of participation in decision-making to reflect the degree of power that people may have, ranging from high participation, where users and carers are actively involved in the decision, to low participation, where they are merely informed of decisions that have been made.

Professional codes of practice and writing around anti-oppressive practice would appear to echo the need for social work intervention that is from an empowering social model perspective (e.g. Thompson, 2005). Indeed, the fact that social work degree programmes advocate involvement by service users and carers is evidence of a commitment to empowering practice from such a perspective. This can also be demonstrated when looking at how person-centred planning has underpinned personalization.

Person-centred planning applies particularly to work with people with learning disabilities. The way in which learning-disabled people have not been consulted or given choices has been well documented (Race, 2002; Thomas and Woods, 2003; Williams, 2009). The 2001 White Paper *Valuing People* (Department of Health, 2001b), mentioned above, advocated the use of person-centred planning by care professionals. Rather than services being organized for people, services are organized with people. From a social model perspective, people's rights and choices are discussed.

There are, however, drawbacks. Many staff have not received training around person-centred planning, and lack of appropriate and independent advocacy services means that disabled people, particularly those with severe learning disabilities, may not receive the appropriate support to make their wishes and opinions known (Oliver and Sapey, 2006). The availability of independent advocacy services is therefore critical for empowering social work practice.

Disabled people and their families have viewed advocacy positively. Advocacy helps disabled people to challenge structural oppression and to access services. Increasingly, with the pressures on resources, social workers and care managers have been less directly involved in providing advocacy services, but signposting people to and working positively with advocates is one way of putting social model ideas into practice. It is also a way of responding positively to the experiences of disabled people.

Oliver and Sapey (2006) discuss the lack of advocacy services, while French and Swain (2012) highlight how advocacy services are struggling financially in the current economic climate. This is also something that has been picked up by organizations such as Mencap (n.d.). Thomas and Woods (2003) discuss how advocacy can enable learning-disabled people to participate in society. Particularly with this group, it is a positive way of challenging social exclusion, which all too often exists. Organizations such as People First (*http://www.peoplefirst.org.uk*) provide opportunities for people with learning disabilities to self-advocate or advocate on behalf of others.

One of the tensions for social workers is being able to advocate for service users, where resource constraints and other pressures may conflict with this role. There is no easy answer to this ethical dilemma, but it is important that you are aware of local advocacy services and can signpost service users and carers to them. Thus (particularly where there are conflicts) social workers can facilitate access to the appropriate support. Being informed about this kind of debate is seen as necessary when reflecting on and considering such ethical dilemmas (C. McDonald, 2006).

Working alongside disabled people

Working alongside disabled people and disabled organizations challenges oppressive practice. Disabled organizations can be seen as controlled by disabled people themselves, relating to the ladder of participation, where such levels of control give a higher level of empowerment. Payne (2005) has discussed the importance of community social work, and the recent agenda in involving users and carers in service organizations is a positive way that social services can work from a social model perspective. However, too often, involving service users and carers can be seen as tokenistic. This involvement needs to be underpinned by a critical understanding of the social model of disability.

There are now programmes where people with disabilities are actively involved and equal partners in training courses, degrees and indeed running courses for social care staff and others (Race, 2002). Social work degree programmes are actively seeking to involve users and carers in social work education, which is a positive way of working alongside people with disabilities. However, Roulstone (2012) argues that critical perspectives relating to disability are often not core to social work degree programmes and present as a specialist option. This may impact upon an understanding of disability rights and studies, which in turn affects practice within adult social care services. So what are the important issues for social workers to consider in relation to disability studies?

Critical perspectives and the social model of disability

We have explored how the social model of disability has challenged the 'tragedy' or individual model of disability. The focus is on challenging the social, political and economic context which is the lived experience of disabled people, as a means of achieving change and dismantling barriers to citizenship and rights. If these barriers are removed, then disabled people can participate in society. Marxist perspectives on sociological thought are important here. The social model of disability argues that disabled people are oppressed because of the capitalist society within which they live. The process of industrialization led to a key relationship between those who owned the means of production (capitalists) and those who worked for them (labour force) (see Chapter 1). As society is about the relationship between capital and labour, the disabled person is of no use or value and is removed from the means of production (Oliver and Sapey, 2006). Impairment meant that the disabled person could not easily work, and, as stated earlier, this led to institutionalization and exclusion. Institutions were therefore an effective way of controlling and segregating disabled people within state structures (Oliver and Barnes, 2012b).

While social welfare and community services have led to changes for disabled people, these are still located within an economic context which oppresses disabled people. Oliver discusses how this has worsened rather than improved within the current global economic climate (M. Oliver, 2013). Priestley (1999) argues that services have traditionally been located within the concept of needs rather than rights. This then means that services can be withdrawn or rationed according to economic imperatives. The neo-liberal context of community care is important here in relation to personalization. A focus on individual services and entitlements negates the need for collective action and collective change. A social model perspective argues that this narrow focus undermines wider change concerning the structural oppression of disabled people. While supporting personalization and independent living, disability commentators have highlighted that a personalized approach alone does not mean that citizenship and rights have been achieved (Dodd, 2013).

There is now a comprehensive range of literature on the social model of disability that has sparked considerable debate (see, e.g., Oliver 2004). The term 'social model' can be heard frequently in discussions with care professionals about how they work with disabled people. Roulstone (2012) discusses the frequent use of terminology relating to the social model within legal and policy imperatives concerning health and social care, but notes that this is often descriptive rather than analytical. Social workers and other health and social care professionals therefore need to deepen their understanding of the social model.

Additionally, social model theory and approaches tend to be presented within this discourse as one-dimensional. However, there are a variety of critical perspectives relating to the social model amongst commentators. Some disabled writers have criticized the social model as being based on a white middle-class perspective and not taking account of the particular needs of disabled women or disabled people from an ethnic minority background. Writers such as Fawcett (2000) and Thomas (1999) have sought to focus on the needs of disabled women. Ideas from both the sociology of disability and the sociology of gender are relevant, and of particular concern are issues around sexuality and childbearing and motherhood. Abortion and birth control, for example, can be seen as divisive issues. Although many feminist writers have broadly welcomed testing during pregnancy, giving women control over reproduction (e.g. Sheldon, 2014), disabled women writers have been critical of antenatal screening, seeing this as new eugenics. Some commentators have argued that these debates have become polarized, and that more discussion needs to take place (e.g. Shakespeare, 1998).

There is also criticism of the social model for generally not taking account of difference. Writers such as Crow (1996) and French (1993b) feel that personal experience of disability (and impairment) is important. This in turn has been criticized as 'turning back the clock' to a focus on the individual rather than the wider social and political constructs for disabled people.

Banton and Singh (2004), writing about race and disability, argue that the social model has begun to take account of factors in addition to the disability, such as social divisions. Variables such as class, race, gender, sexual orientation and age create different experiences for disabled people from particular groups. For example, Asian disabled people using community care services may have a particular experience, and there may be evidence that they do not access community care services in a particular area. The needs of disabled Asian people therefore need to be seen in the context of broader social and economic divisions.

Oliver (2004) summarizes this debate. He is critical of the ongoing discussion about whether the social model can accommodate social divisions, arguing that the model itself is not flawed and time would be better spent on adapting it. He also argues that the debate about whether impairment is a factor is divisive.

Disability and the body

The body has become the focus of increased sociological theorizing, and there has been an emerging discussion about how the body relates to experience of disability within society. While there is agreement that structuralist perspectives are important, there has been a debate about the social construction of the body. Shakespeare and Watson (2001) argue that the sociology of disability needs to include an understanding of the sociology of the body. Impairment is not just biological, and aspects of medical and social perspectives can be complementary, as stated earlier.

A sculpture by Marc Quinn of artist Alison Lapper during her pregnancy was displayed in London's Trafalgar Square between 2005 and 2007, and a large-scale replica featured in the 2012 London Summer Paralympics opening ceremony. (© Dave Rutt/Flickr)

Our bodies are the subject of much discussion across the media, with advice on how to look, lose weight and be fit (see Chapter 1). Thus perspectives on the body are influenced by social structures and the prevailing norms of the day. This process influences the view of the disabled body, and the image and perception of the body are issues for disabled people (Shakespeare and Watson, 2001). Writers do not dispute the impact of social oppression, but also believe that cultural and stereotypical factors influence how disabled people are perceived. There was considerable debate and criticism when a statue of the disabled artist Alison Lapper was exhibited in Trafalgar Square. The public showing of a statue of a disabled, pregnant woman challenged stereotypical notions of beauty (Milmo, 2004).

The body and its functions shape the lived experiences of disabled people. For example, being in constant pain will affect how people cope with daily living. It is argued that the issues are therefore wider than structural oppression. Ideas about our bodies, impairment and pain all impact upon the disabled person.

So there has been debate about how the social model treats disabled people as one homogeneous group. What this appears to point to is that there are variations amongst disabled people and disabled writers about how they view the sociology of disability. Ideas around the sociology of the body argue for a social relational understanding of disability as well as social oppression.

There have been calls for a debate between these two perspectives. Thomas (2004) discusses how some writers see both social oppression and impairment as issues for disabled people. Thomas and Woods (2003) discuss the importance of working with health professionals to support people with learning disabilities in obtaining appropriate treatment. They see this as enabling and allowing people to access resources in society, and argue that this process is different from working according to a medical model perspective. Social workers need to understand the debates within disability studies, and these can then be applied to issues within practice.

The social model and the global context

Disability rights can be seen to have developed globally within Western societies in the 1960s, with disabled people challenging oppression and seeking rights and citizenship. This involved challenging segregation and calls for changes to institutional care models. Swain and French (2014) discuss how the social model of disability arose as a riposte to the individual model of disability experienced by disabled people within the Western world. Here we can see some commonalities in terms of the social policies and welfare services that were the lived experience of disabled people. We can also see disabled people organizing user-led organizations and independent living models across a number of societies (French and Swain, 2012).

The 2011 *World Report on Disability* highlighted the differences in the experience of disabled people across the world (World Health Organization, 2011). However, Oliver and Barnes (2012a) have been critical of the report for not focusing sufficiently on the inequalities experienced by disabled people in relation to economic, political and social deprivation. They refer to a growing body of evidence relating to these issues. For example, Ghai (2001) highlights the impact of poverty on the marginalization of disabled people in India. She argues that this has led to significantly higher rates of some disabling conditions. The lived experience of disabled people is thus different according to cultural context. Where there are issues relating to poverty, there may well also be issues relating to survival. Moore (2013) discusses how the lived experiences of disabled people where there is conflict or war are not easy to document, as potential contributors will be affected by fear of reprisal within their community. There will also be differing perspectives within cultures concerning the social construction of disability. Oliver and Barnes (2012b) discuss how disability may be viewed as a 'punishment' within some societies, clearly then shaping attitudes to disabled people. The impact of stigma and labelling, explored earlier in the chapter, is highly significant here.

However, we can see an international perspective relating to human rights which includes the rights of disabled people. Issues of poverty and development within individual societies which impact on the availability of social welfare services generally may affect this. As has been discussed throughout the book, the global context of economic austerity has hit certain groups within society. Disabled people have been affected like other excluded groups in relation to the availability of social welfare and support services (including social work) as a consequence of global recession (Oliver and Barnes, 2012a). Swain and French (2014) discuss how this in turn impacts upon the identity of disabled people in terms of risk and disability being perceived within the individual model. The global context of risk and vulnerability is therefore important for social workers to engage with and understand.

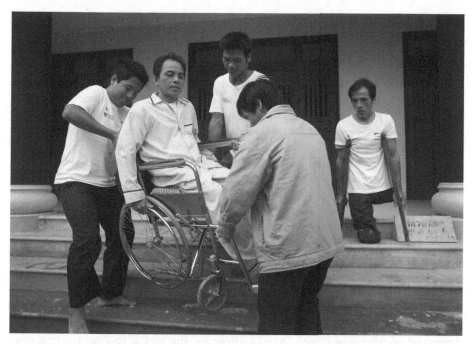

Disability needs to be examined within a global context concerning rights and citizenship. This image shows part of an emergency evacuation drill in Dong Phuoc, Vietnam. (© UN ISDR/Flickr)

Risk and disability

Social workers need to develop a critical understanding of risk in working with disabled people. Risk assessment within processes for safeguarding adults has become a key element of social work engagement with disabled people. With the pressure on resources and consequent eligibility criteria, services are often tailored towards people who are perceived as vulnerable. Ross and Waterson (1996) have argued that the focus on risk appears disproportionate and risk assessment often seems to be in conflict with a social model perspective. Brown (2009) argues that vulnerability is socially constructed. She highlights the case of Stephen Hoskins, a young man with learning disabilities who was victimized and then murdered. He had been excluded from services and was seen as having challenging behaviour (Healthcare Commission, 2006). If we explore this from a social model perspective, we can see how attitudinal barriers relating to disability impacted upon this situation. Stephen's conduct was assessed from an individual model perspective, problematized and related to anti-social behaviour. Gaylard (2008) suggests that support from within the voluntary sector, such as an advocate, might have enabled Stephen to deal with the difficulties he was experiencing.

Disabled people may also be vulnerable to abuse from family or friends or from the workers who are supposedly there to support them. The inquiry about learning disabilities services in Cornwall in 2006 highlighted poor practice and risk issues for people with disabilities (Healthcare Commission, 2006). Similarly, the more recent events into abusive practices at the private Winterbourne View hospital in

Gloucestershire demonstrated the difficulties in monitoring poor practice within the independent sector (Department of Health, 2013b). According to social model theorists, risk issues are often related to resources, poor training and workers with negative attitudes to disability (Oliver and Sapey, 2006). As care is often provided by a variety of agencies, part of the social worker's job is to ensure appropriate support. Challenging negative attitudes towards disability and abusive practice should be a central part of the social worker's role. However, it is significant that the Healthcare Commission (2006) reported that social workers did not feel able to challenge health care professionals within the National Health Service in Cornwall. Does this reflect the power balance between the social and the medical models and difficulties in working in partnership?

There have been recent debates about further legislation relating to the safeguarding adults. The review of the *No Secrets* guidance (Department of Health, 2000) in 2009 highlighted that there was a divide between those who wished for further legislation (e.g. right of entry to safeguard a vulnerable adult) and those who were concerned about the impact of professional power were new legislation to be developed (Department of Health, 2009b). There is also a need for a debate concerning the interface between the independent living agenda and the safeguarding of adults, particularly around the social construction of issues such as risk, vulnerability and capacity. There was some mention of this in the consultation into the review of *No Secrets* (Department of Health, 2009b). However, the review has not led to further significant changes within the Care Act (2014).

Social workers need to understand the social construction of risk. More recently, the idea of positive risk taking has been discussed. Close (2009) stresses that a positive approach to risk needs to be taken when considering self-directed support schemes, rather than focusing on negatives. Instead of seeing what disabled people cannot do, the focus should be on enabling people to be independent. This very much fits with a social model perspective of working in partnership with people to overcome barriers.

Risk assessment and adult protection work is a key ethical dilemma for social workers in applying social model and social relational perspectives. There is no one answer to this issue, but it is about balancing rights, positive risks and negative risks. Balancing risk and protection and empowerment can be problematic, as social workers are often working within inter-professional teams and other professionals may be operating to different risk criteria.

Case study

John is a 55-year-old man with learning disabilities who has lived in a group home for about 10 years. Previously, John lived in the local hospital for people with learning disabilities. Plans are underway for John to move into his own flat using an individual budget. John's family are resistant to this proposal as they don't think John will manage. Staff at the home say John does not voice his opinions on independent living and they are concerned he won't eat properly or look after himself.

- How can sociology help us to understand this situation?
- How could a rights-based approach be used to look at the challenges for John of independent living?

Challenges for social work practice

Social work has been criticized for being too heavily influenced by the medical model (French and Swain, 2012; Morris, 2004; Oliver and Sapey, 2006). Far from empowering disabled people, social workers are seen as encouraging dependency and being preoccupied with risk. Catherine McDonald (2006) discusses how it has become the responsibility of social welfare services to manage risk on society's behalf. Perhaps part of the issue, as has been discussed, is a lack of awareness about disability studies and sociological thought about disability. This may reflect that in recent years there has been little specific literature on social work with disabled people.

There are wide variations in how social work support to disabled people is organized between local authorities. Adult social care services have become more involved in 'gate-keeping' resources, which means that assessment can be experienced negatively by service users (Mantell, 2009). Social workers work within organizations which can be seen as oppressive to disabled people. Here services appear to be designed around things *for* people rather than with them. This relates to an individual model approach rather than a social model approach. Mantell (2009) has highlighted the need for social workers to learn new skills in relation to personalization and self-assessment. There is a need for partnership working and inclusive communication with disabled people. We have also explored in this chapter issues relating to independent living and community care.

From this discussion, it would appear that social work is more influenced by an individual than by a medical model perspective. Function, assessment of needs and resources govern the services that disabled people receive. The focus in assessment is seen as related to needs and risks. Morris (2004) and Priestley (1999) discuss how the focus on care management within social work has created an agenda that is about care needs rather than rights. From this perspective, if your needs are unmet, then you do not receive a service and therefore the structural oppression of many disabled people has not changed. This presents a rather gloomy picture for social work interaction with disabled people. However, we return here to the need for critically informed practice. Morris (2004) argues that a focus on rights would have a greater impact on quality of life. For example, a right to independent living would mean that community care services would have to be provided to support this. Priestley (1999) discusses the benefits of user-led services where disabled people are in control of budgets and services. Woodin (2014), however, explores how the current austerity measures in Western societies have further impacted upon the availability of care services to disabled people.

Fundamentally, social work needs to say more about social work with disabled people, and social work students and practitioners need to be positive about effective social work practice with and alongside them. Oliver et al. (2012) suggest a number of strategies to support this. Amongst these, they argue for greater awareness of disability and disability studies amongst social workers. This would increase understanding of social model perspectives. Secondly, despite resource constraints, personalization represents an opportunity for social workers to work in partnership with disabled people. Finally, Oliver et al. argue for social workers to have a critical awareness of their role within organizations and in working with communities.

Conclusion

This chapter has explored sociological perspectives on disability, and in particular the relevance of the social model of disability and the lived experience of disabled people to social work practice. We have seen how this creates ethical dilemmas for social work practice and examined how this impacts upon contemporary policy and services. There are tensions for social workers and social care services between the 'choice' agenda (e.g. individual budgets) and the 'protection' agenda (e.g. risk management and adult protection) (Department of Health, 2007b). A sociological understanding of risk is important here. There is not always an answer to these ethical dilemmas, but it is important to understand the challenges in working in the area of disability and how sociological perspectives can help develop our understanding. It often appears that it is not possible for social workers to challenge structural inequalities, but the discussion in this chapter offers an alternative discourse about social work practice with disabled people. Examining our own values and attitudes, using sociological thought, can support a more informed and critical approach to practice.

Summary points

- The structural oppression of disabled people is rooted within a historical context of segregation and institutional care practices.
- There are a range of post-modern sociological perspectives on health and disability. Different language can be used by health, social care and disability studies commentators to describe these perspectives.
- There are two key models, the social model and the individual or medical model of disability. The two are frequently seen as polarized, but a critical understanding of perspectives is needed.
- Social workers are seen as lacking awareness of disability issues, and this creates practice which is risk-averse. This needs to be seen within a global context.
- Social workers can promote empowerment for disabled people through working with the personalization agenda, although this can conflict with resource management and risk assessment and safeguarding adults.

Questions for discussion

- Do you think there have been significant changes in how disabled people are treated within society?
- Do you think disabled people need social workers?
- Given the current pattern of resource constraints, assessments and eligibility criteria, do you think empowering practice with disabled people is possible?
- How do you think the current global economic context impacts on the lived experience of disabled people?

Further reading

Glasby, J. and Littlechild, R. (2009) *Direct Payments and Personal Budgets: Putting Personalization into Practice.* Bristol: Policy Press

This book provides an overview of implementing the personalization agenda within health and social care.

Oliver, M. and Barnes, C. (2012) *The New Politics of Disablement.* **London: Palgrave**

This text provides a good overview of how the current political and economic context impacts on the lived experience of disabled people.

Oliver, M., Sapey, B. and Thomas, P. (2012) *Social Work with Disabled People.* **4th edition. London: Palgrave**

This is the fourth edition of a source that discusses the issues relating to whether social work can work in an empowering way with disabled people in the current climate.

Swain, J., French, S., Barnes, C. and Thomas, C. (2014) *Disabling Barriers – Enabling Environments.* **London: Sage**

This book provides an overview of the key issues within disability studies and disability sociology.

6 Sexuality and Sexual Exploitation

Introduction

Talking about sex is still something that makes some health and social care professionals uncomfortable. Yet, sexuality and sexual expression can often be an issue for user and carer groups that social workers engage with (Green, 2005; Hicks, 2009). The difficulties for professionals in discussing sexuality reflect wider attitudes in society about sexuality, sexual activity and sexual orientation. It is interesting to note that it is only more recently that general sociological texts have incorporated a specific section on the sociology of sexuality. Giddens and Sutton (2013) argued that one of the reasons we study sociology is so we can be 'enlightened' about issues such as difference and diversity. This is certainly important when we look at notions of 'normal' and 'abnormal' in relation to sexuality. This chapter will explore how the study of sexuality has developed and examine issues of power and the social construction of sexuality. We will also examine the impact of social movements and critical sociological perspectives which have challenged the discourse concerning sexuality (Weeks, 2010; Wilton, 2000). Throughout the chapter, the discussion concerning sociological thought and sexuality will be related to contemporary and relevant issues within social work practice. The chapter will also examine the global context of sexuality and sociological thought.

The key issues that will be explored in this chapter are:

- defining sexuality
- the historical and structural context of sexuality and sexual expression
- social constructionism and deviant sexualities
- social action and social interaction – the lesbian and gay movement and the impact of homophobia
- the development of critical perspectives on sociology and sexuality
- sexuality and the social work role within a global context.

By the end of this chapter you should be able to:

- explain what is meant by the terms 'sex', 'sexuality' and 'sexual orientation'
- discuss the ways that deviant sexual identities are constructed in societies
- explain the relationship between oppression, social control and sexual identities
- explain the impact of homophobia on the experiences of lesbian and gay people worldwide

- demonstrate a global understanding of the lesbian and gay movement in promoting diversity and challenging homophobia
- explain the role of social workers in working with issues of sexuality, sexual identity and sexual exploitation with a range of service users.

Defining sexuality

Many writers discuss how talking about sex is a highly sensitive and taboo area (e.g. Jackson and Rahman, 1997). This perhaps explains why health and social care professionals may find it difficult to discuss sex with their patients/service users. This can particularly be seen in relation to certain groups within society whose sexual identity is seen as 'deviant' and makes other societal groups uncomfortable (Climens and Combes, 2010). It is also inevitably affected by what we think about sex ourselves. Is it possible to define sexuality? Hogan (1980: 1299) defines sexuality as 'a quality of being human, all that we are, encompassing the most intimate feelings and deepest longings of the heart to find meaningful relationships'. This quote illustrates how difficult it is to define sexuality, as definitions are inherently subjective and shaped by our own values and opinions. In this quote, sex is clearly linked to expressing emotions and feelings, although other definitions stress the physical act of sexual activity. In many cultures, for example, sexual activity has been linked to reproduction. A singular definition of sexuality would imply that there is one common sexual identity, but sexual expression and activity are variable and the way that sexuality is expressed is affected by the cultural and social norms of a given period. Herdt (1981) argues that what constitutes a sexual act cannot be defined without looking at cultural and social norms, a view shared by the majority of contemporary sociologists (e.g. Giddens and Sutton, 2013). However, initially, biological and medical perspectives concerning sexuality dominated.

As sexual behaviour came to be more carefully studied in the nineteenth century, beliefs concerning 'normal' and 'abnormal' sexual behaviour began to develop. For Foucault (1979a), this stemmed from sexuality being classified and defined as part of a 'discourse of sexuality'. This has heavily influenced how an individual's sexual preferences, activity and orientation are expressed. Foucault's ideas around language and discourse shaping how sexuality is viewed are important when we think about helping professionals to talk about sex to service users and carers. How are our interactions shaped by what is perceived as 'normal' sexuality? For example, do we see disabled people engaging in sexual activity as abnormal? The historical and structural context concerning how a discourse on sexuality developed is important here.

Exercise: talking about sex

- What is your immediate reaction to talking about sexuality and sexual issues?
- How do you think this would affect your interactions with service users and carers?
- What do you think you need to do to develop your skills in this area?

The development of a sexuality discourse

Throughout history, people have been required to conform to certain patterns of sexual behaviour and expression. Certain sexual behaviours may be seen as deviant or shocking in one culture and not in another. However, sociologists have argued that in the last two centuries, there have been significant changes to our contemporary view of sexuality in Western society. To understand why this has occurred, we need to look at the relationship between science and sexuality.

Discourses concept used by Foucault to illustrate how language shapes our thinking. Foucault believed there is no such thing as absolute truth, but at any one moment in time a dominant 'way of seeing' exists, shaping our understanding.

Foucault (1979a) saw the nineteenth century as the starting point for *discourses* on sexuality. Prior to this period, sexuality and sexual expression were connected closely with religious morality. Moral regulation through religious institutions was therefore more significant than secular and state regulation and intervention concerning sexual matters. Notions of 'normal' and 'abnormal' sexuality had not been clearly defined, as religious beliefs and social order governed sexual behaviour. Weeks (2010) discusses how Christian religions established a conflict between the mind and the body where sex was concerned. While sexual activity existed outside marriage, this tended to be limited to certain groups. For example, some wealthy men engaged in sexual relationships outside marriage, but for the vast majority of the population (and particularly women) sexual expression was part of marriage and reproduction within the family, and adultery was a sin, with moral and social consequences.

Sociologists see the rise of science and medicine in the nineteenth century as leading to a debate about normal and abnormal sexual behaviour. In this period, sexual behaviour began to be classified according to a predominantly biological and medicalized notion of sexuality. Jackson and Rahman (1997) see classification as leading to labelling according to natural and unnatural sexuality. This was affected by social and cultural norms of the period and had significant social implications in the nineteenth century that are still felt today.

The emphasis on sexuality and biological process is another form of essentialism (see p. 86). An essentialist perspective sees sexuality as biological, fixed and given. Macionis and Plummer (2012) argue that biological factors have historically taken precedence over social and cultural constructs in theorizing sexuality. For Foucault (1979a), the scientific discourse around sexuality led to social control, where science defined sexuality in terms of normal and abnormal sexuality, which then permeated throughout society, leading to cultural and social norms around permissible sexual identity and activity. Foucault's analysis is referred to as 'biopower', the core principle being that the science of sexuality became associated with power and control. As sexuality became classified, state regulation and intervention concerning sexual matters increased.

Sex, the family and the state

Sociological theories that focus on the impact of systems or structures within society have traditionally located sexual roles within a discourse about the family (Foucault, 1979a). Men and women had clearly defined sexual roles, related to biological processes of reproduction. Functionalists such as Parsons (1951) and Murdock (1949) saw sexual roles as necessary in the socialization of children and for stable family environments. Gender and sexuality are closely linked, as the function of the family was also a basis for the sexual division of labour between men and women (Haralambos and Holborn, 2004). Wilton (2000) sees the link between sexuality and family as inherent within social policies which are still relevant today. The stable function of the family unit is therefore also beneficial for the state as it supports wider functions within society.

Bilton et al. (2002) also point to the necessity of stable families for capitalism to function. For Marx, sexual relationships provided the basis for the reproduction of the labour force. Engels (1902) developed Marxian perspectives concerning sex and the family. He saw society as responsible for regulating sexual behaviour (which was naturally promiscuous). He also saw the monogamous nuclear family developing as private property and state structures developed. Men needed to protect their property and their inheritance, and monogamous marriage provided a clear 'blood' line enabling this transmission of property. Women 'sold' their sexual and reproductive services in order to be provided with material stability. Engels regarded communism as providing a solution to women 'selling' themselves, and he can be seen to have recognized that gender roles were heavily associated with sexual behaviour. Marxist feminist perspectives further examined the link between gender, sex and family (e.g. Benston, 1969). Gramsci (1971) discusses how industrialists such as the Ford Company were concerned with the sexual affairs of their employees in order to maintain a stable workforce.

The scientific classification of sexuality served to treat as well as reinforce cultural and social norms. From this perspective, sex and sexual activity are socially controlled and have a structural function to enable stable families to contribute towards a stable society (Foucault, 1979a). Sexual activity was thus primarily about reproduction.

Essentialism and the body

Biological perspectives concerning sexuality led to an emphasis on reproduction, and this connects with issues around the 'sociology of the body'. Turner (1992) argued that the institutions of medicine, law and religion are involved in regulating the body, particularly in relation to birth and death. Thus sanctions can be placed on families in order to control them: for example, in China the relationship between the benefit system and the number of children in the family is used to attempt to contain population growth. Equally, families who conform to ideal types can accrue positive rewards through legal, economic and status privileges: for example, they can acquire financial benefits through the tax system.

While it can be argued that women are now more in control of their own reproduction, regulation is still a factor. Nettleton (2013) discusses the correlation between the control of female sexuality and the control of reproduction and the impact of new reproductive technologies. There is an economic, social and political context to issues relating to reproduction now: for example, the availability of contraception and sex education. Issues of sexual deviancy relating to the sociology of body are still relevant, as we will explore later in the chapter. Historically, those who did not conform were seen as deviant and this influenced sexual expression for a number of groups in society, as we shall now see.

Essentialism and sexual deviancy

In the late nineteenth and early twentieth centuries, biological and reductionist perspectives concerning sexuality had profound implications for certain groups in society. For women, the medicalization of sexuality led to a discourse about 'good' and 'bad' sexual behaviour. 'Good' sexual behaviour was related to modesty and chastity, whilst 'bad' sexual behaviour was seen as provocative and amoral. Because of these definitions, sexuality and gender have become a focus for feminist debate and critical sociology, as we examine later in the chapter. For feminist commentators such as Rich (1980) and Sherry (1973), women's natural, innate sexuality was controlled and defined by male scientists. Men were seen as sexually active, whereas women were passive within the sexual process. The sexual function for women was to reproduce and run the family. Sexual violence within marriage was also hidden, and often seen as the result of women being provocative. Related to this is the view of male sexuality as uncontrollable, one which it is argued is still prevalent in how rape cases are processed (Brown et al., 1993; Lees, 1993).

Biological and religious perspectives are both concerned with the control of women's sexuality. Biological factors provided the classification and justification for what is normal and abnormal. Women who were seen as having 'unnatural' sexual desires became the focus of psychological and psychiatric intervention. In the nineteenth and early twentieth centuries, women who were seen as having 'unnatural' sexual desires or men who were seen as deviant because of homosexual identification were the subject of study by sexologists and psychiatrists. Sebastian Faulks' novel *Human Traces* (2006) features a number of female characters who are referred for assessment and medical intervention owing to 'hysterical' and sexualized behaviour. Nymphomania was the medical term given to women who were seen as having 'unhealthy' sexual desires or fixations. The condition was also seen to affect women's genitals, and in some cases led to clitoridectomies (removal of the clitoris). Goldberg (1999) discusses how women were subjected to a range of treatments to cure abnormal sexual desires, so here we see a clear link between abnormal sexual behaviour and mental health treatments. White (2009), meanwhile, discusses how gynaecology defined sexual and reproductive problems in a medical framework. In particular, problems in these areas were seen as a result of a rejection of femininity.

This reflects the dual sexual role of women, as 'madonnas' or 'whores'. Women who stepped outside conventional sexual roles were outcasts, but still 'used' by men. For example, prostitutes operated on the periphery of society, often subject to danger and physical and emotional violence. Women who had illegitimate children found themselves socially disgraced or at worst incarcerated in asylums. This reflected male power and control over sex and sexual relations (Goldberg, 1999). From a structuralist perspective, behaviour outside conventional norms and structures was punished as deviant.

The development of a science of sexuality is also seen as damaging to those who were not heterosexual, as a binary expression of sexuality was conceptualized within a medical framework. Heterosexuality was conceptualized as normal behaviour, whilst homosexuality was seen as abnormal. Norton (1992) discusses how, before the eighteenth century, homosexuality was simply seen as not existing in Western societies. With a biomedical model, however, came a political and legal framework with laws against sodomy across Europe. State intervention concerning homosexuality became common, with harsh punishments for deviancy that continued well into the twentieth century (and still do in some societies). The behaviour of homosexuals was classified, with sexual 'perversions' being examined and defined (Weeks, 2010). When we examine the global context concerning sexuality and sexual identity, we will see that there are signs that this kind of state intervention is returning. Biological reductionism can be seen to be used by the state as justification for intervention.

However, studies such as those by Kinsey et al. (1948, 1953) and the work of sexologists such as Havelock Ellis (1946) showed that sexuality or sexual expression does not have a fixed pattern, but is variable and fluid. Kinsey et al.'s study of sexual behaviour in America indicated a wide range of difference of sexual expression. This work was ground-breaking at the time as it indicated that sex and sexual expression were far from being simply about reproduction; nor were they fixed between a heterosexual and homosexual identity. Sexual expression, however, was often hidden and influenced by social construction. The interactions between individuals also influenced sexual activity and behaviour. This reflects the work of contemporary sociologists who have argued that sexual eroticism became taboo in capitalist society (Weeks, 2010).

While not ignoring biological perspectives, the focus of these studies was on how sexual behaviours were expressed and how this impacted upon sexual development. However, to a degree, this led to the development of a biomedical model of sexual orientation. For example, Ellis (1946) discussed homosexuals as 'inverts', and his writings led to other theorists using these perspectives to support medical treatments and cures for sexual orientation, although Wilton (2000) argues that this was not his intention.

In the nineteenth and twentieth centuries, sexologists, psychologists and psychiatrists continued to treat sexual behaviours that were considered outside 'the norm'. Sexual behaviours that were not heterosexual were seen within a 'deviant' framework. One of the most well-known figures here is Sigmund Freud. There has been much debate about the writings of Freud and whether he saw homosexuality as arrested development, particularly in relation to the Oedipus complex. However, twentieth-century doctors used his ideas as a method to look at how problems with parents prevented a child from developing a heterosexual identity, leading to a medicalization of homosexuality. Until 1973, the American Psychiatric Association defined homosexuality as a mental disorder.

Many of Freud's followers (e.g. Melanie Klein) saw homosexuality as a disturbed form of sexual expression. *Psychoanalysis* can also be seen to be partly responsible for labelling lesbians and gay men as deviant, and historically it led to interventions based on 'curing' people of homosexuality. More recently, however, it has been argued that Freud's work has been misinterpreted in this area (see, e.g., Davies and Neal, 1996) and that

> **Psychoanalysis** the treatment and study of psychological problems and disorders, developed initially by Sigmund Freud.

he did not see homosexuality as a deviation. Gay and lesbian psychologists such as Isay (1989) have reframed Freud's initial thoughts on homosexuality to demonstrate that psychoanalysis can be a positive tool to support people who have issues with a lesbian or gay identity. We explore this further later in the chapter

E.M. Forster in his posthumous novel *Maurice* (1971, originally written in 1913–14) discusses medical intervention concerning homosexuality and its effect on his principal character in the early twentieth century. It is telling that Forster did not feel able to publish this novel while he was alive, because he himself had kept his sexuality hidden, as was often the case with lesbian and gay identities until recently. Oscar Wilde is an example of someone whose sexual preferences became the subject of public disgrace, leading to a prison sentence at the turn of the twentieth century. Indeed, even in the later part of the twentieth century, public figures and celebrities who were homosexual still struggled with a lesbian and gay identity. The popular entertainer Kenneth Williams records the dilemmas associated with his sexual orientation in his diaries, published posthumously in 1994 (Davies, 1994).

Jeyasingham (2008) highlights how lesbians have historically not been visible in society. This was reflected in literature, art and other forms of creative media. This historical marginalization has also had a significant impact on the identity of lesbians, which we explore later in the chapter. It also relates to how biomedical perspectives classified sexual behaviour, which contributed to how sexuality was viewed and expressed within society

Social constructionism

A social constructionist approach challenges essentialism and has led to the development of critical sociological thought concerning sexuality. While acknowledging biological differences, the key issue is the way in which society and its structures have impacted upon how sexuality develops and, most importantly, how it is expressed. Sociologists such as Weeks (2010) argue that sexuality and sexual identity have been shaped by the historical, social, political and cultural norms and values of a given period. These forces influence what sexuality means and how individuals behave. While state regulation concerning sexual matters is important, however, the responses of individuals, groups and communities concerning sexual behaviour are also highly significant.

There are some broad themes that shape social constructionism and sexuality. Expression of sexual identity is connected to the dominant 'discourse of sexuality'. The fact that sexual identity has been closely linked to the family is seen as socially constructed and linked to power and control. Connell (1987, 1995) discusses the predominance of male-dominated heterosexuality, and refers to this as 'hegemonic masculinity'. At the top of the tree are white, heterosexual men, whilst at the bottom are lesbian women (subordinated femininities). This relates to the earlier discussion about how gender roles relate to sexual activity. Because men are more powerful, their sexual behaviour is regulated in a different way from that of women.

Factors such as race, disability and class further shape power relations in sexual relationships. For example, in the early years of the twentieth century, there was a general preoccupation with over-population and poverty, which can be seen to have informed the development of the eugenics movement (see Chapter 5). Wilson (2006) refers to a letter written by the author D.H. Lawrence concerning the potential genocide of certain groups in society (a view echoed by other authors and intellectuals of the time) to alleviate this issue. In a given period, sexual behaviour may need to be regulated and controlled for a variety of reasons. Social constructs shape how sexual activity is expressed, and this in turn is related to issues of power, control and disadvantage in a number of ways.

Social constructionism and the body

In terms of the sociology of the body, we have discussed how reproduction was focused on supporting the family and thus stability within society. It also follows that social constructs shape how the body is 'used' in this process. Femininity is constructed around the notion of desirability constructed within patriarchal ideologies, so that women can attract a suitable mate for procreative purposes (see Chapter 3). In terms of healthy bodies, sexual attractiveness and desirability are also closely connected to body image, which is heavily influenced by societal norms. Being overweight, for example, is generally seen as sexually unattractive (although this has not always been the case). Magazines, TV and books are dominated by discussions about how to 'sell' yourself as a sexual product. This commodification is wide-ranging in terms of staying young and desirable. The impact of consumer culture on the body and sexuality is therefore highly important (Featherstone, 1991).

Gender and sexuality are closely inter-related. It therefore follows that there will be social and cultural constructs concerning what men in particular are looking for in their 'mate'. While there are biological and anatomical issues to consider, the way in which sexual attractiveness is commodified and constructed can be seen as significant. For example, how do we think sexual attractiveness is rated if you are an overweight person with mental health problems? How does this affect perceived reproductive potential? If a person is not perceived as sexually desirable or having reproductive capacity, how does this affect the way that sexual behaviour and identity are viewed?

The image of the body for women is closely associated with consumer culture.
(© ana reinert/Flickr)

Social constructs concerning normality have been applied to disabled people concerning the development of both sexual identity and sexual activity. As with older people, disabled people are often seen as asexual. Bonnie (2014) points to how disabled teenagers and adults can often be dressed in babyish or androgynous clothing. Alternatively, disabled people can be seen as sexually threatening. At the beginning of the twentieth century, one of the primary reasons for an asylum model of care for people with learning disabilities was to control sexual relationships between them (Race, 2002). Social and cultural constructs also manifest themselves in a fear of abnormality in relation to disability (Barnes, 1991). Field (1993) describes the dual oppression of being disabled and a lesbian. This can be extended to stereotypes around disability and sexual activity, which may be perpetuated by portrayals of disabled people as asexual in popular culture. As Morris (1989: 80) cites one disabled person as saying: '. . . many people assume we are asexual, often in order to hide embarrassment about the seemingly incongruous idea that such "abnormal" people can have "normal" feelings and relationships.'

Bonnie (2014) discusses how disabled people have challenged sexual stereotypes more recently through media representation of their sexuality. She also argues that disabled people are fighting for the right of sexual expression and sexual citizenship. This connects with a rights-based approach to disability, explored further in Chapter 5.

There are also particular issues related to women with disabilities and reproduction. Bonnie (2014) discusses how, historically, disabled people have been sterilized (especially women) and access to sexual health and contraceptive advice may have been hampered by the inability of families to see disabled children/teenagers as sexual beings. Sheldon (2014) highlights the debate about prenatal screening and foetal abnormalities. From a feminist perspective, this is giving women control of their bodies and a choice about abortion, but for disabled writers, prenatal screening can be seen as a new form of eugenics (Shakespeare, 1998). There are therefore particular issues about disabled women's sexuality both in terms of attitudes towards reproduction and concerning parenting support.

Nettleton (2013) discusses the impact of chronic health conditions on the development and maintenance of sexual relationships. Again, professionals are seen as poor at discussing the impact of health problems on sexual relationships. For example, multiple sclerosis may lead to erectile problems for men and the use of catheters can affect sex for both men and women.

Social and cultural taboos around sexual activity and older people also relate to the sociology of the body. Older people are often seen as asexual, devoid of sexual feelings and needs (Lynch, 2014), an image that television programmes, literature and other forms of popular culture often perpetuate (McDonald, 2010). Pickard (1995: 268), for example, says that: 'Sexuality in old age is a subject which is enveloped with secrecy and half-knowledge and referred to in society in general with embarrassment and by joking allusions, that is if it is not dismissed altogether, the old so patently being "past it".'Older women may be particularly disadvantaged here, as we live in a society that constructs images around the symbolic value of the body. Women who are past the age of reproductive ability are seen as 'past it', and therefore their sexuality may not be acknowledged by society (see Chapter 10). Indeed, older women who express their sexuality may be labelled as deviant (Lynch, 2014). Men are able to father children throughout the adult life-course, although declining motility of the sperm and erectile performance may diminish this capacity. Therefore, there is less evidence of men being viewed as asexual, although there is social pressure to not acknowledge this. Older men who are open about sexual activity may be viewed as 'dirty old men', with social sanctions placed on them to conform to dominant ideals.

Social constructionism and sexual orientation

Weeks (2010) defines a number of ways in which social and historical constructs impact upon sexuality and sexual identity, which can be related to sexual orientation in the following ways:

- *Family/kinship*: The experiences of 'coming out' to family.
- *Economic and social organization*: Across the world, lesbian and gay people tend to congregate in large urban centres, where they are better able to work and lead their chosen lifestyle. Sometimes, gay ghettos develop (e.g. Soho/San Francisco), resulting in a perception of 'safety in numbers'.
- *Social regulation*: It is only relatively recently that legislation has been repealed which disallowed teaching about lesbian and gay lifestyles within UK schools. Lesbian and gay organizations such as Stonewall have been concerned with changing structural positions towards lesbians and gay people. For example, the Civil Partnership Act (2004) (*http://www.opsi.gov.uk/ACTS*) and the Marriage (Same Sex Couples) Act (2013) (*http://www.legislation.gov.uk/ukpga/2013/30/contents/enacted*) were the product of many years campaigning for the legal rights of lesbian and gay people.
- *Political interventions*: Sometimes, governments intervene to promote the sexual norm. The rise of the New Right led to the promotion of a traditional agenda of family and heterosexual marriage. Within institutions such as the Armed Forces, until recently, there has been politically sanctioned intervention regarding sexual orientation. Later in the chapter, we examine the global context of political intervention.
- *Identity and resistance*: Lesbian and gay people's identity is shaped by their interaction with the world around them. Adverse reactions, bullying, hate crimes and rejection by families may affect the psychosocial development of lesbians and gay men. Goffman (1968) identified the importance of stigma and labelling on health and well-being (see Chapter 11).

If we accept that society regulates our behaviour, then we begin to see the problems that arise when our identity does not 'fit'. This identity crisis for lesbians and gay men has become known as *internalized homophobia*, which may manifest itself in institutions as 'institutionalized homophobia'.

> **Internalized homophobia** homosexual men or women may self-loathe or self-hate owing to their sexual identity.

Homophobia

Homophobia can be defined as a fear of or aversion towards lesbians and gay men. As sociological thinking on sexuality has developed, so has the debate on the impact of internalized homophobia. The way that our sexuality can be perceived as regulated can have a powerful and detrimental effect on lesbians and gay men. There are many studies and articles detailing the impact of homophobia upon the development of a lesbian and gay identity (e.g. Brown, 1998; Wilton, 2000). Comstock's (1991) study showed that violence towards gay men, in particular, was seen as more socially acceptable than violence towards other groups. It is particularly interesting that violent homophobic attitudes appear in institutions where hegemonic masculinity is at its most dominant.

Bywater and Jones (2007) discuss how homophobia can lead individuals to promote heterosexism as the normative discourse. Here assumptions are made that individuals are heterosexual and societal practices are built around this assumption. This then leads to lesbian and gay people experiencing oppression and discrimination as societal structures are built around heterosexism. Power is significant here as lesbian and gay people attempt to challenge societal attitudes and values (Giddens and Sutton, 2013) and experience marginalization. The strength of these normative attitudes has been such that it is only relatively recently that lesbian and gay people have become more visible within mainstream society in the UK.

There is evidence to suggest that health and social care professionals generally are influenced by cultural norms and beliefs in relation to homosexuality. The National Health Service has recognized this in the production of training standards for staff on sexual orientation (Cree and O'Corra, 2006). This report discusses research showing the way in which homophobic attitudes have affected how lesbians, gay men, and bisexual and transgender people have been treated in the NHS. Research is quoted to show that 33% of gay men, 25% of bisexual men and 40% of lesbian women experience a negative response from mental health professionals on disclosing their sexual identity (King and McKeown, 2003).

Social movements, sexuality and moral panic

The social constructs concerning sexuality have been increasingly challenged in the last 30 years, particularly in relation to 'deviant' or 'abnormal' sexualities. This has related to social movements concerning feminism and disability explored in previous chapters. In terms of sexual orientation, the development of the lesbian and gay movement has been highly significant. In the late 1960s, homosexuality was de-criminalized in England and Wales and a few years later it was officially de-classified as a mental disorder by the American Psychiatric Association. These changes were reflected within wider societal changes connected with gender roles and sexual identity and behaviour. Lesbians and gay men began to develop a more visible and collective identity. The attack by police on the Stonewall bar in New York in 1969 saw a fight back at police brutality. One of the key civil rights organizations for lesbians and gay men in the UK, Stonewall, is named after this incident. Lesbians were also organizing themselves politically as part of the feminist movement and separately from gay men. Gay Pride marches and lesbian and gay organizations developed throughout the 1970s and 1980s.

This political mobilization of lesbians and gay men can be seen as a resistance to sexual regulation and classification. Weeks (2010) talks about 'cultures of resistance' taking place throughout history in response to moral codes and regulations. Political and social movements such as the lesbian and gay movement are part of the

This photo typifies the way in which people have challenged negative portrayals of lesbian, gay, bisexual and transgendered people through Gay Pride events. (© Ian Palmer/Flickr)

campaign to recognize a more pluralist society and challenge the fixed and biological perceptions of sexuality.

The challenge from the lesbian and gay movement can be seen to have led to social anxiety and 'moral panic' in the 1980s. There was a reassertion of heterosexual 'family' values by political, social and religious institutions. For example, in the UK, the Conservative administration introduced legislation prohibiting the promotion of same-sex relationships and lifestyles within education. There was also a concern about the impact of HIV/AIDS on sexual activity, leading to social anxiety, particularly about the behaviour of gay men, in this period. However, moral panics can act as a great lever for changes in societal attitudes, as well as leading to repressive measures by political and social organizations in society. For example, asylum care for people with learning disabilities arose from a moral panic about poverty and over-population. There was a concern that people with learning disabilities would affect genetics and reproduction at this time (Race, 2002). This can be seen as a response to a concern about sexual activity, class and population and resulted in repressive measures.

Weeks (2010: 114) discusses moral panics as 'flurries of social anxiety' that arise when groups challenge the general social values and norms. He further discusses how they usually occur when the boundaries of 'normal' behaviour are loose and flexible (see Chapter 7). HIV/AIDS occurred at a time, the early 1980s, when changes in attitudes towards lesbians and gay people were evident. Homosexuality had been de-criminalized and lesbians and gay men had become more visible. However, the identification of HIV/AIDS was seen as a punishment or curse for the sexually promiscuous behaviour of gay men. This connects to Goffman's work around stigma (see p. 109) where some conditions can have negative moral attributes. This can lead to active discrimination against those with the particular condition (Scambler, 1997).

Certainly, in the early 1980s, there was a very hostile reaction to gay men, which was given impetus by the outbreak of HIV/AIDS. Religious and moral groups talked about a 'gay plague', and this approach reinforced the attitude that homosexuality was abnormal and deviant. A moral panic can be seen to have resulted from fears that HIV/AIDS was going to be become endemic. In terms of the media in general, reactions were mixed. Some celebrities and political figures were supportive of the needs of people with HIV/AIDS, and, ultimately, the 'moral panic' led to some changes in approaches and attitudes towards people with HIV/AIDS and also was important in galvanizing the lesbian and gay movement (Bywater and Jones, 2007).

The lesbian and gay movement can be seen to have led to significant political, social and economic changes:

- Legislation concerning teaching about same-sex relationships in schools has been repealed.
- Many state institutions have changed working practices towards people with same-sex orientation (e.g. the Army).
- The Civil Partnership Act (2005) and the Marriage (Same Sex Couples) Act (2013) have given same-sex couples entitlement to legal and property rights.
- The age of consent for same-sex relationships has been lowered.

The above reflects how the lesbian and gay movement has campaigned for citizenship rights which can be seen to challenge social exclusion and disadvantage (Richardson, 1998).

Critical sociological perspectives

Contemporary social movements concerning sex and sexual identity can be seen to have challenged the structuralist and medicalized perspectives which had dominated debate about sexuality for centuries. Weeks (2010) outlines how social movements in relation to gender, sexuality and sexual orientation have questioned the lack of control women have over reproduction; tackled issues relating to sexual preference, sexual harassment and abuse, male violence and power; and challenged homophobia and the dominance of heteronormative practices within societal structures. This has led to an international lesbian and gay movement which campaigns for sexual rights based on equality and citizenship.

The language and discourse concerning sexuality has also been critically applied to the contemporary context. The use of the term 'queer' has been reclaimed by academics writing about sexual orientation and sexual identity. Queer theory rejects fixed identities of sexuality and offers new perspectives on sex and gender within Western societies (e.g. Butler, 1990; Warner, 1993). Jackson and Rahman (1997) see queer studies as deconstructing the relationship between sex, gender and desire. Therefore, rather than a fixed (and heterosexual) notion of sexual identity, sexuality is fluid and diverse. Queer theory also challenges a discourse about sexuality by redefining language and the labelling of sexual preference (Richardson, 2000). However, queer theory is seen as being expressed within minority groups, and to have not changed a majority heterosexual culture. Wilton (2000) also discusses how some sections of the lesbian and gay community see essentialist perspectives as valuable, particularly in relation to the search for the 'gay gene' as a basis for equality.

There has also been criticism of the role of religion within contemporary debates concerning sexuality. As explored in Chapter 1, social action theorists such as Weber saw religion as potentially socially transformational. Feminist, lesbian and gay critical sociological perspectives, however, see religion as oppressive. Weeks (2010) discusses how a number of faith perspectives have continued to dominate debate and discussion concerning sexual morality. This can be seen in the recent contentious debate about same-sex marriage in the UK and the position of a number of faith groups regarding this. Faith groups here are seen not as transformatory but as reactionary. Kandaswamy (2008) explores the polarized positions of the state and religious and community groups within American society concerning same-sex marriage. Here, we can see elements of moral panic arising about the impact of same-sex marriage and the perceived breakdown of marriage as an institution. The lesbian and gay movement has continued to argue vociferously for marriage as a civil right which should be available in all societies (see Weeks, 2010 for further discussion).

It is also important to relate the lesbian and gay movement to social disadvantage, class and social exclusion. The movement has campaigned for citizenship rights and there have been significant changes for many lesbians and gay men. However, social workers often work with those people who have been marginalized and excluded. It is therefore important that you are aware of your own values and attitudes in relation to sexuality and the support services available.

Critical sociology of sexuality and social work practice

There is considerable evidence about the impact of social constructs on the sexual identity and behaviour of certain groups within society. Social workers need awareness of these issues. As discussed, a critical sociology of sexuality has developed which has challenged essentialism and sexuality. Issues of power and control are important here, as there are also particular issues for groups who are socially disadvantaged. This makes it important that health and social care professionals engage with sexual issues, as there may well be structural factors that are oppressive and inhibit expression of sexual identity for service user or carer groups. Our personal values need examination, as social and cultural constructs can be seen to lead to sexual stereotypes. We cannot assume that because they are 'signed up' to social work values and ethics, social workers are aware of issues of sexuality and sexual orientation. Social workers need to be informed about organizations such as Stonewall that promote the citizenship and equal rights of lesbian and gay people.

Exercise: Stonewall

Have a look at the Stonewall website – *http://www.stonewall.org.uk*.

- Does this challenge your own values and attitudes towards sexual orientation?
- How do you think you could use a website like Stonewall positively within your own practice?
- How might organizations like Stonewall help you to work in partnership with lesbian and gay service users?

Homophobia is also evident within social services and social work. Hicks (2009) draws attention to the fact that homophobic attitudes have often been addressed within the generic framework of anti-discriminatory practice, although this is insufficient. Brown (1998) has looked at how lesbian and gay identity has been perceived within social work theory and concludes that lesbian and gay issues are not appropriately addressed in social work education. There is also a range of research looking at homophobic attitudes within particular service user and carer groups (e.g. Green, 2005; Hicks, 2009; Manthorpe, 2003).

Studies highlight a range of attitudes towards working with sexual issues with different user and carer groups. Service users and carers may also have issues about sexual development and identity arising from poor relationship experiences, abuse, physical or mental health problems or exploitation. Sociological perspectives concerning sexuality explored in this chapter can aid our understanding in a number of ways.

Sexuality and mental health

It would appear that a variety of user and carer groups find it difficult to talk about sexual issues with health and social care professionals. For example, in mental health services, some lesbians and gay men do not disclose their sexual orientation to health providers for fear of being stigmatized (Harris Interactive, 2002). Other mental health studies have echoed this view (Golding, 1997). This may be a particular issue for people who are socially disadvantaged, as Davies and Neal (1996) note that lesbians and gay men are more likely to seek support from the private sector with mental health issues. Income may therefore be an important factor in terms of accessing support.

There is evidence that lesbians and gay men are over-represented within the mental health system (Tew, 2011). The idea that a lesbian and gay identity is 'abnormal' has led to some people with a same-sex orientation seeking support from mental health services. Lesbians and gay men are also more likely to experience issues with alcohol misuse (Herbert, 1994), and Paul (2002) suggests that lesbians and gay men are more likely to attempt suicide. Although, relatively recently, the biomedical model has been challenged and therapeutic approaches have been advocated, it should not be assumed that changes in how sexual orientation is viewed in contemporary society mean there are no identity issues for lesbians and gay men. Attitudes, culture, values and religion can all impact upon the mental health of lesbians and gay men.

Sexuality and disability

Williams (2009) highlights the need to support people with learning disabilities concerning sexual relationships and sexual identity, work which is often hampered by professional attitudes towards discussion of sexual issues with them (Grant et al., 2010). As the Baring Foundation (2006) showed, parents with a learning disability are more likely to have their children taken into care and to not have access to a range of support services. Sexual identity and disability appears to be something generally that professionals struggle with, perhaps as part of the legacy of asylum care and a denial about the sexual needs and feelings of learning disabled people. Shakespeare et al. (1996) relate this to societal attitudes towards the body and the fear of disability. Social workers need to be aware of stereotypes in their work with disabled people. For example, Lipton (2004) discusses the impact of chronic illness on lesbians and gay men. Social workers need to be aware of how 'layers' of oppression may interact with service users where sexual identity and disability may be inter-related.

Social workers frequently work with users and carers where risk is a key issue, and issues of power affect the way in which risk is 'managed'. A negative example of this is forbidding or controlling sexual relationships between people with learning disabilities. In a general discussion of sex and disability, Oliver and Sapey (2006) highlight that workers may need to facilitate sexual activity for disabled people by, for example, putting a person in bed in with another person. Social workers engaging with the social model of disability (see Chapter 5) may need to support service users to take positive risks around sex. Ballan (2008) highlights attitudinal barriers relating to disability and sexuality within social work education and the need for a social model approach. Hicks (2008) discusses the need for affirmative practice.

Sexuality and older people

Older people may be disadvantaged in achieving a fulfilling sexual and/or emotionally intimate relationship through bereavement of a partner. The opportunities for meeting new partners may be limited owing to societal taboos and a focus on youth in the field of dating. The consequences of the social image of asexuality in old age can also have far-reaching consequences. If physical changes are impacting on sexual ability, older people may feel embarrassed to seek help, thus being denied the possibility of a fulfilling physical relationship. Although physical changes in later life may make it necessary to make adjustments in order to participate in sexual intercourse, a loving and intimate relationship can be a positive experience and any difficulties can be faced together within the context of a mature and trusting relationship.

Understanding the sexual needs of older people is essential to assessment and person-centred care. There are research and anecdotal examples of older people in acute care and long-term care sectors being denied the possibility of an intimate relationship, either with an existing partner or through the development of a new relationship (Roach, 2004). An understanding of the importance of sexuality and intimate relationships can help social workers and care managers to address this.

Social workers also need to be aware that there is an even greater taboo around lesbian and gay older people. Manthorpe (2003) discusses how lesbian carers are more likely to have problems accessing services. This may be related to fear of professional reactions, family issues or lack of awareness of what is available. Quam (1997) discusses a case example of a lesbian couple whose relatives sought to separate them at a time of illness. This highlights the need for social work to be sensitive to family and sexuality issues in work with lesbian and gay older people. More recently, organizations such as the Alzheimer's Disease Society and Age UK have started to recognize the needs of older lesbians and gay men, with the latter producing a comprehensive guide for older same-sex couples (Age UK, 2011b). This is one example of how knowing what is available in local communities can counteract exclusion (Ben-Ari, 2001).

Sexuality, children and young people

Issues of sexual identity are particularly relevant to social work with children and young people. Sexual development in children and young people is a complex area. Robinson (2005) discusses how assumptions are made about the sexual identity of children and young people, and this can particularly be the case where sexual orientation is concerned. Green (2005) examines the importance of gender in responding to issues about sexuality and sexual abuse within residential childcare services. In addition, professionals need to be sensitive concerning issues of sexual orientation for looked after children (Thomas, 2005). Social workers need to be particularly sensitive to how an emerging sexual identity can be compromised by abuse and exploitation, which can often be a particular issue for looked after children. Children may also need empowering to deal with sexual issues (Green, 2005).

Sexual identity can affect children and young people in their interaction with peers. A number of studies have explored the impact of homophobia on bullying in schools (see, e.g., Rivers, 1995), and links have been made between developing sexual orientation and bullying. Stonewall found that over half of the lesbian, gay and bisexual pupils surveyed in 2012 had experienced direct bullying. They also pointed to how the use of homophobic language is endemic within school culture, as well as a lack of awareness and discussion of sexual orientation (Stonewall, 2012). Stonewall also discuss how homophobic bullying can lead to truancy and mental health issues. There is evidence to suggest that homophobic bullying and problems within families can lead to young people entering the care system. The Albert Kennedy Trust in Manchester was formed in 1990 following the death of a 16-year-old teenager who had run away from a children's home and was fleeing homophobic attackers. It specifically exists to counter homophobic attitudes and address issues such as addiction, homelessness and mental health problems that lesbian and gay men may experience. The Trust works closely with social services to protect young people who are at risk. Its website details some moving testimonials of young people that the organization has placed in safe supportive environments because of bullying and harassment.

Offering support can be vital to positive practice. Trotter (2000) sees social workers as being in a good position to help young people with issues of sexual identity. Social workers can give support, avoid pathologizing 'deviant' behaviour and offer an accepting and affirming approach to the sexual development of children and young people.

Sexuality and lesbian and gay parenting

Heteronormative values can be seen in relation to lesbian and gay parenting. Bywater and Jones (2007) discuss how some lesbians and gay men may be parents from previous heterosexual relationships. We explore some of the issues relating to surrogacy in the next section of this chapter. Again, the lesbian and gay movement can be seen as highly significant in campaigning for the rights of lesbian and gay parents.

Increasingly, lesbian and gay people have also looked to foster, adopt and have children. Fostering and adoption by lesbian and gay people is part of legislation and discrimination should not occur (Adoption and Children Act, 2002). Hicks has written extensively concerning the issues relating to lesbian and gay adoption and fostering. He argues that lesbian and gay prospective adopters have experienced discrimination by social workers and other professionals based on heteronormative practices (Hicks, 2005). While this position has improved with more lesbian and gay people adopting, there is not consistency within the practice context. Wider attitudes concerning lesbian and gay parenting are also important.

The global context of sexuality

As well as considering issues within the UK, social workers and other health and social care professionals also need to place the sociology of sexuality within a global context. As explored in other chapters, we need to be aware of the predominance of Western cultural perspectives. While critical sociological perspectives have challenged the social construction of sexuality and sexual orientation, we should not assume that this diversity discourse is universal or universally agreed upon, even within Western culture and societies.

Critical sociological perspectives and global social movements relating to gender and sexuality also continue to debate some contentious issues relating to sexual identity, sexual activity, sexual violence and sexual expression. There is not sufficient space within the chapter to explore all these issues in depth, but sociological thought is helpful for understanding these debates. Weeks (2007) talks about the global world of sexuality, with 'flows' of people, issues and debates shaping a world where sexual activity and expression cannot be ignored because of the international nature of the changes that globalization has brought.

Issues relating to sexuality and faith continue to be topical within contemporary societies. Wilton (2000) discusses how both Islamic and Christian fundamentalist religious perspectives impact on women's sexuality and sexual practices. For example, right-wing Christian groups are against abortion and sex outside marriage. Islamic fundamentalists see women's sexuality as related solely to monogamous heterosexual marriage, although in some Islamic cultures men are able to marry several times. Religious beliefs therefore shape responses to sexual morality and sexual orientation in many cultures and societies. However, at the same time there has been an increased secularization of Western cultures in particular. This has led to a separation of religious and sexual values, which has had an impact on morality and arguments concerning 'right and wrong' (Weeks, 2010).

Earlier in the chapter, we explored how HIV/AIDS led to a moral panic concerning same-sex orientation in the UK. While the lesbian and gay movement was able to support changing attitudes within the UK, this has not been the case in all contemporary societies. Weeks (2010) discusses how President Mugabe of Zimbabwe has been able to exploit this agenda in relation to hostility towards gay men. Relevant here is how risk is socially constructed. Bywater and Jones (2007) explore how discriminatory attitudes towards HIV/AIDS relate to notions of deviant sexuality reflected in the blame and stigmatization of certain groups. Also relevant here are changes within Western cultures concerning the spread of HIV/AIDS within African countries. The moral panic can be seen to have diminished in the West as medication and treatments have become available, unlike in African countries (Weeks, 2010).

Debates about reproductive practices continue within a global context. Peterson (2004) discusses how the practice of lesbian parents obtaining sperm from donors has led to certain groups (e.g. American right-wing religious organizations) calling for restrictions. Additionally, lesbian women who have the economic means may be more able to use donor services. This is also the case relating to wealthy gay men who are able to use surrogacy services to have children. As with issues relating to same-sex marriage, issues relating to lesbian and gay parenting are also contested, as explored elsewhere in the chapter in relation to fostering and adoption.

The rights of transgendered people in a number of societies have led to continued debate between feminist, gender and queer theorists. Morgan (1999) highlights how there is a dilemma in relation to trans people in that, in order to support obtaining rights and citizenship, rights to treatment concerning transsexuals have been argued for. Playdon (2004) has claimed that generally gender boundaries have been a key part of the challenges to heteronormativity (e.g. drag kings and queens). However, in some societies, transgendered people can be seen to be sexually exploited and part of sexual tourism.

The marketing of sexual activity and sexual expression has led to the development of sexual tourism and consequent exploitation. As explored in Chapter 3, this has had a significant impact on prostitution and issues relating to forced migration for the sex trade. This is occurring on a global scale (Altman, 2001). Technology and the internet are key factors in the marketing and exploitation of sex. There are significant issues here for young people in terms of sexually harmful behaviours and risks of exploitation (Myers, 2008). This is particularly pertinent for social workers engaging with young people in the context of forced migration or unaccompanied asylum-seeking children and young people.

Conclusion

Sexuality is an important issue for all of us. Sexual identity and behaviour have historically been linked predominantly with heterosexuality, located within monogamous marriage and related to issues of gender and reproduction. Abnormal or deviant sexual behaviour has been classified with significant consequences for many societal groups. A sound knowledge of critical sociological perspectives on sexuality can help social workers understand how social constructionism has challenged essentialist perspectives on sexuality, and can inform positive practice with a range of user and carer groups. It is therefore essential that social workers engage with issues described in this chapter, and training and input from users and carers are important issues here. For example, people with learning disabilities have been involved in some degree programmes (Race, 2002), and, more generally, Hicks (2005) talks about the need for a more explicit discussion about sexuality within the overarching framework of anti-oppressive practice as currently this is often inadequate for understanding the full impact of sexual identity issues. Cocker and Hafford-Letchfield (2010) also discuss the need for social workers to respond positively and affirmatively to the equalities agenda. Affirmative practice here is key.

Summary points

- Sexuality was classified into 'abnormal' and 'normal' definitions in the nineteenth century, which had significant consequences for groups in society who were considered a 'threat' to dominant social and cultural norms.
- Social constructs concerning sexuality have particularly affected disabled people, older people, women and lesbians and gay men.
- People with a same-sex identity can experience structural oppression and internalized homophobia resulting from heteronormative assumptions.
- Social movements have been instrumental in promoting the interests and civil liberties of lesbian and gay people.
- An understanding of sexuality and sexual identities is an important aspect of empowering social work practice. This needs to be placed within a contemporary global context

Questions for discussion

- How do you think we become sexual beings?
- Do you think that there are still certain groups in society where the discussion of sexual issues is a moral taboo?
- In contemporary society, which forms of sexual behaviour and expression are permitted and which are regulated?
- How does this relate to the global context of sexuality?
- What issues would need to be discussed on a training day looking at empowering social work practice in relation to sexuality?

Further reading

Bywater, J. and Jones, R. (2007) *Sexuality and Social Work.* **Exeter: Learning Matters**
This text provides a foundational introduction to the relationship between contemporary perspectives on sexuality and social work practice.

Dunk-West, P. and Hafford-Letchfield, T. (2011) *Sexual Identities and Sexuality in Social Work.* **Farnham: Ashgate**
This collection discusses critical perspectives on sexuality and sexual identity in relation to marginalized groups and examines the importance of these perspectives for social work practice.

Weeks, J. (2010) *Sexuality.* **3rd edition. London: Routledge**
This text provides a comprehensive discussion of the development of the sociology of sexuality. This is effectively linked to contemporary societal issues regarding sexual morality and behaviour.

7 Deviance and Crime*

Introduction

All societies have norms of behaviour and views of what is right and wrong, and how to deal with deviations from these norms (Henslin, 2010). The legal system passes laws that define legal and illegal behaviours, and in the UK the criminal justice system is the institution responsible for the management of crime and criminal behaviour (Bochel et al., 2009). However, deviant behaviour may also be dealt with under the mental health system, and it may sometimes be the role of the courts to determine whether the deviance should be managed by mental health services or criminal justice services (see also Chapter 11). The way societies construct and manage deviant behaviours is therefore shaped within the specific social, cultural and historical context of a given society (Henslin, 2010).

There is a long history of the relationship between social workers and criminal justice policy from the nineteenth century through till the present day (Epperson et al., 2013), and arguably social work involvement in criminal justice work has developed in the twenty-first century owing to the increased interest in rehabilitation and preventative work (van Wormer et al., 2008). Social workers come into regular contact with people whose behaviour may be described as deviant. For example, social workers in the UK are employed as members of multi-agency *Youth Offending Services* to work directly with young offenders (Ellis and Boden, 2004). They are also employed in Children's Services where a child or young person's behaviour may become criminal, or where an adult may be a perpetrator of criminal behaviour within their relationship with a child (Spicker, 2011). Social workers may also work directly with adults in such settings as *Sex Offender Treatment Programmes*, and social workers with adults will engage with service users with learning disabilities or mental illnesses who may well commit crime (Adams et al., 2009). The risk that such people pose to communities has become the subject of much inquiry and policy formulation, and our prisons are said to be over-represented with people who should be in a hospital environment rather than a penal one: 72% of convicted males and 70% of convicted females suffer from two or more mental health disorders, and 20% of all sentenced prisoners suffer from four of the five major mental health disorders (Prison Reform Trust, 2013).

> **Youth Offending Services** multi-agency teams dealing with young offenders; created by the UK Crime and Disorder Act (1998). Youth Offending Teams' members can be from health, social care or other professional backgrounds.
>
> **Sex Offender Treatment Programmes (SOTP)** designed to treat people convicted and sentenced in the UK for sexual offences. SOTP often involve group work and have therapeutic elements,

---

* This chapter was originally written for the first edition by Terry Thomas, Visiting Professor of Criminal Justice Studies at Leeds Beckett University.

> ## The key issues that will be explored in this chapter are:
>
> - classical sociological theories in relation to crime and deviance
> - labelling theory and the social construction of deviance
> - critical perspectives on crime and deviance, including feminist and anti-racist perspectives
> - the creation of moral panics and societal responses to deviant behaviour
> - the relationship between crime, deviance and labelling and social stratification
> - the punitive and labelling framework within which social work takes place, which conflicts with empowering practice.

> ## By the end of this chapter, you should be able to:
>
> - demonstrate an understanding of the major sociological theories of crime and deviance
> - demonstrate an understanding of labelling theory and its relevance in the construction of categories of deviance
> - explain the sociological concept of the moral panic
> - discuss the social response to deviant behaviour
> - explain the relationship between crime and deviance, on the one hand, and social disadvantage and divisions, on the other.

Criminology

The branch of sociology that covers criminal behaviour is usually described as criminology, which is a social science analysis of offending behaviour that seeks to stand back and understand that behaviour. Criminology sets the offender, and the offending behaviour, in the context of the social dynamics of their life and the communities they live in (McLaughlin and Muncie, 2013). Over the years, the study of crime and criminals has been taken up by professionals in other disciplines, such as psychologists, biologists, legal philosophers and political scientists. Psychologists and biologists, for example, look for the explanations of criminal behaviour within the individuals themselves, rather than within social elements (Hall, 2013). These other disciplines all contribute to our greater understanding of offending behaviour, but here we are looking only at the sociological analysis.

Classical criminology

In the eighteenth and nineteenth centuries, crime and criminality were understood in terms of an individual's free choice to decide what behaviour they wanted to engage in. This was tied in with wider attempts to produce a clear and legitimate criminal justice system so that proportionate punishment could be applied to behaviour that was considered criminal (McLaughlin and Muncie, 2013). Implicit in *classical criminology* was Durkheim's notion that society had an agreed

Classical criminology the earliest philosophical ideas about crime (eighteenth/nineteenth century), which envisaged the offender as having 'made a mistake' in departing from collective social norms and as someone who required punishment to correct their deviant behaviour.

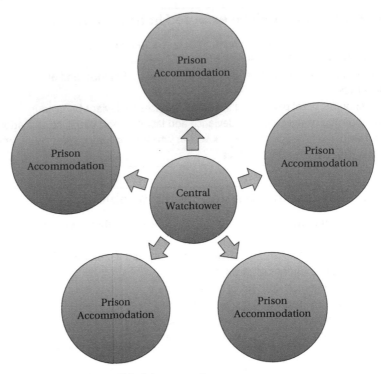

Figure 7.1 Diagrammatic model of the panopticon.

collective set of values or goals and there were no conflicting groups or aims (see Chapter 1).

These ideas are prevalent in the deterrent and punitive model of crime management, through a penal system based on power and control. In his work on prisons, Foucault (1979b) identified a particular way in which these institutions were built. He used the term *panopticon* to denote a prison built around a central watchtower so that inmates could be potentially observed at all times (see Figure 7.1). Even if they were not actively being observed, the fact that they could be had the same effect and demonstrated the power of prison staff in controlling behaviour to comply with collective norms and values. CCTV and speed cameras fulfil a similar function today, working on the principle of the control of behaviour through their presence and potential for operation, irrespective of whether they are actually operational at a given time (Coleman, 2004).

Panopticon a prison model which was built on a central design, so that all could potentially be observed at all times.

The ideas of the 'classical school' are still evident in theoretical thinking on crime. The American criminologist Marcus Felson has taken what he calls 'the rational choice perspective' to show how crime can emerge from everyday life. The implication is that crime is inevitable and constant unless we take steps towards crime reduction and prevention (Felson, 1998). Felson's ideas have helped formulate the so-called '*routine activity theory*' or '*rational choice theory*' of crime. The motivation to

Routine activity theory a theory whereby crime is seen to emerge from the routines of everyday life and is therefore almost inevitable and constant; this leads to notions of crime prevention.

commit crime is given as an ever-present factor that is trig-gered in everyday life by the availability of suitable 'targets'. In this way the theory posits three variables as leading to crime:

1 motivated offenders – usually young males
2 suitable targets – in the form of a person or property
3 the absence of a capable 'guardian' against the crime.

> **Rational choice theory** choices made by potential offenders based on a rational calculation and decisions made within the constraints of time, ability and the information available.

The convergence of these three variables takes place in the routines of everyday life, and offers the opportunity for the criminal act. These routines include travelling to work or school, recreational activities, shopping, and so on. Sometimes the term '*opportunity crime*' is used to describe this behaviour, and crime prevention policies seek to reduce the number of suitable targets and increase the presence of the capable 'guardian' (Hall, 2013).

> **Opportunity crime** crime that emerges from situations that offer the opportunity to those inclined to take it.

In his study of street crime, Hallsworth demonstrates the degree of rationality and thought that goes into street robbery (or 'mugging'), including a thorough assessment of the 'suitable targets': '. . . they would know, for example, when specific individuals would congregate in areas amenable to robbery . . . know the time and days when they would have been paid . . . know that businessmen often stop outside tube stations to check for messages on their mobile phones' (Hallsworth, 2005: 113). However, research by the Cambridge Institute for Criminology found that evidence did not support the notion of opportunist crime amongst young people. In a 10-year study of adolescent crime in Peterborough, they found that only a small proportion of youths (about 4%) were responsible for most of the crimes committed. They concluded that crime resulted not from 'youthful opportunism', but from a combination of personal and environmental characteristics (Wikström et al., 2012).

Nevertheless, since the 1980s there has been a renewed interest in the 'classical school' of criminology and rational choice theory. It has particularly been taken up by politicians of a right-wing persuasion and has been described as 'right realism'. In essence, the idea is that rational, calculating criminals who know what they are doing should be met by suitable sanctions (*just deserts*) that will stop them doing it. Fear is seen as the one factor that will stop people committing crime, and prison is the most severe (fearsome) penalty we have in the UK. Therefore prison should be used more because 'prison works', a mantra

> **Just deserts** making punishment proportionate to the crime; builds on classical theories.

that is particularly associated with Michael Howard when he was Home Secretary in the 1990s, evidenced by the fact that reported crime had fallen as the prison popula-tion increased (Cavadino and Dignan, 2002). A similar argument is made in relation to the death penalty in certain US states, although criminologists dispute the deter-rent factor of this punishment, citing evidence that the murder rate in non-death penalty states has remained consistently lower than in states that use the death penalty (see Figure 7.2).

In political terms this hard-line 'law and order' approach in the UK has grown in pop-ularity since the 1980s. Politicians started to intervene more directly with the criminal

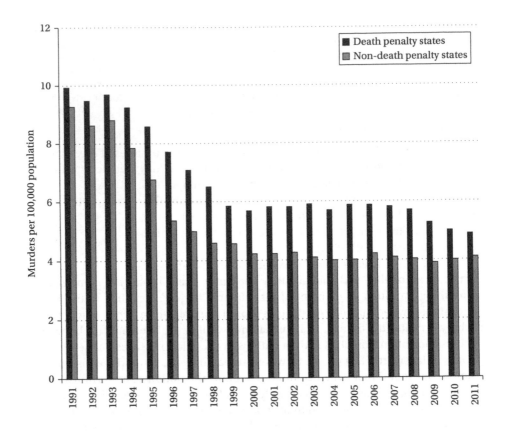

Figure 7.2 Murder rates in US states with and without the death penalty, 1991–2011. *Source:* Death Penalty Information Center, n.d. Available at *http:/www.deathpenaltyinfo.org/ deterence-states-without-death-penalty-have-had-consistently-lower-murder-rates.*

> **Popular punitivism** a term coined in the mid-1990s to describe a swell of public opinion demanding ever more punitive (and disproportionate) sanctions against those convicted of crime; in practice, politicians then exploit this swell to ensure their own popularity.

justice system, and the concept of '*popular punitivism*' was formed to explain the new right-wing drift (Bottoms, 1995). The 2012 White Paper *Swift and Sure Justice* proposes reforms to the criminal justice system based on quicker and more efficient court processes and sentencing, under-pinned by a system of effective punishments.

Justice must also be *sure*, in the sense of commanding public confidence, if it is to provide an effective punishment and deterrent. Criminal justice services must do more to get a firm grip on offenders, making them face up to the consequences of their crime, taking action which both punishes them and supports them to address their offending behaviour. (Ministry of Justice, 2012c: 7)

For social work, however, an emphasis on deterrence and punitive justice creates a tension between a political agenda focusing on punishment and the social work role of enablement and providing access to services and support.

Crime and social construction

At the end of the nineteenth century, the French sociologist Émile Durkheim put forward the idea that crime took place in areas of social disorganization, where the normal rules and regulations did not apply. Durkheim believed that societies functioned effectively where there was a collective consciousness, with consensus about an agreed set of rules. The opposite was a disorganized society that experienced what Durkheim called *anomie* (see Chapter 1). Without an adequate social structure to act as a guide to behaviour, individuals were inclined to criminality. Durkheim was clear that no society could be free of some criminal elements, but the presence of good education, recognized lines of authority and the emergence of a social structure that most people would want to be part of was the starting point for a reduction in crime.

In the 1920s, the Chicago School brought a scientific framework of understanding to why certain parts of Chicago had more crime than others. Cities began to be studied as ecological systems that 'produced' crime in certain neighbourhoods. In particular, academics in 1920s Chicago noted 'zones in transition' as areas prone to criminality. These zones were areas where industry expanded at the expense of housing, which became run down and marginalized. People moved out of these areas and only new immigrants, too poor to live anywhere else, would live there. Weakened families and communal ties equalled more 'social disorganization' and therefore more possibilities for crime (McLaughlin and Muncie, 2013). (See also discussion of Murray's concept of the underclass in Chapter 2.)

These ideas of 'zones in transition' have resonance with much more recent thinking on crime and disorganized areas. The so-called 'broken windows' thesis suggests that areas that are allowed to become run down because of broken windows, damaged property, graffiti, and so on, are likely to attract people who see these as signs of disorganization and lack of regulation. In turn they bring their criminal or anti-social behaviour and take the area further down and past a 'tipping point' from where it descends into an area of crime that people avoid. The policy answer is to make sure the 'tipping point' is never reached and the area is maintained and not allowed to go down (Wilson and Kelling, 1982).

In recent years, there have been attempts to halt this urban decline through public and private investment (Sloan, 2011). This, however, can also lead to greater social polarization, as those living in the areas continue to be disadvantaged, whilst seeing at first hand the privileged position of others, which may lead to greater opportunities for crime.

The 'broken windows' thesis has informed contemporary UK policies to address anti-social behaviour:

> If a window is broken or a wall is covered in graffiti it can contribute to an environment in which crime takes hold, particularly if intervention is not prompt and effective. An abandoned car, left for days on end, soon becomes a burnt-out car; it is not long before more damage and vandalism takes place. Environmental decline, anti-social behaviour and crime go hand in hand and create a sense of helplessness that nothing can be done.

(Home Office, 2002: para. 1.8)

What exactly constitutes anti-social behaviour has been a point of dispute. It has variously been called 'low-level' crime, 'public nuisance' and 'youth annoyance'. Generally, anti-social behavior includes vandalism and graffiti, drunk and rowdy behaviour, intimidation and harassment which impacts on the lives of particular individuals or groups of individuals (Home Office, 2012a). Whereas the criminal law lays down a clear-cut line that, if transgressed, defines a criminal act, no such clear line exists for anti-social behaviour. Whilst some practitioners have welcomed this 'flexibility', others (especially lawyers) are concerned about this subjective departure. However, there can be a fine line between anti-social behavior and more serious criminal offences. Hate crime, for example, has been identified in law in Section 146 of the Criminal Justice Act (2003), and figures show a huge increase in the recorded incidents of this crime. In 2010, 48,127 hate crimes were recorded by police forces in England, Wales and Northern Ireland. Of these:

- 39,311 were racist crimes
- 4,883 were based on sexual orientation
- 2,007 were religious hate crimes
- 1,569 targeted disabled people
- 357 targeted transgender people.

(Home Office, 2011)

This has implications for those social workers who are working with vulnerable victims of anti-social behavior or hate crimes. Section 146 of the Criminal Justice Act (2003) places a duty on the courts to increase the sentence of anyone who is found guilty of a crime aggravated by hostility based on difference in personal characteristics, and social workers may have a role to play in safeguarding, advising and advocating for the vulnerable person. They may also be involved in supporting people who are seen as vulnerable witnesses, so that their voices may be heard in any criminal proceedings (Ministry of Justice, 2011).

The policy of 'zero tolerance' policing has also been supported by the 'broken windows' thesis, premised on the idea that if you ensure that all crimes, however minor, are dealt with seriously, you send out a message that deters the more serious crime. This re-emerged following the riots in Britain in 2011, when the Prime Minister encouraged police forces to take a 'zero tolerance' approach to any street crime in order to deter social unrest (Hennessy and d'Ancona, 2011).

Strain theory

Strain theory suggests crime is the result of individuals being 'blocked' in terms of mainstream society from reaching certain goals; under the consequent strain they seek deviant or criminal ways to reach those goals.

Another elaboration on the theories of social disorganization and areas of disproportionate crime levels is that of Robert Merton's '*strain theory*', in which he explored the way in which individuals could be frustrated or blocked in achieving their aspirations and ambitions in life (Merton, 1938). These aspirations and ambitions could be quite legitimate goals and, indeed, were often the same goals that everyone else had. But whereas others achieved through education, employment opportunities and application to the various steps necessary to

Table 7.1 *UK Christmas crime, 2012 (£ million)*

Shoplifting	522.5
Employee theft	430.6
Supply chain fraud	46.6
Total crime	999.7

Source: Centre for Retail Research: *http://www.retailresearch.org/shopliftingforxmas. php.*

get them, some people could not do this. As a result, they experienced a 'strain' and resorted to illegitimate or criminal channels.

In today's consumer society, Merton's ideas are even more pertinent. In a culture that celebrates material success, consumer goods, status and authority, the inability to achieve these goals places a strain on increasing numbers of people (Jordan and Drakeford, 2012). Surrounded by media and advertising that promote the consumer society, some may feel that only a deviant adaptation is going to get them its benefits. Strain theory does not, of course, explain why some people who do not experience 'strain' turn to crime or why some people who do experience strain do not turn to crime.

There has been concern that the recession and austerity measures will lead to increases in theft as people struggle to cope with rising costs of living. Although not broken down by social class, the Christmas retail crime figures in 2012 for the UK show a rise of 3.45 since 2011 (Table 7.1).

Others have taken Merton's original thesis further to show how strain theory can lead to other deviant adaptations. 'Blocked' individuals may, for example, vent their frustration on others (using violence that appears random) or retreat from society in order to avoid the strain. The latter group may turn to drug dependency to 'forget' their position and effectively 'drop out' of society altogether (Agnew, 1992).

In 2011/12, an estimated 8.9% of people between 16 and 59 in the UK had taken illicit drugs (Home Office, 2012a), and although not all of these people will have committed crimes, there is a clear relationship between illicit drug taking and criminal behaviours (Drugscope, n.d.).

The British criminologist Jock Young has described how rising crime rates have resulted from societies' tendency to exclude more of their members. Modern forms of communication can expound the virtues of the consumer society, but not everyone can partake of it. The result is a class of people culturally included to share the values of the consumer society but structurally excluded and 'blocked' from joining in (Young, 1999)

A number of recent studies have identified the link between social exclusion and higher levels of criminal behaviour (Hall, 2013; McAuley, 2007). Allen et al. (2007), for example, found that 50% of convicted criminals came from the poorest 12% of the council wards.

Case study

Jodie, aged 15, lives on an inner-city council estate. She has a history of truancy and sees lots of people in her local community without work. Jodie and her friends have started to target students who live in the adjoining neighbourhood as they feel invaded by them. They resent the fact that the students have phones, iPods, and so on, and all the things that the local people do not have. The street robbery of 'soft' students gives direct access to some of these commodities.

- How would theories of social exclusion help us to explain Jodie's behaviour?
- Do social theories offer an excuse or an explanation for this behaviour?
- As a social worker, what strategies could you employ with Jodie?

Strain theory or status frustration has also been theorized as a cause of problems for young males trying to achieve an adult male status. If adult masculinity is perceived as involving independence, dominance, toughness and respect from your fellow citizens, the failure of young males to achieve these traits may cause them to look for deviant adaptations. This invariably involves a search for an ill-defined masculinity that gives adolescents a degree of self-autonomy (rather than independence), involves acts of violence (rather than dominance or toughness) and may involve the carrying of weapons (to invoke respect). Gang cultures may help support these deviant adaptations (Messerschmidt, 1993).

Hallsworth noted these particular 'masculine' traits in his study of young men who commit street crime – an adaptation 'forged out of a symbiosis between activities celebrated in the wider society and those condemned by it' (Hallsworth, 2005: 135): 'this vision of masculinity . . . reaches into the detail of life. It is there in the physical presentation of self to the world: it is evident in the clothes, in the language, in the walk, and in speech itself. It is evident in acts and deeds, in what is spoken about, and what is celebrated in speech' (Hallsworth, 2005: 135–6).

Deviant adaptations caused by strain theory are sometimes supported by gang cultures that maintain the deviant value systems and give approval to the resultant criminal behaviour. This role played by gangs has been particularly researched in the USA, where the influence of gangs appears to be stronger than in the UK. Work by Cohen (1954) outlined how gangs could give individuals status that they could not find elsewhere and enabled members to take pride in their deviant adaptations, such as being tough and 'hard'. The gang also allows members to use 'techniques of neutralization' to justify and excuse their criminality (Matza, 1964).

In the UK, the evolution of gangs has been less pronounced, and attention has been paid more to sub-cultures. Sub-cultures may not necessarily be overtly criminal but more symbolic and simply oppositional to the established order (Hall and Jefferson, 1976). However, more recently, there has been increased concern about violent crimes amongst youths which may be related to gang culture (Centre for Social Justice, 2009, 2012), whilst a report into knife crime amongst younger people concluded that gang culture was one of the significant factors (Kinsella, 2011). Young people may be attracted to the idea of being in a gang, as it gives social identity and a sense of belonging to a social group (see Chapter 1). Other incentives may include safety, friendship, money, peer pressure, drug use and a sense of power and control (Cox, 2011). One young gang member describes his experiences as follows:

> I started out holding on to drugs and knives for the older gang members when they were getting chased. They knew the police wouldn't search someone so young. To thank me for what I'd done they would just give me a few pounds. That was it. From that point I got really sucked into it. I would go around on my bike carrying a lot of drugs and cash. (*Daily Mirror*, 21 March 2012)

Research by the Joseph Rowntree Foundation (2008) explored the formation of gangs and territorial activity in six geographical areas and concluded:

- Territorial behaviour emerged where young people's identity was closely associated with their neighbourhoods and they gained respect from representing them.
- Young people often had positive motivations for becoming involved in territorial behaviour, such as developing their identity and friendships. But territorial identities were frequently expressed in violent conflict with territorial groups from other areas.
- The negative impact of territorial behaviour on young people included constrained mobility, problems with access to amenities, and the risk of violent assault and criminalization.
- There was evidence in some places that low-level territorial behaviour could be the foundation of criminal gangs involved in violent crime and distributing drugs.

There is a racialized discourse surrounding gang culture in the UK, and Joseph and Gunter (2011) provide an analysis of race and gang culture. They argue that there has been a narrow focus of analysis on structural causes of criminality, which has failed to engage with issues of identity and street culture. There is continuing debate amongst sociologists about the relationship between gangs and the ethnic composition of an area. Explanations for the disproportionate representation of knife and gun violence amongst black youths remain a contested area, although Kinsella (2011) concluded that the majority of young people carry knives out of fear as opposed to defending an area or community.

The overwhelming majority of gang members are male, although it has been estimated that 12,500 girls or young women are involved in gangs in the UK (Pearce and Pitts, 2011). The role of females in gangs may be ancillary, where they are used to carry drugs and guns and for sexual exploitation by the male members of the gang, as the following case study demonstrates.

Case study

The young girl grew up living with her father and three younger siblings on a housing estate in the UK. When she was 11 years old she started dating a 14-year-old boy she met at school and who was in a gang. He often tried to persuade this girl to have sexual intercourse with him, and by the age of 12 she agreed.

Soon afterwards the girl found out that he had filmed them having sexual intercourse on this boy's laptop. . . . this boy's attitude towards her changed dramatically and he became aggressive and cold. The boy threatened to show her father the footage and post it on various social networking sites for all of their friends to see. The idea of this

happening terrified the young girl and she begged him not to do it. He agreed . . .
on one condition: that she must always be available to both him and any other gang
member for sex. . . . From this moment on the 12-year-old girl's life descended into one
of regular abuse and sexual exploitation. She was raped on a weekly basis, and many of
these crimes were filmed and played back to her by her rapists.

(Centre for Social Justice, 2014: 7–8)

- How does a sociological understanding of identity and belonging help to explain this girl's position?
- How can an understanding of gang culture and relationships of power inform social work assessment and understanding?

There have been a number of high-profile cases of child sexual exploitation by groups of men throughout the UK. Although slightly different from the case above, as the perpetrators are groups of men who target vulnerable girls, there are clearly similarities in the social work role when working with victims of sexual exploitation. The Serious Case Review into child sexual abuse in Rochdale concluded that there had been a series of failures over a number of years by both police and social workers.

> Children's social care was found to have failed to act appropriately on multiple occasions. When it was first alerted to the problem in 2006 by sexual health workers who told them of their belief that a gang of men were sexually exploiting young people, the service concluded that no strategy meeting or assessment was needed due to inadequate evidence, despite it being 'incumbent' on the service to inform the police and start a Section 47 enquiry.
>
> The council's policy of investing in non-qualified social work staff, born of a desire to save money and a belief in moving towards a more diversely qualified workforce, meant that initial assessments were not carried out by highly experienced and qualified social workers as required by statutory guidance. (Donovan, 2013)

The riots, August 2011

The four days of rioting in the UK following Mark Duggan's death in August 2011 provide a good case study for the exploration and application of theories of crime and criminal behaviour. Mark Duggan was a young black man who was shot by police who claimed that they thought he was armed and they were acting in self-defence. This sparked a series of riots, initially in Tottenham where Duggan lived, but which quickly spread to other areas of London and then to other cities throughout the UK. The cost of damage from the riots is estimated at £370 million (Nwabuzo, 2012). From a structural perspective, sociologists have argued that the riots were indicative of social unrest associated with disaffected youth, who saw them as a way of mobilizing resistance and protest against the capitalist system in general and the police in particular. However, this does not account for the wide variety of people involved in the riots: evidence from statistics of those who were arrested shows that it was not just the disaffected working classes who were taking part. Other accounts of the riots suggest that these were opportunistic crimes, as people took the opportunity to loot shops and cause civic unrest. However, neither of these perspectives can explain why there was rioting and unrest in only some areas of

London and why it only spread to some other cities and not others. The interim report into the causes of the riots concluded that there was no single cause and therefore no single solution (Nwabuzo, 2012). However, there were concerns that all sense of proportion was lost as the courts pushed people who had been arrested through the criminal justice system, favouring harsher penalties, such as custodial sentences.

Labelling theory, deviancy amplification and moral panics

Behaviour only becomes criminal when someone defines a particular act as such. Much has been said about the Labour Government passing numerous laws between 1997 and 2006 which rendered whole areas of behaviour criminal that were previously not considered so (Dwyer and Shaw, 2013). Labelling theory looks at how the social response to crime is made and how certain behaviour comes to be considered deviant or criminal. Labelling theory also goes one step further, to suggest that the very imposition of social judgements on certain individuals helps push those individuals further down the paths of criminality that have been identified. The labelling thus becomes a self-fulfilling prophecy.

Defining deviance is not necessarily an objective process, and sociologists are interested in the ways in which deviance is constructed within and between societies. The symbolic interactionist school of sociological thought is helpful in exploring the social context of deviance. Symbolic interactionists such as Chambliss (2010) use the term 'relativity of deviance' to explain how different groups have different norms to explain why something may be deviant in one group and context but not in another. Sociological concern, therefore, is more focused on the understanding of why certain acts, individuals or groups are seen to be deviant.

In the USA, Becker outlined how the making of criminal laws defines certain people as 'outsiders' and then the enforcement of those laws (the social response) enables the police, the courts and others to impose the deviant/criminal label on those people. The outcome is the creation of negative stereotypes around those considered as criminal (Becker, 1963). Interventions such as police cautioning, reprimands and final warnings seek to lower the degree of labelling by keeping offenders – especially first-time offenders – out of court and 'out of the system'.

Deviancy amplification extends the ideas of labelling to demonstrate how social reactions to crime, in the way of policing, courts and penal policies generally, can lead to the furtherance of criminal careers. At its most simple, the prison system, with the goal of reducing crime and producing good citizens, often does exactly the opposite. Offenders leave prison and return to crime more readily than before. Young (1971) used the term 'deviancy amplification' in his analysis of drug users in London during the 1960s. Much of this activity was low-level and relatively harmless, but the press interest, followed by police crack-downs and court punitiveness, had a 'loop-back' effect. What had been a peripheral activity for some people now came to personify their identity against conformism and authority. The social response had given it more significance as a form of rebellion rather than restricting it (Young, 1971).

Today we might compare crack-downs on under-age drinking as having a similar unintended consequence. Thirty years ago, such drinking was largely ignored and seen as an age-related rite of passage. In current society, there is much concern about 'alcohol-related' crime, which typically involves 18- to 30-year-old males, but also an increasing number of young females, and often occurs in entertainment areas of town and city centres (Alcohol Concern, 2011). Contemporary interventions see it as a major problem requiring appropriate policing, possible use of ID cards and severe sentences on those selling the alcohol. A rise in under-age drinking results as young people rebel against the crack-down and accord the activity more significance than before. Although many young people may enjoy drinking alcohol, a report in 2007 found that among 35 European countries, the UK has the third-highest proportion of 15 year olds who report having been drunk 10 times or more in the past year (Alcohol Concern, 2011). Almost half of all 15 year olds had been involved in some form of fighting or violence (Alcohol Concern, 2010).

As labelling and deviancy amplification cause problems and unintended consequences for individual offenders, so moral panics have similar influences on the wider public perceptions of crime. Integral to the 'moral panic', a term first popularized by Stanley Cohen (1972) in his studies of the social reaction to fights between groups of young people in British seaside towns during the 1960s, is the way the media take hold of a crime 'story' and reports it in such a way as to strike a chord with public concerns (Goode and Ben-Yehuda, 1994). The media reporting interacts with the social response to the crime – especially policing and court sentencing – to create an escalating spiral of 'panic' that requires someone to do something now before something else happens. At the heart of the 'moral panic' is a kernel of truth that 'something' has happened, but that original truth can be lost in the distortions that accompany its reporting, and the resultant social reaction can be overly hostile and disproportionate in its implementation.

The media often report gangs in a negative light, and murders associated with knife and gun crime and gangs feature prominently in news headlines. Whilst this is clearly concerning, there is also evidence that the number of homicides is decreasing (ONS Crime Statistics, 2013) and there are concerns that the media reporting gives a distorted picture.

The 'moral panic' – and its 'folk devil' – can change frequently and as suddenly as it appears. Over the years the phenomenon has attached itself to 'single-parent families', 'teenage mothers', 'football hooligans', 'muggers', 'dangerous dogs', 'paedophiles' and others. When 2-year-old James Bulger was killed by two 10-year-old boys in 1993, it triggered concerns about the behaviour of young people, law and order, and appropriate responses, to the extent that *The Times* newspaper commented 'Britain is in the grip of one of those moral panics that afflicts every nation periodically' (Editorial, *The Times*, 3 March 1993).

Marsh and Melville (2011) explore the contemporary context of moral panics and demonstrate the media role in developing these. They identify the fact that certain crimes become massive media stories, and use Innes's (2003) concept of 'signal crimes' to explore the relationship between media, crime and moral panics. These signal crimes reflect the mood and interest of a particular period and the intense and excessive media reporting add to the societal reaction that goes beyond the case itself. The reporting of a number of killings of young people such as Rhys Jones (2007), Anthony Walker (2005), Holly Wells and Jessica Chapman in Soham (2002), Damilola Taylor (2000), Sarah Payne (2000), Stephen Lawrence (1993) and James Bulger (1993) is used as an illustration of how the media coverage contributes to a societal concept about the safety of young people.

Case study

Brian's parents divorced when he was 12 years old and he remained living with his mother. His mother later formed a new relationship with Ken, who moved into the house when Brian was 14. When Brian was 15, he had a huge argument with Ken. The argument took place at the same time of year that Brian's father had originally left his mother and memories came flooding back. In a fit of pique, Brian took the family car and went for a midnight drive.

He was picked up by the police as he was driving in circles in the car park of a nearby supermarket. A Youth Court placed Brian on a supervision order and he started reporting to the same social worker. The social worker assessed Brian as having minimal problems and the supervision was perfunctory. This changed following Brian's arrest for shoplifting along with some youths he had met at the Youth Offending Team when he had been reporting. More reports and more court hearings followed and Brian's 'fear' of the court decreased.

- How can labelling theory be used to understand this chain of events?
- Does the social work role conflict with the punitive focus of the criminal justice system in this case?

Critical criminology

A new criminological school of *critical criminology* emerged in the 1960s that applied a far more political analysis to the explanations for crime. Key aspects of strain theory and 'labelling' theory were developed to look at the factors involved in determining when an act was judged to be deviant in the first place. This took the focus away from the individual engaged in crime and deviancy and looked at the social system that surrounds us. *Conflict theories* of deviance took strain theory and labelling theory forward by pointing out that these theories had presupposed a consensual set of values in society. Conflict theorists held that this was not necessarily so and that society was actually composed of numerous groups that interacted with and were often in conflict with each other. Many groups challenged the dominant societal values that they saw others as imposing upon them. Crime and criminalization took on a new perspective, where the process of criminalization was a form of social control by the more powerful groups in society and thus a way of maintaining the existing social order. The power to 'label' was critical in this interaction between groups, and not any sort of neutral application.

In the 1970s, sociologists of a left-wing persuasion used conflict theory to build a

> **Critical criminology** an attempt to broaden the analysis of crime to its context and to wider notions of social justice and human rights, as well as to the structural relations of production and distribution, reproduction and patriarchy.

> **Conflict theory** accepts that there are not necessarily any collectively agreed norms in society and that to understand crime we have to understand the interests served by criminal law and the way power is used in society.

Left idealism a Marxist approach to crime and punishment analysing the processes of criminalization and the social responses to crime.

new criminology that explained crime in Marxist terms. A seminal book in the UK was called *The New Criminology* (Taylor et al., 1973), and this new perspective on crime would later be known as '*left idealism*'. The fusion of a Marxist analysis with criminological theories appeared to give a better explanation of what was going on in the field of crime and the social response to crime. This analysis was premised on the law being a mechanism drawn up and designed by the ruling class to perpetuate the capitalist economy and keep the working class in a subservient position. The following arguments were therefore made:

- The ruling class define what is a criminal act, based on their interests.
- The ruling class can break laws whenever they see fit but the working class will be punished if they do so.
- Criminal behaviour is a form of resistance to the oppression and excesses of capitalism.
- As long as capitalist societies promote inequality and class conflict, crime will always be present.

The mode of economic production therefore promotes crime as we experience it and is the basic explanation for criminal behaviour. The new criminology could see through the existing pictures of crime and criminality that we had been presented with and offered the structural injustices, inequalities and exploitation of the working class as the wider view. Its critics responded that it was possibly too utopian in its outlook, seemingly dependent on a re-ordering of society before we could get to grips with crime and its realities for the victims of crime.

The demonization of youth

Much has been written about youth culture and the demonization of youth, epitomized in the stereotype of the '*chav*' (Marsh and Melville, 2011). These 'chavs' (also sometimes referred to as hoodies) are seen as a symbol of 'broken Britain', as they are often associated with areas of urban social deprivation and anti-social behaviour, crime and violence (see also Chapter 2). Catherine McDonald (2006) argues that the main motivation for the crimes committed by these groups of youths is to relieve boredom, rather than to obtain material goods, which seems to contradict the strain theory that people are motivated by need.

Kemshall et al. (2009) argue that the concepts of youth and risk are meshed together and there are concerns about the relationship between youth culture and crime. Social capital is an important sociological concept for understanding both the relationship between youths and crime and the route out of a social context that may precipitate criminal behaviour (see also Chapter 8). To understand this, we can explore the concepts of bonding social capital and bridging social capital. Bonding social capital refers to the inward social networks that give a sense of belonging and identity, such as family, local neighbourhoods and friends. Whilst these networks can give a sense of inclusion and security, however, they can also limit opportunities to escape social exclusion and disadvantage (MacDonald and Marsh, 2001). Bridging social capital refers to the outward-looking social connections that enable people to become more

Trayvon Martin was a black 17 year old from Florida who was shot and killed in 2012 when walking home from a local shop by a white neighbourhood watch volunteer who judged that he looked suspicious. The case brought racial and other stereotypes and prejudices to wider public attention, prompting many calls for justice, such as in this 'Million Hoodies March' in New York City. (© Andrew Dallos/Flickr)

socially mobile with diverse ranges of groups in order to negotiate transitions (Holland et al., 2007). The challenge, then, for social workers and other professionals working with young people is to help them to engage with social networks that will enable them to negotiate these transitions and explore opportunities for future actions. This offers a different view from the traditional demonizing and pathologizing approach and argues that adolescence and growing up is a difficult time of transition. Rather than blaming young people, we should provide them with opportunities for a range of legitimate opportunities, supported by appropriate adults.

'Left realism' remains a strand in the schools of criminological thought, and its advocates argue that it can provide theories that can be used now to help groups struggling against oppression. In this way, work on prisons, policing, 'mugging', violence against women and deaths in custody has been informed by left idealism (see, e.g., Hall et al., 1978; Scraton, 1987).

In the mid-1980s, a number of UK criminologists – including some who had been part of the 'new criminology' – reacted against 'left idealism' as being too utopian and too distant from the realities of crime experienced by many in the working class. In particular, criminologists based at Middlesex Polytechnic (later University) proposed a new '*left realism*' to take criminology forward (Lea and Young, 1984; Matthews and Young, 1986). The 'left realists' were not only parting company with the 'left idealists', but were also anxious to provide opposition to the rise of 'right realism' (see above) with its ideas of more severe sentences and greater use of incarceration as the appropriate punishment.

> **Left realism** a UK school of criminological thought emerging in the mid-1980s in reaction to the perceived utopianism of left idealism and the reactionary policies of conservative thinking on crime.

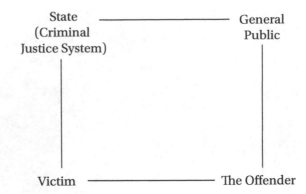

Figure 7.3   The square of crime.

Square of crime a theoretical device created by left realists that is made up of four sides (the state, the general public, the victim and the offender) stressing the interaction between the police and other agencies of social control.

The 'left realists' regarded themselves as taking crime more seriously than the 'left idealists' and providing a more complex analysis. This included the siting of crime more firmly in its social context. The '*square of crime*' was used to illustrate this social context (see Figure 7.3).

The 'left realists' criticized other theorists for focusing on the social construction of crime rather than on the crime itself. Using the 'square of crime', the criminal act can be viewed from various perspectives and the varying different theoretical positions can be brought to bear:

> to control crime from a realist perspective involves intervention at each part of the square of crime: at the level of the factors which give rise to the putative offender (such as structural unemployment), the informal system (such as lack of public mobilization), the victim (such as inadequate target hardening), and the formal system (such as ineffective policy). (Young, 1986: 41)

The victims of crime

The Crime Survey for England and Wales (Home Office, 2012a) estimated that 8.9 million crimes had been committed against adults in the year ending September 2012. In addition it was estimated that in the same time period there were 0.8 million crimes committed against 10 to 15 year olds. The victims of crime have traditionally been the neglected players in the criminal justice system, but in recent years attempts have been made to rectify this position and the voice of the victim has been given more prominence.

The media construction of the victim is often that of the elderly and defenceless person or the very young – and equally defenceless – child. The reality of victims, however, is that many of them do not fit these ideal media portrayals. Many victims of crime are young men who in other circumstances may well be the perpetrators of crime. A new post of Police and Crime Commissioner was introduced in England and Wales in 2012, and these Commissioners will be required to consult victims of crime when making future plans and in the future will also have budgets and powers to determine local services for victims.

The media portrayals of the ideal victim nonetheless persist and reinforce widespread 'fear of crime' amongst parents (for their children) and elderly people who are afraid to venture out at night. Policies and resources are then targeted at these groups to offer 'reassurance', and to tackle the 'fear' rather than the substance of crime.

Criminologists have also noted how victims and their supporters have improved their position in actually defining crimes. When new activities start causing problems for a community, there is a need to define them; sometimes there is agreement on that definition and sometimes there is not. Criminologists refer to the concept of 'dominion' to reflect this struggle over who has the right to define what is going on.

The position of men who have offended against children provides a case study. In the 1970s these men were seen as sad and rather pathetic individuals who were punished and released back into the community. In the 1990s, public opinion turned against such offenders – now more often referred to as paedophiles – and differences emerged about the best way to respond to them. Practitioners such as doctors, social workers and others saw their behaviour as dysfunctional and needing to be treated, while the general public saw it as an 'untreatable' affliction that required offenders to be incapacitated by long-term imprisonment. Women's groups saw it as a problem of masculinity. Yet other groups, including politicians, had to make judgements on the appropriate ways of achieving public protection and proportionate punishments. This whole struggle of definition is referred to as the problem of 'dominion'.

Crime and gender issues

Until the 1960s and 1970s, sociologists studying crime invariably looked at male offenders and not at women offenders. The study of female offenders was neglected or treated with indifference and at best they were seen as committing a limited number of crimes (e.g. shoplifting), often under the influence of hormonal imbalance (women's 'problems'). At worst, as Smart (1977) noted, the female offender was simply 'invisible'. Smart's work evolved from the women's movement of the 1960s and 1970s and was an attempt to correct the 'distortions' that appeared to be taking place.

Why women committed less crime than men has been attributed to the additional socialization and controls that are placed on women but not on men (Walklate, 1995). Although women appeared in the criminal courts far less often than men, the fact that they appeared to be sentenced more harshly was studied. The conclusion was that women were sentenced 'twice': firstly for the offence and secondly for the fact that they were women and therefore 'deviants' from the law-abiding role they should adopt as good wives or mothers (Heidensohn, 1985).

There is some evidence of the courts responding to ideological constructs about femininity and crime. The Corston Report (Home Office, 2007) into the deaths of six women in Styal Women's Prison in Cheshire found that women's offending behaviour had changed very little and yet the female prison population had increased.

Far greater attention has been given to women as victims of crime – especially violence and sexual offending (see, e.g., Dobash and Dobash's [1979] study of domestic violence against women and Cameron and Fraser's [1987] study of women as victims of murder and manslaughter). Evidence from the Crime Survey for England and

Wales study (Home Office, 2012a) found that men are more likely to be victims of crime than women:

- Three in every 100 adults were victims of crime in 2011/12: 2% of women and 4% of men reported being a victim of violent crime.
- 5% of girls aged 10–15 reported being victims of violence, compared to 11% of boys.
- 201 females were victims of homicide compared with 435 males.

There was a reverse in this trend in the numbers of females reporting intimate partner violence compared to males (7% compared to 5%) (Ministry of Justice, 2012a).

The incidence of domestic violence and the police response to it is a particular area of current concern (see also Chapter 3). Both men and women can be victims of domestic violence, and it is estimated that between 2012 and 2013 there were 269,000 domestic-abuse-related crimes in England and Wales, and in the same period 77 women were killed by their partners or ex-partners (Laville, 2014). The report that issued these figures also criticized police forces for their handling of domestic violence cases, concluding that only 8 of the 43 police forces responded well.

Domestic violence may not always be immediately apparent, and social workers have a key role to play in helping to identify women and children who are vulnerable. Keeling and van Wormer (2012) used a narrative approach to hear the stories of survivors of domestic abuse. Participants in the research felt that they had been let down by social workers, who were judgemental and victim-blaming. It is important for social workers to build a supportive relationship with the victims of domestic violence, as well as directing them to specialist services that can provide further support. As Davis and Lockhart (2010: xxvi) say:

> A cornerstone of professional practice in both professional social work and the domestic violence field is the concept of empowerment practice. Within the domestic violence field, empowerment practice is addressed first as a strategy to assist individual women to take control of their lives and second, as a strategy for taking action against domestic violence in certain communities.

(See Chapters 3 and 9 for further discussion of the impact of domestic violence.)

The racialization of crime

With regard to the relationship between race and crime, sociologists have considered explanations for the over-representation of black and minority ethnic groups in the criminal justice system and for the greater likelihood of African Caribbean people being involved in the criminal justice system than other BME groups.

The following evidence demonstrates that African Caribbean people are more likely to be stopped and searched by police, there are a higher proportion of arrests following these searches, and they receive harsher treatment in the courts and in sentencing procedures.

- Adults from a mixed-race background have a higher incidence of being a victim of personal crime than other ethnic groups.
- Per 1,000 population, black people were stopped and searched seven times more than white people.

- In 2009/10 there was a decrease in the number of arrests of white people, but an increase of 5% and 13% in the number of arrests of black people and Asians, respectively.
- Overall, black people were 3.3 times more likely to be arrested than white people and a higher percentage were sentenced to immediate custody for indictable offences.

(Home Office, 2012a)

In seeking to explain these inequalities, sociologists and criminologists have claimed that crime has become racialized, in that this is not just an indication of inequalities in the criminal justice system, but reflects a reproduction and perpetuation of perceived racial differences (Keith, 1993). Institutional racism operates within the criminal justice system, where stereotypical beliefs about racial differences (based on phenotypical differences) become ingrained and mediated through the police, the courts and the penal institutions (see also Chapter 4). Racial stereotypes are used to link black people with certain crimes (e.g. sex crimes, aggravated burglary and violent crimes) and serve to legitimate exclusionary practices. As Gilroy (1982: 215) puts it: 'Black law breaking supplies the historic proof that blacks are incompatible with the standards of deviancy and civilization which the nation requires of its citizenry.'

The use of stop and search has been a highly controversial aspect of policing as a result of the disproportionate number of black men who were stopped in the 1980s and 1990s. The impact of the Macpherson Report in 1999 and an acceptance of institutional racism by the Metropolitan Police led to a reduction in the use of stop and search. However, in 2005, following the 7/7 bombings in London, stop and search increased by 14%, with terrorism-related searches increasing by 9%. These figures have since decreased, although the majority are still in London (Home Office, 2012a; see also Table 7.2). In 2009, the European Court of Human Rights ruled that police using stop and search powers under Section 44 of the Terrorism Act (2000) without

Table 7.2 *Stop and search rates and disproportionality ratios, England and Wales, 2007/8*

	England and Wales	England and Wales excluding London	London
Rates per 1,000			
White	16.9	14.0	40.8
Black	128.8	67.7	167.8
Asian	39.7	25.8	62.6
Other	32.1	15.0	55.4
Total	21.6	15.5	60.4
Disproportionality ratios			
Black/white	7.6	4.8	4.2
Asian/white	2.3	1.8	1.5

Source: Equality and Human Rights Commission, 2010

reasonable grounds for suspicion were infringing people's freedoms and human rights and were acting unlawfully.

The Centre for Crime and Justice study (Garside, 2006) identifies socio-economic status as an explanatory factor for the over-representation of young African Caribbean males compared with other ethnic minority groups who are involved in the criminal justice system. The inquiry noted that there are strong links between black people being the victims of crimes as well as the perpetrators of crime owing to their position in areas of social deprivation. Garside (2006: 47) suggests that:

> Some poor and disadvantaged people do commit crime because they are poor and disadvantaged. Some of them end up in our prisons and courts as a result. This does not mean that the poor and disadvantaged commit most crime. Nor does it mean that disadvantage is the cause of most crime. But some of the grossest victimizations are concentrated among the poorer members of society, and it is reasonable to conclude that the poor will often be perpetrators as well as victims.

The inter-relationship of crime, race and socio-economic status is further highlighted by the position of black women in prison. African Caribbean women demonstrate a similar over-representation as men, and 15% of the prison population are foreign nationals from under-developed countries, with many serving long sentences for the importation of drugs (Prison Reform Trust, 2013).

There are 6,679 ethnic minority police officers (March 2012), which accounts for 5% of all officers compared with 4.8% in March 2011, and there has been a steady increase since 2003, although this figure is still unrepresentative of the population it serves (Home Office, 2013a; see Figure 7.4).

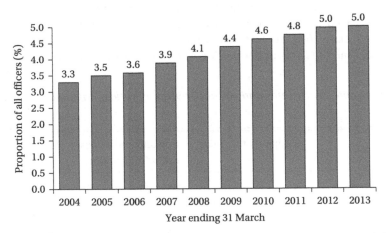

Figure 7.4 Minority ethnic officers as a proportion of all officers as at 31 March in the 43 police forces of England and Wales (excluding central service secondments), 2004–13

Source: Home Office, 2013a.

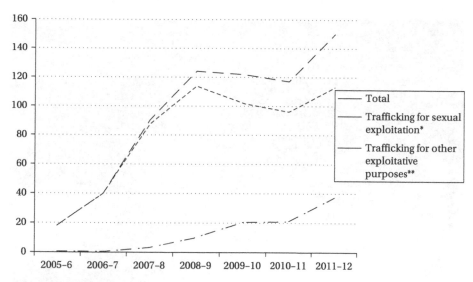

Figure 7.5 Trafficking offences, UK, 2005–12.
*Sections 57, 58 and 59 Sexual Offences Act 2003
**Section 4 Asylum and Immigration (ToC) Act 2004
Source: Home Office, 2012c.

Globalization and crime

As well as opening up markets for legitimate trade and exchange between countries worldwide, the globalization process has also opened up markets for illegal trade and activity. There are transnational criminal markets in drugs, arms, people trafficking (especially women and children, but by no means exclusively), toxic waste, natural resources or protected animal parts (such as elephant tusks for the ivory trade). The numbers of people being trafficked for economic and sexual exploitation is increasing exponentially, as Figure 7.5 demonstrates. Organized crime costs the UK between £20 and £40 billion a year and involves around 38,000 people operating as part of about 6,000 criminal gangs (HM Government, 2011).

An additional global problem is the international drug trade, with 73.7 metric tonnes of heroin being seized globally in 2008 and an estimated 16–17 million cocaine users throughout the world (United Nations Office on Drugs and Crime, 2013).

These global crime figures clearly impact on social workers working with vulnerable people who may be misusing substances (see Chapter 11) or who are being sexually exploited or enslaved (see Chapter 6).

Cyber crime

The internet also opens up possibilities for crime, with cyber crime estimated to cost the UK £27 billion per year. The internet is used for a variety of crimes, including fraud, identity theft, theft of financial information and corporate intellectual property, and child exploitation. The internet is a profitable and low-risk channel for committing crimes, and because it is borderless, criminals can base themselves in

Social workers need to be aware of the complex web of social relations that can lead to placing people in vulnerable situations, including issues of global crime such as sex trafficking and exploitation. (© Chris Schmidt/iStock)

countries where they are less likely to be prosecuted. Thus the global context of crime leads to constantly shifting boundaries between states and new opportunities for pursuing criminal activity.

The challenge for social work is to promote a human rights perspective with people who are the victims of crime and to challenge the context within which human rights violations exist. However, there have been questions as to whether this in itself is enough if the legal frameworks are not available to enforce compliance.

The global context of crime and deviance also raises questions about sentencing practices and human rights. Throughout the world, the death penalty is still used for some crimes (especially in the USA, China and many African states) and raises questions and tensions with social work practice and values within an international context.

Sentencing theory

Contingent upon the various explanations for crime offered by sociology are the various theories of sentencing that are used by the courts. These different theories of sentencing have also evolved over the years, as have the different schools of thought identified with them. They were formalized and put into UK criminal law as recently as 2003 by the Criminal Justice Act of that year (Section 142). In essence they are as follows:

- *Retribution* (also known as 'just deserts'): i.e. the imposition of a sentence to reflect the seriousness of the crime committed (the 'classical' school of criminology and rational choice theory).
- *Rehabilitation* (also known as treatment or the 'welfare' model): i.e. recognizing the deficits experienced by the offender and attempting to prevent the commission of future crimes (strain theory, 'labelling', etc.).
- *Restorative justice*: i.e. recognizing the 'wrong' committed against an individual or the community and endeavouring to correct that wrong with suitable activities and communication with the offender (an integrating of theories). Surveys have found that 85% of victims who participated in restorative justice programmes found them helpful and were satisfied with the experience (Ministry of Justice, 2012b).
- *Public protection*: emphasizing the social control and 'incapacitation' element of sentencing.
- *Incapacitation*: a punishment that removes the offender's ability to commit further crimes, e.g. imprisonment.

One of the methods used in 'restorative justice' involves the bringing together of offender and victim in forms of mediation. This could involve the young person from a low-income family and a community with poor schools, poor housing and poor health facilities having to explain their criminal activity – and even apologize for it – to someone with none of these disadvantages and deprivations. Such an apology fits uncomfortably with proponents of left idealism.

When it comes to such sentencing theories as 'restorative justice', left idealism would question the validity of trying to recognize 'wrongs' committed by juveniles against an individual or the community and then trying to correct those 'wrongs' by suitable activities on the part of – and communications with – that juvenile offender. Not only does such an approach appear to ignore children's rights in its informal approach, but it also overlooks the wider 'wrongs' committed against the juvenile by the social disadvantages inherent in capitalist societies.

Social workers working with people likely to be sentenced will need to recognize these different theories of sentencing. A recurrent theme in contemporary sentencing is the idea of 'risk assessment'. Social workers and other practitioners are asked to assess the risk that individuals may pose in terms of further offending. This is clearly necessary for exercises in 'public protection', but is also a factor in rehabilitation and restorative justice. The process of 'risk assessment' involves the weighing up of factors about an individual and their social circumstances and includes, for example, previous criminal record, psychological profiles, intelligence, use of drugs and alcohol and degree of self-insight. The factors are usually divided into static and dynamic categories, with the latter more liable to change and more amenable to change (see Milner and Myers, 2007).

The 'risk assessment' seeks to inform sentencing decisions, parole decisions and other decisions within the criminal justice system. This attempt to effectively predict the future has been assisted by various 'instruments' introduced to assist practitioners (Baker and Kelly, 2011).

Conclusion

In this chapter we have explored the main sociological contributions to understanding crime. In terms of crime reduction, the big challenge is to take this understanding into appropriate policy changes. A series of sentencing theories have been formulated to reflect the different explanations. For the social worker the challenge is to locate his or her practice within this wider picture of how behaviour becomes classified as criminal and the subsequent social responses to that behaviour.

To bring the picture completely up to date, we should make reference to the sociology of crime as it presents itself at this stage in the twenty-first century. The growth of a politics of 'law and order' and the creation of what has become known as 'popular punitivism' has already been noted. Garland (2002) has outlined a series of features that now characterize what he calls the contemporary 'culture of control'. According to Garland, these features surround our current criminal justice policies and those who work for them. At the start of this chapter, for example, probation officers were referred to as coming from a tradition of being 'social workers to the court'. Now the probation service has 'de-emphasised the social work ethos that used to dominate their work' and they have been repositioned 'as providers of inexpensive, community-based punishments, oriented towards the monitoring of offenders and the management of risk' (Garland, 2002: 18). The same might be said of social work itself as part of the wider community safety partnerships now seen as necessary to combat crime. The challenge for social workers may be to resist pressures on them to limit themselves to the delivery of 'community-based punishments' and to renegotiate the space available to them to practise the values of the social work role. As Horner (2013: 113) summarizes the situation: 'It is . . . fair to say that the relationship between social work and the criminal justice system is one of tension and flux.'

Summary points

- There is no single sociological perspective on crime and deviance, but a range of viewpoints that help us to understand and analyse the nature of crime.
- The media are instrumental in constructing discourses around crime and deviance.
- Poverty and social exclusion are important variables in relation to crime and deviance.
- Social work has been marginalized in the area of crime and deviance, but has an important role to play in prevention as well as rehabilitation.

Questions for discussion

- Is it right to divert young offenders away from the criminal justice system on the grounds that it only exaggerates the problem?
- Why do some young men become street robbers to obtain money and possessions (e.g. mobile phones) when others use legitimate avenues to obtain the same things?
- How can we prevent some urban areas descending into areas of criminality and anti-social behaviour?
- Do social workers experience a tension between a punitive role in the criminal justice system and their empowering and supportive role?

Further reading

Hale, C., Hayward, K., Wahidin, A. and Wincup, E. (eds) (2008) *Criminology.* **2nd edition. Oxford: Oxford University Press**
There are contributions from a team of criminologists in this text, which provides a useful source for students of criminology coming to the subject for the first time. The book looks at different forms of crime and historical and contemporary understandings of crime and criminal justice. The book is accompanied by a website.

Hall, S. (2013) *Theorizing Crime and Deviance: A New Perspective.* **London: Sage**
This book engages with a wide range of criminological theories to provide a useful analysis of current patterns of crime and harm.

Laing, L., Humphreys, C. and Cavanagh, K. (2013) *Social Work and Domestic Violence.* **London: Sage**
This is a valuable source that explores the theoretical debates about domestic violence and a range of social work interventions to support vulnerable women and children.

McLaughlin, E. and Muncie, J. (eds) (2013) *Criminological Perspectives: A Reader.* **3rd edition. London: Sage**
This is an internationally acclaimed book that provides a global perspective on criminological issues.

8 Family and Community

Introduction

Standard 5 of the Professional Capabilities Framework for Social Work states that qualifying social workers should 'understand psychological, social, cultural, spiritual and physical influences on people; human development throughout the life span and the legal framework for practice. They apply this knowledge in their work with individuals, families and communities' (College of Social Work, 2012a). This will cover a wide range of disciplines, but included within it is the need for a sociological understanding of family formation and function, concepts of community and the impact of these structures on individuals and groups.

In Chapter 1 we explored the way that the functionalist sociologist Parsons viewed society as a set of social institutions that operate together to achieve social cohesion and to unite people. The purpose of this chapter is to explore the social institutions of family and community, the changing nature of these and their function. Conflict perspectives of the family and an exploration of the inequalities and disadvantages that may be a feature of some families will be offered as an alternative to the functionalist perspective of cohesion and harmony.

The key issues that will be explored in this chapter are:

- definitions of the family and explanations and debates about the function of families within the social system
- the structure, composition and size of families, exploring notions of continuity and change in the nature of the family in modernity and post-modernity
- notions of the *troubled family* or *dysfunctional family* and the implications of this for social work practice
- the role of social work in relation to family intervention and social control.

By the end of this chapter you should be able to:

- describe different family types
- discuss the nature of family and the roles of family
- discuss the relationship between disadvantage, oppression and family life
- explain what is meant by the term 'dysfunctional family units'
- discuss the nature of risk within the family
- explain the importance of sociological understanding for informing social work practice with a variety of family types.

What is the family?

Exercise: how do you understand the family?

- Before reading the next section, think about who you would class as your family.
- Compare your list with someone else.
- Are there similarities and are there any differences?

For sociologists, the family is a key social institution in society, and traditional definitions focus on ideas about cooperative groups based on the notion of kinship ties and marriage with the purpose of overseeing the upbringing of children (Macionis and Plummer, 2012) In the exercise above, you may have conceptualized your family as a small group of people who are bound together by marriage and blood ties and who live under the same roof – usually a small group of individuals, including adult(s) with or without dependent children. Alternatively, you may have viewed your family as a wider social grouping than this, including people who are related through marriage or blood ties, but who do not necessarily live under the same roof. In the traditional sociological literature, the former is known as the *nuclear family* and the latter is known as the *extended family* (Henslin, 2010)

The concept of family may also be used in a broader way, to incorporate the notion of a set of shared values. Institutions may then use this to inculcate the notion of a collective set of beliefs and ethics: for example, the church family or family of workers. A family is 'a grouping that consists of two or more individuals who define themselves as a family, and who over time assume those obligations to one another that are generally considered an essential component of family systems' (National Association of Social Workers, quoted in Vosler, 1996: 13). This definition of the family is what is termed a *phenomenological* definition. It is based on people's lived experiences and the meanings that they themselves attach to the concept of family. It also allows for a dynamic view of family life, seeing the family unit not as something that is fixed and static, but as something that transforms over time to reflect changing social circumstances and sets of ideas. The family is defined in a broader context of groups of people who have a mutual obligation to each other, who may or may not necessarily live under the same roof. This is known as the family of choice, where two or more individuals assume mutual obligation to one another, not necessarily on the basis of marriage, blood ties or kinship ties (Macionis and Plummer, 2012). Therefore the family may be made up of groups of friends or a communion of individuals, such as members of a church or other religious/spiritual organization. From this phenomenological perspective, family becomes associated with a sense of identity or belonging and forms the basis of existential questions such as 'Who am I?' Perhaps this can be most clearly evidenced by accounts of individuals who have been adopted and, as they grow older, may seek to find or find out about their biological parents in order to

Nuclear family small family unit that consists of a man and woman in a monogamous marriage and their dependent children.

Extended family a family form that includes members outside the immediate parent and child relationship such as grandparents.

Phenomenology to study and observe behaviour in order to understand its meaning.

understand their historical and genetic location within society. There is a growing interest in genealogy and ancestry, linking the past with the present. Thus, family is not just about living arrangements, but constitutes an important part of social identity (see Chapter 1).

Therefore, when sociologists talk about the family, they are looking beyond different living arrangements, and seeking to explore the multiple levels of meaning that the family has in post-modern society, as well as explanations for changes in the nature and structure of families and the social construction of particular family forms as normal or problematic (Heaphy, 2011).

Changing family structures

Broadly speaking, our location within some form of family structure is a general feature of human societies. However, the constitution, structure, size and function of families vary over time and across cultures. There are a wide variety of family forms throughout the world, but there are common functions in terms of:

- economic production
- socialization of children
- care of the sick and aged
- recreation
- sexual control
- reproduction.

In the Western industrialized world, the family unit has been based on an understanding of the legitimacy of monogamous marriage, but this is not a universal principle. We can see from the discussions in Chapter 6 about civil partnerships and gay marriage, adoption and child-rearing that social and cultural practices impact on our understanding of what constitutes a family. In addition, the constitution of the family is undergoing major transformations in Western societies, based on changes in marriage, divorce and new family structures, as evidenced in the following Office for National Statistics (2012a) figures:

- In 2012, there were 18.2 million families in the UK. Of these, 12.2 million consisted of a married couple with or without children.
- The number of opposite-sex cohabiting couple families has increased significantly, from 1.5 million in 1996 to 2.9 million in 2012. The number of dependent children living in opposite-sex cohabiting couple families doubled from 0.9 million to 1.8 million over the same period.
- In 2012, 38% of married-couple families had dependent children, compared with 39% of opposite-sex cohabiting couple families.
- There were nearly 2.0 million lone parents with dependent children in the UK in 2012, a figure that has grown steadily but significantly from 1.6 million in 1996.
- There were 26.4 million households in the UK in 2012. Of these, 29% consisted of only one person and almost 20% consisted of four or more people.

'Never mind what Susie's mother said. Two-parent families are *not* a cult!' (© 2001 by Randy Glasbergen. www.glasbergen.com)

Structural perspectives

From a functionalist perspective (see Chapter 1), the family is an important social institution that reinforces the norms and values of the society. In pre-industrial times, the family would be concerned with functions such as education and work. However, industrialization saw the transference of these functions to specialist institutions (e.g. the schooling system and the factory system of capitalist production). Thus, the family took on different specialist functions, namely the socialization of children and the stabilization of adult personalities (Parsons and Bales, 1955).

The family continues to serve an important societal role in the reproduction of social and economic functions which are required for the maintenance of stability and social order. As Levitas (1998: 28) puts this: 'Strong families build the social cohesion of our nation and its communities. Families are primarily institutions of social control and social welfare.' This can be related to the function of the family as a unit of reproduction, reflecting a socialized concept of the family as the ideal place for the rearing of children. Historically, we can see how society has sanctioned this function of the normal married family. For example, prior to the 1959 Mental Health Act, women who gave birth outside the institution of marriage were often incarcerated in the asylums of the mental health system (Rogers and Pilgrim, 2010).

For Parsons, the family is a site for the reproduction of the prevailing social order, through the socialization of a moral blueprint and the reinforcement of cultural norms and values. In this respect, the family has two important functions:

1   the primary socialization of children
2   personality stabilization for adult members.

Primary socialization is concerned with the teaching and learning of social values and cultural norms.

Exercise: primary socialization

List the things that families may do in order to teach their children about social norms and values.

You may have included the following in your list: eating and nutrition; speaking and language; clothing; religious and cultural practices; sleep patterns; inter-personal relationships; respect for others and discipline; health-related practices – for instance, dental care or personal hygiene – as well as illness behaviours (the socialization of responses to illness and help-seeking behaviours – see Chapter 11). This notion of primary socialization and the dominant norms and values of society reflects Foucault's (1979b) notion of disciplinary power in which individuals self-regulate their behaviours and actions, but these are reinforced through professional ideologies. An example of this can be seen in discussions about the family and health-promoting behaviours, particularly in relation to family eating patterns and current concerns about levels of obesity. The Department of Health (2011b) concludes that overweight and obesity constitute the most widespread threat to health and well-being in the UK, with one of the highest levels of obesity in Europe and little evidence of significant and sustained decline: 23% of adults are obese and 61.3% are either overweight or obese, while 23.1% of 4 and 5 year olds and 33.3% of 10 and 11 year olds are overweight or obese (Department of Health, 2011b).

Studies have identified a link between family eating patterns and healthy eating. Christian et al. (2013) studied the relationship between home food environment, parental attitudes and children's fruit and vegetable consumption patterns and found that where families regularly ate meals together, children were more likely to consume the recommended daily intake of fruit and vegetables, as parents model good behaviours and act as role models to reinforce good habits.

Adult personality stabilization is concerned with the emotional assistance of adult family members and reflects an ideological and normative construct of the ideal family type. Within the discourses of the normative family unit, marriage is seen as an important adjunct to the stable family unit: 'Marriage between adult men and women is the arrangement through which adult personalities are supported and kept healthy' (Giddens and Sutton, 2013: 175).

Hockey and James (2003) argue that the functionalist approach to an understanding of family is based on an understanding of power and authority relations through a hierarchical structure of family formation. This over-emphasis on consensus and conformity fails to acknowledge processes of conflict, inequality and abuse within families. The incidence of domestic violence and family abuse exposes the myth of the family unit as one of stability and harmony (see also Chapters 3 and 7). In 2011/12, 15% of all violent incidents in the UK were as a result of domestic violence, with a third of all women and nearly one-fifth of all men stating that they had been the victim of one form of domestic abuse since they were 16 (emotional, financial or physical abuse, sexual assault or stalking by a partner or family member) (Strickland,

2013). The Women's Aid organization, however, has argued that official statistics underestimate levels of domestic violence as they only record reported cases and do not account for the hidden victims in society.

Case study: the impact of domestic violence and abuse on a family's housing situation and their emotional and physical well-being

Mum and her two children aged 9 and 1 years old were living with their in-laws in very overcrowded accommodation. Mother was verbally abused by her husband and his parents and made to do all the household chores. Her movements were restricted, the family lived in one bedroom and shared a double bed and there were no toys in the house. Mum had had postnatal depression following the birth of her youngest daughter. This was compounded by ongoing domestic violence by her husband who was physically and sexually abusive. The Shelter worker described Mum as being 'worn down' when they first met.

The family's Health Visitor referred them to Shelter and Shelter worked with them for 16 months. A significant amount of time was required in order to establish a trusting relationship between the Shelter worker and the Mother. The eldest daughter was very protective of her Mum and was withdrawn. The youngest daughter also seemed very unhappy and was not thriving.

The family had an urgent need to be re-housed away from the abusive husband. Mum had no access to finances and was very vulnerable. She was on high levels of anti-depressants and was often confused. She had threatened to kill herself and her children.

(Shelter, n.d.)

This case study demonstrates the impact of domestic violence not only on the individual, but also on wider family members and relationships. It is also acknowledged that family members can be complicit in domestic abuse and violence by not intervening to prevent it, and there have been changes in the law to take account of this. The Domestic Violence Crime and Victims Act (2004) introduced a new criminal offence of familial homicide, where a family member is guilty of causing or allowing the death of a child or vulnerable adult, which is punishable by up to 14 years' imprisonment. In Leeds in 2007, Shazad Khan was imprisoned for the murder of Sabia Rani. Four members of his family were sentenced for familial homicide (BBC News, 2008).

The impact of domestic abuse on both women and children is acknowledged in contemporary policies through commissioning practices that recognize the connections between the two (Goulding and Duggal, 2011), and social workers have a key role to play in supporting vulnerable people. Narrative research by Keeling and van Wormer (2012) found that women who experience domestic abuse may be reluctant to inform social workers, fearing that their children may be taken into care. Therefore an understanding of family relationships and the impact of domestic abuse on both women and children is fundamental to good safeguarding practices so that social workers can adopt supportive and individualized approaches.

Marxist perspectives

There is a difference between household and family. However, many definitions of the family conflate the two to construct a normative definition of the family, the conjugal nuclear family, based on the monogamous marriage of heterosexual partners, with one or more dependent children. Gail Lewis (1998) argued that this normative construction of the nuclear family addressed the needs of modernity and the industrializing society.

Marxists have argued that stable families are needed for capitalism to function. Labour power is produced and reproduced within the family, through reproduction, maintenance of health, education and the socialization of dominant values and ideological systems. Engels (1902) developed a Marxian analysis, arguing that the private domain of the nuclear family and the dominance of monogamous marriage developed as a result of private ownership of property (see also Chapter 6). Married men were able to protect their property through the production of heirs, and women traded their sexual and reproductive functions to their husbands in return for material protection. In this way, Engels argued, the traditional family form promoted patriarchy, with women being seen as the sexual and economic property of men. Marxist feminists have further argued that women contribute to the capitalist economy through their unpaid labour in the domestic sphere (Oakley, 1974) and as a reserve army of labour to be employed in the secondary sector of the dual labour market (Mann, 1985). From a Marxist perspective, the family also contributes to the capitalist economy through patterns of consumption. Theories of consumer behaviour and decision-making have identified the importance of the family or household unit for two reasons:

1   Many consumer products are purchased by a family unit.
2   Individuals' buying decisions may be heavily influenced by other family members through socialization and role-modelling processes.

Household consumption practices are important for the economy as well as being directly influenced by changing economic circumstances. In 2008, UK households spent £9.6 billion weekly, with spending on transport, recreation, culture, housing, fuel and power accounting for nearly half of this (Office for National Statistics, 2010a).

The various roles of family members will influence the purchase and consumption practices within the household, which may be related to gendered constructions of family roles (see Chapter 3). One member of the household, for example, may take responsibility for the purchase of items which may then be consumed by the whole family/household unit (e.g. food and toiletries). Within a consumer society, advertising and marketing are important, with the UK advertising industry estimated to be worth £7.8 billion in 2008 (Department for Culture, Media and Sport, 2011).

Exercise: advertising and family roles

Next time you are watching commercial television, make a note of the adverts.

• How many of the adverts are aimed at family units of production?
• How far do these adverts reflect gendered constructions of family roles?

Social action theory

Micro-sociology is concerned with the way that individuals see the world and the ways that individuals both influence and experience family life. Hockey and James (2003) identify the family as an important source of identity formation. Identities are constructed throughout the life-course with the mixing of ages and generations within the family, so that social roles are partly determined by relationship to other family members and therefore people may have a range of social identities. For example, a woman may have a role as mother to the children in the family, daughter to her parents, wife or partner, sibling, and so on. Work and work relations intersect with family roles, with identities being shaped further by the relationship between the public and private sphere of life (the public sphere being the arena of paid employment and the private sphere being the domestic arena). Powerful ideologies are played out through these identity formations via the social construction of normative roles (see also Chapter 3). Although there may be many different forms of family unit in contemporary Western societies, the gendered roles within the family remain relatively stable (Elliott, 1996). Despite a growing number of women in paid employment outside of the home, there has generally been little change in the division of labour within the family unit, reflecting continuing patriarchal ideologies and the notion of the male breadwinner society (Equal Opportunities Commission, 2006).

Relationships and identities within the family also reflect wider social processes and constructions. In traditional family forms, members may be organized within an extended family structure where elders are revered and respected for their wisdom and sagacity. Extended families may be extended vertically and/or horizontally (Figure 8.1a, 8.1b). Vertical extension includes grandparents and great-grandparents, whereas horizontal extension includes aunts, uncles and cousins. Thus the extended family can be a complex grouping of individuals – the concept of the family tree with multiple branches and sub-branches, united by a central trunk.

The extended family (or some form of it) may reside under one roof. However, there may also be what is referred to as a modified extended family, where there is a series of separate nuclear families who may not have much physical contact, but who may come together for a shared purpose: for example, a celebration such as a christening or golden wedding.

Historians are not in entire agreement about the extent to which there has been a decline in the significance of the extended family type in modernity and post-modernity in Western industrialized societies. Some historians have argued that there has been an exaggeration of the extent of the extended family type historically, portraying a halcyon vision of a lost sense of values. Others, however, have argued that the processes of modernity have led to increasing geographical mobility, resulting in a greater physical segregation of families (Macionis and Plummer, 2012). In addition, there have been ideological changes, with young people being encouraged to move away from the nuclear family at particular times of life-course transition (e.g. many school leavers being encouraged to move away from the parental home to pursue a college or university education or married couples moving away from parental homes to set up their own homes). This is reflected in the historical concept of the dowry and the bottom-drawer concept of the acquisition of consumer durables in order to help people with this transition. This second example demonstrates the

Figure 8.1   Simplistic diagram of a family tree based on:
(a)   vertical extension

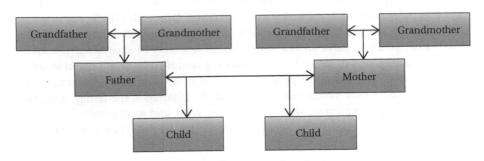

(b)   horizontal extension

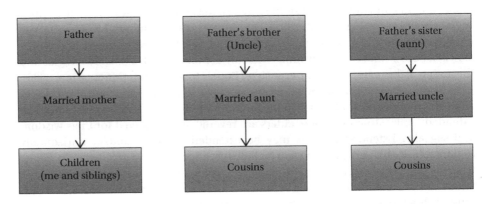

associated changes of individualism and consumerism, as individuals are encouraged to be independent and self-determinate, entering the world of the housing market (through either the property-owning democracy or access to the private rented sector predominantly, although some may also occupy public sector or social housing).

Community

It is difficult to separate families from sociological concepts of community, especially when exploring important principles of social identity formation and social networks. Yet the definition of community is not straightforward and can have a variety of meanings. Community can be defined as a description of social networks related to place, interest or communion, or as a set of shared values, although often the two broad categorizations overlap. In general, what can be said about communities is that the members have some sort of shared interest or something in common with each other, and that this distinguishes them from other groups. Cohen (1985) argues that the desire to see oneself as different from some people and having a common identity with others is central to the concept of community. This is a phenomenological perspective of community, focusing on the lived experiences of individuals

A Bar Mitzvah ceremony. (© Daniel Lawson/Flickr)

in constituting their social identity. The identity of a community is often expressed in terms of symbols and rituals. A good example of this is religious communities, which have ritualistic practices that symbolize the belonging to that community: for example, the Bar Mitzvah ceremony marking a Jewish boy's transition into adulthood in the Jewish faith, or the confirmation ceremony, which signifies full membership to various Christian communities.

Lee and Newby (1983) use the term 'communion' to define community, where locality is far less important than the sense of identity and belonging and shared value systems. Thus a geographically disparate group of individuals such as the Countryside Alliance would be seen as a community. The relationships can be between groups of individuals who are located near to each other, or who are geographically distant and may not even be in physical contact (e.g. internet communities). The nineteenth-century French thinker Alexis de Tocqueville (1994) used the term 'habits of the heart' to explain that values and norms affect decisions about whether to engage with a community. Tolerance, reciprocal relationships and social trust are important values that can determine the sense of belonging and identity within a community and are significant in terms of the social networks that people develop. Putman (2000) uses the term 'social capital' to explain the connections amongst individuals over time which create social bonds.

> Whereas physical capital refers to physical objects and human capital refers to the properties of individuals, social capital refers to connections among individuals – social networks and the norms of reciprocity and trustworthiness that arise from them. In that sense social capital is closely related to what some have called 'civic virtue.' The difference is that 'social capital' calls attention to the fact that civic virtue is most powerful when embedded in a dense network of reciprocal social relations. A society of many virtuous but isolated individuals is not necessarily rich in social capital. (Putnam, 2000: 19)

In a study of American society since the 1950s, Putnam argued that there had been a significant decline in social bonding in families and communities, alongside a fall in the membership of other social networks, such as religious organizations and recreational groups. Social capital is an important sociological concept in the understanding of identity and relationships and the ways that people use social networks, engage in reciprocal social relationships within them and derive value for attaining their personal goals. Boeck and Fleming (2011) identify inward-looking connections and social bonding in terms of the family and close friends, and outward-looking connections within the wider community. In their study of youth offending, they argue that people use outward-looking connections for transitions into work, but inward-looking connections for emotional support. These social bonds are important to an individual sense of belonging and demonstrate how family and community processes intersect. Children do better where there are strong reciprocal social relationships between families, schools and wider social networks such as community centres. This underpins contemporary policies for community engagement and regeneration. The concept of social capital can also explain why some people may become dislocated from communities through, for example, homelessness or enduring mental health problems, leading to stigmatization, marginalization and social exclusion (see Chapters 2 and 11).

The Families in Focus project in Camden, London, is a community-based pilot project, using both interventionist and preventative strategies to work with children and young people. Through this, workers gain the trust of families and are able to provide intense support to address some of the problems that the local residents experience. An important aspect of this project is that it is based in a small locality and builds on the strengths of local residents and empowers them to make decisions and changes to their lives. Community-based officers work with local residents and help them to regain a sense of community and social cohesion (Wigfall, 2006).

Critical sociology and the family

Post-modernist theorists take pluralism and the notion of continuous change and instability as their starting point, and argue that traditional notions of the family are inadequate for an understanding of the many family types that co-exist in contemporary societies (Cheal, 1988). Morgan (1996) has suggested that the concept of 'doing family' is more useful in understanding the nature of diverse forms of contemporary family lives. Families need to be understood in terms of their fluidity, and as a set of relationships built around common purposes. For Morgan, analysis of what goes on in families is important in terms of intimate connections, the routine of everyday activities, and the connection between history and current lives.

Beck and Beck-Gernsheim (1995) suggest that our age is characterized by a much more complex series of negotiations. Marriage is now entered into voluntarily (in the main) rather than for economic reasons, and the nature of roles has changed, not least because an increasing number of women have entered the paid labour market. Therefore, family life is not just about the negotiation of roles within the private sphere, such as domestic roles, sexual relations and childcare, but also about negotiating paid work and economic inequality. Thus family lives are seen as more chaotic and the 'battle of the sexes' is the 'central drama of our times'. This has resulted in an increased breakdown of relationships and all the issues that are related to this.

A rise in the divorce rate and other demographic changes mean that an increasing number of families are living in what are termed reconstituted units. Changes in legislation have been significant in allowing people to divorce, and since the 1960s there has been a dramatic rise in the number of divorces. Between 2009 and 2011, there was a 4.9% increase in divorce in England and Wales, rising from 10.5 to 11.1 per 1,000 married population. In 1995, 33% of marriages had ended in divorce by the time of the fifteenth wedding anniversary, compared to 22% in 1970. In 2010, the highest number of divorces was in the 40- to 44-year-old age group (Office for National Statistics, 2010a).

Some concern has been raised about the effect of divorce on children, although it is generally accepted that children derive more benefit from being cared for within a happy environment (see Chapter 9). One area of concern about divorce has been the adversarial nature of the family legal system, which may contribute to acrimonious relationships, and has the potential to affect both the divorcing couple and any dependent children. The rising divorce rate has also caused some concern that divorce is too readily available and that this may discourage people from trying to work through problems together. The breakdown of traditional support and mutual benefit systems and the concomitant rise in individualism have resulted in a growth in the welfarist approach to problem solving and problem management between couples and demonstrate the ideological position that a family is the best unit for the rearing of children. The Tavistock Centre (a charitable trust), for example, offers a programme called 'Parents as Partners' that provides 16 counselling sessions to both parents to improve parental relationships and children's well-being and opportunities for success. The programme is aimed at vulnerable families and offers a whole-family approach to tackling the problems of poor relationships.

Family Links programme

Many children do not have happy family lives and fail at school.

Family Links helps change this by training thousands of health, education and community professionals to use the Nurturing Programme so that:

- parents create a calm, kind, healthy, hopeful family life
- children succeed and nurture their own children.

The Nurturing Programme is a springboard for robust emotional and mental well-being in all adults and children: the foundations for a positive life at home, in school and society (see https://www.familylinks.org.uk/The-Nurturing-Programme).

Black perspectives

Black theorists have been critical of mainstream sociology in relation to the family, pointing to the implicit racism that is embedded in the Eurocentric approach that is largely adopted. Through constructions of the normative family, alternative family forms come to be seen as deviant and alien (Elliot, 1996). In addition to this, the focus on the family as a unit of oppression (particularly for women) ignores the positive elements that the family provides within the context of wider community hostility (Bhavnani and Coulson, 1986) and diverts attention away from other structural and institutional processes that contribute to black women's continued oppression (Thorogood, 1987).

Black perspectives on the family have also highlighted the enduring myths of family formations amongst black and minority ethnic populations. Although families in South Asia may often live in an extended family structure, this is not replicated within South Asian populations in the UK (Dobbs and Burholt, 2010), and yet stereotypical assumptions have often influenced policy decisions about provision of support to dependent relatives in the community. The result of this is greater social isolation and a poor quality of care (Ahmad and Walker, 1997). Caballero et al. (2012) have also questioned stereotypical assumptions about the constitution of mixed-race families. They argue that attempts to find a single benchmark for understanding the experiences and identities of children brought up in mixed-race families have failed to account for the wide diversity and complexity of family formation.

Feminist perspectives of the family

Egalitarianism a philosophy associated with the promotion of equal opportunities in society.

Feminist perspectives of the family have been important for challenging notions of *egalitarianism* and harmony within the family, seeing families as a potential source of disharmony and unequal power relations, related to the domestic division of labour, unequal power relationships and the ideology of caring. These three important themes emerge from feminist writings on households and families. Work and family roles and relationships are inextricably linked, and changes in labour market patterns have led to increased sociological interest in work/family relationships. A significant shift has occurred in the labour market in the post-Second World War period, with increasing numbers of women taking on paid employment outside the private sphere of the home.

In addition to these changes, globalization and the global recession have led to increased pressures on businesses to cut costs to achieve greater profit margins (Burchielli et al., 2008), and to employees being expected to work longer hours. This, coupled with the increase in the numbers of women entering the paid labour market, has raised questions about work/life balance and the impact of work environment on family life and family relations. The Office for National Statistics' 2005 Time Use Survey found that working parents on average spent 19 minutes a day looking after children. Working mothers were found to spend less time sleeping and relaxing than non-working mothers, whilst working fathers with young children were found to work more hours, have less sleep than other men and take on a higher proportion of domestic tasks. Thus both the quantity and quality of time spent in family relationships is compromised through these new patterns of work/family relationships.

Although some households may reflect a unit with shared roles and responsibilities, the trend remains one of segregated roles between adult members of families, with a disproportionate burden of housework, childcare and family care falling on women (Equal Opportunities Commission, 2006). Women continue to provide 75% of housework alongside 38% of hours of paid work, while men's paid and domestic work has remained largely unchanged (Harkness, 2008).

Emotional labour and ideologies of caring

There is a social construction of the notion of caring, based on gendered roles and socialization processes (see Chapter 3). Ideologies of caring are reinforced through social policies in relation to the family, with child settlement policies/procedures often favouring the woman and maternity care and maternity leave being structured around norms of female care (Pascall, 1997). Ideologies of family care are embedded in current community care policies (National Health Service and Community Care Act, 1990), which has led to an increase in provision of informal care within families, where family members provide unpaid care for other dependent family members (see also chapter 3). It is estimated that 6.4 million people in the UK are providing unpaid care for an older parent or disabled or seriously ill family member (Office for National Statistics, 2013b). Carers UK estimates that 2.3 million adults give up work to provide this care, with a further 3 million reducing working hours, with resultant impacts on family finance and increased levels of debt.

Carers UK (2011): key findings about the cost of care

- *Choosing to eat or heat*: over 45% were cutting back on essentials like heating or food.
- *Falling into debt*: 4 in 10 were in debt as a result of caring.
- *Sick with worry*: the stress of money worries had affected the health of 1 in 2.

Although many carers enter into a caring relationship voluntarily, the costs of caring must not be underestimated. The current model of community care is premised on the notion of a mixed economy of welfare in which informal care plays a fundamental role (Dwyer and Shaw, 2013), and yet this ideology of family care fails to recognize the damaging effects on carers. More recently, policy imperatives in adult social care have stressed the importance of carer assessments and the key role of social workers in assessing carers' needs (Davies, 2012; see also Chapter 10).

Social disadvantage, risk and moral panics

The discussion above demonstrates that, although the family is an important subsystem of society, the idealized image of the family hides a number of damaging effects of family life and promotes a normalized version of it that no longer reflects many people's experiences. Denzin launched a scathing attack on the American family in post-modernity, arguing that the traditional model of the family is no longer applicable to many people's circumstances. He defines the modern family as 'a single-parent family, headed by a teenage mother, who may be drawn to drug abuse and alcoholism' (Denzin, 1987: 33). He further suggests that the family is far less significant in terms of childcare, with the institutionalization of care through day-care provision. Thus the state and statutory providers have become increasingly important in terms of the primary socialization of children and children's development. This could be reflected in Government policies about extended schools and wrap-around care (Every Child Matters – see Chapter 9).

Denzin also points to the role of television in many children's lives, and in the development and perpetuation of cultural myths. Sigman (2012) suggests that the average 10 year old will spend more time watching TV than being at school. Denzin concludes that in post-modernity a child is 'cared for by the television set, in conjunction with the day-care center' (Denzin, 1987: 33). Thus it is argued that the nature of family life is in chaos as day-care providers are unable to provide children with the emotional guidance that they require as they offer more limited emotional investment (Leavitt and Power, 1989).

The discussion above clearly identifies a number of concerns about the stability of the family unit and the extent to which the decline in traditional family forms has contributed to the breakdown in social cohesion. Rather than providing stability and serving the functions of the wider society, families have increasingly been blamed for the problems of society. Children are seen to be vulnerable to the damaging effects of poor parenting (Furedi, 2002), with a number of childhood health problems being viewed as a consequence of parental action. Hehir (2005) has argued that nurturing, socialization and early stimulation may be viewed as contributory factors to child morbidity patterns, and family breakdown in particular is associated with the rise in mental health problems in children (Bramlett and Blumberg, 2007).

Families, poverty and social exclusion

Social exclusion and poverty are often related to the income levels of the adult partners within the household, and thus the entire family unit experiences the impact of income and material deprivation. Distribution of resources within the family may not always be equal (Himmelweit et al., 2013), and there is some evidence that women will often go without when resources are scarce in order to ensure that children and male partners are provided for. Lifestyle practices and risks are inculcated within the family through the function of primary socialization, where that socialization may involve learning of poor lifestyle choices, for example in relation to diet and leisure, with implications for health status.

A key Government priority since the 1990s has been to tackle child and family poverty and social exclusion (see Chapter 2), and yet recent austerity measures to tackle the economic problems associated with the global recession have resulted in increased family poverty and deprivation. The effects of these measures can be seen in the fact that around 400,000 more children will experience relative poverty by 2015/16 and 500,000 will experience absolute poverty in the same time frame (based on definitions in the Child Poverty Act, 2010). This will disproportionately affect families with three or more children, those living in private rented accommodation and households with younger children, all of which have above average levels of poverty. The absolute and relative poverty rates rise for children from Pakistani and Bangladeshi households by more than 5% (Family and Parenting Institute, 2012). Children living within single-parent families are also more likely to experience the impact of poverty and social exclusion. Such families constitute 26% of households with dependent children (Office for National Statistics, 2012a), and this figure has remained fairly consistent since the 1990s. Of these, around 8% are headed by single fathers (Office for National Statistics, 2012a).

The Family and Parenting Institute (2012) conclude that the changes in the tax benefit system are one factor that is contributing to this rise in family poverty. The introduction in 2013/14 of the cap in benefits that families can receive will particularly impact on large families, and reforms to the Child Tax Credit and Working Tax Credit will especially affect families with young children.

> Overall, low-income households with children, particularly non-working lone parent households, lose more as a percentage of income on average from tax and benefit changes to be introduced over this period than pensioners, those of working age without children and richer households with children. (Family and Parenting Institute, 2012: 3)

The rising divorce rate has provided grounds for concern, with questions being asked about the nature of family life in post-modernity and signs of some form of moral panic about the breakdown of the family as a sub-system. This, in turn, has led to concerns about the breakdown of society and traditional values. However, the remarriage rate remains high, and it is difficult therefore to draw the conclusion that the institution of marriage has significantly reduced in popularity as a form of social organization.

The remarriage rate, however, has implications for family structure in contemporary society, as an increasing number of children live with a biological parent and a step-parent and may also live with step-siblings or half-siblings. Step-families constitute 11% of all families in the UK with dependent children (Office for National Statistics, 2014). Children and adults may spend time in two different reconstituted family arrangements, constantly having to negotiate boundaries and their place within the family unit.

The rise in lone-parent families has led to much discussion about absent parents, and Bradshaw and Millar (1991) have argued that a significant minority of children in lone-parent families lose contact with the absent parent. Owing to the ideological model of the maternal role in bringing up children, this has given rise to particular concerns about absent fathers. The *Dad and Me* report (Glynn and Addaction, 2011) found the following problems for children where fathers were absent from their lives:

- They are often isolated, unsupported and likely to partake in negative behaviours, such as crime or substance misuse.
- They lack a positive image of themselves, causing problems that can manifest themselves differently according to gender.
- They describe a daily struggle with their emotions and a frustration at not having the opportunity to resolve negative feelings.
- They need to establish trusted links with older generations, and express a need to engage with positive, older role models in their communities.
- They are rarely held accountable for their actions.

The rise in lone-parent families and the ideological model of child-rearing being a maternal activity have led to concerns about more children growing up with absent fathers. (© antoniogiorgio.photoshelter.com/Reproduced with the permission of the photographer)

The Fathers for Justice pressure group has highlighted some of these issues, claiming that the rights of absent fathers have been rather overlooked in recent history, although this may be starting to change. Chawla-Duggan (2006) reports on a project which uses father development workers to support early years learning, acknowledging the important role that fathers have to play, and how their involvement can lead to improved social, educational and emotional outcomes.

Although less than 2% of single parents are teenagers (Office for National Statistics, 2012a), there have been moral panics associated with the perceived rise in teenage mothers, with some social commentators seeing this within the context of pursuit of social housing. (See, e.g., Charles Murray's discussion of the 'underclass' in Chapter 2.) The reality, however, is much more complex than this, with the rise in teenage motherhood being related to a number of different factors (Phoenix, 1991; Smith-Battle, 2000). It is also a misrepresentation to see all teenage mothers as a drain on society and the welfare system. The majority live within their parents' home and continue to be supported emotionally, functionally and financially by their family.

Dysfunctional family a term used in society to refer to families that are not operating according to society's expectations and are seen to disrupt social cohesion and the smooth organization of society.

Nevertheless, the notion of the family as a stable unit which has a positive influence over the smooth functioning of society has come under increasing criticism, with a growing concern about the family as a dysfunctional unit, both for society as a whole, and for the individual members of the family. The term *'dysfunctional family'* is one that has been used by sociologists and policy makers. Although social workers may well find themselves working with such families, the language of dysfunction does not fit easily with social work values and principles of anti-oppressive practice. Labelling a family as dysfunctional, or a problem family, tends to pathologize the members of that family, and it is a negative and disempowering term.

A family is seen to be dysfunctional when there is constant conflict, misbehaviour and/or abuse. This may be by one or more members of the family, but may lead to accommodation of these behaviours by other family members. Dysfunctional behaviour becomes reinforced within the family unit, with a cycle of behaviours emerging. The common elements of the dysfunctional family are:

- under-functioning by adult members of the family unit
- little guidance and few boundaries for behaviour
- children being left to fend for themselves
- inconsistency and violation of basic boundaries of behaviour
- difficulties in controlling own behaviour or reacting to the behaviour of others, with a consequent undercurrent of violence and violent response to behaviours
- a model of family violence.

Dysfunctionality of the family breeds hatred and conflict, which is then reflected in wider society (Vogel and Bell, 1968). Thus social problems and anxieties about the moral values of a society become rooted in the dysfunctional family. The stability of the family was brought into sharp focus in the aftermath of the riots in the UK in August 2011. Many youths and young adults were involved in the riots, leading to questions about family functioning, with the Coalition Government raising concerns about poor parenting, and shortly afterwards setting up the Troubled Families Initiative (Churchill, 2013).

In 2012 Louise Casey was appointed to investigate the nature of troubled families. She interviewed 16 families to try to get a picture of the problems that they encountered and concluded that a history of poor family relationships, violence and abuse and parents having children at a young age were common factors that led to entrenched family problems, social exclusion, anti-social behaviour and crime (Department for Communities and Local Government, 2012).

> Linked to shifting family structures is a broader set of often dysfunctional relationships – between parents themselves; between them and their children, with their friends and extended family, and even the relationship with professionals assigned to them. Many of the people interviewed were just not very good at relationships – unsurprising perhaps in light of their own upbringings.
>
> Their inability to form effective and positive relationships was often pivotal and played out across their lives with regard to their relationship with their partners, as parents, with their neighbours, friends and associates – and indeed with the myriad of agencies and services that work with them. (Department for Communities and Local Government, 2012: 48)

The media reporting of child deaths, youth crime and dysfunctional families has led to a number of concerns about the stability of the family unit and the extent to which the decline in traditional family forms has contributed to the breakdown in social cohesion. Rather than providing stability and serving the functions of the wider society, families have increasingly been blamed for the problems of society

(Department for Communities and Local Government, 2012). Policy interventions in social work practice and education reflect this moral panic, with a primary focus on safeguarding children, based on a rather limited evidence base, mainly from atypical cases.

Exercise: media reporting of child deaths

Have a look at reports of child deaths in newspapers. (These can be accessed from the archives of individual newspapers. Try *http://www.dailymail.co.uk/*; *http://www.mirror.co.uk*; or *http://www.theguardian.com/uk*.)

- What is the dominant view of families within these reports?
- What do they tell us about the public perception of social work intervention in family life?

Family interventions

In recent years, there have been attempts to reverse processes of disadvantage, and family intervention has been seen as important in building community solidarity and a collective consciousness (see Chapter 2). Urban regeneration programmes, such as dockland developments to attempt to rebuild communities and work with families, have been used as a way of uniting communities and promoting a sense of social cohesion. For example, legislation has been passed which introduces parenting orders and contracts which can force parents to engage with family and youth services. The penalty for not complying with these orders is imprisonment, as a response to concerns about anti-social behavior, youth offending and truancy. Social workers have a key role here in terms of family interventions to promote family relationships.

Social workers may be involved in family group conferences. The emphasis here is on empowering families and supporting them to find solutions to their problems. The families, therefore, and not the professionals, are the decision makers, and this is consistent with social work values to empower and enable people. (See NSPCC, 2009, for further information.)

There are many examples of social and policy principles being mediated through the family to socialize children into the norms and values of the society and which construct normative expectations of good parenting roles. Under a 2000 amendment to the 1996 Education Act, parents can be arrested and charged if their children persistently truant. In 2011, 12,800 parents in England and Wales were taken to court for failing to ensure their child went to school, with 9,800 being found guilty and sentenced. The majority of those who were punished were given fines, but nearly 500 were given community service punishments and 11 were jailed (Ministry of Justice, 2011). This reflects wider Government concerns about the scale of the problem of truancy, the long-term impact of this on societal cohesion and economic well-being, and the role of the family as one of a series of measures to tackle the problem (see also Chapter 7).

Exercise: childhood obesity

According to Public Health England (2014), one in five children in reception class is overweight or obese (boys 23.2%, girls 21.2%), as is one in three children in Year 6 (boys 34.8%, girls 31.8%). A number of commentators have argued that obesity in children is a child protection issue and that social workers have a duty to intervene (Griffiths, 2010).

- Do you think that social workers should intervene to protect children who are obese?
- What are the arguments for and against this intervention?

Donzelot (1980) has argued that family policy has increasingly focused on 'policing of the family', with the family being seen as a site for normalization and moralization. He argues that the patriarchal domination of the private family unit by the father has been replaced by a patriarchal surveillance of the family through state intervention. Social workers, the education system, psychiatry and philanthropy are all seen as agents of the state, responsible for the surveillance and protection of families, and thus contribute to the perpetuation of the dominant set of social values and morals. However, Donzelot also provides a critique of Marxist and feminist perspectives on the family, arguing that state policies and professional interventions have shaped family roles in very different ways for mothers from different social backgrounds.

Donzelot's notion of the policing of the family continues in current policy interventions through reform programmes such as Work for Welfare and Sure Start. Originally New Labour's family policy was concerned with getting mothers back into paid employment in order to reduce family (and, in particular, child) poverty. Current family policy continues to emphasize the role of professional intervention in the family, with a primary focus on safeguarding children (see also Chapter 9). The recent change in the title of the Government Department responsible for family policy to the Department for Children, Schools and Families reflects the welfare partnerships in relation to children and families, and the Coalition Government's key priorities for family policy clearly demonstrate the commitment to and direction of welfare provision for families, with an emphasis on early intervention, supporting parents and parental relationships, and safeguarding children (HM Government, 2010b).

Globalization and the family

Belonging and having a sense of identity are universal needs and can be seen in global patterns of family and community organization. However, there are many different forms of family and community organization, and contemporary studies help us to understand 'how relatedness and ideas of kinship may be composed of various components – substance, feeding, living together, procreation, emotion' (Carsten, 2000: 34).

One way that we can explore this is through the institution of marriage and how this reflects a set of traditions, values and beliefs within a society. Throughout the

Polygamy – a type of marriage involving three or more people.

Polyandry – the marriage of one woman to two or more men.

Polygyny – the marriage of one man to two or more women.

Monogamy – system of marriage between a man and a woman.

world we can identify different types of marital organization. *Polygamous* marriages relate to marriages of more than two partners: *polyandry* involves one woman and several men, whilst *polygyny* is where a man has more than one wife. These types of marriages often exist in societies where there is a marked difference in the numbers of men and women (Macionis and Plummer, 2012). *Monogamy* refers to a marriage between one man and one woman (Murdock, 1949), and until March 2013 this was the legally accepted type of marriage in the UK. Since that time, same-sex marriages have been legal. Usually, partners choose marriage of their own free will, but some cultural practices favour arranged marriages, where parents of individuals will choose partners for them. If social workers are to be culturally competent, they need to understand these different forms of marriage and family relationships.

Table 8.1 demonstrates the pluralist nature of families throughout the world and different models of family structure and relationships. Whilst this diversity enriches societies, with the increased mobilization of populations in a globalized world it can also lead to conflicts and oppression. For example, the principle of arranged marriage prevalent in traditional societies is a consensual arrangement where individuals can choose whether or not to accept the partner chosen for them, but the process of forced marriage has led to abuse, conflict and oppression of women throughout the world.

Table 8.1 *Cultural themes and marriage*

Characteristic	Traditional societies	Industrial and post-industrial societies
Structure	Extended (married spouses embedded within a wider kinship network of explicit obligations)	Nuclear (fewer obligations towards the extended kinship network)
Authority	Patriarchal	Some patriarchal features but authority divided more equally
Number of spouses at one time	Mostly one spouse, but some have polygamous relationships	Monogamous
Who selects the spouse?	Usually the parents	Individuals select their own spouse
Inheritance	Rigid set of rules, which are usually related to the father's line of descent	Highly individualistic

Source: Adapted from Henslin, 2010

A fifth of all girls in the developing world are married by the age of 18 and one in seven before the age of 15. In certain countries (Niger, Chad, Mali, Bangladesh, Guinea and the Central African Republic), over 60% of girls are in early or forced marriages. Early and forced marriages are also prevalent in Europe, with the highest rates in Georgia (17%), Turkey (14%) and Ukraine (10%). It is estimated that, in 2010, 400 girls and young women in Britain were forced into marriage, with the majority of cases involving families from South Asia. Forced marriages can also involve kidnapping, physical abuse and rape. Legislation in England and Wales makes it a criminal offence to force a person into marriage and parents could face up to two years in jail (Strickland, 2013). Social workers need to understand the oppression and disadvantage that women may experience in order to support and advocate for them.

A further aspect of relationship and family formation is related to global processes of the technological revolution, which has opened up opportunities for on-line dating, cyber relationships and cybersex. Whilst this can be advantageous for many and demonstrates new forms of communication and social engagement in the global world, it can also increase vulnerability and exploitation. Although much of the literature on on-line grooming and exploitation focuses on children and adolescents, there is some evidence that vulnerable adults are groomed on-line, with people with bipolar disorders being particularly susceptible to on-line relationship abuse. Cybersex can also cause problems in families as it may lead to relationship breakdown and divorce (Schneider, 2000).

Conclusion

This chapter has explored the institution of family and its central place within the ideological and policy context of society. There are both continuities and change in the nature and structure of the family. Cree (2000) has argued that there is an institutionalization of practice in relation to the family, but much social work practice remains structured around an outdated model of the family and fails to reflect the experiences of many service users. This is an important issue for social workers to address in their role as advocates and in looking at ways to empower some of the most vulnerable people of society.

The changing nature of the family and the move away from the normative conjugal family model has led to some commentators arguing that the family is in crisis or decline. However, the family remains a central feature of government policy and welfare intervention. Since 1979, all UK governments have focused on family values as a cornerstone of policy and ideology, reflecting a functionalist perspective of the role of the sub-system in social stability. Thus the family is not just a private institution, but is located within a political environment and dominant set of ideas.

Until the late nineteenth century, the family unit was seen as a private domain, but throughout the twentieth century and into the twenty-first, there has been increased state involvement in family policy and family development. State care of children in the early 1960s and 1970s was largely in residential homes, which were small and mirrored family units. In the 1980s, social work intervention with families demonstrated a preference for family-based care (e.g. foster care, as opposed to residential care). There were lots of initiatives to close down residential homes (based on the notion that they were not good for children, owing to the impact of institutionaliza-tion and concerns about residential home abuse, which was highlighted through various scandals).

Saltiel (2013) argues that the vast majority of families that social workers work with experience some form of uncertainty and complexity, and Farmer et al. (2013) argue that there is a long history of children being brought up by members of the extended family when parents are not able to look after them. Thus it is impor-tant for social workers to understand the range of family networks that co-exist in post-modernity and how these might impact on family relationships and experi-ences.

Summary points

- Families have changed, but the majority of children still live in two-parent fami-lies.
- An understanding of sociological perspectives on the family helps us to look at our own values and acknowledge that people may not have the same networks of support.
- Family has become idealized and is often seen as a safe and secure place. However, abuse and disadvantage occur in some families. This may lead to moral dilemmas and tensions for social workers in practice.
- Caring is an important function of the family and in community care policies, but is structured around a particular notion of family formation and family roles.

Questions for discussion

- Is the family still the best place to bring up children? Justify your response to this question.
- There is evidence to suggest that your own experience of family affects how you perceive the nature of family life. How can sociological perspectives on the family help you to understand the diverse nature of family life?
- To what extent does the professional role with families adopt a surveillance or a supportive function? Are the two necessarily mutually exclusive?
- Government policy reflects a commitment to the promotion of safer communi-ties. What evidence is there that the community and family contribute to the stability of society or that there is a breakdown in the structure and function of these sub-systems?

Further reading

Chambers, D. (2012) *A Sociology of Family Life*. Cambridge: Polity
This book provides a comprehensive introduction to key sociological issues about the family and community. It provides a useful discussion of historical changes in family formations, as well as engaging with current issues, such as issues of morality and the role of the family.

Gilchrist, A. and Taylor, M. (2011) *The Short Guide to Community Development Processes.* **Bristol: Policy Press**

This is a very accessible book that introduces the reader to key contemporary issues about the politics and practices of community development and provides useful insights into the nature of community.

Kemshall, H. and Wilkinson, B. (2011) (eds) *Good Practice in Assessing Risk: Current Knowledge, Issues and Approaches.* **London: Jessica Kingsley**

This is a collection of contributions based on current research into risk and assessment. The chapter by Boeck and Fleming is particularly helpful for understanding issues of social capital.

9 Children and Young People

Practice with children and their families has consistently been a dominant and controversial aspect of social work practice for the past 70 years, but the concept of childhood as a distinct social category is a relatively new one. The sociology of childhood is a fast-growing body of sociological knowledge, and an understanding of key concepts and theories is an important aspect of understanding the nature of social work practice with children and young people.

> ## The key issues that will be explored in this chapter are:
>
> - childhood as a unitary and global concept
> - the social construction of childhood as a social category
> - social disadvantage in relation to the category of childhood
> - risk and childhood
> - the particular issues that face children who are seeking asylum
> - the importance of sociological understanding in informing social work practice with children in contemporary society.

> ## By the end of this chapter, you should be able to:
>
> - identify childhood as a distinct social category and a form of social division that exists within society
> - consider the differential childhood experiences that exist within contemporary British society and globally
> - explore sociological theories of childhood with a view to understanding the changing social meanings of childhood in society
> - discuss the modern child as a focus of state social concern and its relevance for contemporary social work practice.

Childhood as an area of sociological inquiry

While modern sociology has explored and developed theories concerning social divisions such as class, gender, race and the family, the period of existence known as childhood has until the past 20 years or so been largely ignored as a concern for sociological inquiry. It would be fair to say that when children have been subject to concern, this has usually been subsumed under the categories of 'the family' or 'education'. Corsaro (2011) views the marginalization of children within sociology as an extension of the marginalization of children within society as a whole. This takes place within social and academic worlds occupied and dominated by adults. More recently there has been a growth of sociological interest in the lives of children, which has arisen as a part of sociology's concern with minority and socially excluded groups within society. Hence sociology's rediscovery of childhood is a part of a wider phenomenon of the sociological study of the biographies and experiences of excluded minority groups such as disabled, gay and lesbian and older people in our society. As children have become more visible, this has been as a reflection of their status as 'becomings' rather than 'beings', as the dominant approaches within sociology and social welfare focus upon what types of adults children will become (Qvortrup, 1991).

More recently, however, as reflected in the children's rights movement and new areas of academic study entitled childhood studies, the lives and experiences of children in terms of who they are as opposed to what they may become have become legitimate areas of inquiry. This chapter will illustrate how sociological perspectives on the construction of childhood provide a useful means for understanding our assumptions about children and how these assumptions have influenced social work practice.

The emergence of childhood

Early sociological and historical interest in the study of childhood is characterized by an analysis of the emergence of childhood as a distinct social role in society. The work of Ariès (1962) has been influential in gaining an understanding that conceptions of childhood have varied over time and are culturally and historically situated. Childhood as a social role and category separate from adulthood began to emerge in the late eighteenth century. A protectionist view of childhood emerged with concerns about the moral and physical welfare of children, leading to numerous legislative controls and much regulation. This recognition of childhood and the acknowledgement of children's welfare and rights were highlighted by specific pieces of legislation and policy, primarily concerned with the protection of children from abuse. In addition, in the mid-nineteenth century, laws were passed to prevent children from working in factories, accompanied by a framework for the education of children and the recognition of the need for specific interventions in the case of juvenile delinquency (Fraser, 1984). This period was significant as children were no longer wage earners, but were school pupils. Nevertheless, class divisions in childhood remained firmly embedded (Hendrick, 1992). While many welfare initiatives offered genuine protection for children, they also demonstrated increasing state control and regulation over children's lives. Working-class children particularly came under increasing scrutiny from the state and its agencies, and out of these reforms emerged the early activities of modern social work (Horner, 2013).

Through the state's focus upon improving the lives of working-class children, there appeared to emerge a consensus on the notion of what constitutes an ideal or natural childhood: a childhood that is good and beneficial for children, families and society as a whole, or, as Hendrick (1992) states, 'a maturing bourgeois domestic ideal' which constructed children as vulnerable, innocent and in need of protection by adults.

What is childhood?

There is no single, agreed definition of childhood as its meaning changes in relation to the social context in which it is created. The questions about what is childhood and when it begins and ends may seem straightforward, but they involve challenging 'taken for granted' assumptions about childhood and exploring a range of differing theories and perspectives across the social sciences. It may be worthwhile here distinguishing between the notion of being a child and the concept of childhood itself. In biological terms, a child is someone who is biologically immature or has not yet reached puberty. In legal terms, a child may be defined as a *minor*, someone who does not exercise specific legal rights and responsibilities by virtue of their age. Being a child can be seen as a biological and physical state characterized by certain physiological and psychological stages (see Freud and Piaget). Wyness (2011) suggests that childhood is an abstract set of ideas or conceptions, and children are the grounded physical manifestations of childhood. The ideas that we hold about the nature of childhood are said to define children's lives and the relationship they have with others in society, whether they be real or imagined. The perspective that although children exist, childhood is socially constructed will be discussed later in this chapter.

The term 'childhood' implies a period of existence which is fixed and essentialist. *Fixed* suggests that there is an assumed consensus that childhood begins and ends at particular ages, that this is unchanging, and that this period called childhood can be viewed over different historical periods. In this sense, it could be argued that the stages of childhood are the same in twenty-first-century Britain as they were in Victorian Britain. When sociologists refer to the notion of something being *essentialist*, it is suggested that there are particularly defining characteristics or traits associated with it.

Exercise: defining features of childhood

- List 10 of the essential features and characteristics associated with childhood.
- Compare with a fellow student or colleague.
- How many do you have in common? Are these features or traits common to all children and to all societies?

This may have proved a more challenging exercise than you first thought, as you realize that many of the traits associated with childhood tend to be culturally specific and tend to describe your own experience of childhood, your perception of your children's childhood or what you hope childhood is or wish it was like. What might have emerged from your own discussions are images of different childhoods based upon different childhood experiences rather than a period of life which is characterized by common distinguishing features. Some insight into understanding childhood can be gained through comparative studies which demonstrate the way in which different societies develop different conceptions of childhood, adding further weight to the argument that childhood is socially constructed. What determines childhood and what distinguishes childhood from other stages such as adulthood is an interesting and challenging question and alludes to the perspective that childhood is neither natural nor essential and the distinction of adulthood from childhood is predominantly a false one.

Several definitions of childhood tend to define it in negative terms: that is, a child can be defined as a young human or someone who has not reached puberty or adulthood, the period between infancy and adolescence. Hence some of the defining characteristics of childhood are described by the absence of something as opposed to common unifying traits. It could be argued that these definitions tend to define adulthood rather than childhood, as they imply that adulthood signifies the period in which human beings are recognized and acquire status and standing in society.

For sociologists and for social workers and other practitioners who work with children, what becomes evident in understanding the history and discourses concerning childhood is that it is almost impossible to avoid adult interpretations, adult concerns and adults' constructions of those histories and experiences. For sociologists, researching childhood in itself can be problematic, as the sociology of childhood becomes adults' constructions of childhood experiences. Ensuring that knowledge and research are constructed through the engagement of children and through the employment of a child-centred methodology remains a challenge for sociologists.

To many people, this image of a child smoking crosses the line between appropriate adult and child behaviour. (© Alexander Hafemann/iStock)

Childhood as a social construct

The view that childhood is a social construct is relatively new, and an area in which Ariès (1962) and Denzin (1987) have been particularly influential. Ariès (1962) examined literary and artistic representations of children and put forward the theory that childhood did not exist in medieval society, and it only emerged around the fifteenth century. By examining the depiction of children in art and literature, Ariès argued that, prior to the fifteenth century, children were viewed as miniature adults who wore similar clothes to them, were treated like them, worked in factories or on the land and did not engage in playful activities. He concluded that there was no distinct period known as childhood, and there was little separation between the adult and child worlds. Ariès was eager to assert, however, that although childhood was not recognized, this did not mean that children were not liked or cared for. He believed that children were nurtured until around the age of 7 and they were then deemed ready to join the adult world. He drew a distinction between the lack of concern for the physical and mental well-being of children in medieval society and the obsessions regarding the moral, physical, educational and sexual problems of the modern child.

Ariès's work has, however, been challenged and undermined, with critics accusing him of a flawed methodology due to his depen--- --- on artistic and literary representations of children, which can b--- --- --- ve and unreliable (Hendrick, 1992). This evidence can be ---- --- --- he images and writings about children may --- --- --- --- --- --- children should be viewed as opposed to --- --- --- --- --- ice. While methodologically flawed, Ariès --- --- --- --- t in the study of childhood and for the v--- --- --- --- --- velopmental notion that is important w---

Jenks (2--- --- --- --- --- ersal, and sees the distinction betw--- --- --- --- --- nson (in Best, 2005: 306) views the --- --- --- --- ood is seen as a route to adulthood --- --- --- --- which children are constructed as --- --- --- --- ood and adulthood are seen as bir--- --- --- --- another. For example, adulthood --- --- --- --- responsibilities, work, voting, an--- --- --- --- of these factors.

Structur---

Sociologica--- --- ---erning 'agency' and 'structure' are also reflected within the range of theories and perspectives that seek to explain the phenomena of childhood. The ability of children to be self-determining is fundamental to social work practice; however, the extent which children are recognized as social actors who possess the capacity to respond to shape their own future and determine for themselves is a matter of debate within modern welfare.

Functionalist perspectives on childhood

Some structural theories of childhood tend to focus on the role of socialization within society as a way of preparing future citizens (see also Chapter 8). These predominantly functionalist theories regarding the role of socialization have dominated much of sociological thinking in understanding children and childhood. Functionalist perspectives identify childhood as a distinct stage from adulthood, emphasizing the role of socialization and suggesting that childhood plays a preparatory function in becoming an adult. Socialization as performed by society's institutions of the family and school plays an essential role whereby children absorb the values, standards and norms of the society in which they live.

Most theories (e.g. Parsons and Bales, 1955) emphasize the early socialization which takes place in the family, in which children are passively moulded into hopefully responsible members of society (see Chapter 8). This view offers a rather deterministic view of childhood in which children are passive recipients in the process and play no role in shaping their future or creating the society of which they are a part. Children's capacity for agency is ignored as adults become the active participants in the process, whether as parents in the family or other adults in the form of teachers, religious leaders or social workers.

Functionalist models tend to describe the process of socialization rather than focus upon how and why children become integrated into society. Within this approach Parsons viewed children in two ways: either as a threat or as a potential benefit to society, depending upon how successfully they were socialized into being responsible citizens (Parsons and Bales, 1955). However, socialization is not a one-way process, and these theories have been challenged for being overly deterministic and ignoring the part that children play in society. Children may actively resist attempts to incorporate them into the dominant culture and create counter-cultures.

Marxist perspectives on socialization

Marxist perspectives also focus on the importance of socialization in understanding childhood and its role in producing a future workforce. They view socialization as the transmission of capitalist, patriarchal and racist values and ideology. As far as children are concerned, the welfare state represents a process of state socialization in which public space is created for children in the form of nurseries and schools. Children are thus socialized into adopting dominant values and beliefs. Mackie (1987) states that the main purposes of gender socialization are to protect the interests of patriarchy and to maintain the inequality between men and women. Hence socialization is important in reproducing inequality and power within society in relation to gender, race and class as well as other forms of social division.

The structural location of childhood

Societal concerns and sociological interest regarding the experiences of children in society have led some sociologists (Corsaro, 2011; Qvortrup, 1994) to view childhood as a structural category or a social division that is a permanent part of society. Though childhood is a social construct, this does not mean that childhood does not exist. Best (2005) goes a step further in recognizing the concept of childhood as a *state-sponsored* social division. He suggests that the period of childhood is something that is not biological or naturally occurring, but a period of life which is socially constructed. To a certain extent it is constructed by the modern state through legislation and social policies and the instructions of the criminal justice system, the education system and health and social welfare services.

The significance that is attributed to the state of childhood is one that does not necessarily reflect the status and value of children in society. What emerges is a rather contradictory and dichotomous position where the activities of the state through legislation and social policies and state institutions could be argued to be more concerned with promoting adults' concerns and interests and those of society as a whole, which may not be consistent with the interests, wishes and needs of all children in society. The recognition of the needs and rights of children and their compatibility with the rights and needs of adults is a common ethical and professional dilemma that challenges practitioners in the field of social work. This can be seen in relation to Government responses to childcare, in which plans to extend the school working day may be of benefit to the state, employers and possibly working parents, but may have different implications for children who could be looked after in day care from 7.30 a.m. to 6.00 p.m.

Childhood as a structural division is inter-related with other social divisions such as class, gender and race, and there are also further intra-structural divisions within the category of child, such that the diversity of childhood experiences in Britain challenges the notion that childhood is a fixed entity. As James and Prout (1997: 8) put this, 'childhood is a variable of social analysis. It can never be entirely divorced from other variables such as class, gender, or ethnicity. Comparative and cross-cultural analysis reveals a variety of childhoods rather than single and universal phenomena.'

Although the child population in Britain had been in decline since the 1970s, recently this has begun to change. Whilst there were approximately 12.1 million children in Britain in 2001, the child population is expected to rise to 13 million by 2035 and varies regionally and across ethnic groups (Office for National Statistics, 2011). The effects of net migration of men and women of childbearing age are seen as the main reason for this. The child population is greater in Northern Ireland than in South-West England, and the ethnic minority population is younger than the majority white group. One in three children are from an ethnic minority group, and this trend is set to continue with a decline in birth rate among white middle-class families and an increase in accompanied and unaccompanied children seeking asylum. Children of mixed parentage represent the fastest-growing ethnic category (see Chapter 4) and are the fourth category after white, Pakistani, and Indian. Over 50% of the mixed population in the UK is under 16 years of age (Office for National Statistics, 2011).

Of particular significance for social work is a picture within British society of not one childhood, but many different childhoods characterized not by innocence, or images represented in Enid Blyton books, but by differences and diversity in relation to class, ethnicity, migration status and wealth. The state, through the activities of social workers and other occupations, is concerned with intervention in and regulation of childhood, and evidence suggests that social workers are more likely to be

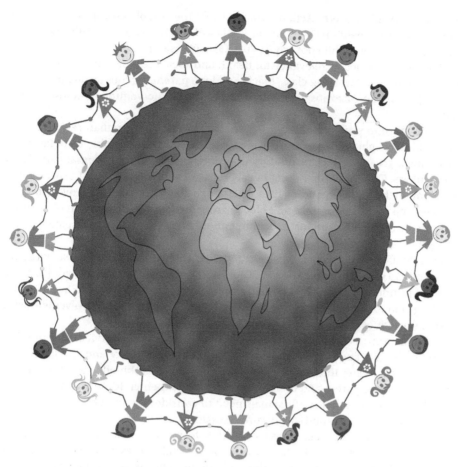

A symbolic representation of the diversity of childhood across the globe – although what childhoods are missing from this image? (© prawny/iStock)

involved in work with children and families from specific socio-economic groups and ethnic backgrounds (Davies, 2008; Owen and Statham, 2009). There is no national research evidence concerning referral rates of minority ethnic families to social services departments; however, the significance of race and ethnic categorization is an important factor in working with black and minority ethnic children and families (see also Chapter 8).

The concept of childhood as a single entity is not reflected by the diversity of experience of children in contemporary British society. The 2011 Census highlights differential childhood experiences regarding family structure, ethnicity, poverty and housing. The problems associated with defining and understanding poverty have been discussed in Chapter 2. Child poverty can be measured by the number of children living in households with less than 60% of median income. Despite Tony Blair's intention that 'our historic aim will be for ours to be the first generation to end child poverty' (Blair, 1999), as well as specific attempts by Labour governments to reduce child poverty, the number of children living in such households remains at

3.6 million (Child Poverty Action Group, 2012). The Joseph Rowntree Foundation predicts that the Coalition Government's policy of cuts in welfare spending will result in a significant rise in child poverty by 2020 (MacInnes et al., 2013).

Poverty has particular relevance for health and social care practice as 'disproportionate numbers of working class, black, and lone parent families attract the gaze of state agencies and are exposed to state-directed family interventions' (Goldson, 1997: 24).

Babies born to poorer families are more likely to be born prematurely and to be of low birth weight. They are more likely to experience health problems in later life, including a greater risk of respiratory infection, gastro-enteritis, dental caries and tuberculosis. Children from poorer households are at increased risk of experiencing accidents in the home, including fires. As Holman (1978: 193) notes: 'In overcrowded homes, chip pans, knives, pills and bleach are more likely to be in reach of children . . . parents on income support . . . cannot afford a fireguard . . . a stair gate . . . or a playpen.'

Poverty affects children's self-esteem and their ability to participate in social activities, and can have a long-term legacy. Children raised in poverty are, as adults, more likely to be unemployed or in low-paid employment, are more likely to live in social housing, and to have a greater risk of alcohol and drug abuse and involvement with criminal activities (Child Poverty Action Group, 2012).

Children from poorer backgrounds are unlikely to receive the services they require. Despite what we know about the correlation between poverty and the likelihood of experiencing care, there are no longitudinal studies of the effects of poverty on parents' ability to parent and their experiences while their children are looked after. Social workers and other professionals need to consider the impact poverty has on the lives of service users and social work assessments.

There is tension between those who wish to protect children from the adult world and those who see the best protection for children as recognizing children as independent beings and giving them the same rights as adults. Firestone (1971: 70) regards childhood as an institution of oppression, stating that 'for women and children to become fully human they need to be liberated from childhood'. Goldson (1997) argues that the structural relationship between adults and children is characterized by power and dependency. This is presented as natural and good for social order. Within this relationship, adults are mature, rational and strong and they provide and protect, whereas children are immature, irrational, they receive, consume and are in need of protection. On this view, age is seen as a fundamental determinant in the distribution of rights, power and participation. Goldson goes on to discuss how the social, economic and political position of childhood in capitalist societies is based upon exclusion and marginality. Childhood is characterized not just by interpersonal dependency but also by structured dependency. The notion that children do not belong in the public space is an important consideration in the maintenance of boundaries between the adult and child worlds. Lee (2001) discusses how throughout the nineteenth and twentieth centuries children were gradually removed from the streets and the workplace through education and early social work, and how the concept of a 'child out of place' is used to refer to children who do not conform to middle-class, Western ideals that children are dependent and require adult supervision, particularly in public places.

The separation of the adult and child worlds is a complex and contradictory one as some sociologists and political commentators bemoan the early demise of childhood. Their concerns are centred on a consumerist culture in which children are bombarded with marketing and advertisements. On the other hand, for some young people the effect of economic and education policies is to prolong their dependency on adults in order to secure a home and reasonable living conditions.

Social action theories

The view that children are social actors is consistent with that of interpretative sociologists who regard socialization as an interactive process and stress the part played by individuals in shaping society. Emphasis is placed on how individuals create, resist and act upon different roles (see Chapter 1). Socialization is seen as a complex process in which children are free to make choices, although those choices may be constrained (Cree, 2000). The social institutions of the family, school and health and social care play a powerful role in regulating childhood.

The concept of a *tribal child* (James and James, 2012) provides a framework for discussing how children actively construct their own cultural worlds and participate in society. This view acknowledges the difference in status between adults and children and describes how children and young people develop their own hierarchies, language and culture. It has influenced the use of ethnographic approaches in research with children, as illustrated by Iona and Peter Opie's work in the 1950s and 1960s regarding children and play (Marsh and Bishop, 2014). Stanley Cohen in his seminal work *Folk Devils and Moral Panics* (1972) provides a framework for understanding the societal reaction to youth culture, and Angela McRobbie (1977) addresses the gender blindness of study in this area in exploring girls and sub-cultures (see Chapter 7).

Critical perspectives

Critical perspectives provide a reconstruction of childhood built on the premise that children are active social agents and that power relations exist between adults and children (James and Prout, 1997). The view that children are experts on their own situation promotes child-led research. Whilst adults may possess more knowledge, children have a better understanding of what it means to be a child; both adults and children possess competence – just different ones.

This section considers children as active agents in decision-making and in relation to ages of responsibility; in the following section we will then explore the issues raised for children as active agents in care-giving or children as carers.

The ways in which children participate in society can be viewed through the ways in which they assume responsibility for their actions. This is a highly contested matter and is linked to our ideas and perception of childhood. If children are perceived as being innocent, shy and immature, then they will assume very little responsibility for their actions. On the other hand, if children are deemed to be capable, rational and confident, then it could be said that they are responsible for their own actions. Levels of childhood responsibility are linked to debates around children's rights and are of particular relevance for practitioners working with children, especially in social work, education and health.

The following exercise highlights the different ages at which children are afforded certain adult rights and choices and reflects the lack of clarity that exists in legislation defining and governing childhood.

Exercise: childhood and the age of responsibility

- From what age can a child have a bank account?
- What is the age for compulsory school attendance?
- What is the age of criminal responsibility in (a) Scotland, (b) England and Wales?
- From what age can children be given an Anti-Social Behaviour Order?
- What is the sexual age of consent for (a) heterosexual and (b) same-sex relationships?
- From what age can children work?
- From what age can children buy cigarettes?
- From what age can children enter the armed forces?
- From what age can children learn to drive a car?
- From what age can children marry without parental consent?

One of the most controversial areas in which children are expected to assume legal responsibilities for their actions is that of criminality. Following the murder of the toddler James Bulger in 1993 by two 10-year-old boys, the release of his killers in 2000 and the torture and attempted murder of two young boys by two other boys (aged 10 and 12) in Edlington, South Yorkshire, in 2010, there has been debate regarding the age of criminal responsibility in Britain. There are many who believe that the age of criminality is set too low in Britain in comparison with other European countries. A report for the Centre for Crime and Justice Studies by Allen (2006) calls for the age to be raised from 10 to 14, as too many children are prosecuted and criminalized. It calls for greater emphasis on the educational, social and mental health needs of children and suggests care proceedings should be used for younger offenders. The report recommends the phasing out of the use of prison for 15 and 16 year olds and the use of restorative justice. The United Nations Standard Minimum Rules for the Administration of Juvenile Justice (the Beijing Rules) also caution against setting the age of criminality too low:

> The minimum age of criminal responsibility differs widely owing to history and culture. The modern approach would be to consider whether a child can live up to the moral and psychological components of criminal responsibility; that is, whether a child, by virtue of her or his individual discernment and understanding, can be held responsible for essentially antisocial behaviour. If the age of criminal responsibility is fixed too low or if there is no lower age limit at all, the notion of criminal responsibility would become meaningless. In general, there is a close relationship between the notion of responsibility for delinquent or criminal behaviour and other social rights and responsibilities (such as marital status, civil majority, etc.).

> (United Nations, 1985)

However, at the time of writing it is unlikely that the age will change, as the age of responsibility is not set in isolation but reflects society's history and construction of childhood and is linked to other aspects of rights and responsibilities for children.

The issue of children's rights is a matter of contentious debate amongst politicians, policy makers, parents, children and welfare practitioners. British childcare policy is centred on notions that children are vulnerable and need support and protection, and these principles are embodied in legislation and policy (Children Act, 1989; Every Child Matters, 2004; Children Act, 2004). Situations where children are abused, neglected, not listened to, not trusted and not believed have led to a growing realization that adults do not always protect children, nor do they always make decisions that are in their best interests. The perception that children are possessed by adults, are dependent upon them and thus in need of their protection is slowly changing to one that recognizes that not only do children have needs, but they also have the right to have their needs met (Lansdown, 2001). The adoption by Britain of the UN and European Charter of Children's Rights reflects this change, and a view that children are capable of becoming self-determining agents with the ability to make their own informed choices is a central feature of the children's rights movement. The United Nations Convention on the Rights of the Child defines a child as *every human being under the age of 18* unless the legal age of majority in a country is lower. The main principles are as follows:

- All rights apply to all children without exception or discrimination of any kind (Article 2).
- The best interests of the child must be a primary consideration in all actions concerning children (Article 3).
- States have an obligation to ensure that as far as possible every child's survival and development are promoted (Article 6).
- Children's views must be taken into account in all matters affecting them (Article 12).

However, while Britain has ratified both policies, the earlier discussion on differential childhood experiences suggests that it has a long way to go to fully realize these principles in practice. Article 12 poses a particular challenge for adults in working with children as to the age at which and how far children are able to make decisions for themselves. However, Revans (2007) reports on a project where seven local authorities are working with looked after children and involving them in care decisions in order to improve the quality of their lives.

Under the Children Act (2004) the first Children's Commissioner was appointed in Britain, with a remit 'to promote awareness of views and interests of children. He is expected to raise the profile of the issues that affect and concern children in England, and promote awareness and understanding of their views and interests among all sectors of society, both public and private' (Department for Education and Skills, 2004).

Critical perspectives promote children as being relatively autonomous and competent, and there are many issues in social care and health practice in which children's rights to self-determination are crucial. Social workers may find themselves in a hospital setting, working with children suffering with long-term or acute conditions where consent to treatment is both a legal and an ethical issue. There are occasions where a social worker is the lone practitioner who is advocating on behalf of a child who does not wish to consent to treatment.

The concept of 'Gillick competence' or the 'Fraser test' is the benchmark by which professionals have to ascertain the ability of children to provide consent. In 1985, the House of Lords controversially ruled that children under 16 years old could be given contraceptive advice or treatment without parental knowledge or agreement (NSPCC, 2014a). A person who has reached the age of 16 years should be regarded as competent to give consent unless there is evidence to the contrary. Competence should be assessed in the same way as it is in adults. The rules were revised by the Department of Health in 2001, stating that the 'Gillick' or 'Fraser' test is about a child's capacity to consent and not about what other people consider right. It recognizes that it is good practice to involve families of 16 and 17 year olds in the decision-making process unless the young person specifically requests that this should not happen. It also states that attempts should be made to persuade the young person to confide in their families, but stresses that confidentiality should be maintained unless there is a risk of harm.

The rights of children to make decisions about their lives and also to participate in adult arenas challenge notions of childhood and children's rightful place. The UN Charter has ensured that children's rights are now a global concern. Lee (2001) suggests that the UN Charter represents an abstract set of principles without any practicable applications, and makes several promises of providing global spaces for all children. Rather than extending the rights of children across the world, he suggests that such a charter creates more ambiguity regarding the position of children and their relationship with adults throughout the world.

Exercise: children and consent

You are a hospital social worker. Max, aged 15, has been diagnosed with terminal cancer and after several long spells in hospital has told you that he no longer wishes to continue with his treatment.

- What do you consider are the main issues in enabling Max to make a decision about his treatment?
- What other areas within social work practice may involve a child's capacity to give consent?

Children as active care-givers

The concepts of formal and informal caring have been studied within sociology, primarily with respect to women (see Chapter 3), yet children have cared for relatives for centuries. However, it was not until the 1980s that the extent and nature of the informal care provided by children was identified through research. The issues that young carers face highlight the strengths and abilities that many children possess, rather than emphasizing their vulnerability and lack of responsibility. The issues facing children who care for parents or siblings have remained relatively hidden in social work practice, though the consequences of caring can have a major impact on their experiences of childhood and later life.

The proportion of children involved in caring has risen significantly. In 2001, the Census identified over 175,000 young carers in Britain, whereas estimates in 2011 suggest that the number is near to 700,000.There are a further 3 million children in the UK who have a family member with a disability. Approximately a quarter of a million young people in the UK live with a parent who is misusing a Class A drug, and 920,000 young people in the UK are children of alcoholic parents. It is most likely that the official statistics for young carers under-represent of the numbers of children involved (Children's Society, 2013).

Although many young carers are hidden from education, health and social services, the Children's Society (2013) identifies some of the factors that can identify that a child is a young carer. These include underachievement at school, suffering depression or tiredness, school absence, inability to take part in extra-curricular activities and a parent who often misses appointments. The largest survey to date of young carers in the UK has been conducted by Dearden and Becker (2004) on behalf of the Children's Society. Their *Young Carers' Report* found that the amount of time spent caring ranged between 10 and 20 hours a week, with a small minority of children working over 50 hours, leading to significant implications for schooling and educational difficulties. Caring can be a very long-term commitment for many children, and can start at an early age. One-fifth of young carers and their families receive no other support except for their contact with a specialist young carers' project, and usually social services support is the most common external service received.

The experiences of young carers challenge our ideas of an appropriate childhood. Children may be seen as in need of care and protection, particularly when it is judged that the roles of parents and children have been reversed. Children as carers can be assessed under the Carers Recognition Act (1995) and under Section 17 of the Children Act (1989) as a *child in need*. At the time of writing, the Children and Family Act (2014) requires local authorities to treat young carers as having the same rights to a full assessment of their needs as adult carers. However, in relation to involvement with social workers, children are more likely to be assessed if they are living with a lone parent or if they are caring for an adult with drug or alcohol problems (Dearden and Becker, 2004). Such a referral to social services may reflect potential child protection concerns, and the risk of being accommodated by social workers can represent a real fear for young carers and their relatives and prevent them from seeking support.

Case study

Ravinder is 12 and lives with his mother and younger sister, Kuldeep, aged 9. His mother has suffered from severe depression for 10 years and Ravinder has provided care for his mother and sister. Lately his mother has been having difficulty sleeping at night and most days she stays in bed until 11 a.m. A typical school day for Ravinder involves him waking at 6 a.m. to get himself and Kuldeep ready for school. He takes Kuldeep to school and usually arrives at his own school late. On their return from school, Ravinder does some housework and prepares the family meal. Ravinder loves his mother and appears very protective towards her. He says that he is her best friend.

- What impact may Ravinder's caring responsibilities have on his personal well-being, education and social life?
- What responsibilities do you consider appropriate for children to assume?
- How does this compare with your and your fellow students' experiences?
- As a social worker, what do you consider to be the individual needs of each member of this family?

Childhood, globalization and risk

The ideas associated with a risk society (Beck, 1992) permeate contemporary sociological thought and current welfare practice in terms of the assessment and management of risk, and nowhere is this more evident than in the area of social work practice with children and their families. Within social work with children, risk is strongly associated with the potential for harm and is defined in relation to physical, emotional and sexual harm and neglect. The risks of harm for children by their parents are highlighted by the Cawson Report (Cawson, 2002), which suggests that:

- 7% of children experience serious physical abuse at the hands of their parents or carers during childhood.
- 1% of children experience sexual abuse by a parent or carer and 3% per cent by another relative during childhood.
- 6% of children experience serious absence of care at home during childhood.
- 16% of children experience serious maltreatment by parents, of whom one-third experience more than one type of maltreatment.

The rather narrow focus of safeguarding children from harm as enshrined in child protection law and policy in England and Wales fails to recognize child protection as a global concern. According to UNICEF (2006), *child protection* refers to the prevention of and response to violence, exploitation and abuse against children – including commercial sexual exploitation, trafficking, child labour and harmful traditional practices such as female genital mutilation/cutting and child marriage. Welfare organizations in the UK have at times failed to respond to the needs and safety of children who are subject to forms of child abuse that go beyond Eurocentric norms and definitions. However, the risks associated with modern childhood appear to be more extensive. There are major concerns regarding the risk associated with food and obesity, 'stranger danger', road traffic accidents, alcohol and drug use, mental heath problems, mobile phone use and use of the internet.

What do you think this photograph suggests about societal attitudes to childhood, risk and responsibility? (© Drew Geraets/Flickr)

Reflection

The effects of globalization on the lives of children can be witnessed by the numbers of children who seek asylum and the proportion of women and children who are illegally trafficked. Amnesty International suggests that half the world's refugee population are children (*http://www.amnesty.org*). Social work with asylum-seeking children and their families is a rapidly growing area of practice and one for which many social workers feel ill prepared, though this may change as they become more familiar with it. In 2011, there were 19,804 asylum applications to the Home Office and 1,277 of these were from unaccompanied minors (Wright, 2012). There are different legal responsibilities for social services depending upon whether children seeking asylum are accompanied or unaccompanied. According to the UK Border Agency (2013), an unaccompanied asylum-seeking child is a person who, at the time of making the asylum application:

- is, or (if there is no proof) appears to be, under 18
- is applying for asylum in his or her own right
- has no adult relative or guardian to turn to in this country.

Grady (2004: 134) also notes that 'the concept of family is a problematic one concerning asylum as little is done by immigration officials to check the relationships of the adults who accompany children. So whilst adults may accompany children, it is not clear whether the adults have responsibility for them.'

Despite the children's rights agenda, British childcare policy continues to be based primarily upon principles of welfare and protection for children, but there is genuine concern that these values are not afforded to all children, particularly in relation to children's immigration status. As Masters (2003) notes: 'The social work response to unaccompanied refugee children offers a good gauge to reflect on how much our professional value base and practice has been compromised by resource-led thinking and the prejudices with which we become stained through the creeping influence of the wider political agenda – both on a local and national level.'

There are concerns that the British Government's responses to accompanied and unaccompanied children contravene the UN Charter on Rights of the Child. Grady (2004) argues that the Government is able to prevent children from legally seeking support from social services as the Nationality, Immigration and Asylum Act (2002) states that families who seek support from the Secretary of State via the National Asylum Support Service (NASS) are not eligible for support from social services under the Children Act in relation to a child in need. NASS's primary function is one of housing and financial support and as an agency it is not in a position to offer support and protection to asylum-seeking children.

The Audit Commission Report *Another Country* (2000) concluded that though children may present as being mature and capable, this may hide post-traumatic stress disorder and other mental health conditions brought about by their experiences of separation and loss.

Trafficked children may be frequently confused with 'smuggled', 'separated' or 'unaccompanied asylum-seeking children', and there exists a culture of disbelief

Table 9.1 *Minors by UK country and exploitation type*

	England	Northern Ireland	Scotland	Wales	Total
Domestic servitude	20	–	1	1	22
Labour exploitation	94	–	7	1	102
Sexual exploitation	60	8	3	1	72
Not recorded	35	–	1	2	38
Total	209	8	12	5	234

Source: Home Office, 2012b

that surrounds child trafficking (NSPCC, 2012). In the UK, the number of trafficked children rose from 489 in 2011 to 549 in 2012, an increase of 12% (NSPCC, 2014b). The main reason for trafficking of girls is for sexual exploitation, followed by forced labour (Home Office, 2012b; see also Table 9.1). An emerging development in Britain and Europe is the trafficking of mainly Roma children, who are forced to beg on the streets.

A multi-agency response involving immigration staff, the police and social workers is crucial in identifying victims of child trafficking. Many children may enter the country on a false premise and with false ID and are themselves unaware of the reasons as to why they are being brought into the country. Once in the country, '50% of children go missing', and in 2011 the Government issued additional guidance safeguarding children who may have been trafficked. There is also a growing recognition of the links between child exploitation and trafficking. Immigration officers have a responsibility to inform children's services if a child's documentation is incorrect or if they have concerns about the child; however, this opportunity is missed in many situations. Social workers who conduct age assessments have a further opportunity to identify a trafficked child, but many social workers lack knowledge and they require training to recognize indicators of trafficking. This has been recognized by the Centre for Social Justice (2013: 110), which argues: 'The newly established College of Social Work should be aware of the gap in training on trafficking for social workers, and should recommend that it be added to the curriculum for student social workers.'

Case study: domestic servitude and private fostering

A 14-year-old Nigerian girl was identified by immigration services at Manchester Airport as possibly having been trafficked when suspicions were alerted about her immigration status. Immigration staff called children's social services. On calling the girl's father in Nigeria, he explained that she was on holiday with an uncle to visit friends. However, the uncle did not show up. This raised concerns that the young girl may have been trafficked for domestic servitude. The girl was housed in children's social services emergency accommodation. However, she was deported back to Nigeria a month later even though the father tried to block his daughter's return home.

(Save the Children, 2007)

- What are your reactions to the responses by the statutory agencies?
- How may attitudes and assumptions regarding race and culture affect professional responses in such a situation?
- How can social workers intervene to safeguard the welfare of the young girl?

Conclusion

An understanding of the social construction of childhood provides a useful framework within which to understand and articulate some of the issues and debates that concern social work with children and their families. The view that adults do not always know or act in the best interests of children, and the recognition that children have rights as well as needs, challenge the dominance of the welfarist approach in social work. Many adults, including parents, social workers, police officers and teachers, share the resistance to the recognition of children's rights. In social work, however, empowering children does not mean that they are able to do anything they want without consideration of their competence; rather, child-centred practice means involving children of all ages in the matters and decisions that affect them. As Lansdown (2001: 7) says, 'a commitment to respecting children's rights does not mean abandoning their welfare'.

Summary points

- Childhood is not a unitary concept; rather, a diverse range of childhoods are experienced within society.
- Childhood is socially constructed and is shaped by adults and children alike.
- Sociological perspectives are relevant in understanding contemporary debates concerning the nature of childhood within a global context.
- Social work with children and families is characterized by poverty and social exclusion.
- Recognition of the rights of children, and a willingness to work in partnership with them and their families, is essential for child-centred practice.

Questions for discussion

- Frones (1994) suggests that childhood has become more individualized, as children become consumers in their own right, with their own books, magazines, television programmes and games. Could this be seen as children acquiring greater rights and adult status, or does such individualization represent a greater division and separation between the states of being an adult and being a child?
- Are children free and innocent, or are they now blighted with adult responsibilities and concerns?
- What evidence is there to suggest that childhood is a global concept?
- How can sociological perspectives of childhood enable social workers to promote the empowerment of children?

Further reading

Corsaro, W. (2011) *The Sociology of Childhood.* **3rd edition. London: Sage**
An accessible book that provides a comprehensive overview of key sociological
theories.

James, A. and Prout, A. (1997) *Constructing and Reconstructing Childhood:*
Contemporary Issues in the Sociological Study of Childhood. **2nd edition.**
London: Falmer Press
This second edition is a useful book for students seeking a discussion of a wide range
of contemporary issues regarding the construction of childhood in a global context.

Parton, N. (2006) *Safeguarding Children: Early Intervention and Surveillance in*
a Late Modern Society. **London: Palgrave**
Incorporating contemporary social theory, this book examines the latest developments in social work policy and practice.

Wyness, M. (2011) *Childhood and Society.* **2nd edition. Basingstoke: Palgrave**
A sociological discussion of childhood within a global context that includes discussion concerning technology, education and child labour.

10 Old Age

Introduction

There is a global trend of population ageing, with a particular trend towards increased populations of people over the age of 85 (Rau et al., 2008). This continuing trend is related to decreases in fertility and mortality rates, and has shifted the ratios between older and younger people in many countries across the world (Martin et al., 2012). For the first time in 2001, according to UK statistics, the numbers of people over 65 exceeded the numbers of people under 16 (Office for National Statistics, 2001). This global trend raises a number of questions about policies for provision of older people's services and provides dilemmas and opportunities for social workers. As Weiss (2005) states, ageing populations present a global social work challenge, with the need for social workers to take greater responsibility for the care and well-being of older people. Sociological perspectives can help us to understand the social context of older age, so that we can identify solutions and best practices to work with older people in a valuing and anti-discriminatory way. Although much of the discussion in this chapter is located within the UK context, the key issues of structural context, lived experience, risks and positive approaches to old age have universal application and can contribute to a global understanding of old age to equip the social work practitioner with knowledge to adopt a cross-cultural approach and work across boundaries.

The key issues that will be explored in this chapter are:

- social definitions and context of ageing in contemporary Britain
- ageism and stereotypes of older people
- discriminatory practices in relation to older people, which relate to anti-oppressive practice and the role of social work
- social disadvantage, disempowerment and social exclusion of older people
- factors that promote positive images and experiences of older age.

By the end of this chapter you should be able to:

- identify the social construction of old age as a distinct category of adulthood
- critically explore the concept of chronological age as a basis for service provision
- demonstrate an understanding of the concepts of ageism and age discrimination
- explain the sources of disadvantage and oppression for older people
- demonstrate an understanding of positive ageing and the role of social work in the empowerment of older people.

Defining old age

Although terms such as 'older people' and the 'elderly' are widely used in both lay and academic language, the precise definition of what constitutes old age is more problematic (Victor, 2005). Traditional approaches to understanding phases in the life-course have focused on transitions between different life-stages, and one of the most frequently used definitions of old age in the Western industrial world is based on the notion of *chronology*, which views old age as a particular phase in the life-cycle, character-ized by transition from independent adulthood through retirement (Victor, 2005). Different theoretical perspectives use different criteria and approaches to explain this transition. Medical definitions of old age see this transition within the context of biological changes, whilst psychological definitions are more concerned with adaptation, moti-vation, self-esteem and resilience (Green, 2010; Heath and Schofield, 1999). Sociological definitions, on the other hand, are concerned with the social context of ageing and the construction of the life-stage through social attitudes and policies. (See Phillips et al., 2006, for further discussion of definitions.) Although it is widely acknowledged that the concept of old age is defined in cultural context and any defi-nition is open to question, in the UK chronological age is often used to identify older people as a distinct category in the life-course. (See World Health Organization, n.d.a, for a discussion of the global application of definitions of ageing.)

> **Chronology** chronological age is a measure of age related to the number of years since a person was born.

There have always been older people in societies, but in the twentieth and twenty-first centuries they have become more visible (Martin et al., 2012; Wilson, 2000). People are living longer and, at the same time, the birth rate is declining, leading to a shift in the balance of the population and in the ratio of economically active to economically inactive (Martin et al., 2012). Lower fertility rates and the increase in divorce have led to a change in the structure and size of families, and to an increase in solo living in older age, which has implications for informal care for older people. Across the industrialized world, countries have pursued policies of de-institutionalization of older people's care, which raises further issues about how as a society we care for an ageing population (Martin et al., 2012).

The demographic context

Based on a chronological definition of ageing, we can see that the number of older people in the UK is increasing and is predicted to continue to increase (see Figures 10.1 and 10.2).

Population ageing is significant as it has a number of political, economic and social implications that impact directly on social work practice. It is clear that people are living longer, although these are general figures and mask regional and socio-economic group differences. However, what is also significant is that, in general, healthy life expectancy has not risen as fast as life expectancy, creating greater demands on health and social care services. Although old age and ill health are not inextricably linked, National Health Service spending on the 65+ age group is almost double that for the under 65s (although it must be noted that there are wide variations amongst the over 65s that are not accounted for by this broad figure) (UK Parliament, 2010).

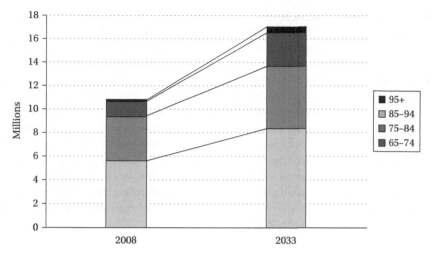

Figure 10.1   Predicted population increases 2008–33.
Source: UK Parliament, 2010.

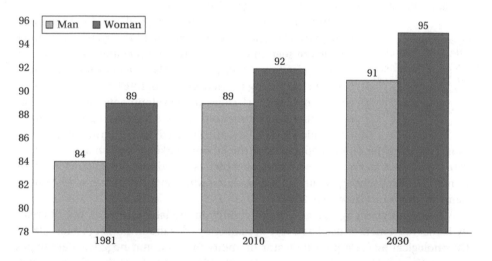

Figure 10.2   Trends in average life expectancy for men and women in the UK.
Source: UK Parliament, 2010.

Alongside the increase in life expectancy, the birth rate, as noted above, is decreasing, which is significant as the ratio of under 16s to over 65s is also changing, with over 65s outnumbering under 16s since the 2001 Census. It is predicted that, by 2035, there will be 4 million more people over 65 than under 16 (Rutherford, 2012). In 2008, there were 3.2 people of working age for every person of pensionable age. This ratio is projected to fall to 2.8 by 2033 (UK Parliament, 2010). (For further demographic statistics, go to World Health Organization, n.d.b.)

These demographic changes raise political and economic concerns about the sustainability of current models for providing health and social care for older people

(McDonald, 2010) and have been the subject of a number of recent policy reports and white papers in the UK (Department of Health, 2010, 2012, 2013a).

The recommendations set out in these reports shape the policy agenda and have implications for social work practice in terms of decisions that are made about people's eligibility for and access to services and the role of social workers in assessing and planning services to address needs. Although the focus of this chapter is on the sociology of ageing, the way that the social context is shaped provides an important backdrop for understanding older people's experiences. Two broad types of sociological perspectives can help to provide a greater understanding of older age. The first of these are structural perspectives, which explore the social patterning of society and how old age is structured within a capitalist society, leading to inequalities and differences. The second broad set of theories are social action theories, which explain experiences from an individual's perspective, identifying the role of interactions with others (see Chapter 1) (Victor, 2005)

Structural perspectives

Structural perspectives are concerned with the way that societies are structured and divided, and early social theories of ageing took this focus.

Disengagement theory older people disengage from society and other people disengage from older people. This is seen as mutually beneficial.

Within a broad theory of chronological age, Cumming and Henry (1961) proposed a *disengagement theory*, whereby older people are seen to disengage from society and society is seen to disengage from older people. This is seen as mutually beneficial in facilitating the acceptance of role changes associated with chronological changes and developments. However, it has been criticized as it sees old age in a negative light of reduced economic productivity, and is based on the normative premise that it is natural for older people to leave the labour market at a given age (J. Powell, 2001). This is in fact a social construction which is based on the capitalist need for human resource management and is associated with the introduction of systems of pension provision (Llewellyn, 2009).

A fixed retirement age suggests some rigidity in the labour market, but the reality is that retirement is used as a way of managing the labour market (Victor, 2005). Chronological age is a poor indicator of ability to work, and negative stereotypes are used as justification for the exclusion of older people from the labour market (Phillipson, 1998). Disengagement theory also fails to account for some of the other roles that older people may take on when they leave paid employment, for example grandparenting and volunteering. With regard to the latter, 30% of people aged 65–74 and 25% of people over 75 are engaged in some form of formal volunteering, whilst older people account for the second largest group in society involved in informal volunteering (Centre for Social Justice, 2010). Volunteering can help people to adjust to other losses in life, giving them a sense of purpose and fulfilment (Baldock, 1999), and can contribute to social inclusion and social citizenship (see below).

Older people may also provide important support as grandparents, who are increasingly playing a part in the care of pre-school children and in after-school and holiday care of older children. In 35% of families, grandparents provide the main source of childcare arrangements (Statham, 2011). This is supported by

Government policies, which stress the importance of the grandparenting role in the light of other demographic changes, such as the growth in the number of lone-parent families and increased female participation in the paid labour market. In 2006, grandparents provided informal childcare for 31% of lone-parent families and 32% of two-parent families (Age UK, 2014). In terms of social work practice, it is also important to note that grandparents play a significant role in caring for children who no longer live with parents owing to abuse, neglect or other child protection issues.

A counter-theory to disengagement theory is *activity theory* (Havighurst, 1963), which argues that rather than older people being increasingly inactive, old age is a period of activity and engagement in different pursuits. Laslett (1989) was one of the first theorists to offer a more positive perspective of ageing in his theory of the Third Age. The Third Age is defined as a period

> **Activity theory** the view that the ageing process is delayed and quality of life is enhanced when old people remain socially active.

of personal achievement and fulfilment (Laslett, 1989), and Laslett argues that, although not exclusively related to retirement, this is often a period when people are relieved of work and caring responsibilities. Therefore within this theory, old age is not a period of social and physical inactivity, but, with the increasing longevity of the population, an increasing number of people are able to enjoy an extended period of fulfilment in retirement (Centre for Social Justice, 2010).

The Third Age concept has been subjected to a number of criticisms, not least that it fails to take account of social divisions based on political and economic factors and health status (Tinker, 1992). Many have argued that Laslett offers a halcyon account of old age which does not reflect the reality of people's experiences based on structural and ideological divisions (McKee and Stuckler, 2013). Nevertheless, the theory has some value in that it provides a counter-view to the prevailing view of inevitable dependence in old age, and questions the assumption that older people cannot/do not make a useful contribution to society.

There is certainly evidence that activity can contribute to positive experiences of older age, and it has been on the policy agenda at various international and national levels (Mendes, 2013). The Department of Health has established guidelines for activity in adulthood and believes that older people will benefit from activities that help them to keep moving and maintain mobility, and from exercise that promotes strength, balance and coordination (Department of Health, 2011c). Activity also involves meaningful occupation and can contribute to the well-being of older people. Dorrestein and Hocking (2010) argued that meaningful activities that account for individual preferences can increase functional abilities of older people in residential care settings.

Despite the advantages of activity in later life, activity theory has been criticized as it is seen as prescriptive and normative and fails to acknowledge social divisions and social circumstances (e.g. poverty and poor health) which may impact on an individual's ability to participate in activities (Ray et al., 2009). Thus, the notion of a prescribed norm of activity as proposed by this theory is in danger of victim-blaming those who are unable or unwilling to participate.

Disengagement and activity theories have been criticized for failing to take account of the impact of political and economic processes on the experiences of ageing (Ray et al., 2009), and an analysis of class, gender and ethnicity as variables that contribute to differential experiences of ageing is largely absent. Conflict theories, on the other hand, are concerned with the macro-level analysis of the political and economic context of ageing and can be seen to derive from Marxist and Weberian sociological perspectives (see Chapter 1).

Age stratification theory

Age stratification theory assumes that people can be grouped together, with the assumption that people of a similar age will have similar experiences and age-related abilities. Three basic themes are relevant in this theory:

1 The meaning of ageing and the position of older people are situated within a particular social context.
2 Transitions within the life-cycle are related to social definitions of ageing. Thus, retirement as a particular social construction defines the experiences of age-related cohorts.
3 Processes for the allocation of resources between different groups are related to social definition.

Homogenization viewing a group as sharing the same characteristics.

The allocation of age-related roles and the assumption of age-related abilities leads to the *homogenization* of older people, assuming common experiences and circumstances, which fails to recognize diversity in old age (Llewellyn, 2009). However, this theory does help us to understand the relevance of power in structural explanations and the hierarchies of values that are constructed in societies. Evaluation of each group is based on dominant social values, and the marginalization of certain groups can therefore be seen to reflect the relative power that different groups hold (Vincent et al., 2008).

Political economy theory

Political economy theory challenges the biomedical and individualistic approach to ageing and argues that experiences of ageing are structured within a given political and economic context. In advanced capitalist societies, old age is seen within the context of the division of labour and the inequalities that are structured through this. Thus, rather than being a time of harmony and homogeneity, older age is characterized by divisions which are based on class, gender and ethnicity. There is a social creation of structured dependency in old age based on the notion of forced retirement and the pensions system (Townsend, 1981).

Estes (1979) argues that this leads to age barriers for older people, where there is a mismatch between their abilities and the resources and opportunities that they experience. She further argues that there is an ageing enterprise in capitalist society, where older people are treated as commodities to be cared for. Policies segregate older people from other adults, leading to social divisions and stigmatization. Thus social policies, rather than ameliorating social problems, may contribute to continuing social divisions and inequalities.

Within structural theories of ageing, there has been an over-emphasis on ageing as a negative process, where older people are seen to be a burden on the welfare state.

The *burden of dependency thesis* may lead to intergenerational conflict, as groups become segregated and compete against each other for resources. In particular, concerns have been raised about the relationship between workers and pensioners, and the priorities for different groups (Philllipson, 1998) and notions of crisis in funding statutory provision for older people continue to underpin policy debates in relation to income maintenance and health and social care provision (Victor, 2005).

> **Burden of dependency thesis** the theory that older people are dependent on the state and this creates a burden on the welfare system.

Social action theories

Structural theories have been criticized for their over-emphasis on class as the basis for divisions and inequalities (Ray et al., 2009) and for failing to explore the experiences of older age for individuals, and their meanings, interpretations and interactions within society (Walker, 1994). In contrast, social action theories focus on the ways that people interpret and experience their old age (see Chapter 1). Communication and interpersonal relationships are an important part of person-hood, as we may construct our own perceptions of self through interactions with others. Symbolic interactionism is a reciprocal process (see Chapter 1) where people construct their experiences through interactions with their environment and through the dominant norms of society. Older people may internalize dominant negative values, believing that they have little to offer, thus further marginalizing themselves from mainstream society (Wurm et al., 2013).

Social workers are a product of the culture and environment that they live in and may therefore be influenced by the dominant discourses of that society. Kitwood (1997) illustrates this through his study of communications with people with dementia, in which he identifies a number of negative communications with older people which impact on self-esteem, identity and behaviour. He uses the term 'malignant social psychology' to explore these negative communications, which can manifest in a number of communication processes and impact on perceptions of self. For example, people may treat older people as though they are children, a process which Kitwood refers to as 'infantilization'. An Age UK (2014) survey found that 53% of people feel that they are treated like children when they reach very old age.

Stereotypes and ageism

The aging of society has not significantly changed our perceptions of aging and the elderly. Ageism – the discrimination against individuals based on their age – is widespread, generally accepted, and largely ignored.

(Angus and Reeve, 2006: 138)

In the context of older age, the economic environment in terms of culturally created dependency through policies of compulsory retirement is important, but so too is the social and cultural environment which stereotypes older people and contributes to ageist practices. Stereotypes are the ideas held about membership of particular groups, based primarily on membership in that group. Stereotypes assume that you can universally apply characteristics to a group of people, irrespective of their diversity and interpersonal differences (Hazan, 2000), and reflect negative images of older

A stereotyped depiction of older people. (© jrling/iStock)

people as a social problem. The understanding of old age as a social problem derives from a biological model of ageing, which views old age as a period of inevitable physical decline and increasing dependency. Thus, stereotypical assumptions may be made about the inevitability of physical and mental decline, increased dependence and inability to process information. In addition, there is a pervasive stereotype of asexuality in older age, inhibiting older people's ability to engage in intimate and sexual relationships (Pickard, 1995) (see Chapter 6).

Discourses are also important in shaping dominant sets of ideas, and constructions of power are reflected in the language we use (Foucault, 1979b). In particular, the media are a dominant social institution and have the power to construct symbols and images through language and discourse (Habermas, 1989). In the words of Milner et al. (2011: 26): 'Mass media is a critical platform for communicating the meanings and experiences of ageing between generations, and plays a role in shaping the agenda for discussing ageing issues. Media portrayals of ageing not only reflect the widespread ageism in society, but also largely reinforce negative stereotypes.'

Exercise: Stereotypes of older people

- What stereotypes of older people are evident within the sign pictured on the facing page?
- What other stereotypes of older people can you think of?
- Think of other forms of popular culture (birthday cards, fairy tales, TV programmes – soap operas, sitcoms).
- Are there similar stereotypes portrayed within these different forms of popular culture?
- Why is this relevant to you as a social work practitioner?

Age discrimination

This assumption of generality and universality in old age, and of increasing dependency, has led to particular forms of welfare provision for older people (Phelan, 2010). Health and social care services have developed on a medicalized model of practice, with an emphasis on secondary and tertiary care services provided by professionals (Hugman, 1994). This welfarist model has led to a form of health and social care provision with the emphasis very much on health care needs being met through a service-led agenda. Social care needs are seen as a lower priority and there has been a failure to acknowledge a diversity of needs and abilities among older people (Lymbery, 2005).

Ageist assumptions fail to acknowledge diversity and the impact of social, environmental and psychological factors on the processes and experiences of ageing. Such assumptions lead to discrimination against older people. Ray et al. (2006) define ageism as 'stereotypes and prejudices held about older people on the grounds of their age. Age discrimination is used to describe behaviour where older people are treated unequally (directly or indirectly) on grounds of their age.'

Although the Equality Act (HM Government, 2010a) makes any form of discrimination unlawful, there is still widespread ageism in the UK. A European survey of ageism found that 64% of people in the UK believe that ageism is a serious problem, compared to 44% across Europe as a whole (Age UK, 2011a). Social workers are not immune from these processes of discrimination and there is evidence that ageism exists amongst those who provide care and support for older people (Oliver, 2013). This discrimination is manifest in a system of health and social care based on welfarist models of practice which treat older people as dependent and excludes them from decision-making processes about their lives (Lymbery, 2005).

There is evidence of strategies to tackle age discrimination, but the picture remains mixed (Centre for Policy on Ageing, 2009). One area where there have been significant attempts to improve funding and quality of care is dementia care. In 2009, the National Dementia Strategy was published, providing £150 million over the first two years to:

- increase awareness of dementia
- ensure early diagnosis and intervention
- radically improve the quality of care that people with the condition receive.

However, the Centre for Policy on Ageing (2009) report concluded that one reason for continued age discrimination in health and social care is as a result of cumulative ageist attitudes among staff.

Ageing and disadvantage

From a structural perspective, ageing and the experience of ageing are in part based on access to resources. Income and health inequalities of working-aged life persist into older age and are compounded by age-specific factors. For a significant minority of older people, old age is a period of disadvantage, poverty and social exclusion.

Scharf et al. (2003: 78) identify five specific domains of social exclusion that are relevant to an understanding of the social disadvantage that older people may face:

1   Exclusion from material resources.
2   Exclusion from social relations, reflecting the importance attributed to the ability of older adults to engage in meaningful relationships with family, friends and neighbours.
3   Exclusion from civic activities, recognizing the need for individuals to be able to be involved in wider aspects of civil society and in decision-making processes which may in turn influence their own lives.
4   Exclusion from basic services, drawing upon the key role played by access to services in and beyond the home in terms of individuals' ability to manage every-day life.
5   Neighbourhood exclusion, reflecting the contribution made by the immedi-ate residential setting to an individual's sense of self and, potentially, the quality of their lives.

There is great diversity in older age, but a significant number of older people are some of the most vulnerable in society, owing to combinations of poverty, ill health and social exclusion and isolation. Although pensioner poverty has shown a steady decrease since 1979, in 2010/11, over half of all pensioners were classed as having at least one form of poverty (Barnes, 2012). Older people are also more at risk of

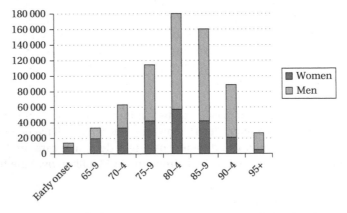

Figure 10.3   Number of people with dementia in the United Kingdom by age.
Source: Compiled with data from Alzheimer's Society, 2007.

suffering the consequences of disadvantage that accumulate over the life-course. Inequalities of income or health throughout the life-course are perpetuated into old age, and nearly 10% of older people have lived in poverty for most of their lives (Scharf et al., 2003).

As stated above, old age does not cause ill health, but there is an increased likelihood of ill health as people age. With the increases in longevity, more people are being diagnosed with a range of life-limiting illnesses and long-term conditions. Dementia, for example, represents a significant challenge for health and social care providers as well as having a significant impact on individuals and their carers. In 2012, there were 80,000 people in the UK with dementia, and this number is projected to increase to over 1 million by 2021 (Alzheimer's Society, 2012; see also Figure 10.3). This condition can lead to social isolation not only for people living with dementia, but also for their carers. This may be further compounded by limited access to resources such as health care and social services, owing to lack of understanding or awareness of the available services. Although three-quarters of people accessing NHS health and social care services are aged 65 and over, only two-fifths of total expenditure is spent on this group (Rutherford, 2012). (For further information about numbers of people living with dementia in the UK, see Alzheimer's Society, 2012.)

Social exclusion and inequality may also be related to losses that older people face. Although not all older people will experience loss and the experience of loss varies between individuals, older people may experience a whole range of losses that are disproportionate to those of other groups in society. There may be loss of income through retirement, loss of health through chronic disabling conditions or the loss of home or partner, leading to adjustments to living alone and increased potential for social isolation. There may also be losses of self-esteem and belief due to ageist practices (discussed below) and loss of a sense of safety and well-being due to social context and processes.

Older people may have strong attachments to their locality and community, and this may make them vulnerable if there is a loss of this community. Social networks are important sources of support for older people, and strong networks can provide the social capital for health and well-being. Wenger (1991) identifies four types of social support for older people:

1 Local, family-dependent systems, based on support from families, neighbours and friends within a locality
2 Local, self-contained systems, where neighbours usually provide support. This is the principle that underpins the formation of retirement villages, for example.
3 Wider-community networks, with a high level of community activities
4 Private, restricted networks where there is the absence of close family and friends. A personal assistant employed through a personalized budget might provide a good example of this type of support. (See Chapter 5 for further discussion of personalization.)

Exercise: social support

Reflect on the types of social support listed above and how they might inform social work practice.

Fragmentation of communities may contribute to social isolation amongst older people, which is a significant problem associated with ageing. More than 50% of people over the age of 75 live alone, and half of older people say that the television is their main form of company (Centre for Social Justice, 2010). In a study by Victor and Bowling (2012), one third of older people reported being lonely over a significant period of time, the impact of which is significant in terms of premature mortality (Cornwell and Waite, 2009) and depression (Windle et al., 2011). Social isolation may be perpetuated through a perception of increased vulnerability to crime and social disorder, leading to exclusion from participation in society (Scharf and Keating, 2012). As one respondent in the Centre for Social Justice Study (2010: 28) commented: 'When we first came here I wouldn't have dreamt of locking a door or even shutting it. Now almost nobody over 60 would think of going into town by themselves at night. I think we have a policeman but I don't think he is ever there.' (For further statistics on the material, health and social circumstances of older people see Age UK, 2014.)

Risk and abuse

As discussed in previous chapters, risk is a key concept in post-modernity (Beck, 1992), which raises a number of questions and issues in relation to the experience of ageing. Associated with the risk society is the concept of abuse, with a rise in the number of reported cases of elder abuse within both domiciliary and institutional care settings. Abuse is defined as: 'Violation of an individual's human and civil rights by any other person or persons' (Department of Health, 2000).

Abuse occurs in different settings and can be found in institutional and domiciliary contexts. Action on Elder Abuse (n.d.) identifies seven types of abuse, although people may experience more than one of these types of abuse and the scale of abuse often escalates:

1 physical
2 financial
3 sexual
4 psychological/emotional
5 neglect
6 discriminatory
7 institutional.

The term 'multiple abuse' is used to describe situations where two or more types of abuse are occurring simultaneously (see also Figure 10.4).

The 2007 prevalence study of elder abuse found that approximately 2.6% of older people in the community are subject to one or more forms of abuse from relatives and care workers, which is line with other international studies (O'Keeffe et al., 2007).

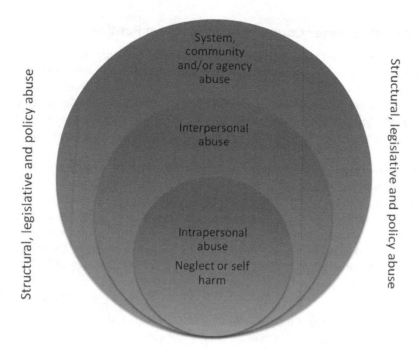

Figure 10.4   Levels of abuse.
Source: Penhale and Parker, 2008: 31.

The figure rose to 4% when neighbours and friends were added to the equation. Prevalence and incidence studies of abuse often rely on self-reported data. However, these may underestimate the true incidence of abuse as people may be reluctant to report abuse owing to fear factors, such as fear of being removed from home or jeopardizing the family's status in the community. The victim may feel that they are dependent on the abuser for basic survival or the bonds of affection may be stronger than any desire to leave the situation.

These figures do not include older people who are being abused in institutional settings, which is increasingly being highlighted and reported. Age UK (2014) estimate that over half a million older people are abused across domiciliary and institutional settings in the UK. The following YouTube clip contains some graphic images that may upset some people, but highlight this growing problem of institutional abuse: *http://youtube/YQHP5u3EIUw*.

There are a number of reasons why the issue of elder abuse has not received the same societal or policy attention as child abuse:

- Older people may not come into contact with external agencies as often as children, making detection more difficult.
- There may be a lack of attention focused on elder abuse compared to child abuse within professional education programmes, reflecting cultural and professional priorities.
- Cultural ideologies the protection of vulnerable children tend to get greater attention, reflecting the emphasis on the values and virtues of youth in Western societies and ageist attitudes to older people.

Case studies: Peter Connelly and Margaret Panting

Peter Connelly was a 17-month-old British boy who died in London in 2008 after suffering more than 50 injuries over an eight-month period. His mother and her boyfriend and his brother were all convicted of causing or allowing his death. Following his death the Laming Report (2009) was produced, exploring progress in child protection and safeguarding processes, and Eileen Munro was commissioned by the Government to review child safeguarding processes and procedures (Munro, 2011).

Margaret Panting was a 78-year-old woman who was taken out of a care home to be cared for by family. She died within one month, and on investigating her death, the pathologist found over 100 injuries on her body, including cigarette burns and lacerations. Her son-in-law and his sons were arrested on suspicion of her murder, but the Crown Prosecution Service decided that there was insufficient evidence to bring charges against them. This death largely escaped the attention of the mass media, and there was no public inquiry to investigate what lessons may be learned from this case.

(Action on Elder Abuse, n.d.)

- Ask colleagues/friends if they have heard of Margaret Panting.
- Now ask if they have heard of Peter Connelly (Baby P).
- Is there a difference in the responses?
- Why do you think there is such a difference between the public and statutory responses to these two incidences of abuse and death?
- Does this reflect an ageist attitude and lack of public concern about older people compared to younger people?
- Does society perceive children as more vulnerable than older people, and therefore in need of a greater amount of protection?

Biggs (1996) argues that the acknowledgement of domiciliary elder abuse presents a paradox to governments who promote the family as a unit of caring within community care policies. It is, however, important to understand the nature and incidence of abuse (in both domiciliary and institutional settings), as the impact of abuse can not only disempower older people, but also compromise their rights to citizenship.

In recent years, the problem of elder abuse has become much more prominent in both the mass media and policy formulation. A number of TV documentaries have exposed both domestic and institutional abusive practices, and Comic Relief drew attention to the abuse of vulnerable older people in 2005 with its TV film *Dad*, starring Richard Briers. This fictional account of elder abuse highlighted the tensions and conflicts between parents and children which can lead to adult abuse. As a dominant form of information and social attitude formation, the media play an important role in raising awareness about elder abuse.

In policy terms, *No Secrets* (Department of Health, 2000) clarifies the role of social service departments and social workers within a multi-agency framework in England, based on principles of collaborative working, empowerment of service users, supporting their rights (the issue of capacity is crucial here) and acknowledging that, in the right to self-determination, older people have the right to take risks, providing these are properly understood.. Health and social care professionals need to address risk in partnership with service users to promote independence, rather than dependence (a clear theme identified in a number of key policy documents: e.g. Department of Health, 2005, 2007a). There is ongoing debate about the efficacy of the quasi-legal framework to protect vulnerable adults, and it is likely that further legislation will be proposed in this area. The review of *No Secrets* in 2009 in England (Department of Health, 2009b) and the Welsh Assembly Government review of the Welsh equivalent of *No Secrets, In Safe Hands* (Social Services Inspectorate Wales, 2000), advocate a safeguarding approach built on empowerment and citizenship, with majority support for a system that puts adult safeguarding on a firmer statutory footing in line with the Adult Support and Protection Act (2007) in Scotland. This is reiterated in the 2011 Law Commission Report, which recommends a modernized statute that provides a clear and coherent social care system with a new legal system to safeguard vulnerable adults and safeguarding boards with a statutory footing. These recommendations have not yet been implemented, but they signify a clear policy shift aimed at empowering vulnerable adults to make safeguarding decisions and providing a legal process to support this.

Dignity in care

Older people may also be disempowered through institutional practices and community care policies. Long-term care needs of older people with varying degrees of dependency have historically been provided for through a system of nursing and residential care homes (Means and Smith, 2003). Whilst there is evidence of much good and innovative practice within this care sector, there is also evidence of institutionalization and a lack of individual care or autonomy, as the following quote illustrates:

> Nothing quite prepared me for the shock of entering residential care. Most of the staff are incredibly patient and kind – and I appreciate their help – but it is the constant bustle and ringing of bells from which one cannot escape . . . and the limited choice about food, activities or even companionship, which I find so hard to take. Then I am not allowed to do anything considered the least bit risky, one understands it is to keep one safe . . . but it's pretty galling at my age, after a life of independence, to find oneself so powerless and constrained. (Cited in McClymont, 1999)

Institutionalization may lead to stigmatization, lack of autonomy, poor material resources and loss of liberty and dignity. In addition, institutionalization is often associated with a medicalized or welfarist model of care, with power being concentrated in the hands of professionals.

Although numerous examples exist of good-quality care for older people in hospitals and care homes, the following extract from the Francis Report (2012) provides an example of the poor-quality care experienced by some older people:

> The next day her daughter visited, her mother was sleeping and her face was partially covered by a sheet. There was blood on the floor and when the patient woke up her daughter saw that she had a very large bruise covering almost the whole of the right side of her face and neck as though 'someone had taken a bat to her'. There was also blood on her nightdress. When her daughter eventually found a nurse she was simply informed that there was no entry in the incident book and given no information

about what had happened. The patient's daughters asked various nurses, the ward sister and the doctor what had happened, but none knew.

To be treated with dignity and respect is a fundamental human right and is enshrined in the UK Human Rights Act (1998). This involves respecting people's right to privacy and dignity in care, and providing care in an appropriate environment that reflects the personal preferences of the care recipient. Thus the environment of care is important in reflecting the quality and social inclusivity of care provision (Social Care Institute for Excellence, 2010). Katz et al. (2011) identify a number of key factors that contribute to quality of life for people with high support needs (see Table 10.1). An understanding of these key quality-of-life measures can help social workers to work in a more positive way with older people in both domiciliary and institutional care settings, addressing issues that contribute to social isolation and social exclusion, discussed earlier.

Table 10.1 *Contributions to quality of life for people with high support needs*

Social well-being	Meaningful relationships *(personal and with paid carers)* Social interaction Making a contribution *(including roles)* Cultural activities *(including religious activities)*
Psychological well-being	Self-determination *(including involvement in decision-making, control, independence, autonomy)* Continuity and adjusting to change Sense of self *(including self-esteem)* Humour and pleasure Mental health *(including existential balance, sense of purpose*
Physical well-being	Safety and security Good environment *(including contact with nature)* Getting out and about Physical health *(including living in an ageing body)* Physical activities

Source: Katz et al., 2011: 7, Table 1

Social gerontology

Social gerontology is a relatively new discipline and adopts a multidisciplinary approach, drawing on theories from the social sciences, the arts and the humanities. The new critical gerontology that is emerging helps us to understand the plurality of experiences that older people have and the impact of other variables such as gender and ethnicity in the biography of the individual. Critical gerontology integrates macro-level and micro-level theories to provide a more comprehensive analysis of old age (Phillipson, 1998) and offers opportunities for exploring the multiple roots of oppression and disempowerment in later years, but at the same time it explores how old age can have or lack meaning for older people and can offer opportunities

Case study

Hannah is an 83-year-old woman who was admitted to hospital three weeks ago with hypothermia and a chest infection. She has lived alone in her two-bedroomed terrace house since her husband died four years ago. She struggles to manage on her pension and her house is in need of some modernization – she has no central heating and the windows are ill fitting. She uses electric fires in the living room and bedroom, which are expensive to run. Hannah rarely goes out as she feels intimidated by the youths in the local area, and she has few visitors.

Hannah is medically ready for discharge and you have been asked to assess her social needs.

- Reflect on sociological theories of ageing and how they might inform your understanding of Hannah's needs.

for empowerment. Estes (2001) has developed an approach to understanding old age which integrates structural factors with the role of the state, and explores the intersection of multiple roots of oppression (class, gender, ethnicity) in the context of citizenship approaches, the ageing enterprise and social inclusion.

Gender and old age

Old age is gendered (Arber and Ginn, 1995), with an intersection between ageing and gender. In older age, women outnumber men and are more likely to live alone (Rutherford, 2012). Men are more likely to suffer from life-threatening illnesses such as coronary heart disease and strokes, leading to a higher premature mortality rate, whilst women are more likely to suffer from life-limiting illnesses such as diabetes and arthritis. There is some evidence that this pattern will change with changing lifestyles and work practices, meaning that the differentials will become less marked in the future (Annandale, 2008). Nevertheless, the experiences of ageing may be very different for men and women. Two-thirds of men receive non-state pensions, whereas three-quarters of women do not. This is significant as non-state pensions offer a better income than state pensions, so the incidence of poverty and social exclusion amongst older women is much higher.

The sexualization of women's value also leads to women's and men's differential experiences of ageing (Ginn and Arber, 1993). Once past the age of reproductive capacity, women's contribution to society becomes devalued as women are judged in terms of physical appearance. Men's physical appearance is less important, as they are valued for their continuing contribution to economic productivity. For women, age-related appropriate behaviours are constructed, particularly in terms of the body and fashion. The *mutton dressed as lamb* simile is a good indication of the age-related expectations in society. This emphasis on appearance becomes commodified through the availability of cosmetic surgery and anti-ageing products (Annandale, 2008). This dual standard of ageing is not just about appearance, but further contributes to oppressive practices in respect of older women. As Bernard and Meade (1993: 2) note: 'It is the structures, policies and ideology of western capitalist society that are the major cause of women's relative social and economic powerlessness. In societies such as ours that are systematically . . . at times sexist, racist and ageist . . . it is hardly surprising that amongst the myriad disadvantaged groups, older women feature particularly strongly.'

Chambers (2004) argues that many studies of gender and old age have problematized ageing, where older women experience ageism and sexism and, despite being higher users of health and social care services, are less likely to be offered individualized care services. Chambers explored the subjective experiences of widows and found multiple narratives of their experiences. Some felt a sense of loneliness and despair, whilst others demonstrated a pragmatic attitude. A third narrative was based on a sense of opportunity, as widowhood and old age were seen as a point of transition. This is important in terms of positive well-being and is a good fit with the current policy agenda, which focuses on ageing well. Social workers are ideally placed to contribute to this through their knowledge and value base so as to empower people and work from a strengths-based and person-centred perspective (Phoenix and Sparkes, 2009).

Ethnicity and old age

There are currently over 500,000 minority ethnic elders in the UK (Age UK, 2014), but this is projected to change as the patterns of migration of the 1950s and 1960s will result in significant population change as minority ethnic groups age (see Table 10.2). Thus minority ethnic elders constitute one of the fastest-growing groups within the older population.

Pensioners from black and minority ethnic (BME) groups are more likely to be in poverty than white pensioners, especially those from Pakistani and Bangladeshi backgrounds. It is reported that 49% of this group are living in poverty (Age UK, 2014) and, with the exception of the Indian population, levels of loneliness across all ethnic groups are higher than for white groups of elders (Victor et al., 2012).

The experiences of minority ethnic elders have to be understood in the context of wider social practices and ideologies in relation to the structural position of minority ethnic populations and the impact of direct, indirect and institutional racism (see Chapter 5). There needs to be a more complex theoretical underpinning to understand the diverse range of experiences that ethnic elders may have, based on racism and ageism, and acknowledging the importance of understanding difference within difference. (Not all older people from minority ethnic backgrounds will have the same experiences, and it is important not to conflate ethnic categories.) This is

Table 10.2 *People over the age of 65 by ethnic group, UK (percentage)*

Black Caribbean	9
Black African	2
Indian	6
Pakistani	4
Bangladeshi	3
Chinese	5

Source: Office for National Statistics, 2001

important for social work practice. Social workers face significant issues in engaging and working with minority ethnic elders.

Older people from BME groups may be particularly disadvantaged and are more likely to suffer discrimination in accessing services, according to the King's Fund Report (2002). Norman (1985) refers to the triple jeopardy for ethnic elders of ageism and racism and the perception of a lack of access to appropriate services. There may also be a fourth jeopardizing factor of not having English as a first language, thus further reducing the accessibility of services. The one-size-fits-all approach can disadvantage ethnic elders, and take-up tends to be low, reflecting a level of unmet need and a lack of awareness of needs amongst service providers. The King's Fund Report concludes that most black elders would prefer to access mainstream services rather than specialist service provision, but may have difficulties because of a lack of awareness amongst service commissioners and providers.

Life-course and biographical approaches

In developing gerontological theory, there is a growing emphasis on a life-course perspective, which sees old age within the context of the whole life journey (Binstock and George, 2001). Life-course perspectives integrate the micro-worlds of individuals and the macro-patterns of institutional organization and social change. Thus the experience of old age is, in part, dependent on other experiences throughout the life-course. Experiences of racism, sexism or other forms of discrimination may affect people's perceptions and experiences in old age, as well as social stratification processes, contributing to their (lack of) income and health status. Thus old age is a period of heterogeneity, with people having very different experiences. As Stoller and Gibson (1994: xxiii) note: 'people's location in the social system, the historical period in which they live and their unique personal biography shape the experience of old age'.

Exercise: your biography

- Write down the things that have affected the patterns of your individual life.
- Now divide these into macro-level societal changes and micro-level individual factors.

The macro-level factors may unite you with other members of an age cohort, but the micro-level factors are unique to you and shape the experiences that you have had and the way that you have responded to them.

Ruth and Kenyon (1996) have identified three benefits of using biographical approaches to the study of old age:

1 They contribute to the development of theories of adult development and old age.
2 They provide a focus on the public and personal way that people develop.
3 They provide an important understanding as to how individuals believe that life can be enhanced.

Biographical approaches shape the way that people age from within, and people's narratives are important for understanding the richness and complexities of lived experiences. Look at the photo on this page and describe what you see. Not surprisingly, you will have described a number of physical attributes, such as grey hair, glasses and wrinkles. Featherstone and Hepworth (1991) argue that we make assumptions about people on the basis of these observable physical processes asso- ciated with ageing, and they refer to these as the mask of ageing. Seeing beyond this mask, through a phenomenological understanding of the meaning of ageing to indi- viduals, helps us to see beyond the negative experiences and engage with individuals as unique human beings (Ballard et al., 2005).

The following poem was found in a locker in a hospital ward. While this is addressed to nurses, and although there is no information about the author, it illustrates the life biography perspective and has relevance for all who work with older people.

'Crabbit Old Woman'

What do you see, what do you see? / Are you thinking, when you look at me – / A crabbit old woman, not very wise, / Uncertain of habit, with far-away eyes, / Who dribbles her food and makes no reply / When you say in a loud voice, I do wish you'd try. / Who seems not to notice the things that you do / And forever is losing a stocking or shoe. / Who, unresisting or not; lets you do as you will / With bathing and feeding the long day is fill. / Is that what you're thinking, Is that what you see? / Then open your eyes, nurse, you're looking at me. / I'll tell you who I am as I sit here so still! / As I rise at your bidding, as I eat at your will. / I'm a small child of 10 with a father and mother, / Brothers and sisters, who loved one another – /A young girl of 16 with wings on her feet, / Dreaming that soon now a lover she'll meet. / A bride soon at 20 – my heart gives a leap, / Remembering the vows that I promised to keep. / At 25 now I have young of my own / Who need me to build a secure happy home; / A woman of 30, my young now grow fast, / Bound to each other with ties that should last; / At 40, my young sons have grown and are gone, / But my man's beside me to see I don't mourn; / At 50 once more babies play around my knee, / Again we know children, my loved one and me. / Dark days are upon me, my husband is dead, / I look at the future, I shudder with dread, / For my young are all rearing young of their own. / And I think of the years and the love that I've known; / I'm an old woman now and nature is cruel /– 'Tis her jest to make old age look like a fool. / The body is crumbled, grace and vigour depart, / There is now a stone where I once had a heart. / But inside this

Anne Llewellyn's grandmother on her 101st birthday. (© Anne Llewellyn)

old carcass, a young girl still dwells, / And now and again my battered heart swells. / I remember the joy, I remember the pain, / And I'm loving and living life over again. / I think of the years all too few – gone too fast. / And accept the stark fact that nothing can last – / So open your eyes, nurse, open and see, / Not a crabbit old woman, look closer – See Me.

Reflection

- Reflect on how this poem made you feel.
- What learning will you take from this for your future social work practice?

Life-course perspectives fit with social work practice with older people, with assessments focusing on strengths approaches, where the current issues are identified within the holistic context of the person's life to understand needs from the person's perspective and identify coping mechanisms. Life-history and reminiscence therapy are approaches used with success in dementia care (Woods et al., 2009). Mackenzie et al. (2006) studied the use of doll therapy with people with dementia. This was done in a therapeutic way where the assessment had suggested that the person might have a nurturing or caring need, and it was reinforced in James et al.'s (2006) study, where people were clearly caring for the dolls and not playing with them. The benefit was that people became more active, less agitated and showed greater levels of interaction with others.

Globalization and older age

Much of the discussion above has focused on Western issues about the ageing population, although some of this discussion is transferable to other contexts. However, population ageing is a global phenomenon and raises issues about new patterns of social disadvantage. As well as this, global processes such as the technological revolution have important consequences for people's experiences and the provision of care. It is predicted that the greatest increase in the proportion of older people globally will be in the less developed countries, with numbers of older people expected to escalate by 140% by 2030 (Martell, 2010). A key feature of this is that life expectancy is also expected to increase, with more older people living into older ages, which could lead to further demands on health care, housing and income maintenance through pensions.

There is a social patterning of life expectancy throughout the world, with poorer life expectancy concentrated in sub-Saharan African countries and countries with poor economic conditions and widespread deprivation. HIV and AIDS have a significant impact on mortality rates in many of the countries with the poorest life expectancy rates. Deaths from AIDS are highest in the 18- to 45-year-old age group, who have sometimes been referred to as the 'missing generation' because of the lost income and caring role for dependent children (Dominelli, 2010). The impact of this is that grandparents are increasingly called upon not only to work, but also to look after their dependent grandchildren, as this quote from a 65-year-old grandfather in Zimbabwe illustrates: 'Looking after orphans is like starting life all over again, because I have to work on the farm, clean the house, feed the children, buy school uniforms . . . I thought I would no longer do these things again. I am not sure I have the energy to cope' (cited in Oduaran and Oduaran, 2010).

Globalization also impacts on old age through accelerated migration and increased urbanization, which can further isolate or disadvantage older people. More than 100 million older people in developing countries are living on less than $1 per day (International Association of Homes and Services for the Ageing, n.d.) and the numbers of older people in poverty across the world are increasing. The model of the extended family (see Chapter 8) in traditional societies is being eroded as economic problems have contributed to family breakdown where families cannot afford to look after dependent older relatives. In 2012, the Inter Press Service reported on a 91-year-old man in India who was tortured and evicted from his own house by his only son for 'not earning any money' (Hari Krishnan, 2012). Global processes such as the technologization of society can also impact on experiences of ageing. Technology can bring new benefits to older people (especially in the Western world) through provision of assistive technologies to facilitate independent living. However, it can also lead to new social divisions through digital exclusion. In the UK, only 36% of the over 65 population have used the internet, and exclusion from technology rises with age, with 79% of the over 75s being non-users (Age UK, 2014). Of course, this may change in the future with the ageing of current populations of younger people who are digitally literate and competent, but the benefits will not be shared equally throughout the world.

Positive ageing

Much of the discussion above seems to paint a rather negative picture of older age. However, recent policy imperatives have sought to promote positive ageing, working in partnership with older people to enable and empower them and maximize independence (e.g. Department of Health, 2001c). Personalization is a key policy imperative in current social care practice focusing on the promotion of independence and self-reliance through the provision of services tailored to individual needs. Allied to this is a need for improved information and advice and investment in preventive services (Burton et al., 2012). Older people are central to this process, as the care is about and for them and they are the experts in their own care needs. Thus the principles of personalization focus on the strengths and resources of older people, rather than service-led provision. Social workers have a crucial role in shaping this personalized agenda, using their skills and knowledge to support older people in their personal, family and social contexts (Burton et al., 2012).

Person-centred care emphasizes individual experience and identity, questioning the taken for granted and unpicking the way that language constructs ideas. Social workers have a key role to play in this agenda, and an understanding of sociological theories and the social construction of old age can help social workers to challenge these assumptions and advocate for the most vulnerable in society.

Successful ageing is related to two key factors:

1   personal relationships, where older people have a feeling of belonging
2   older people feeling engaged in meaningful activity

Figure 10.5   Enacting positive ageing.
Source: Adapted from Department of Health, 2007a.

Primary social networks have been found to engender positive feelings of self in older people (Hunt, 2005), and we have also discussed activity theory and active ageing within this chapter. Duffy and Gillespie (2009) have argued that citizenship should be at the heart of policies for older people and that safeguarding and risk management should be seen in the context of threats to citizenship, which may be multi-causal.

The co-existing factors in Figure 10.5 are important for citizenship, social inclusion and a sense of positive well-being and are important considerations for social work practitioners who are supporting older people in either domiciliary or residential care settings. A focus on citizenship can promote more positive approaches to older age and ageing (see also *http://www.bjf.org.uk*).

Conclusion

The sociology of old age has much relevance for social work practice in providing frameworks for the understanding of the social context of ageing. The sociology of old age is concerned with:

- people over their life-course
- age-related social structures and institutions
- the dynamic interplay between people and structures, as they influence each other.

Old age is not a homogeneous experience, but is socially and culturally diverse. It is important to understand not only the social context and the processes that contribute to older people's experience, but also the current context within the holistic framework of the life-course. A sociological approach to old age can help social work practitioners to understand and challenge systems of oppression and disadvantage and to use their knowledge and skills to promote positive well-being in older age.

Although social work with older people may have been constrained by organizational boundaries, priorities and funding issues, an understanding of gerontological theory and the diverse needs and experiences of older people can help to develop a more emancipatory approach to working with older people. Social workers are ideally placed to witness the inequities and oppressions that people experience and to challenge existing political and economic structures that may shape those experiences in order to truly empower older people. Within the radical social work movement, there has been relatively little attention in relation to older people's services, but demographies and changing ideological contexts make this an area where social workers can really make a difference to people's experiences.

Summary points

- Chronological age is the most commonly used definition of old age and is often used in service provision and social policies.
- Sociological perspectives help us to understand the social construction of ageing as a distinct category of adulthood.
- Structural perspectives locate ageing and the experiences of ageing within the social, political and economic structures of society.
- Social action perspectives help us to understand the experience of ageing from the perspective of the individuals who experience it.
- Experiences of old age are wide and varied, but a significant minority of older people are vulnerable and socially disadvantaged.
- Institutional practices may contribute to the disempowerment and marginalization of older people.
- The concept of positive ageing is important in helping older people to be empowered and valued.

Questions for discussion

- How do the sociological perspectives of old age help us to understand the marginalization of older people in contemporary capitalist societies?
- Is ageing biological or social? How can the structures and institutions of society shape the experience of ageing?
- How can sociological perspectives help us to develop an understanding of ageism and inform anti-oppressive social work practice?
- Have a look at the voluntary sector websites. What services and projects are available to enhance quality of life in old age?

Further reading

Bowling, A. (2005) *Ageing Well: Quality of Life in Old Age.* Buckingham: Open University Press
This book embraces the positive aspects of ageing and explores ways in which professionals can work with older people to enhance their quality of life.

McDonald, A. (2010) *Social Work with Older People.* **Cambridge: Polity**
This is a very accessible text which provides a logical discussion of key issues in social
work practice with older people. Concepts of human rights and social justice
underpin the discussion and help the reader to think about the importance of
understanding diversity in older age.

Ray, M., Bernard, M. and Phillips, J. (2009) *Critical Issues in Social Work with
Older People.* **Basingstoke: Palgrave Macmillan**
As the title suggests, this book takes a critical look at the study of ageing and
social work, exploring issues that are central to older people's experiences. It
merges theoretical discussion with research and encourages a critically reflective
approach to practice.

Victor, C. (2005) *The Social Context of Ageing: A Textbook of Gerontology.* **London:
Routledge**
This provides a good overview of the theorizing of old age within social gerontology,
and also explores issues, such as material resources in old age and family and
caring networks, which are relevant for social work practice with older people.

11 Health and Mental Health

Introduction

Sociological interest in health and illness is a relatively new sub-discipline of sociology, although it has gathered momentum since the 1970s. The sociology of health and illness argues that the biomedical model and subsequent treatment from professionals cannot be seen solely in relation to scientific knowledge and discourse. Social structures and associated factors are highly influential in how disease is produced and experienced within societies. We have examined functionalism and illness in relation to disability in Chapter 5. We will further explore sociological perspectives relating to health and illness in this chapter, in the context of mental health and mental illness. Mental health problems are widespread within society, and adults with mental health problems represent one of the most disadvantaged groups within modern Britain. The impact of health inequalities in relation to mental health is also significant. This can be seen within a global context of poor mental health relating to wider social and health problems (Friedli, 2009).

The chapter will explore definitions of mental health in relation to the biomedical model and its continued importance within psychiatry. We will explore the dichotomy in mental health policy and practice between biomedical perspectives and social and psychological perspectives. The significance of the survivors' movement within mental health as a force for social change and the civil and citizenship rights of people with mental health problems will also be examined. The social movement has been informed by the lived experience of people with mental health issues, and it has led to the growth of recovery and strengths-based approaches. This has contributed to critical sociological perspectives on mental illness. The chapter will conclude by discussing the global context of mental health and health inequalities. The role of mental health social workers is also facing a time of considerable change and tension, and this will be related to critical sociological perspectives.

> ## The key issues that will be explored in this chapter are:
>
> - the discourse concerning mental illness
> - biomedical and sociological perspectives on health and illness
> - structuralism, asylum care and the social construction of mental illness
> - the lived experience of mental illness, including the role of the mental health survivors' movement and challenges to structuralism
> - critical sociological perspectives: the anti-psychiatry movement, narrative, recovery and strengths-based approaches.

> **By the end of this chapter you should be able to:**
>
> - have an understanding of the sociology of health and illness, including the global context of health inequalities
> - demonstrate an understanding of the biomedical approach to mental illness and its relevance in the historical development of mental health services
> - understand structuralist perspectives relating to medicalization, asylum care and the use of power within mental health services
> - discuss social constructionism relating to mental illness and the impact of stigma and labelling on social exclusion and health inequalities
> - understand the lived experience of mental illness and mental distress and the role of the survivors' movement
> - have an awareness of critical sociological perspectives relating to recovery and strengths-based approaches and their relevance to contemporary social work practice
> - have an awareness of the global context of mental health.

Definitions of mental illness

Mental illness and mental disorder are wide and ill-defined areas, which makes definition problematic. As with disability, professionals have used and continue to use a range of terminology and language within professional discourse which can be perceived as labelling in relation to people who have mental health problems and who use mental health services (Golightley, 2011). Taylor and Field (2007) argue that we can distinguish between three different types of overlapping populations who may access mental health services:

1 those suffering from impaired bodily function: for example, people with learning disabilities, people with forms of senile mental confusion.
2 people with behavioural problems such as alcohol misuse and eating disorders
3 people with what are termed mental illnesses: for example, schizophrenia, bipolar disorder and depression.

Whilst these different categories demonstrate the complexity of defining mental disorder and the wide range of populations who engage with mental health services, they are not very helpful in terms of providing an objective definition of mental illness.

A crude distinction can be drawn between biological and social approaches to defining mental illness, although the two approaches are not mutually exclusive. The biological approach formed the basis of much of the early psychiatric approach to mental illness (and retains relevance in contemporary psychiatric approaches). To understand contemporary psychiatric approaches, it is also important to then explore the social structures and processes that have impacted on the treatment of mental illnesses as well as the experiences of service users and their carers. Golightley (2011) discusses how medical perspectives can be seen to continue to dominate the support and treatment offered to people with mental health problems. A broader understanding of health and illness is useful here.

Sociological approaches to health and illness

In other sections of the book, we have explored sociological thought relating to health and illness in terms of disability and the sociology of the body. In this chapter, we further explore these perspectives and relate them to mental health. The *biomedical model* has historically heavily influenced studies of health and illness. Within this perspective, the organization of health and illness has been seen to be very much concerned with treatment and improving function.

> **Biomedical model** the theory that the basis of disease, including mental illness, is physical in origin. Illness can be identified objectively through signs and symptoms and treated scientifically with technology, for example drugs and surgical interventions. The body can be likened to a machine that can be broken down into its component parts.

Kleinman's (1988) model of the three overlapping sectors of health care – the professional sector, the folk sector and the popular sector – is useful for understanding the organization of health and illness. The folk sector includes alternative and complementary forms of health care provision that sit outside the professional biomedical sector. The popular sector is the lay sector of health care, which includes individuals, families, communities and peer influences (Nettleton, 2013). This sector is important in terms of socialization of health and illness behaviours as well as providing informal care. However, in Western society, the professional sector has historically had the most power and influence in determining policy, deciding what is illness and how to treat it, and in managing the nation's health. The professional sector is dominated by the biomedical model, and, in terms of mental health, by psychiatry and medicalization. This model developed historically when acute infectious diseases were the major causes of morbidity and mortality, and it has been seen to dominate the health and social care sector until the present day.

However, sociological perspectives concerning health and illness argue that medical treatment focused solely on biology is reductionist. White (2009) discusses how disease and illness can be seen as socially produced. Factors such as class, gender and ethnicity affect how diseases are 'distributed'. Treatment and knowledge surrounding illness and disease are affected by social structures and the societies in which we live. Critical here is that health inequalities are affected by the political and economic context of society. Thus social structures impact upon, for example, the prevalence of certain diseases amongst certain groups in society. A number of significant reports have drawn attention to the variables relating to disease and prevalence. White (2009) highlights how the Black Report (Department of Health and Social Security, 1980) raised the key issues relating to health inequalities which have continued to dominate health policy. Nettleton (2013) discusses the *Independent Inquiry into Inequalities of Health*, which built on the Black Report (Acheson, 1998). This showed a continuation of higher prevalence rates of disease and earlier mortality across social classes for a number of significant illnesses, for example strokes and heart disease. This led to a number of policy initiatives by the then Labour Government, called National Service Frameworks, to attempt to address these inequalities. However, health inequalities continue to be the reality for many people, including people with mental health problems. For example, a report concerning people with schizophrenia in 2012 highlighted significantly earlier mortality for this group (Schizophrenia Commission, 2012).

Nettleton (2013) also discusses how class, gender, race and geographical location are all factors relating to health inequalities. Later in the chapter we explore inequalities in these areas in relation to mental health. We will see that people with mental health problems experience structural inequalities relating to health and mental health in a binary context. This can be seen as similar to issues relating to disability and health inequalities. However, structural perspectives have focused on biomedical approaches to health and mental health, whereas sociology has developed a discourse relating to social causation and social construction.

Structuralism and the treatment of mental disorder

Biological approaches to health and illness developed during the Enlightenment with the focus on scientific knowledge. This included the development of psychiatry in relation to mental illness, which focused on the classification of mental disorder as a medical condition and on accompanying diagnoses of disorder (Pilgrim, 2009). Mental illnesses increasingly came to be seen as the result of genetics and chemical dysfunction within the brain. Genetic approaches were particularly prevalent, and can be seen as part of the ideological context of the late nineteenth century, based on Darwin's theory of evolution. Genetic malfunctions were believed to be passed down through the generations and to worsen with time. This can be related to the development of the eugenics movement (see Chapter 5). Biological approaches therefore focused on individual abnormality, with surgical and pharmacological treatments. This led to the development of mental health as a profession, with accompanying structures.

Medicalization can be defined as a process whereby processes and experiences that were previously seen as normal have increasingly come under the control of medical practitioners, to be diagnosed, investigated and treated (a classic example of this is childbirth – a normal physiological process, in many instances, that has come to be controlled through the specialisms of obstetrics and midwifery). This established medical authority in relation to mental disorder (Scull, 1979). Medicalization has particular relevance in the arena of mental health problems, as behaviours can be labelled and subject to treatments, acting as a powerful tool of social control. In addition, it is argued that the biomedical approach to the treatment of mental illness not only reduces the importance of structural factors and social causation, but also diverts policy attention away from them.

> **Medicalization** the process of increased involvement of the medical profession in areas previously seen as normal.

Early psychological theories of mental disorder also focused on individual malfunctioning, particularly in terms of personality development and stabilization. Classification concerning abnormality and normality was therefore as important here as within psychiatry. For example, from the standpoint of Freudian psychoanalysis, it was believed that personality stabilization could be achieved through progression through a series of sequential and developmental stages, and that interruption or regression of these stages led to mental abnormality. There is some evidence of this theoretical standpoint more recently in explanations of eating disorders (Bruch, 1973).

Biomedical models of mental illness have been highly influential in the develop-

Biological approaches to health and illness are seen as focusing on treatment, with an over-reliance on medication. (© sdominick/iStock)

Physiology study and science of functions of bodies/organisms.

ment of psychiatric treatments. The belief that mental illness/disorder could be treated at an individual level and the acceleration of research into brain anatomy and *physiology* led to the growth of the asylum system as a means of control, treatment and surveillance of people with mental health problems: 'The establishment of a comprehensive asylum system provided both a rationale for the confinement of lunatics in one place and an opportunity for the close scientific scrutiny of odd behaviour, delusions and delinquencies necessary for the development of a conceptual framework' (Rogers and Pilgrim, 2001: 46).

Asylum care and social control

The growth of the asylum system can be traced back to the 1860s and can be related to a wider context about social control and deviance that applied to other societal groups. Jones (1960) has argued that mental health asylums initially developed as humanitarian retreats located in the countryside. However, the growth of asylums has been particularly associated with developments in industrial capitalism and the need to contain deviance and promote the Protestant work ethic and notions of individual responsibility. As Abbott and Sapsford (1987: 7) note: 'there is a clear relationship between prevailing social structures, dominant ideology and the way society handles its deviants.' Thus the real growth in the asylum model can be seen alongside developments in the Poor Law and as part of the drive to maintain social control. Asylums became colonies for people with learning disabilities and mental health problems. Self-contained, these institutions allowed them to be virtually invisible within their local community.

Foucault (1979b) has argued that the asylum system reflected the post-Enlightenment approach to power and control. Behaviour could be controlled through biomedical surveillance of the population, with the medical profession (and psychiatry in particular) having legitimate authority to determine what was illness and how to treat it. From Weberian perspectives (see Chapter 12), if medical practitioners are given the legitimate authority to diagnose and treat illness, then that deviance can be controlled and compliance is enforced through medical treatments.

Control and surveillance were also manifest through the design of the asylums and the inter-relationships between staff and patients, demonstrating hierarchical patterns of organization. Geographical layout was important, based on the Foucauldian model of the panopticon (see Chapter 1), where the asylum was built around a central watchtower so that inmates could be potentially observed all the time (as in prisons). Individual wards also reflected this panopticon design.

These structural power relations are reinforced by the feelings of helplessness that many mental health service users report. So in these terms, mental distress could be seen as a reaction to powerlessness, whether from institutions, families or communities. Thus mental distress can be experienced as an internalized oppression, reinforced by societal structures. Gould and Martin (2012) discuss how mental health law leading to the containment of people with mental health problems has been a contested area as it can be perceived as discriminatory and part of an oppressive process. As Laurance (2003: 4) puts it:

> The complaint that mental health services are too coercive, too narrowly focused on medication and do not offer the kind of support that people want is widespread among people with mental problems. They see a service focused on containment, with little regard for people's individual experiences, few resources devoted to talking therapies and an emphasis on crisis management rather than preventative care.

However, relating this to structural functionalism (see Chapter 1), the containment of people with mental health problems serves to support order within society.

This psychiatric and asylum model of care dominated mental health service provision up until the final quarter of the twentieth century, when it came under increasing scrutiny from diverse groups, including service users and their carers. The challenges to the asylum model will be explored later in the chapter.

The adoption of a biomedical approach to mental illness has also been increasingly criticized, particularly from sociological perspectives. Although there may be an organic basis to some mental disorders (e.g. senile mental confusion), abnormal behaviour cannot be measured objectively, but is dependent on the social constructions of normality and abnormality. These social constructions are often a product of social and political circumstances and reflect dominant social processes and structures. Notions of abnormality and normality have also led to the labelling of people with mental health problems, and accompanying stigmatization.

Stigma

Stigma severe social disapproval of personal characteristics or beliefs that are against cultural norms. Goffman (1968) describes how stigma can manifest itself, and the damaging effects stigma can have on individual members of society.

The term *stigma* was originally used by the ancient Greeks to denote someone who was different. Stigma referred to the outer bodily signs that indicated deviance (e.g. branding of the skin in the case of criminals). In contemporary Western society, a number of clinical conditions are said to be stigmatized or stigmatizing and mark the individual out as different from other members of the population. Goffman (1968) defines stigma as the relationship between people's actual and perceived social identity. Stigmatizing conditions may be based on discreditable attributes (those that are not immediately visible – e.g. in the case of the mental illness, where it is often the label that marks someone out as being different) or discrediting attributes which are immediately visible (e.g. a facial disfigurement). People with stigmatized conditions come to be seen as inferior or culturally unacceptable (Williams, 1987) and there are negative moral connotations associated with them. Thus stigmas are not commonly associated with an informed and accurate perception of societal groups (Giddens and Sutton, 2013).

Labelling is an important aspect of stigmatization in mental illness, and is not necessarily based on objective criteria, but reflects the dominant stereotypes of society. These stereotypes become reinforced through a number of agencies, such as the criminal justice system, the education system and the medical system. This is related to the power of those in charge of societal structures, who define and label deviant behaviour (Giddens and Sutton, 2013). The media also have an important role to play in the stereotyping and continued stigmatization of people with mental health problems. The label of mental illness is often seen as people's primary defining characteristic in newspaper stories, and pejorative language is deployed to perpetuate the negative image of people with mental health problems. Bogg (2008) discusses how positive images concerning mental health rarely feature within the media. Negative portrayals therefore reinforce concerns about public safety in relation to people with mental health problems (Webber and Nathan, 2012).

Stigmatization can have a profound effect on people's social identity and social relationships. People with mental health problems not only have to manage the symptoms that they experience, but also have to manage societal reactions. The following quote from the Department of Health ShiFT document *Action on Stigma* (Department of Health, 2006: 8) illustrates the attitudes and discrimination faced by people who have been diagnosed with a mental illness.

> When I applied for a job as a cleaner at a care home, the manager called me and wanted to know more about my disability, which I'd declared. She pressed me so I said 'I'll be absolutely open with you. I've got a schizo-affective disorder and I hear the voices of people I know.' There was complete silence on the phone. She didn't say a word. So I said 'Hello, are you still there?' All she said was 'I'll be in touch.' Anyway, a few days later, lo and behold, I received a rejection letter. To me, her silence spoke volumes and I felt very discriminated against.

Structural perspectives

Social drift and social exclusion

Stigmatization and labelling can be seen as important in relation to the social causation of mental ill health. This is connected to the causes of mental illness being located within the structural inequalities of society, and the relationship between processes of stratification and the presence of mental illness. This is particularly important for social workers and other health and social care professionals in terms of the Allied Mental Health Professional (AMHP) role within mental health legislation of considering environmental and social factors impacting upon mental ill health and to look at other solutions than hospitalization. The following are all examples of structural inequalities within society, contributing to social exclusion and social disadvantage for people with mental health problems.

Social class

There is a clear social class gradient within the diagnosis of mental illness. In poorer areas of society, there are higher rates of schizophrenia, alcoholism and psychosis. This reflects the wider picture relating to patterns of mortality and morbidity according to social class (Giddens and Sutton, 2013). In a survey of general practice consultations, Shah et al. (2001) found that for all psychiatric disorders, consultation rates were higher for people from Social Class V. The causes for this are debated. Some have questioned whether it is the poverty that leads to the mental health problem or whether it is the other way round, and mental health problems lead to social exclusion from the labour market, and thus lead to poverty. This is known as the *social drift hypothesis* (Blane et al., 1993). Drift theory can lead to a higher concentration of people with mental health problems in inner cities where visibility is less apparent and services may be concentrated (Golightley, 2011). A number of studies have pointed to the importance of relative deprivation as a precipitating factor in the causation of mental illness.

> **Social drift hypothesis** the theory that people who are disadvantaged drift down the social scale. This is related to social exclusion.

This seems to be related to notions of citizenship and social inclusion (see Chapter 3). Barker and Taylor (1997: 58) note how: 'Relative deprivation has a greater impact on morbidity and GP consultation for stress-related conditions such as depression, anxiety and headache/migraine. . . . Relative deprivation is also associated with poorer mental health for . . . mothers of young children.'

Employment and material conditions

Employment for people with mental health problems continues to be a significant issue within contemporary society, with less than a quarter of people with mental health problems having employment (Mental Health Foundation, 2012). There is a clear relationship between labour market impoverishment and increased mental illness. This picture does not appear to have changed significantly (see, e.g., Social Care Institute for Excellence, 2011b). The statistics in Table 11.1 illustrate the stark difference between overall employment for working-age adults and people with mental health needs.

The stress of poverty is an important contributory factor to mental illness, but

Table 11.1 *Estimated employment rates (over 16 hrs/week) showing differentiation for people with mental health conditions, 2009 (percentage)*

Whole economy working-age employment rate	72.5
People with any disability	47.5
People with any mental illness	13.5
People receiving secondary mental health care and on Care Programme Approach	3.4

Source: HM Government, 2009

so is loss of status in a society that values doing over being. This can also help to explain the increasing morbidity from mental health problems in retirement, as older people become dislocated from economic and social roles (see Chapter 10). Loss of employment can lead to a loss of sense of self, reducing social worth and self-esteem, which may also impact on roles and relationships. Fagin and Little's (1984) research explores the impact of male unemployment and roles within a traditional family structure and concludes that these changes in family dynamics and roles and relationships cause stress and increase the potential for mental health problems in both genders. Furthermore, there is a triangular relationship between material conditions and physical and mental health problems. Those who suffer material deprivation are more likely to suffer from both poor physical and mental health (see Figure 11.1).

There is clearly a relationship between unemployment and mental illness, but also a relationship between work and mental health problems. Role overload, thwarted ambition, bullying and the target-driven economy can all lead to stress in the workplace and alienation (to use Marxist terminology).

Housing
Poor housing conditions and poor layout and design of dwellings have been linked with a higher incidence of physical and psychological problems (Conway, 2000). Littlewood and Tinker (1981) concluded from their research that mothers living in high-rise flats were more likely to experience stress due to the physical conditions of the accommodation. Significant factors included no play areas for children, difficulties in carrying prams and other equipment up flights of stairs and social isolation due to the inability to get out.

Noise and harassment are also seen as contributory factors to stress. The policy to

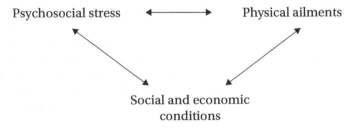

Figure 11.1   Physical and mental health and material deprivation.

house homeless families in bed and breakfast accommodation has been linked to a higher incidence of stress-related problems, not just because of poor-quality living space, but also owing to the effects on intimate partner relationships if there is a lack of defined adult space (Davies, 1993). Recently, problems with poor housing and local communities have been highlighted by policies connected to social exclusion. Correlations between crime, poor housing and problem neighbours have featured strongly in the media (Goodey, 2004). There is evidence to suggest that such fears can impact upon mental health, and there have been policy attempts to deal with community fears about security and harassment.

Social reaction theory and social constructionism

We have explored how social disadvantage relates to causation and experience of mental health problems. The social reaction to mental ill health is also significant. This theory argues that mental illness is not an objective category, but the labelling of mental illness stems from the reaction of others to deviant behaviour. Thus, it is argued, states of normality and deviance are socially constructed within societies. This can be observed within common parlance. Terms such as 'loony', 'nutter' and 'fruitcake' are widely used as terms of abuse for people who are seen as 'different' from others.

Scheff (1966) argues that societies have two sets of rules and norms: those that are regulated through the legal framework and those that reflect the dominant value systems and expected codes of behaviour within society. The latter he refers to as residual rules, and these differ between and within societies and over historical periods. They are constructed through the ruling majority. People are seen as deviant when they break these residual rules, although this is not an objective category. Whether someone is labelled as mentally ill for residual rule breaking depends on a number of factors:

- the degree of marginality of the residual rule breaker
- the perceived seriousness of the rule breaking
- the social distance between the labeller and the labelled
- the tolerance of the society of the deviant behaviour.

Thus labelling is seen as important within the social constructionist approach to mental illness. This can be particularly well demonstrated through the Rosenhan study of 1973. A number of people who had not actually been diagnosed with mental illness were admitted to mental institutions throughout the United States. The only person within the hospitals who was aware that these were not real patients was the medical director. The brief of these 'pseudo-patients' was to get themselves discharged from hospital. Throughout the period of the study, not one of the pseudo-patients was discharged. In fact all of their behaviour came to be seen within the context of the label: for example, one of the pseudo-patients was taking notes of his experiences, and written in his medical notes was the fact that he displayed excessive writing behaviour indicative of his schizophrenic diagnosis (Rosenhan, 1973).

Social constructionism is seen as important for the containment of deviance. A number of case studies demonstrate how dominant social norms have been legitimated through the construction of psychiatric diagnoses and the labelling of 'deviant' and 'abnormal' behaviour in relation to, for example, homosexuality (see Chapter 6). Drapetomania was another psychiatric classification of the late nineteenth century; this was a diagnostic label placed on Negro slaves, the symptoms of which were repeatedly attempting to escape from their masters. Drapetomania and the legitimation of the diagnosis are indicative of the dominant ideologies of the time, which were based on the Darwinian theory of social evolution; African and African Caribbean populations were seen to be inferior to whites and therefore it was acceptable to use them as slaves. Failure to comply with this accepted ideological norm therefore constituted deviance and needed to be managed (White, 2009).

A more contemporary example of social constructionist approaches can be seen through the examination of Attention Deficit Hyperactive Disorder (ADHD), the incidence of which Rogers and Pilgrim (2010) have argued has dramatically increased over the last couple of decades. However, Cooper and Bilton (2002) have questioned whether there has been a real rise in the incidence of ADHD, or whether there has been a rise in the labelling of this condition. In particular, they point to the role of schools and teachers in referring children who are seen as deviant, and question whether this is more about classroom management and social control than a manifestation of a greater incidence of pathology.

Thus social perspectives have questioned the biomedical (psychiatric) approach to mental illness and have instead focused on its social context. In addition, social perspectives tend to be critical of the objectification of the medicalized approach, as this ignores the lived experience of individuals and the importance of agency and social interactions. Social scientists (and this is increasingly reflected in policy and policies) have particularly focused on the concept of stigma in relation to mental illness and the consequences of stigmatization for service users and their carers.

Social stress theory and the lived experience

This perspective is concerned with the adaptive responses of individuals to stressful life events which are located within individuals' social and cultural contexts. Rogers and Pilgrim (2010: 53) note that 'in all social classes, the greater the number of life events, both positive and negative, then the greater the probability of psychiatric symptoms appearing'. However, this is rather simplistic and does not account for the higher prevalence amongst people lower down the social scale, as well as the presence of other variables that may mediate people's ability to manage the life events. Social integration is linked to good mental and physical health and lower mortality rates (Repper and Perkins, 2003). In addition, the presence or perception of emotional support from others improves mental and physical health and acts as a buffer against the impact of major life events. Intimate and confiding relationships provide the most powerful basis for emotional support. Thus it is argued that the breakdown of kinship networks and traditional communities (see Chapter 8) has led to more dislocated people within society without these buffers of emotional support.

Exercise: providing support for mental health needs

Think of a major life event where you have relied on others for emotional support.

- What kinds of support do you think social workers and other professionals can offer to assist people with mental health problems experiencing social stress?
- How can this support empower people to address the issues with social stress they are experiencing?

Social stress and vulnerability can be seen as affecting marginalized groups within society. For example, one of the key criticisms of community care has been that it has led to isolation within the community as opposed to isolation in an asylum. Social stress can also be a key issue for migrants and refugees, who experience displacement, discrimination, hostility and violence within local communities.

There have been two classic studies that have looked at stress and depression and coping mechanisms. The first of these, by Gove and Tudor (1973), explored the apparent prevalence of depression in housewives and offered a number of explanations related to the housewife role. The authors concluded that the stress of the female role in the traditional male breadwinner family was related to depression. Housework was often unstructured and monotonous, not time-limited and with long hours, leading to frustration. This was compounded by fact that the skills required for the housework tasks are often not commensurate with women's qualifications or educational ability. Furthermore, the unitary role of housework offered no opportunity for compensation in other roles to manage the stressors. Ironically, more recent research (Annandale and Hunt, 2000) has shown that as increasing numbers of women have entered the paid labour market (see Chapter 3), they have taken on multiple roles, leading to higher incidences of stress and depression. The traditional roles within the domestic division of labour (housework, childcare and, more recently, informal care of other dependants) have continued alongside paid labour, leading to role overload, feelings of inadequacy and dissatisfaction.

The second classic study in this area, by Brown and Harris (1978), argued that the ability to manage stress was mediated through social factors. In a study of post-natal depression (PND), the authors concluded that women were more likely to suffer from this condition if they had a combination of high vulnerability factors and high provoking agents. Vulnerability factors included low intimacy with husband or partner, loss of mother or poor relationship with her, a previous episode of PND, a previous loss (death or separation) and a lack of employment outside the home. Provoking agents included factors such as loss or threat of loss and long-term difficulties (e.g. poverty and social exclusion), domestic violence and marital breakdown. In addition, Brown and Harris saw personality characteristics as important, based on childhood experiences and low self-esteem.

Social stress theory can also be used to explain the rising incidence of suicide. Suicide is the second most prevalent cause of death for younger men, with concerns being expressed over the past two decades about the growing incidence of suicide amongst this group. In addition, the unemployed, prisoners, people with life-threatening physical illnesses, or who are being treated for mental illness, the recently divorced and separated, farmers and health professionals have a higher than average incidence of suicide. Mental health policy in recent years has sought to address this, particularly in relation to a high prevalence of suicide amongst young males. While this has decreased to a limited extent, the highest rate of suicide is now amongst middle-aged men, which may be caused by the current economic context (Department of Health, 2014).

The experience of mental illness

Not only does stigmatization have an impact on the societal view of mental illness, but it also impacts on people's sense of self when they have been diagnosed with mental illness. Through the process of secondary deviance, people may come to see themselves within the context of their label of primary deviance, affecting their self-image and self-esteem. Thus they internalize the dominant stereotype of society, which impacts on their sense of self-worth and self-belief, with implications for social interaction, as well as help-seeking behaviours. Rogers and Pilgrim (2010) discuss how labelling and stigma impact upon the lived experience of people with mental health problems both internally and within communities. Sociological thought on emotions argues that we learn how to internalize behaviour or actions that are deemed inappropriate within society (Thoits, 1985). This then impacts upon the participation and involvement of people with mental health problems within society.

The cost to the UK economy of mental illness in terms of missed employment opportunities is £23 billion per year, and the summary costs of care, premature death and economic loss amount to £77 billion per year (Office of the Deputy Prime Minister, 2004). The discrimination in employment against people with mental illness is evident in the fact that almost 50% of people who are signed off sick for six months or more with mental illness will never work again. Thus long-term unemployment and the attendant problems of material disadvantage, social exclusion and low self-worth are a particular issue. People who had been diagnosed with a psychotic illness were three times more likely than the rest of the population to have debt problems, to be in social housing provision and to be separated or divorced from their partner (Office of the Deputy Prime Minister, 2004). The following statement expresses the cumulative social problems faced by people with mental illness:

> So we are perceived as a social burden. We lose sight of our potential, and when we try to move on, discrimination and stigma prevent us getting jobs that use our skills and experience and push us out of housing and education. The jobs we do get are poorly paid, and don't utilise our skills and experience. And there are practical considerations – we stand to lose our financial security, whether state benefits or private insurance, when we attempt to rebuild our lives. We also stand to lose the health and social services that we find helpful, so that at the time when we most need support, our coping mechanisms are undermined. Moving back into society becomes a risky business. (Office of the Deputy Prime Minister, 2004: 3)

The experiences of people supporting relatives or friends with mental health problems have also been highlighted within the literature (e.g. Tew, 2011).

Critical sociology and contemporary perspectives

Critical sociological perspectives have challenged biological perspectives of health and mental health. The biomedical model has been seen as reductionist and it has been argued that social causation and social construction of illness are also important. As well as this, commentators have pointed to particular issues for a number of societal groups, including people with mental health problems. Critics of the biomedical model have argued that it does not take account of individual experiences. The growth of alternative medicine is important here in challenging scientific knowledge and interpretations (Giddens and Sutton, 2013). Alongside this, interactionist sociological perspectives are relevant. How people react to and live with illness has become part of health and mental health services in the UK and other countries: for example, supporting people to live with pain rather than just medically treating pain. Strategies to help individuals manage health problems have become an important part of services offered. This also relates to an increased emphasis on the voice of the 'patient' in connection with health and illness.

Social movements, health and mental health

Alongside extensive advice and guidance on health and well-being, the importance of self-management has also developed. The Expert Patient Programme, for example, has encouraged people to be in charge of their own health problems. Rather than listening to professionals, it is about listening to the individual experience (Department of Health, 2001a). This relates to sociological perspectives on narrative and the lived experience. As well as individual treatment, patient and user involvement has also become important generally within health and mental health. We are going to examine here the development of a social movement concerning mental health service users.

Beresford and others have written extensively about the development of mental health user organizations and services (e.g. Beresford, 2002). The mental health user movement, also known as the survivors' movement, has challenged the predominance of a medical and individualized model of mental illness, arguing that issues of power, control, stigma and labelling are seen as essential to understanding and working with people who have mental health difficulties. As with other social movements that have arisen in post-modernity, it has campaigned for civil and citizenship rights. The use of the term 'survivor' is symbolic of how social movements can be seen to challenge organized power (Giddens and Sutton, 2013). The mental health user movement has done this in a number of ways.

Contemporary mental health policy and practice can be seen to have been influenced by the mental health user movement in terms of involving users and carers within the planning and delivery of mental health services. The lived experience of people with mental health problems has also shaped a growing narrative approach which challenges the hegemonic power of psychiatry. Hanrahan (2012), for example, discusses how narrative is part of resistance to dominant discourses. Narrative theory has also had a significant impact on the development of the concept of recovery, which has challenged biomedical approaches (Tew et al., 2012).

Recovery and citizenship

Ideas around personal recovery can be seen to have developed from the lived experience of people with mental health problems (Social Care Institute for Excellence, 2007). This is part of critical sociological thought in relation to the sociology of mental health and illness, by using narrative and lived experience to support social change and transformatory practice. As discussed in Chapter 1, this relates to what Giddens (1991) calls self-reflexivity. Recovery can also be linked to the social model of disability, in also looking at how structural inequalities exclude people from society and advocating citizenship and social participation (Tew et al., 2012). Ralph and Corrigan (2005) identify three aspects to a recovery approach. Firstly, recovery happens naturally without intervention. Secondly, recovery occurs in relation to support and treatment of mental disorder. Thirdly, recovery is a continual process, where individuals are supported with ongoing mental health problems. It is perhaps the latter that is the particular focus of both user-led and professional mental health services. However, there is no one common definition of recovery, but a wide-ranging literature on recovery approaches and on the relationship of social perspectives to mental distress (see, e.g., Tew, 2011).

As we have explored, a mental health diagnosis can lead to stigma and resultant social exclusion. Essentially, people with mental health problems should be supported and enabled to value their own strategies for coping with mental illness. This takes account of the barriers within society that prevent this, similar to a social model perspective (see Chapter 5). Rather than focusing on 'cure' and symptom

Recovery and strengths-based approaches have become integral to partnerships with mental health service users in health and social care. (© Leeds and York NHS partnership Foundation Trust, reproduced with permission)

management, recovery perspectives propose that mental health users have the capacity to find their own solutions. Recovery perspectives therefore support enabling practice, rather than labelling people with mental health problems and providing solely medical treatments. A recovery model stresses the importance of hope and personal resilience, and there is a growing interest in how people's spiritual beliefs can be a source of personal strength (Barker and Buchanan-Barker, 2003). Recovery also relates to ideas of citizenship and social participation of people with mental health problems (Tew, 2011). This challenges structural inequalities relating to stigma, labelling and social stress theory explored earlier in the chapter.

Mancini (2011) discusses the importance of mental health professionals using evidence to support recovery-based perspectives within their practice. He also discusses how a recovery discourse has the potential to transform power relations between mental health service users and professionals. Thinking sociologically, this challenges the stratified system within which inequalities exist. For example, how language, terminology and discourse are used within assessment processes can be seen to have disempowered service users. Professionals have controlled the assessment process, reinforcing structural inequalities by 'gatekeeping' services and resources. How professionals approach intervention from a recovery perspective could significantly change this. Professionals can redirect power to service users by working in partnership in relation to recovery. Social workers can be part of this agenda, although the contemporary role and function of the social worker in mental health services is contested.

Case study

Prisca is a mental health social worker who is working with June, a young woman with mental health problems. June has had a number of compulsory admissions to psychiatric care in the last few years and is seen by professionals as having a 'chaotic' lifestyle. June has one child who is currently being fostered. June has recently moved to a new flat in a new area, as she wanted to put some distance between herself and her ex-boyfriend. She does not know anyone in the area where she lives.

- Conduct an internet search in relation to recovery plans and approaches.
- How might a recovery approach support June?
- What skills would Prisca need to work in partnership with June in relation to this?

Social perspectives and mental health social work

In the latter part of the twentieth century, social approaches to the understanding of mental illness and mental health started to emerge which can be seen as akin to the philosophy and values of social work practice. It is for this reason that it has been argued that the Approved Social Worker (ASW) role has been part of mental health legislation, to provide a balanced approach with other key medical professionals and ensure that social and environmental factors are taken into account when considering compulsory detention for people with mental health problems. Therefore, the social work role has been closely aligned to developing social approaches. Many commentators (e.g. Tew, 2011; Webber, 2012) would argue that social work continues to be in a good position to understand structural inequalities and the social construction of mental illness. A concern was that this would be lost in relation to the changing role of the ASW to Allied Mental Health Professional (AMHP) in the Mental Health Act (2007). The following quote sums up the debate at the time about the distinctiveness of the social work role:

> Social work does bring something distinctive to the mental health arena. The strong support offered to the social work role by service users at the consultation conference is testimony to that. Articulating it is more difficult and the NWW [New Ways of Working] group will be attempting to do that in a succinct way. It is a constellation of values, commitment to social justice, partnership with users and carers, the ability to see the social context of individuals and how this influences both behaviours and recovery, and a commitment to the worth of each individual which meant social workers practised social inclusion before the term had been invented. Above all it stands as a challenge to the traditional medical model of diagnosis, prescription and treatment which does not fully acknowledge the mental health service user as best informed about their needs. (Bamford, 2014)

However, social workers are not the only professionals who are working with social perspectives relating to mental distress. It is important to be aware of the debate on social perspectives as it has been crucial in shaping mental health policy and practice in recent years, and has led to many changes in services. There are new roles such as Support and Recovery Workers and a range of integrated mental health teams (Bailey and Liyanage, 2012). Concern has also been expressed that the changes to the ASW role will dilute the contribution of social work to social perspectives (Ramon, 2009). Currently, out of 5,000 AMHPs in the UK, only 120 are not social workers and there appears to be reluctance for other professionals to take on this role (Webber, 2012). This is seen as leaving social workers acting as AMHPs isolated within integrated teams (Bailey and Liyange, 2012). There continues to be debate about whether mental health social workers should be managed within a local authority or a health service structure (Nathan and Webber, 2010). There is also a reform agenda for social work itself, which may impact further on the mental health social work role (Department for Education, 2012b).

Policy makers have attempted to address professional divisions by advocating partnerships across health and social care. The National Service Framework for Mental Health (NSF) published by the Department of Mental Health in 1999 set targets and standards to tackle mental health problems in five key areas: health promotion and stigma; primary care and access to specialist services; the needs of those with severe and enduring mental illness; carers' needs; and suicide reduction. The review of progress within the NSF in 2004 set further objectives in working with people who have a dual diagnosis, tackling issues of social exclusion, the needs of people from ethnic minority groups, provision of psychological therapies and inpatient care. This has since led to new service models and role changes (Department of Health 2007d). The current Coalition Government also aspires towards preventative mental health policies, promoting recovery and social inclusion (Department of Health, 2011a). However, as explored, there remain tensions, conflicts and dilemmas between social perspectives and psychiatry. The power and influence of mental health social workers are contested within this.

Sociological perspectives enhance our understanding of these dilemmas and uncertainties. As Tew (2011: 9) states: 'It is important to develop a repertoire of concepts and models that may help us beyond the territory of just treating symptoms, and may be useful in giving meaning to experience, and in enabling and supporting recovery.'

It is this more pluralistic model that led to the formation of the Social Perspectives Network, which aims to create debate around social and psychological theories relating to mental health. At the heart of social perspectives is the recognition of people's experiences within society as significantly contributing to the development of mental health problems. Working to empower service users requires professionals to be open and able to embrace new ideas and models. Tew (2011) discusses the importance of not being 'fixed' to a particular model. Whittington (2003) echoes this in research findings concerning what service users expect from social workers. Anti-oppressive practice is at the heart of this process, recognizing how structural inequalities have impacted upon people with mental health problems. We have explored the connections between health inequalities, class and environment and mental health policy and practice. There are also binary issues for social workers to be aware of and explore in relation to gender and race.

Gender and mental health

Most of the sociological discussion about gender in relation to mental health has been about women, although there is a growing body of research about men's mental health.

More women than men either suffer from mental health problems or are diagnosed and labelled as such (Prior, 1999). Mental health issues for women may also be related to caring responsibilities. Taking time away from your own career can have personal stress and financial implications (Evandrou and Glaser, 2003) and caring can restrict personal freedom and lifestyle (Twigg, 1993). Men do predominate in categories of mental illness that involve the outward display of emotions, such as schizophrenia, alcoholism and psychoses (Tew, 2011). This may be related to processes of primary socialization which encourage boys to display anger more overtly, and girls to internalize it (see below).

Various theories have been put forward to explain the gender disparities in mental health, including social causation theories and social constructionist approaches. Women's material position in society, in particular, has been explored, with female material deprivation being related to the male hegemony of male breadwinner society, and horizontal and vertical segregation in the paid labour market (see Chapter 3).

Sex-role stereotyping and gender socialization are also seen as important factors in the explanations of gender inequalities in mental health. Women are socialized to be passive and to direct anger internally and are therefore more likely to be diagnosed with depression and neurotic conditions. Rogers and Pilgrim (2010: 82) note that:

> men's conduct has been more associated with public anti-social acts, violent and sexual offences, drunken aggressive behaviour, and so on. In contrast, women's behaviour has been associated more with private, self-damaging acts, where aggression is directed at the self rather than others. Depression, parasuicide, eating disorders and self-mutilation together summarize this tendency. Men are more likely to

indulge in behaviour that is antisocial, and to be labelled as criminally deviant more than women. This is then reflected within psychiatry, in that men are more likely to have labels which refer to and incorporate the threat of their behaviour.

However, there may also be gender differences in obtaining help. Women are generally more likely to consult GPs (Sandman et al., 2000) and are more likely to engage with health promotion and preventative health strategies (White, 2009) that may impact on earlier detection and/or prevention of serious health problems. Research has also focused on men and their dislocation from traditional roles and the relationship to increased mental health problems (Aldridge, 1998).

Ethnicity and mental health

Ethnicity is now seen as a key determinant of mental health. Whilst there is limited research into the areas of race and mental health, a number of studies (e.g. Brown, 1997) have concluded that overall rates of diagnosis of mental illness are higher amongst African Caribbeans and some groups of Asians, and, in particular, severe mental illness such as schizophrenia. In a study in 1987, McGovern and Cope reported that schizophrenia was diagnosed between 4 and 12 times more often in African Caribbean immigrants and between 7 and 18 times more often in British-born people of African Caribbean descent than amongst the British white population. Black people are 44% more likely than average to be detained under the Mental Health Act and black Caribbean men are 29% more likely to experience physical restraint (Sashidharan, 2003). Furthermore, people from African Caribbean backgrounds are more likely to be detained by the police under Section 136 of the Mental Health Act, even though there is no significant ethnic difference in the use of violent or threatening behaviour (Smaje, 1995). The evidence about incidence and diagnosis of mental illnesses amongst people of Asian descent is less conclusive. Some studies have found a slightly higher incidence of hospitalization for mental health problems amongst Indian and Pakistani immigrants than among white English men (Dean et al., 1981), whilst others have found a lower incidence (Cochrane, 1977). However, Raleigh (1996) suggests that cultural and language differences may lead to an under-reporting of mental health problems among people of Asian background. In addition, there is evidence to suggest that both Asian and African Caribbean people are more likely to receive medicalized rather than psychological treatments (Fernando, 2010).

Social class positioning, racism, disadvantage and social stress (e.g. from migration) are all factors affecting ethnic minority groups. Stereotypical images influence assessment and the services provided. Consequently, people from ethnic minority groups can be seen to avoid service input until a specific crisis is reached. This then reinforces the control aspect of mental health services.

The relationship between race, ethnicity and mental health has been of particular debate in Britain since the 1970s. The nature of this debate has changed from a preoccupation with so-called 'race differences', ethnic and cultural dispositions to particular forms of mental illness, to considering ethnic inequalities in service experience and outcomes linked to the poor experiences of BME groups in British society and its institutions. The Macpherson Report into the death of Stephen Lawrence defined institutional racism as the 'collective failure of an organization to provide an appropriate and professional service to people because of their colour, culture or ethnic origin' (Macpherson, 1999). Following an amendment to the Race Relations Act (2000), institutional racism has become a focus for intervention for public organizations, and recognition of the manifestation of racism has been highlighted by a number of high-profile cases in mental health care. A review following the death in 1998 of David Bennett, an African Caribbean man suffering from schizophrenia who had been forcibly restrained whilst in a mental health unit, concluded that widespread stereotyping, cultural ignorance, institutional discrimination and the stigma and anxiety associated with mental health often combine to undermine the ways in which mental health services recognize, assess and respond to the needs of BME communities (Sainsbury Centre for Mental Health, 2002). Moreover, the independent inquiry into Bennett's death argued that 'if a patient's cultural, social and religious needs are not scrupulously considered, these will inevitably affect his reactions and may exacerbate his symptoms. It is essential that every patient is treated according to his needs' (Norfolk, Suffolk and Cambridgeshire Strategic Health Authority, 2003: 23).

Research in the review mentioned above, *Breaking the Circles of Fear* (Sainsbury Centre for Mental Health, 2002), found that, on the one hand, service users feared using mental health services, which were seen as a part of a coercive 'system' akin to the criminal justice system in terms of regulation, whilst, on the other hand, professionals, fuelled by misconceptions and stereotypes, feared intervention with black people. There continues to be a debate about ethnicity and mental health and the over-representation of ethnic minority groups within mental health services. The impact of labelling in relation to the mental health disorder of ethnic minority groups is still seen as a significant issue within health and social care practice (Fernando, 2010). More recently, the need for social workers and other professionals to work positively with people with mental health problems seeking asylum has also been highlighted (Fernando, 2010). This relates to the global context of health and mental health inequalities.

Global context, health and mental health

In previous chapters we have discussed the increased importance of global sociological perspectives in understanding the political, social and economic context within which societies operate. An understanding of global health inequalities is important within this context. Essentially, people living in high-income countries are healthier than those living in low-income countries (Giddens and Sutton, 2013). Nettleton (2013) also talks about the globalization of information on health and well-being with the development of supranational bodies which have been used to develop consumerism in health care on a global scale. However, this is likely to only be experienced by those in higher-income groups.

Additionally, the impact of conditions such as HIV/AIDS is significant within the global context, with a much higher prevalence in low-income countries (UNAIDS, 2006). The social construction of conditions such as HIV/AIDS is also important (Nettleton, 2013). For health and social care professionals in the UK, the mental health needs of people seeking asylum within the UK have also become increasingly significant.

The World Health Organization's Report *Mental Health: New Understanding, New Hope* (2001) advocated that commonalities were adopted in relation to the treatment and support offered to people with mental health problems across countries. However, the concern here is that this is overly preoccupied with managing risk. Rogers and Pilgrim (2010) argue that the WHO Report serves to reinforce structural inequalities on a global scale by focusing on psychiatric treatment and accompanying laws. They advocate investment in mental health support services on a global scale rather than a focus on risk and safety.

Commentators have argued that the global context of social disadvantage and consequent migration has a significant impact on high levels of psychosis in migrant groups (Morgan and Hutchinson, 2010). Thus issues relating to the social causation of mental illness can be seen as intensified by the experiences of people who are also facing high levels of stress and uncertainty within the social, political and economic context. The issues relating to poverty, disadvantage and class and mental health disorder can also be seen on an international scale (Lorant et al., 2003). The global context of health and mental health can be related to sociological perspectives on disadvantage and social exclusion. As in other areas explored in this book, it is important for social workers and other professionals to have an understanding of this global context.

Conclusion

Sociological perspectives in relation to mental health have a resonance with the value base of social work practice. On the one hand, the role of social factors in mental ill health has been given credence in a plethora of social initiatives, services, policy and good practice guides. On the other, mental health law and policy shows that power and control issues in mental health are still highly relevant. Public concerns about managing risk and media portrayals of people with severe mental health problems continue.

However, there are positive changes within mental health practice. There is a body of work on psychological and sociological perspectives on mental health which can help with understanding and working with people who have mental health problems. Many health professionals have argued that they are working from a 'holistic' model of mental health (Tew, 2011). The National Service Framework for Mental Health (Department of Health, 1999) provides an opportunity for partnership between health and social care services. There are also opportunities for mental health professionals to work with personalization from a recovery and strengths-based perspective (Bailey and Liyanage, 2012). Therefore, seeing all health professionals as working from a psychiatric approach can be reductionist. Indeed, amongst psychiatrists, there is a critical psychiatric movement that sees social factors as more of an imperative than biomedical models. The Critical Psychiatry Movement is influenced by ideas from what is known as the 'anti-psychiatry' movement encapsulated by the work of R.D. Laing in the 1960s which challenged methods used in psychiatry (e.g. ECT, or electroconvulsive therapy, treatment).

It is important that social workers and other health and social care professionals engage and work with critical perspectives. As has been identified in the chapter, this is taking place within changes to integrated working in mental health (Nathan and Webber, 2010). Social workers do and can make a positive contribution to positive practice with people who have mental health problems. Moving away from the 'us and them' debate to working alongside service users sits well with empowering practice and social action perspectives.

Summary points

- A biomedical model of mental illness has dominated treatment and support since the 1860s.
- Structural inequalities influence mental illness, leading to social exclusion and disadvantage.
- Sociological perspectives on social reaction theory, stigma and labelling are important for understanding the social context of mental health problems.
- The mental health user movement has become increasingly important in challenging biomedical perspectives and has influenced the development of the recovery model.
- Critical sociological perspectives have also challenged structural perspectives in relation to inequalities in mental health experienced by a number of societal groups.
- Social perspectives and social workers have a contribution to make within contemporary mental health policy and practice.

Questions for discussion

- Are the biomedical model and the social model of mental illness mutually exclusive, or can they be used in conjunction with each other to empower and enable people?
- Is the role of the social worker in mental health under threat? If so, what might be the implications of this?
- Is mental illness real, or a social construction based on dominant ideas of normality and abnormality?

Further reading

Karban, K. (2011) *Social Work and Mental Health.* **Cambridge: Polity**
This book provides a comprehensive discussion of theoretical frameworks in mental health which help the reader to understand the role of social workers when working with people with mental health problems in a range of settings. There is a strong emphasis on social perspectives, and key sociological concepts such as inequality are discussed in depth.

Laurance, J. (2003) *Pure Madness: How Fear Drives the Mental Health System.* **London: Routledge**
This book is critical of the nature of mental health services, and provides a good critical commentary on the sources of oppression for people with mental health problems.

Rogers, A. and Pilgrim, D. (2010) *A Sociology of Mental Health and Illness.* **4th edition. Buckingham: Open University Press**
This is an accessible book which provides a comprehensive discussion of social theories of mental illness.

Tew, J. (2011) *Social Approaches to Mental Distress.* **London: Palgrave**
This text brings together a range of social perspectives that help us to explore the social context of mental health problems. This is related to contemporary mental health policy and practice.

12 Social Work and Social Context

Introduction

Social work practice is continually changing, with an evolving social context based on economic, social and political factors. In recent years, there has been a focus on reorganization and regulation of social work. The work of the Social Work Reform Board (2010) is being implemented and overseen by The College of Social Work. Alongside this work, the Health and Care Professions Council (HCPC) is now responsible for the monitoring and regulation of social work. The overarching Professional Capabilities Framework (PCF) assessing professional capability from pre-qualification to senior social worker and management level is now the core development pathway for social workers (College of Social Work, 2012a). In Chapter 1, we explored sociological thought relating to social location and status. The current work of regulatory and scrutiny bodies for social workers will impact upon this. Additionally, the recent publication of two reviews of social work education and training is likely to further affect the structure and function of social workers (Croisdale-Appelby, 2014; Department for Education, 2014).

Against this backdrop of changes within the regulation and management of the profession, the impact of recession on social care and social workers can be seen in terms of resource constraints, low staff morale and stress and burn-out (Collins, 2008). As the book has explored, there are particular challenges in work with different user and carer groups. The emphasis of the proposed changes is to improve the calibre of social workers and the knowledge and skill base which social workers use in their practice. However, there is concern within the profession as to how changes can be implemented within the current economic and political context and also within the organizational cultures within which social work operates (Moriarty et al., 2011). As has been explored throughout the book, an understanding of sociological perspectives which connect with the user and carer groups social workers engage with can provide social workers with the potential to be an emancipatory force. However, we have also examined the contradictory tensions in the social work role in relation to function and structural power. Sociological thought concerning organizational theory and bureaucracy, power, identity, emotional intelligence and resilience is particularly relevant here and will be explored further in this chapter and related to contemporary issues within social work practice. The global context of the challenges that social workers face will also be explored, as this can be seen to increasingly impact on the context of UK social work practice (Hamama, 2012).

> ### The key issues that will be explored in this chapter are:
>
> - the current context of social work education, training and professional development
> - structural perspectives and the role and function of state social work
> - power, sociological perspectives and the social work role
> - organizational theory and sociological perspectives in the context of social work practice
> - critical sociology and relationship to social work practice
> - critical social work practice in the social context
> - the global context of social work.

> ### By the end of this chapter you should be able to:
>
> - demonstrate an awareness of social work education, training and development and the relevance of sociological perspectives
> - understand how structural sociological perspectives relate to the role and functions of social workers within the statutory context
> - understand how sociological perspectives on power relate to inherent tensions in the social work role
> - have an understanding of organizational theory, managerialism and social work practice
> - have an awareness of the relationship between critical sociology and critical social work practice
> - have an awareness of the changing nature of social work practice within a global context.

Social work as a profession

Throughout the history of social work there have been numerous attempts to redefine its roles and responsibilities, reorganize the delivery of services and re-educate its workforce. Social work as a profession can be seen in relation to the role and function of a range of professional groups who developed as a result of the welfare state in the 1950s. Whilst there are many theories of professionalism (e.g. Johnson, 1972), a commonly held definition of a profession is an occupational group that displays certain traits. For functionalists, not everyone can hold these traits, and therefore we place our trust in the professionals (e.g. doctors and lawyers) to use their expert knowledge for our benefit. Professional groups have tended to promote their role in organizations through acquiring a knowledge base and thus status. In terms of the sociological perspectives discussed in Chapter 2, social work is part of a professional middle class. However, some of the main tenets of professionalism (e.g. a monitoring professional association) have only recently been achieved. Thinking about social stratification, this can be seen to have impacted upon the status and professional power of social work (Giddens and Sutton, 2013). It is only recently that social work has become a degree-level qualification, and this has been later than for many health and social care professional courses. The regulation and accreditation of social work training and regulation are currently divided between two organizations and the clarity this gives to the professional status of social work has been questioned (Department for Education, 2014). The new College of Social Work has been established to give social workers a clear national voice and to provide direction for the profession. The College has provided a professional development framework as well as developing standards. For example, Brindle (2014) sees it as positive that The College of Social Work has published advice on the social work role and task.

As well as the development of The College of Social Work, a new training scheme for social workers has been piloted. Frontline provides a fast-track training scheme separate from standard university training. Frontline has seen 25 applicants for each place and half of these are drawn from Russell group universities (Brindle, 2014). Referring back to Chapter 2 and structural theories on class, Frontline can be seen as promoting educational meritocracy within social work education and training as it looks to recruit academic achievers. As such, it has been criticized for being elitist and it has been argued that fast tracking will not necessarily improve the quality and retention of social workers (Cooper, 2013). However, it can also be seen to be improving the professional attainment of some social worker trainees.

Exercise: professional development and the Professional Capabilities Framework

Have a look at Figure 12.1 (also available at *http://www.tcsw.org.uk/pcf.aspx*). Find your level within this development framework and ask yourself the following questions:

- How do you see yourself developing as a professional within this process?
- What do you see that you have achieved as a professional, and what has helped you to do this?
- Do you feel you have professional status as a student or qualified social worker?

The debate concerning what kind of professional makes a good social worker is at the heart of much of this chapter. Sociological perspectives are helpful in placing this debate within a social context. The focus on the regulation of social work can be seen as focusing on a structural view of professionalism. Carey (2014) discusses how social workers see a significant gap between the rhetoric of professionalism and the reality of front-line social work practice. This relates to a neo-Marxist perspective concerning labour and work alienation within capitalist economies, and the argument that social work has become 'state' social work. Jordan and Drakeford (2012) discuss how the development of social policy and social welfare has been closely related to the provision of such 'state' social work. The provision of social work services (particularly by the local authority) has therefore been closely connected with other public services such as council housing, welfare benefits and government employment and training programmes.

Lymbery and Butler (2004) suggest that continual changes to social work, social welfare and social policy have led to social work becoming more focused on a reactive and reductionist model of professional practice which is limited to statutory roles

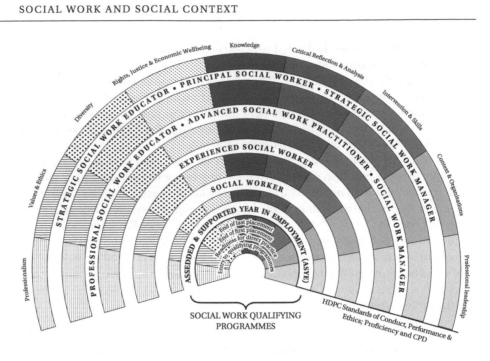

Figure 12.1   Professional Capabilities Framework for Social Workers.
Source: © The College of Social Work. Accessed 8 April 2014: correct at time of going to press. (The PCF is subject to regular updating.)

and responsibilities. The specialist role relating to safeguarding within child protection work is a good example of this. Hafford-Letchfield (2006) discusses how this relates to a hierarchical system of work which is closely managed and specialised. This emphasis on process can be seen to have connections with the theory of *scientific management* and labour production developed approximately a century ago by theorists such as Taylor (1911). While this described a mechanistic view of labour production, scientific management theory can be seen as relevant to the systematic model being adopted within health and social care today (Pinnock, 2004). This is because professional social work within this model has become task-orientated and closely supervised. As such it has been seen as deskilling, a discussion to which we return later in this chapter

> **Scientific management** a scientific approach to industrial economy where workers are tightly managed within a mechanized process.

There have also been criticisms that this model of social work practice has responded to media and public concerns about the immediacy and efficacy of social work practice: for example, the media 'scandals' concerning child protection which have occurred over the past 40 years (see Chapter 9). Social work commentators continue to argue for the need for social work values and emancipatory practice to support social workers in resisting this reductionist view of professional social work (e.g. Ferguson and Woodward, 2009). As we will explore, this also relates to the debate between the structural context of social work practice and critical sociological perspectives.

Despite the tensions described, social work has remained a prominent career choice within the helping professions as we have moved into the twenty-first century. This has been assisted by its becoming a degree-level profession and by the provision of state funding for social work training. Hill (2010) highlights how social work still remains a popular career choice, despite students being aware of the challenges of the structural context of social work. Furness's research shows that applicants for social work training are still motivated by a desire to help others and that social work is seen as a satisfying and morally rewarding career (Furness, 2007). However, there has been concern that despite buoyant recruitment to social work programmes, social workers' analytical skills and knowledge are being devalued as individual practitioner autonomy and decision-making are being reduced. Morley and Dunstan (2013) explore how social work identity in relation to empowerment and supporting change for service users is being eroded by the economic context of social work practice. This is impacting upon social work practice in a number of Western democracies. Stanford (2010) refers to a contemporary organizational context of fear and blaming which impacts upon the individual experience of social workers. The chapter will explore how 'best' practice can be promoted despite this contradictory context. However, we first look further at structural issues which impact upon social work practice and their connection with sociological perspectives.

State social work and structuralist perspectives

As outlined in Chapter 1, sociological perspectives concerned with the functions of societal structures are still relevant when we look at the state or statutory functions of health and care professions such as social work. There are currently considerable challenges for social workers in relation to their professional role and responsibilities. This has had a significant impact on how social work is perceived within society and on the social and professional identity of social workers, whether student or qualified (Stanford, 2010). Hughes and Wearing (2007) discuss how the current emphasis on business and performance culture within health and social care organizations also needs to be analysed when looking at organizations, power and professional identity in social work. This needs to be understood with reference to neo-liberalism and the impact that this had on the economic context within which social work operates.

In discussing the political, economic and social context of contemporary state social work practice, the impact of neo-liberalist thinking is important. Penna and O Brien (2013) summarize this debate. Within neo-liberalist thought, market forces predominate. Trade in a global context is allowed freedom from individual state control, which is seen as supporting wealth creation and individual freedom. Crucially for health and social care services, governments also need to reduce public expenditure on public services and social welfare.

The impact of cuts on public services is significant at the present time. Neo-liberalism is an economic and ideological approach to policy delivery, focusing on deregulation and the adoption of private management principles and public sector cuts. In the UK, it can be traced back to the 1970s, with the ideological shift in the management of public sector institutions, reflecting the Thatcherite principles of freedom and liberty. The new right advocated rolling back the frontiers of the welfare state and reducing dependence on the public sector. This created a mixed economy of welfare and saw private sector management principles being adopted by public sector organizations. This has continued with successive governments since the 1970s. The impact of marketization and consumerism is discussed below. The neo-liberalist and new managerialist policy direction of governments in Western democracies has developed since the 1990s, and was amplified under New Labour policies in the UK (Geyer, 2012). Neo-liberalism involved minimal government intervention, a focus on empowering people to self-help and the supremacy of the private market in welfare.

Neo-liberal policies reflect a profound change in public sector management principles, with an emphasis on cost reduction and privatization, leading to new forms of public management. New Labour embarked on a programme of modernization of public services, which can be seen in a number of policy documents concerned with the development of social work and social work services. *Modernising Adult Social Care* (Department of Health, 2007c) is one example of this, with an increased emphasis on competitiveness.

This has been significant for state social workers in changing the landscape of public services available to them in their work. It has also led to an audit culture, which has flourished in the last two decades (Lauder et al., 2012) with an emphasis on performativity and targets. This has resulted in significant changes in policy delivery with a triangular process of management, through strategic development of policy through centralized government, operationalization through a civil service that is accountable for policy development and local implementation (Geyer, 2012).

Neo-liberalist policies have led to a 'mixed' economy of care, where there has been a reduction in public provision of social care services and a concomitant rise in provision from private companies (Healy and Meagher, 2004). Significant changes in residential care and day and home care services have also resulted from this modernization process. This reduction in state-provided social care services directly relates to the challenges that social workers are currently facing within statutory services (C. McDonald, 2006). In a mixed economy of care, social workers are using their legal and statutory responsibilities to provide services to vulnerable people from both public and private sector providers. They are also providing services to those most affected by a reduction in social welfare services. As we go on to explore later in the chapter, this has impacted upon the ability of social workers to be emancipatory in their practice.

Changes to public services have led to significant restructuring of social work services, which has left social workers feeling constrained by the organizations within which they work (Wilson, 2013). This has created uncertainty about the future of the social work role in a number of areas. It is important to state that adult social work and children's social work now involve separate organization and management, which impacts upon the sense of a generic context within which social work operates. The structural context of practice within children's services has been heavily influenced by a number of high-profile inquiries into the death of children under the care and support of social work services (Department for Children, Schools and Family, 2009b; Department of Health and Home Office, 2003). Children's social care services are working with some of the most marginalized and excluded families within society and responding to safeguarding issues rather than using legal and statutory responsibilities to provide support to families (Department for Education, 2011a).

As well as being subject to a transformational agenda of modernizing services, adult social care has witnessed a change in care philosophy. As outlined in Chapters 5 and 10, there is a current emphasis on personalized and self-directed services (Leece, 2012). This has created ongoing uncertainty about the future role and remit of adult social workers (Lymbery and Postle, 2010). Additionally, while the ethos of personalization is about promoting individual empowerment, it has been argued that there is also a neo-liberalist policy agenda to service changes (Leece, 2012). At the same time, social workers within adult social care service are working to safeguard vulnerable adult groups (Holloway and Lymbery, 2007).

Some areas of adult and children's social work have seen the increased prominence of the third sector and a reduction in state social work services. For example, work with homelessness and substance misuse now tends to be provided by a range of agencies across a number of sectors (Nelson, 2012). This reflects the impact of a mixed economy of care and a consequent reduction in the social work role in these areas. It also highlights that there are now a range of professionals involved in providing social welfare services to a number of excluded groups and communities.

State-provided social work services are therefore going through a period of profound change with demarcations arising between statutory adult and children's services as well as the outsourcing of functions and responsibilities to the third sector. This has led to some discussion about changes to the social work degree and moves away from a generic social work qualification. Lymbery and Postle (2010) argue that this would result in a fragmentation of social work practice, and they emphasize the importance of core generic social work values, knowledge and skills. They also emphasize the importance of qualified practitioners able to manage complex uncertainties.

Social work and power

The current ability of social workers to support emancipatory practice has been questioned. As state services have been reduced, it can be argued that social workers are seen as 'agents of the state' using power to control and direct marginalized groups. Thinking sociologically, social work power is used to control and sanction deviant behaviour (Giddens and Sutton, 2013). Social work can be seen as having become more concerned with monitoring and surveillance underpinned by a range of legal responsibilities (Jordan and Drakeford, 2012; see Chapter 7). Here social workers are operating between state structures associated with social and welfare services (e.g. housing) and a policing role (e.g. benefits and monitoring young offenders). This shapes the interactions of social workers with service users rather than fostering social action and emancipatory approaches where social workers are working in partnership with individuals. Intervention based on power and control is likely to continue where reduced state services are focused on the most vulnerable and excluded. Pollack (2010), for example, discusses how social workers spend their time in child protection working with 'high-risk' families. Smith (2008), meanwhile, discusses how, because social workers are part of state structures, responses to service users are shaped by this structural context. Therefore power is used in a collective and oppressive way to reinforce inequalities rather than in an individual way to support change. Promoting access to opportunities is also important here. As explored in Chapter 2, social workers operate as part of social stratification and social divisions where position within a social hierarchy determines not only employment, but also access to a range of benefits. This serves to create hegemonic relationships between state social work services, social workers and service users. Within this context, it is seen as legitimate to use power and authority given by the state to monitor marginalized and excluded groups. Fred Powell (2001) argues that this therefore makes social work a political activity as it is intervening between the state and individuals. Later in the chapter, we will explore power in relation to social action theories, where power can be utilized in different ways within the individual relationship with service users.

There are a number of instances where the connection between state power and social work power can be seen within this structural context: for example, attendance parenting skills groups as part of 'penalities' where children and young people do not attend school and imprisonment of parents of persistent truants (see Chapter 8). Here social workers may feel expected to focus on the control mechanisms such social orders give rather than on wider structural factors such as poverty (Smith, 2008). This analysis is particularly pertinent to safeguarding children and work with youth offenders, although it needs to be located within the broader economic context discussed earlier. The inner-city riots of 2011 and the governmental and state response to this led to a focus on working with deviant and socially excluded families (Jordan and Drakeford, 2012; see Chapter 8). A number of social policy measures have been proposed here which it can be argued relate to using power to monitor rather than to achieve emancipatory change.

Social work and risk

Previously in the book, we have explored sociological perspectives on the social construction of risk in relation to a range of user groups social workers engage with. The emphasis on monitoring within social work practice is seen as increasing a defensive and risk-averse work culture with an emphasis on recording decisions and an over-reliance on rules and procedures (Beddoe, 2010). Supervision as a management activity within the work place is therefore about ensuring that individual workers are managing risk within a procedural context. This relates to the social context of social work, where preoccupations with risk, safety and the wider security of society as a whole are paramount (Webb, 2006).

Stanford (2010, 2011) argues that this focus leads to social work being practised within a culture of fear for many individual practitioners. This creates a reactive climate for practice, where social workers feel they have to justify every action in the context of managing risk rather than assessing needs and promoting rights and social justice. This then impacts upon professional confidence and the ability to manage stressful and complex dilemmas. Stanford's research also demonstrates how preoccupation with risk influences both personal and professional identity for social workers within Western societies (Stanford, 2010). A significant part of assessment of individual needs has therefore come to be about measuring and defining risk (Webb, 2006). This involves a bureaucratic context to practice with an emphasis on technical skills within clearly defined systems, relating back to the previous point about scientific management (Kemshall, 2010). As resources are constrained and demands increase, this emphasis is likely to continue with accompanying changes to public management and organizational culture.

Exercise: risk self-audit

Think about your own practice as a student or qualified social worker and identify a situation where risk has been a factor:

- Was the recording and monitoring of risk a concern in this situation?
- Did this affect the work undertaken and any specific outcomes?
- Might alternative approaches to risk have been employed?

Organizations, management and social work

As outlined earlier, organizational systems and processes are important for the contemporary social work professional. Hughes and Wearing (2007) argue that social workers need to be aware of the importance of organizational analysis to be expert and informed practitioners. Organizational theory is important for contemporary social work practice in a number of ways. It enables us to understand how organizations are structured and the political, economic and social context that shapes this. This therefore means that we can understand the culture of health and social care organizations and factors such as authority, hierarchy, status and management. This discourse also needs to be located within an understanding of the impact of neo-liberalist thought on how health and social care organizations are reacting to the current economic context concerning resource management. Increasingly, as demand has increased and resources have contracted, this has led to a hierarchical approach to managing social work services and the loss of individual worker accountability in the practice environment (Hafford-Letchfield, 2006).

For Max Weber (see Chapter 1), the most efficient way to organize large-scale organizations was through bureaucracy, based on hierarchy. While he agreed with structuralists that institutions, classes and groups were important elements of society, he was also interested in the way in which individuals influenced and created the structural elements of society (Weber, 1976). Weber argued that capitalism needed efficient administrative structures for managing processes and tasks, and bureaucratic organizations were the way to achieve this. The bureaucratic approach can be seen to exemplify many aspects of contemporary social work organization: eligibility criteria regarding needs; allocation of work; panels to decide resource allocation; processes for managing safeguarding decisions. Later in the chapter we explore whether and how individuals may be able to influence these bureaucratic processes. Weber's concept of rational-legal authority, where organizations are governed by rules and regulations, is significant here, based on a hierarchical management structure. This creates an automated response to practice in terms of, for example, presenting requests for services to resource panels. Relating this to the work of Taylor, Braverman looked at the 'de-skilling' of work which could result from a scientific management approach to labour. It can be argued that social workers have become de-skilled, as they have lost the power to make discretionary decisions within the current context (Braverman, 1974). However, social workers also need to be able to make an articulated and informed case for resources, which does require skills within the same process. A scientific approach also does not take account of

Social workers feel increasingly under pressure from bureaucratic and time-consuming processes. (© AVAVA/iStock)

the individual experience regarding motivation and personal qualities, for example (Hafford-Letchfield, 2006).

Organizational change has been significant within social work services, as it has been across the health and social care economy. Local authorities have also 'contracted out' aspects of their legal and statutory responsibilities to a specialized third sector (e.g. carers' assessments). There has also been the development of integrated services and teams with health professionals. This has raised a number of issues in particular sectors about management, pay, resource allocation and work conditions which have been identified as problematic (see, e.g., Bailey and Liyanage, 2012, regarding mental health social workers, as discussed in Chapter 11).

This has meant that change within social work organizations has often been viewed by front-line staff not as positive and benefiting workers or service users but as being about public service cuts and service reorganization. This can be seen in relation to social worker support for personalization, which has decreased over the past few years (Dunning, 2011). Change is seen as being about more about private sector principles within a mixed economy of care, where service users and workers have few choices and change is not part of a collaborative process. For example, social workers within adult social care are fearful of a loss or de-skilling of their jobs due to changes within personalization and self-assessment (Davies, 2012).

At the same time as there has been concern expressed about the social work role, there has also been an entrenchment of management hierarchies within social work causing a reduction in practitioner autonomy. This relates to the neo-liberalist policy agenda discussed earlier in the chapter. Writers refer to this as the 'new managerialism' of social services (e.g. Adams et al., 2009; Healy, 2002), which would appear to embed structuralism in social services. Financial responsibility and control is important, particularly given the reduction in budgets in recent years. There has also been an emphasis on managing individual performance, specific timescales for assessments and the role of monitoring and quality processes. Performance management of both outcomes for service users and measurement of staff performance has been identified as complex given the day-to-day changes experienced by many of the people social workers engage with (Healy, 2002). Bailey and Liyange (2012) also highlight the difficulties with management systems in relation to integration between health and social work services, with a number of barriers being identified relating to strategic leadership, finances and individual staff areas of responsibility.

Change management theory is a key concept within the private sector, and has now become influential within public sector management and leadership. Lewin (1951) developed a process where organizations adapt to change and then stabilize into new processes and structures guided by effective leadership. The almost constant nature of change within the public sector has been seen to make it difficult to follow such a process. The extent of change within the public sector has seen a call for strategic leadership, with managers needing to further develop their skills to support change management (Hafford-Letchfield, 2006). The way in which students are prepared (or not) for taking on leadership roles later in their careers has also been an area of discussion (Healy, 2002). Supervision, too, has been highlighted as an area where individual workers need further support from skilled leaders and managers (Tsui, 2005). The adoption of leadership as one of the domains of the Professional Capabilities Framework would also seem to see the development of leadership as necessary in the current context of social work practice. The focus here is on learning leadership skills, indicating a view of leadership wider than managing processes (College of Social Work, 2012a).

Munro has called for changes to the current management culture within child protection and social work in general. She discusses the need to reinforce professional judgement and decision-making skills within an ethical framework, not one based on a culture of compliance. This is critical of the procedural and managerial context within which child protection work has been operating (Department for Education, 2011b). Munro argues that social work should 'help professionals move from a compliance culture to a learning culture, where they have more freedom to assess need and provide the right help' (Department for Education, 2011b: 7).

Sociological thought can help support social workers in their learning and development within this current context. Social action theories and critical sociology put the focus on how individuals can shape change and practice and move beyond the confines of the structures and organizations within which they operate.

Social work and social interactionism

There are a number of ways in which the actions of social workers can have an impact despite the contradictory context of their work. Social workers can use their knowledge, skills and values to support individuals within this context: for instance, supporting access to services and support. Key current policy imperatives can also be seen to support this: for example, enabling service users to lead more independent lives through personalized services promotes individual rights. Working with the current equalities agenda may enable social workers to support the citizenship and rights of marginalized groups (Oliver et al., 2012). Throughout the book, we have explored the development of social movements in relation to a number of user groups and how this impacts upon social work practice. An understanding of social movements can support positive social work practice.

Through a clearer understanding of the interface between organizational, personal and professional identity, social workers can more ably deal with the dilemmas and uncertainties of their role within the organizations they operate in (Hughes and Wearing, 2007). Therefore social workers are not 'passive' participants in alienating practice environments but are able to influence and support change, finding solutions to complex problems. How might this occur?

Social interactionism and power

Power determines the structural context within which social work practice occurs. Pollack (2010) discusses how, because of the structural context of power, social workers are often in a position where they are 'translating' for service users in seeking to empower or support them in accessing services or gaining support. From a social action perspective, the way in which social workers carry out this task is critical to the individual experience. However, this may often be shaped through the need to reinforce the regulatory functions of the state rather than through enablement or empowerment. Smith (2008) highlights that, despite being part of state structures, social workers can use relationships to support differing 'outcomes' for service users based on values, knowledge and skills. Relationship-based social work has thus been advocated by commentators as an important part of social work practice (Ruch, 2005). Therefore power is not 'fixed' but can be used or influenced in a number of ways.

Exercise: power and social work assessment

Joan is a student on placement in a learning disability team. On her first home visit, she takes an assessment form with her and fills this out throughout her assessment. The visit does not go very well and Joan's practice educator invites her to think about the reasons for this.

- How has Joan used her professional power in this assessment?
- What learning could Joan utilize from this experience?

Social interactionism and organizations

Social workers work within organizations, which are multi-faceted. There may be contradictions in how individuals behave within organizations. For example, front-line managers may empathize with the experiences of front-line staff while being directed to 'manage' performance targets, and so on (Hughes and Wearing, 2007). The actions of individuals can be seen as particularly important in 'human service organizations', where there is a need to uphold moral parameters to behaviour as well as to meet business targets and ensure efficiency (Hasenfield, 2000).

As well as understanding that social workers are part of state structures, we need to look at how individuals and organizations attempt to influence how social services are organized and managed. Weberian ideas concerning bureaucracy, which were discussed above, are important here. For Weber, as we noted, the most efficient way to organize large-scale organizations is through bureaucracy, based on hierarchical organization. As such, bureaucracies provide a clear 'top-down' chain of command, with rules governing the way in which organizations are run (Weber, 1976). Bureaucracy is seen as the epitome of the expression of instrumental rational action, where the organization is divided up into a series of rational tasks and actions, with individuals being assigned to a place within the organization based on their skills and abilities (There is some overlap with functionalist theory here.) *Bureaucratization* is a rational process, and, as with technological advances, it provides the best way of organizing complex tasks and functions. However, Weber was concerned that organizations could wield unlimited power, and therefore argued that they need to be subject to political control. Weber's theory on organization remains highly relevant today. Professionals in health and social care will often refer to organizations being 'too bureaucratic'. One of the key concerns for contemporary social work writers is that the running of social services organizations has become more important than the key tasks of social work itself. Using Weber's theory, it could be argued that social services have become too preoccupied with the organization of their functions, with control of resources and managing user and carer expectations, creating inflexibility. And this certainly seems to be the case when we examine research on social work experiences on the front line.

> **Bureaucratization** method of work organization characterized by regulation and hierarchy of tasks.

For Weber, bureaucratization is a consequence of increasingly complex organizations in modern society. This leads to divisions of labour in which tasks are broken down on the basis of ability rather than personality and relationships. Weber (1976) identifies an 'iron cage of bureaucracy' where the achievement of organizational goals becomes an end in itself rather than a means to an end. This can be seen, for example, in the use of standardized frameworks for assessing risk through e-assessment tools in social work practice. Whilst these tools have been developed to assess and manage risk, Peckover et al. (2011) argue that these standardized assessment frameworks have become increasingly formalized through the use of electronic systems, thus reducing the potential for practitioner judgement. In their research of structured approaches to risk management in social work with children and families in five local authority areas, they found that the tools could become an end in themselves, rather than a means to an end, and that practitioners were frustrated at having to complete duplicate or unnecessary assessments in order to progress to the part of the tool that was particularly relevant to their assessment. Whilst the respondents in Peckover et al.'s study were committed to electronic forms of assessment, they felt that the tool had become a tick-box exercise and limited social workers' professional judgements and interactions with children and families. Therefore it appears to be having a direct impact on the relational nature of social work practice. This is further illustrated by the following quote from a service user: 'It seems like they have to do all this form filling, their bosses' bosses make them do it, but it makes them forget about us' (Laming Report, 2009: Section 3).

However, social work intervenes at a number of levels within organizations. Hasenfield (2000) discusses the differences between business organizations and human services organizations. Social workers have traditionally worked with individuals within this context, managing caseload and resultant relationships. This context is still relevant, despite the way in which caseloads may be increasingly directed by managers. Also important here is the impact of workplace culture, which shapes relationships within and without the organization. Individuals have influence within the workplace culture, and this can be positive or negative (Hughes and Wearing, 2007). The interactions with service users, carers and other professionals all have to be considered, as well as the structural context. Social workers also need to consider how they work and engage with user- and carer-led organizations and partnership working generally.

Social work and the lived experience

Throughout the book, we have examined narrative approaches concerning the lived experience of user and carer groups that social workers engage with. Understanding narrative is seen as supporting partnership working. Yet, as has frequently been discussed, partnerships with users and carers can frequently be seen as tokenistic (Beresford and Croft, 2004). There are also challenges of partnerships that can cause stress and burnout for individual social workers. The pressure to manage complex relationships within the constraints of the organization and resources available presents difficulties for social workers (Evans and Harris, 2004). However, this should not mean that social workers and teams should not work to manage challenges and find solutions. The experiences of social workers of trying to manage these challenges within bureaucratic organizations can certainly be seen as a significant factor in why social workers do not stay in the profession. Perrott (2009) discusses how many social workers appear to leave the statutory or 'state' sector for the voluntary sector, where it is believed that more emancipatory practice can occur. Healy and Meagher (2004) refer to social workers feeling 'de-professionalized' by the way in which statutory social work is organized and delivered. They encourage social workers to adopt a more collective approach to their work through engagement with agencies and organizations. Critical sociological perspectives can assist social workers with different approaches.

Critical sociology

Critical sociology and the context of social work

Who are social workers accountable to? Social workers can often feel caught between the needs of employers and agencies and the needs of service users (Hill, 2010). On the one hand, social workers are concerned with ideas of social justice. On the other, social workers are answerable to organizations and, through a range of legal and policy imperatives, to the state. Social workers are also accountable for professional standards, as outlined earlier (College of Social Work, 2012a). Public accountability is also significant here in how social work organizations have responded to public concerns about social work performance (Department for Education, 2011b).

In a time of austerity, commentators have been critical of how reductions in social welfare services have impacted upon social work and care services. Lymbery and Postle (2010) discuss how community care has led to changes in the social work role generally, with an increased involvement in managing and rationing expenditure. This is juxtaposed with the role to enable and empower service users through personalized services and early intervention. Lymbery and Postle discuss how social workers are caught between the financial reality of community care and the political rhetoric of personalization. As outlined in Chapter 5, disability studies commentators are critical of the care management role for disempowering service users.

The impact of changes in personalized services on carers is also worth noting. Care is increasingly being commodified, with a policy shift from payments to carers to payments to care users. Thus individuals become empowered to pay for their own packages of care, which fundamentally shifts the relationship between the family, the market and the state. In terms of balancing work between users and carers, there is a breakdown of the boundaries between the gift relationship (Cheal, 1988), where care is provided within the context of a personal relationship, and the market economy, where care becomes a commodity. Moran et al. (2012) have highlighted that carers' rights are not always considered within this process.

Critical sociology and critical social work

Gray and Webb (2013) provide a useful summary of critical thought concerning social work. This can be seen as linking to critical sociological perspectives in challenging structural inequalities and power relations within social work practice. Gray and Webb outline that there are a number of components relating to critical perspectives within social work: for example, the service user and carer movement, explored within a number of chapters within this book. Additionally, 'best' practice in social work is linked to critical thinking and analysis about the social work role (Jones et al., 2008). Ideas around critically reflective practice also advocate a critical stance in relation to social work practice (see, e.g., Fook, 2002). In previous chapters, we have explored ideas relating to empowerment and advocacy in social work. This can be seen to deconstruct power relations and work to empower service users (Braye and Preston Shoot, 1995). Gray and Webb (2013: 103) discuss how critical social work uses post-modernist sociological perspectives and critical theory as 'strategies of thought' to support critical practice. Ideologies of power, structural oppression and emancipatory practice can be examined within this context.

Social work commentators have also been critical of the neo-liberal context within which social workers operate, which is seen to reinforce structural inequalities. Pollack (2010) discusses how, rather than perceiving power to be 'top-down', social workers need to examine how they can 'translate' state power to the benefit of people whom they work with. Hence the ways in which social workers use their authority and power are crucial to their interactions with service users.

Radical social work has been concerned with how social workers can use power to support transformation. Marxist perspectives on social division and exploitation (explored in Chapter 2) are relevant here in exploring the contradictions between being an 'agent of the state' and also working to promote social justice. Ferguson and Woodward (2009) explore how radical social work perspectives from the 1970s are still relevant to the social work role and task now. The focus on anti-oppressive practice can be seen to be located in a social work context which challenges structural inequalities and is still advocated across social work practice (see, e.g., Thompson, 2005). Ferguson and Woodward (2009) argue that radical social work perspectives can support 'best' practice, working alongside users and carers as well as supporting collective action and campaigning within social work, social welfare and social policy. For example, social workers can draw management attention to issues with resources, assessment, and so on. So, rather than being passive recipients of 'top-down' power, social workers can challenge organizational practice and context. Using information and knowledge about radical social work can assist this process. (See, for example, *http://www.radical.org.uk/barefoot/*, which provides alternative perspectives on social work issues, dilemmas and 'scandals' from a radical social work perspective.)

Critical sociology, risk and social work

As earlier discussed, health and social care services have been perceived as becoming risk-averse, rather than focusing on needs and rights. The risk discourse within social work literature highlights the issues. It is argued that health and social care services focus on the negative impact of risk by being preoccupied with negative outcomes. Therefore, risk management is shaped by generic probability factors used within risk assessment tools rather than by individual risk assessments and the individual experience (Duff, 2003). This is affected by a preoccupation with 'getting it wrong' that is affected by a social construction of risk. Risk management then becomes about surveillance and control rather than working with individuals. Stanford (2010) discusses how there is a need for further research around how social workers experience risk on the front line, which would support critical awareness of dealing positively with risk. Workers need further support on how to challenge and work with the moral dilemmas of risk. This relates to the development of emotional intelligence and emotional resilience. The Munro Report stressed that defensive risk-averse practice does not reduce the prevalence of risk but leads to displacement onto children, young people or the professionals they work with (Department for Education, 2011b). Munro talked about social workers reconnecting with the skills to work with children, young people and their families, as discussed in Chapters 8 and 9.

Critical sociology and professionalization

Earlier we discussed professionalism and social work identity. Social work commentators have called for a 're-professionalization of social work' (Healy and Meagher, 2004). That is, social work needs to reconnect with the political and social context of social work as well as the current preoccupation with the economic context. Lymbery and Butler (2004) state that the key challenge for social workers is in negotiating their organizational responsibilities with their professional role and standards. The 'practice realities' of managing resources alongside service user expectations can become difficult. It is this tension that can cause the 'emotionally intelligent' social worker to become overly stressed or 'burned out'. Tension is also acute in relation to adherence to social work values and emphasis on social work role in relation to social justice (Hughes and Wearing, 2007).

The changes relating to the supported year in employment and the support offered to newly qualified social workers is intended to support the transition into practice and to support students in terms of managing professional identity (*http://www.skillsforcare.org.uk/asye/*). The management of an emergent professional identity is likely to be critical upon qualifying. Smith (2008) explores the connections between personal and professional identity in the use of power within the social work role. Here the use of power relates to understanding of self, values and attributes and how self-identity shapes professional identity. For example, a risk-averse practitioner may be using their authority and power through defensive rule-bound practice. Smith (2008: 49) refers to this as using 'positional' power within the context of bureaucratic organizations. The critically reflective practitioner would be seeking to balance power relations with an understanding of self and professional identity. Thus practice would be informed by emotional intelligence.

Critical sociology and social work practice

Adamson et al. (2012) discuss how the term 'emotional resilience' can be interpreted in a number of different ways. Resilience is used in connection with a strengths-based approach in work with service users, particularly in relation to mental health. Resilience within social work practice can refer to personal identity, but is also about how social workers manage themselves within the workplace. The context of social work is therefore important to understanding emotional resilience. Thinking sociologically, how an individual interacts with this context will shape their actions and practice.

However, resilience must be related to an understanding of emotional labour and emotional intelligence (Adamson et al., 2012). Hochschild's work on emotional labour is useful here (Hochschild, 1983). Her study of flight staff showed how staff were trained to manage emotion and feelings within their public role. She called this concept 'emotional labour' (see also Giddens and Sutton, 2013). Public sector work involves a very significant degree of interaction with individuals, groups and communities. The ability to manage feelings and 'perform' a public role is important for social workers. However, at what point does this become suppressing emotions and feelings, rather than managing the self? Social work is a stressful profession at the 'coal face' of difficult and complex problems. This relates both to work with vulnerable and marginalized groups as well as the organizational context of practice discussed earlier in the chapter.

Emotional intelligence supports developing skills and strategies to manage self in the complex and contradictory world of social work (Morrison, 2007). A good example of this would be the ability to maintain a skilled approach to work with service users, despite resource pressures and caseload management. In their research, Adamson et al. (2012: 9) identified that resilience involved interplay between self (e.g. values), a range of 'mediating' factors such as work/life balance and the context within which practice occurs. Structural factors such as organizational culture were important in determining individual actions and responses to stress. So emotional resilience cannot be easily defined and is dependent on a range of factors relating to personal and professional identity, role, organization and the context of social work practice. Carey (2014) offers an interesting perspective on how cynicism within social work practice can be used to provide a grounded resistance to organizational demands, change and competing priorities. In this context, resistance can be positive.

The need for emotionally intelligent social workers has been highlighted as part of the current changes to social work (Department for Education, 2011b; Social Work Reform Board 2010). Munro discusses the need for emotionally intuitive practice as opposed to a focus on monitoring and surveillance, which she argues too often characterizes social work practice (Department for Education, 2011b). Such an approach would allow for a more thorough assessment of risk based on relationships with parents and children. While this discourse relates to work with children and families, all areas of social work practice require emotionally intelligent and reflective practitioners who are thinking critically about their role and responsibilities. Morrison (2007) has argued that the concept of emotional intelligence has been little applied to social work and social work practice. While acknowledging that emotional intelligence can be linked to performance management, Morrison also argues that emotional intelligence can support positive practice for social workers. Ingram (2013) examines this further in relation to how the relatively new concept of emotional intelligence can be applied to relationship-based social work practice and support the challenging of proceduralism and managerialism. While ways of defining and measuring emotional intelligence can be contested (Matthews et al., 2002), it can be seen as highly relevant to social workers because of the emotional context of their work.

Emotionally intelligent practice can therefore support critical practice. While social workers need to use legitimate power and their state authority, this can be underpinned by emotionally intelligent and skilled practice. For example, empathy has been highlighted as key to both communication skills and emotionally intelligent practice (Ingram, 2013). Partnership working with service users can be fostered using this approach.

Emotional intelligence and identity are therefore key to how social workers both critically challenge and manage themselves in social work practice. Critical practice can be enhanced by a critical understanding of sociological perspectives, as outlined within this chapter. The reflective process underpins critical practice, and Fook and Gardner (2007) discuss how emotionality underpins a more critical approach to reflection. The process of reflexivity is widely seen as necessary for social workers to manage conflict, particularly between organizational self and personal identity (Fraser and Matthews, 2008). Wilson (2013) discusses how the term 'reflective practice' is used extensively within social work practice but is not always clearly understood. A number of reflective approaches are used within social work practice (e.g. Schon, 1983). Wilson's study explores students' understanding of reflective practice and the challenges of reflective practice within contemporary social work organizations. However, critically reflective practice can support critical practice, as discussed earlier in the chapter. Social workers need to think more widely than the immediate context of practice. An understanding of the global context of social work practice is also important here.

Exercise: reflection and problem solving

Examine a piece of reflection you have completed in your training or professional development. Deconstruct the incident described focusing on the following:

- How has reflection helped you understand the incident?
- Has the reflection involved looking at different perspectives (e.g. theory, reflective models, approaches to conflict)?
- Has the reflection helped you to problem-solve?

The global context of social work

> We live in a society defined by risk, polarization, global markets, chronic change and fragmentation.
>
> (Fred Powell, 2001: 14)

Social work literature, research and commentary all operate within a discourse between academics and others in a number of Western economies. There is therefore some commonality in terms of the ideas explored in this chapter. As we have explored throughout the book, social work engages with marginalized groups and communities. The neo-liberal economic and political context shapes social policy and social welfare within a global context (Pollack, 2010). Economic factors relating to free trade, fiscal prudence and corporate business affect societies across the globe. This in turn impacts on the provision of social care and social welfare services. Western societies have implemented programmes of cuts to social care and social welfare services, which impact upon the social work role within a number of countries (Jordan and Drakeford, 2012).

The global nature of risk management is also significant. Technology concerning the management of information allows for closer monitoring of risk and risk behaviour. Social work commentators in a number of countries have discussed ideas concerning the risk society and the impact that this has on risk management within social work (e.g. Stanford, 2011). This points to commonalities in how Western societies respond to risk-averse and defensive responses to risk management within social work practice. Stanford's work highlights that the moral and ethical issues for social workers in Western societies are similar. Risk dilemmas exist for social workers in a number of Western societies, with complexities in terms of managing these dilemmas from an ethical perspective. This relates to issues such as race and asylum, as explored in Chapter 4.

Smith (2008) explores how much of the discussion about globalization has focused on the economic and political context and subsequent cuts to social welfare and social work services. However, there is the opportunity for transformatory practice for social workers in responding to global forces: for example, how social workers respond to working with issues such as sexual exploitation and forced migration. The use of power in this practice context can be particularly important in terms of how power is 'translated' (Smith, 2008).

However, study of international and global perspectives relating to social work within social work education can be seen as variable. Hugman (2010) discusses how social work exists as a profession in 90 countries, and this has led to the development of global standards relating to social work education and training. The International Federation of Social Workers' definition of social work seeking to promote social change and social justice is significant within social work education and training (*http://www.ifsw.org*). It also stresses that social workers interact with individuals in their own groups and communities. This would appear to support ideas that social work engages with the lived experience of individuals to achieve change.

An interest in international social work and the global context can be seen as part of the critically reflective practitioner. Healy (2008) sees an international discourse for social work as an opportunity to share perspectives and understanding. This can particularly be seen in relation to issues relating to cultural awareness and under-standing. Dominelli (2007a) argues that social workers need to critically analyse the global context of social work in relation to values, and human rights in particular. This is so that social workers can clearly understand how certain groups are excluded and marginalized because of global forces. Social workers need to practise with an understanding of oppression and its global impact: for example, an awareness of post-colonialism in many countries and how this then relates to the global context of managing risk, migration and exploitation (Hugman, 2010).

Conclusion

At the beginning of this book, we discussed how a range of sociological perspectives can develop an understanding which can support social workers in their practice. This chapter has explored how the role of social workers in supporting change is made complex by the social context within which social work practice operates. As well as this, throughout the book we have referred to social work practice with a range of user and carer groups. Each chapter has been supported by discussion of socio-logical perspectives relating to the area of discourse.

What is common to these discussions is that a range of critical perspectives influ-ence 'best' or 'good' practice. A critical application of sociological perspectives is part of this process, enabling social workers to think critically. Jones et al. (2008) argue that social work is too often concerned with a deficit or negative model of practice. They argue instead for a reflective and evaluative style of practice which draws on examples of positive practice and problem solving. Important here is con-necting with the 'lived' experience of people whom social workers work and engage with.

This chapter has also examined how current and potential reforms of social work education, training and development can be related to sociological perspectives. In particular here, critical sociological perspectives can help to evaluate contemporary

Poster from ENSACT Conference: Social Action in Europe, Dubrovnik, 2009. (© Sharon Schneider/Flickr)

social work policy and practice drivers. Certainly, this is complex in terms of the interplay between neo-liberal policies and the management of public services. However, returning to the Professional Capabilities Framework, a number of the domains would appear to highlight the possibility of critical practice. For example, Domain 4 is concerned with supporting social justice and advancing human rights and economic well-being (College of Social Work, 2012a).

The challenge is how social workers choose (or not) to engage with the widespread changes to the profession. Wilson (2013) has highlighted the need to understand the contradictions and tensions within the current social work context by understanding and implementing critically reflective practice. At the time of writing, it remains to be seen how social workers will respond to new developments within education and training. There is an opportunity to use sociological perspectives as explored within this book as part of this process. Thinking sociologically could make a significant contribution for social workers in understanding the complex power relationships within existing practice and their role in attempting to support social change in the current organizational context.

Summary points

- Social work is going through a period of intense change relating to education, training and post-qualifying practice.

- This is taking place within a structural context where the social work role and task are being specialized and re-focused in both adults' and children's services.
- This creates tensions between social work principles relating to social justice and human rights and the statutory responsibilities social workers have.
- This has led to public service management based on private sector principles, with an emphasis on systems and processes.
- Critical sociological perspectives can assist with critical social work practice which attempts to work with these dilemmas and contradictions.
- This creates a need for emotionally intelligent and reflective practitioners.
- Many of the issues facing social workers are affected by the global context of neo-liberal Western economies.

Questions for discussion

- Thinking about sociological perspectives on power, do you see it as positive that The College of Social Work serves as a national voice for social workers?
- Consider structural functionalism (discussed in Chapter 1). How does this relate to the current statutory function of social work?
- Can critical sociology assist social work practice with working alongside users and carers in partnership?
- How can emotional intelligence be supported by critically reflective practice?

Further reading

Hughes, M. and Wearing, M. (2007) *Organizations and Management in Social Work.* **London: Sage**
This book provides a comprehensive view of how organizational theory relates to social work practice and the challenges for social workers in working within contemporary social work organizations.

Jones, K., Cooper, B. and Ferguson, H. (2008) *Best Practice in Social Work.* **London: Palgrave**
This text provides a helpful overview of how critical perspectives relating to social work practice can support 'best' or critical practice. The text is related to ethical dilemmas and tensions within the social work role.

Smith, R. (2008) *Social Work and Power.* **London: Palgrave**
This book provides a detailed overview of theoretical perspectives on power relations, including sociological perspectives. This is related to the social work role and task and provides further material for discussion.

Useful Resources

Databases

AgeInfo (database from the Centre for Policy on Ageing) at *http://www.cpa.org.uk/ageinfo/ageinfo2.html*

Social Care Online at *http://www.sci-socialcareonline.org.uk*

Social Trends at *http://www.ons.gov.uk/ons/rel/social-trends-rd/social-trends/index.html*

SWAP Subject Centre News at *http://www.swap.ac.uk/news/*

Government bodies

Care Quality Commission at *http://www.cqc.org.uk/*

Department for Education at *http://www.gov.uk/dfe* – the Government Department responsible for children and families

Department of Health at *http://www.dh.gov.uk* – the Government Department responsible for health and social care

Every Child Matters at *http://www.everychildmatters.co.uk* – covers a whole range of issues in relation to family and child policy

Northern Ireland Executive: Department of Health, Social Services and Public Safety at *http://www.dhsspsni.gov.uk/*

Northern Ireland Social Care Council (NISCC) at *http://www.niscc.info/*

Scottish Government, Health and Social Care at *http://www.scotland.gov.uk/Topics/Health*

The Scottish Social Services Council at *http://www.sssc.uk.com/*

The Welsh Government: Health and Social Care at *http://www.wales.gov.uk/topics/health/?lang=en*

Websites

Action for Children at *http://www.actionforchildren.org.uk*

Action on Elder Abuse at *http://www.elderabuse.org.uk*

Age UK at *http://www.ageuk.org.uk* – addresses current issues about older people's services and needs

Albert Kennedy Trust at *http://www.akt.org.uk* – a site which supports lesbian, gay, bisexual and trans homeless young people in crisis

Alcohol Concern at *http://www.alcoholconcern.org.uk* – advice, support and information on the impact of addiction

Barefoot Social Workers at *http://www.radical.org.uk/barefoot* – the voice for radical social work in Britain

Barnardo's at *http://www.barnardos.org.uk* – addresses issues about children's needs and services

British Association of Social Workers at *http://www.basw.co.uk* – site of association representing social workers

Carers Trust at *http://www.carers.org* – provides information for carers

Centre for Mental Health at *http://www.centreformentalhealth.org.uk/*– includes publications and briefing papers to improve quality of life for people with mental health problems

Child Poverty Action Group at *http://www.cpag.org.uk* – includes useful statistics and publications on child poverty

College of Social Work at *http://www.tcsw.org.uk/home/*

Community Care at *http://www.communitycare.co.uk* – features articles as well as other information about contemporary social work

Disability Rights UK at *http://www.disabilityrights.uk/org* – body formed from the unification of the Disability Alliance, Radar and National Centre for Independent Living

Equality and Human Rights Commission at *http://www.equalityhumanrights.com/* – includes useful statistics and publications on race and ethnicity and the promotion of equality and citizenship for disabled people

Health and Care Professions Council at *http://www.hpc-uk.org*

Institute for Public Policy Research at *http://www.ippr.org.uk* – independent think-tank, exploring policy responses and promoting social justice and democratic participation

Joseph Rowntree Foundation at *http://www.jrf.org.uk/* – includes publications on a range of social issues

Law Society at *http://www.lawsociety.org.uk* – useful for legal aspects of family policy

Make Poverty History campaign at *http://www.makepovertyhistory.org* – provides facts and details of campaigns to tackle poverty globally

MENCAP at *http://www.mencap.org.uk* – offers a range of advice for people with learning difficulties

MIND at *http://www.mind.org.uk* – campaigns on issues for people with mental health problems

NACRO at *http://www.nacro.org.uk* – a useful website which explores issues about rehabilitation

National Children's Bureau at *http://www.ncb.org.uk*

National Society for Prevention of Cruelty to Children at *http://www.nspcc.org.uk*

Shelter at *http://www.shelter.org.uk* – charity for housing and homelessness

Stonewall at *http://www.stonewall.org.uk/* – provides clear information about citizenship rights for lesbians, gay men and bisexuals

Selected journals

Ageing and Society
Body and Society
British Journal of Social Work
Child & Family Social Work
Children and Society
Community Care
Disability and Society
Journal of Children and Poverty
Journal of Gender Studies
Journal of Mental Health
Journal of Poverty and Social Justice
Race and Class
Social Identities
Social Work Education
Sociology
Sociology of Health and Illness

References

Abbott, P. and Sapsford, R. (1987) *Community Care for Mentally Handicapped Children*. Milton Keynes: Open University Press

Abbott, P., Wallace, C. and Tyler, M. (2005) *An Introduction to Sociology: Feminist Perspectives*. London: Routledge

Abel-Smith, B. and Townsend, P. (1965) *The Poor and the Poorest*. London: Bell and Sons

Abrams, M. (1978) *Beyond Three-Score and Ten*. Mitcham: Age Concern

Acheson, D. (1998) *Independent Inquiry into Inequalities in Health: Report*. London: HMSO

Action on Elder Abuse (n.d.) Available at *http://www.elderabuse.org.uk*

Adams, R. (1990) *Self Help, Social Work and Empowerment*. Basingstoke: Macmillan

Adams, R., Dominelli, L. and Payne, M. (2009) *Critical Practice in Social Work*. 2nd edition. London: Palgrave Macmillan

Adamson, C., Beddoe, L. and Davys, A. (2012) Building resilient practitioners: definitions and practitioner understandings. *British Journal of Social Work*. Advanced Access published 10 October. doi: 10.1093/bjsw/bcs142

Advisory Council on the Misuse of Drugs (2010) *Consideration of the Anabolic Steroids*. London: The Stationery Office

Age UK (2011a) *Ageism in Europe: Findings from the European Social Survey*. London: Age UK

Age UK (2011b) *Lesbian, Gay or Bisexual: Planning for Later Life*. London: Age UK

Age UK (2014) *Later Life in the United Kingdom*. Available at *http://www.ageuk.org.uk/Documents/EN-GB/Factsheets/Later_Life_UK_factsheet.pdf?dtrk=true*

Agnew, R. (1992) Foundations for a general strain theory of crime and delinquency. *Criminology* 30(1): 47–87

Ahmad, W.I. and Walker, R. (1997) Asian older people: housing, health and access to services. *Ageing and Society* 17(2): 141–66

Alcock, P. (2008) *Social Policy in Britain*. 3rd edition. Basingstoke: Palgrave Macmillan

Alcohol Concern (2010) *Right Time, Right Place: Alcohol-Harm Reduction Strategies with Children and Young People*. London: Alcohol Concern

Alcohol Concern (2011) *Young People and Alcohol Factsheet*. London: Alcohol Concern

Aldridge, D. (1998). *Suicide: The Tragedy of Hopelessness*. London: Jessica Kingsley

Allen, R. (2006) *From Punishment to Problem Solving: A New Approach to Children in Trouble*. London: Centre for Crime and Justice Studies

Allen, R., Jallab, K. and Snaith, E. (2007) Justice and reinvestment in Gateshead: the story so far. In R. Allen and V. Stern (eds) *Justice Reinvestment: A New Approach to Crime and Justice*. London: International Centre for Prison Studies

Alsop, R., Fitzsimons, A. and Lennon, K. (2002) *Theorizing Gender: An Introduction*. Cambridge: Polity

Altman, D, (2001) *Global Sex*. Chicago: University of Chicago Press

Alzheimer's Society (2007) *Dementia UK: The Full Report*. Available at *http//:www.alzheimers.org.uk/site/scripts/download_info.php?fileID=2*

Alzheimer's Society (2012) *Dementia Statistics*. Available at *http://www.alzheimersresearchuk.org/dementia-statistics/*

Ambrogi, S. and Abbas, M. (2011) British riots spread on third night of violence. Reuters News, 8 August. Available at *http://www.reuters.com/article/2011/08/08/us-britain-riot-idUSTRE7760G820110808*

Andersen, M. (2008) *Thinking about Women: Sociological Perspectives on Sex and Gender*. 8th edition. New York: Allyn and Bacon

Angus, J. and Reeve, P. (2006) Ageism: A threat to 'aging well' in the 21st century. *Journal of Applied Gerontology* 25: 137–54

Annandale, E. (2008) *Women's Health and Social Change*. London: Routledge

Annandale, E. and Hunt, K. (2000) *Gender Inequalities in Health*. Buckingham: Open University Press

Anthias, F. and Yuval-Davis, N. (1998) *Women – Nation – State*. Basingstoke: Macmillan

Arber, S. and Ginn, J. (1995) *Connecting Gender and Ageing: A Sociological Approach*. Buckingham: Open University Press

Ariès, P. (1962) *Centuries of Childhood*. London: Jonathan Cape

Aspinall, P. (2009) 'Mixed race', 'mixed origins' or what? Generic terminology for the multiple racial/ethnic group population. *Anthropology Today* 25(2): 3–8

Atkinson, D. (2005) Research as social work: participatory research in learning disability. *British Journal of Social Work* 35: 425–34

Atkinson, D. and Warmsley, J. (1999) Using autobiographical approaches with people with learning difficulties. *Disability and Society* 14(2): 203–16

Audit Commission (2000) *Another Country: Implementing Dispersal under the Immigration and Asylum Act, 1999*. London: Audit Commission

Bailey, D. and Liyanage, L. (2012) The role of the mental health social worker: political pawns in the reconfiguration of adult health and social care. *British Journal of Social Work* 42: 1113–31

Baker, K. and Kelly, G. (2011) Risk assessment and young people. In H. Kemshall and B. Wilkinson (eds) *Good Practice in Assessing Risk: Current Knowledge, Issues and Approaches*. London: Jessica Kingsley

Baldock, C.V. (1999) Seniors as volunteers: an international perspective on policy. *Ageing and Society* 19(5): 581–602

Ballan, M. (2008) Disability and sexuality within social work education in the USA and Canada: the social model of disability as a lens for practice. *Social Work Education* 27(2): 194–202

Ballard, K., Elston, M. and Gabe, J. (2005) Beyond the mask: women's experiences of public and private ageing during midlife and their use of age-resisting activities. *Health: An Interdisciplinary Journal for the Social Study of Health, Illness and Medicine* 9(2): 169–87

Bamford, T. (2014) *Social Work: New Ways*. Available at *http://www.spn.org.uk/index.php?id=1003*

Banton, M. and Singh, G. (2004) 'Race', disability and oppression. In J. Swain, S. French, C. Barnes and C. Thomas (eds) *Disabling Barriers – Enabling Environments*. London: Sage

Baring Foundation (2006) *Finding the Right Support? A Review of Issues and Positive Practice in Supporting Parents with Learning Difficulties and Their Children*. Available at *http://www.baring foundation.org.uk/Findingrightsupport.pdf*

Barker, D. and Taylor, H. (1997) Inequalities in health and health service use for mothers of young children. *Journal of Epidemiology and Community Health* 51: 74–9

Barker, P. and Buchanan-Barker, P. (2003) *Spirituality and Mental Health: Breakthrough*. London: Whurr

Barnes, C. (1991) *Disabled People in Britain and Discrimination*. London: Hurst

Barnes, C. (1992) *Disabling Imagery and the Media: An Exploration of the Principles for Media Representations of Disabled People*. Halifax: British Council of Organisations of Disabled People/Ryburn Publishing

Barnes, M. (2012) *Poverty in Later Life*. London: Age UK

Barrett, M. and McIntosh, M. (1982) *The Anti-social Family*. London: Verso

Barrientos, S., Kabeer, N. and Hossain, N. (2004) *The Gender Dimensions of the Globalization of Production*. Geneva: International Labour Organization

Barron, C. and Lacombe, D. (2005) Moral panics and the nasty girl. *Canadian Review of Sociology and Anthropology* 42(1): 51–69

Barron, R.D. and Norris, G.M. (1976) Sexual divisions and the dual labour market. In D.L. Barker and S, Allen (eds) *Dependence and Exploitation in Work and Marriage*. London: Longman

Barton, L. (ed.) (1996) *Disability and Society: Emerging Issues and Insights*. Harlow: Addison Wesley Longman

BBC News (2006) Racism row lecturer is suspended. 23 March. Available at *http://news.bbc.co.uk/1/hi/education/4838498.stm*

BBC News (2008) Family jailed for allowing death. 13 March. Available at *http://news.bbc.co.uk/1/hi/england/west_yorkshire/7295048.stm*

BBC News (2011) England rioters 'poorer, younger, less educated'. 24 October. Available at *http://www.bbc.co.uk/news/uk-15426720*

Bebbington, A. and Miles, J. (1989) The background of children who enter local authority care. *British Journal of Social Work* 19(5): 349–68

Beck, U. (1992) *Risk Society: Towards a New Modernity*. London: Sage

Beck, U. (1999) *What is Globalization?* Cambridge: Polity

Beck, U. and Beck-Gernsheim, E. (1995) *The Normal Chaos of Love*. Cambridge: Polity

Becker, H. (1963) *Outsiders: Studies in the Sociology of Deviance*. New York: Free Press

Beckett, C. (2006) *Essential Theory for Social Work Practice*. London: Sage

Beddoe, L. (2010) Surveillance or reflection: professional supervision in 'the risk society'. *British Journal of Social Work* 40(4): 1279–96

Beechey, V. (1982) The sexual division of labour and the labour process: a critical assessment of Braverman. In S. Wood (ed.) *The Degradation of Work? Skill, Deskilling and the Labour Process*. London: Hutchinson

Ben-Ari, A.T. (2001) Homosexuality and heterosexism: views from academics in the helping professions. *British Journal of Social Work* 31(1): 119–31

Benjamin, O. and Sullivan, O. (1999) Relational resources, gender consciousness and possibilities of change in marital relationships. *Sociological Review* 47(4): 794–820.

Benston, M. (1969) The political economy of women's liberation. *Monthly Review* 21: 13–27

Beresford, P. (2002) Thinking about 'mental health': towards a social model. *Journal of Mental Health* 11(6): 581–4

Beresford, P. (2012) The 'overclass' is the real threat to society. *Guardian*, 3 April. Available at *http://www.theguardian.com/society/2012/apr/03/overclass-threat-society*

Beresford, P. and Croft, S. (2004) Service users and practitioners reunited: the key component of social work reform. *British Journal of Social Work* 34(1): 53–68

Bernardi, F. (2009) *Globalization, Individualization and the Death of Social Classes: An Empirical Assessment for 18 European Countries*. Working Paper no. 15. Bamberg: Trans Europe Project

Bernstein, B. (1975) *Class, Codes and Control*. London: Routledge and Kegan Paul

Bernard, M. and Meade, K. (eds) (1993) *Women Come of Age: Perspectives on the Lives of Older Women*. London: Edward Arnold

Best, S. (2005) *Understanding Social Divisions*. London: Sage

Bhavani, K. and Coulson, M. (1986) Transforming socialist-feminism: the challenge of racism. *Feminist Review* 23: 81–92

Bidet, J. and Kouvelakis, S. (eds) (2009) *Critical Companion to Contemporary Marxism*. Chicago: Haymarket Books

Biemann, U. (2002) Remotely sensed: a topography of the global sex trade. *Feminist Review* 70: 75–88

Biggs, S. (1996) A family concern: elder abuse in British social policy. *Critical Social Policy* 16(2): 62–83

Bilton, T., Bonnett, K., Jones, P., Stanworth, M., Sheard, K. and Webster, A. (2002) *Introductory Sociology*. 4th edition. Basingstoke: Macmillan.

Bindman, J. and Doezema, J. (1997) *Redefining Prostitution as Sex Work on the International Agenda*. Available at *http://www.walnet.org/csis/papers/redefining.html*

Binstock, R. and George, L. (eds) (2001) *Handbook of Aging and Social Sciences*. 5th edition. San Diego: Academic Press

Black and In Care (1985) *Black and In Care, Conference Report*. London: Blackrose Press

Blair, T. (1999) *Child Poverty Speech*. The Beveridge Lecture, 18 March. Toynbee Hall, London

Blane, D., Smith, G.D. and Bartley, M. (1993) Social selection: what does it contribute to social class differences in health? *Sociology of Health and Illness* 15(1): 1–15

Blaxter, M. (1976) *The Meaning of Disability*. London: Heinemann

Blewett, J., Lewis, J. and Tunstill, J. (2007) *The Changing Roles and Tasks of Social Work: A Literature-Informed Discussion Paper*. London: Synergy Research and Consulting

Bochel, H., Bochel, C., Page, R. and Sykes, R. (2009) *Social Policy: Issues and Developments*. 2nd edition. London: Prentice Hall

Boden, S. (2006) Dedicated followers of fashion? The influence of popular culture on children's social identities. *Media, Culture and Society* 28: 289–98

Boeck, T. and Fleming, J. (2011) The role of social capital and resources in resilience to risk. In H. Kemshall and B. Wilkinson (eds) *Good Practice in Assessing Risk: Current Knowledge, Issues and Approaches*. London: Jessica Kingsley

Bogg, D. (2008) *The Integration of Mental Health Social Work and the NHS*. Exeter: Learning Matters

Bonnie, S. (2014) Disabled people, disability and sexuality. In J. Swain, S. French, C. Barnes and C. Thomas (eds) *Disabling Barriers – Enabling Environments*. 3rd edition. London: Sage

Bottoms, A. (1995) The philosophy and politics of punishment and sentencing. In C. Clark and R. Morgan (eds) *The Politics of Sentencing Reform*. Oxford: Clarendon Press

Bourdieu, P. (1986) *Distinction: A Social Critique of the Judgement of Taste*. London: Routledge and Kegan Paul

Bourdieu, P. (1988) *Language and Symbolic Power*. Cambridge: Polity

Bovenkerk, F. (1984) The rehabilitation of the rabble: how and why Marx and Engels wrongly depicted the lumpenproletariat as a reactionary force. *Netherlands Journal of Sociology (Sociologica Neerlandica)* 20(1): 13–42

Bowling, B. and Phillips, C. (2002) *Race, Crime and Criminal Justice*. London: Longman

Bradshaw, J. and Millar, J. (1991) *Lone Parent Families in the UK*. Department of Social Security Report, No. 6. London: HMSO

Brager, G. and Sprecht, H. (1973) *Community Organizing*. New York: Columbia University Press

Bramlett, M. and Blumberg, S. (2007) Family structure and children's physical and mental health. *Health Affairs* 26(2): 549–58

Braverman, H. (1974) *Labor and Monopoly Capital: The Degradation of Work in the Twentieth Century*. New York: Monthly Review Press

Braye, S. and Preston-Shoot, M. (1995) *Empowering Practice in Social Care*. Buckingham: Open University Press

Brewer, J. and Wollman, H. (2011) Sociologists' offer to unravel the riots. *Guardian*, 11 August. Available at *http://www.theguardian.com/uk/2011/aug/11/sociologists-offer-unravel-riots*

Brindle, D. (2014) Social work stakes out its territory. *Guardian*, 18 March. Available at *http://www.theguardian.com/society/2014/mar/18/social-work-stakes-territory-advice-note*

Bristow, J. (2013) Reporting the riots: parenting culture and the problem of authority in media analysis of August 2011. *Sociological Research Online* 18(4): 11

Britton, J., Gregg, P., Macmillan, L. and Mitchell, S. (2011) *The Early Bird. . .: Preventing Young People from Becoming a NEET Statistic*. University of Bristol: Department of Economics and CMPO. Available at *http://www.bristol.ac.uk/cmpo/publications/other/earlybirdcmpo.pdf*

Bronfenbrenner, U. (1979) *The Ecology of Human Development: Experiments by Nature and Design*. Cambridge, MA, and London: Harvard University Press

Brown, B., Burman M. and Jamieson, L. (1993) *Sex Crimes on Trial: The Use of Sexual Evidence in Scottish Courts*. Edinburgh: Edinburgh University Press

Brown, D. (1997) *Black People and Sectioning: The Black Experiences of Detention under the Civil Sections of the Mental Health Act*. London: Little Rock

Brown, G.W. and Harris, T. (1978) *Social Origins of Depression: A Study of Psychiatric Disorder in Women*. London: Tavistock

Brown, H. (2009) Safeguarding adults. In R. Adams, L. Dominelli and M. Payne (eds) *Social Work: Themes, Issues and Critical Debates*. London: Palgrave

Brown, H.C. (1998) *Social Work and Sexuality: Working with Lesbians and Gay Men*. Basingstoke: Palgrave Macmillan

Bruch, H. (1973) *Eating Disorders*. Houston: Basic Books

Bulmer, M. and Solomos, J. (1998) Introduction: re-thinking ethnic and racial studies. *Ethnic and Racial Studies* 21(5): 819–37

Burchardt, T. (2000) *Enduring Economic Exclusion: Disabled People, Income and Work*. York: Joseph Rowntree Foundation. A summary version is available at *http://www.jrf.org.uk/Knowledge/findings/socialpolicy/060.asp*

Burchielli, R., Bartram, T. and Thanacoody, R. (2008) Work–family balance or greedy organizations? *Industrial Relations* 63(1): 108–33

Burr, V. (2003) *Social Constructionism*. London: Routledge

Burton, J., Toscano, T. and Zonouzi, M. (2012) *Personalization for Social Workers: Opportunities and Challenges for Frontline Practice*. Maidenhead: Open University Press

Bury, M. (1997) *Health and Illness in a Changing Society*. London: Routledge

Butler, J. (1990) *Gender Trouble: Feminism and the Subversion of the Identity*. London: Routledge

Bywater, J. and Jones, R. (2007) *Sexuality and Social Work*. Exeter: Learning Matters

Caballero, C., Edwards, R., Goodyer, A. and Okitikpi, T. (2012) The diversity and complexity of the everyday lives of mixed racial and ethnic families. *Adoption and Fostering* 36(3–4): 9–24

Calder, M. (2011) Organizationally dangerous practice: political drivers, practice implications and pathways to resolution. In H. Kemshall and B. Wilkinson (eds) *Good Practice in Assessing Risk: Current Knowledge, Issues and Approaches*. London: Jessica Kingsley

Callender, C. (1992) Redundancy, unemployment and poverty. In C. Glendinning and J. Millar (eds) *Women and Poverty in Britain: The 1990s*. London: Harvester Wheatsheaf.

Callinicos, A. (1999) *Social Theory: A Historical Introduction*. Cambridge: Polity

Cameron, D. and Fraser, E. (1987) *The Lust to Kill: A Feminist Investigation of Sexual Murder*. Cambridge: Polity

Campbell, A. (2009) Life story work and life review. In T. Lindsay T (ed.) *Social Work Intervention*. Exeter: Learning Matters

Cangiona, A., Shutes, I., Spencer, S. and Leeson, G. (2009) *Migrant Care Workers in Ageing Societies: Research Findings in the United Kingdom: Report*. COMPAS, University of Oxford

Carers UK (2011) *The Cost of Caring*. Available at *https://www.vocal.org.uk/assets/files/downloads/The_Cost_of_Caring_1.pdf*

Carey, M. (2014) Mind the gaps: understanding the rise and implications of different types of cynicism within statutory social work. *British Journal of Social Work* 44(1): 127–44

Carr, S. (2008) *Personalization: A Rough Guide*. Report 20. London: Social Care Institute of Excellence

Carsten, J. (2000) Introduction: cultures of relatedness. In J. Carsten (ed.) *Cultures of Relatedness: New Approaches to the Study of Kinship*. Cambridge: Cambridge University Press

Carter, J. (2003) *Ethnicity, Exclusion and the Workplace*. Basingstoke: Palgrave

Castells, M. (1997) *The Power of Identity*. Oxford: Blackwell

Cavadino, M. and Dignan, J. (2002) *The Penal System: An Introduction*. London: Sage

Cawson, P. (2002) *Child Maltreatment in the Family: The Experience of a National Sample of Young People*. London: NSPCC.

Central Council for the Education and Training of Social Work (1991) *The Rules and Requirements for the Diploma in Social Work*. London: CCETSW

Centre for Contemporary Cultural Studies (1982) *The Empire Strikes Back*. London: Hutchinson.

Centre for Policy on Ageing (2009) *Ageism and Age Discrimination in Social Care in the United Kingdom: A Review from the Literature*. London: Centre for Policy on Ageing

Centre for Social Justice (2009) *Dying to Belong: An In-Depth Review of Street Gangs in Britain*. London: Centre for Social Justice

Centre for Social Justice (2010) *Breakthrough Britain: The Forgotten Age. Understanding Poverty and Social Exclusion in Later Life*. London: Centre for Social Justice

Centre for Social Justice (2012) *Time to Wake Up: Tackling Gangs One Year after the Riots*. London: Centre for Social Justice

Centre for Social Justice (2013) *It Happens Here: Equipping the United Kingdom to Fight Modern Slavery*. London: Centre for Social Justice

Centre for Social Justice (2014) *Girls and Gangs*. London: Centre for Social Justice

Chambers, P. (2004) The case for critical social gerontology in social work education and older women. *Social Work Education* 23(6): 745–58

Chambliss, W. (2007) The saints and the roughnecks. In T. Henslin (ed.) *Down to Earth Sociology: Introductory Readings*. 14th edition. New York: Free Press

Chand, A. and Keay, L. (2003) *Child Protection and Its Impact for Black Families Living in the UK: Research into Practice*. Conference Report

Chawla-Duggan, R. (2006) Exploring the role of father development workers in supporting early years learning. *Early Years* 26(1): 93–109

Cheal, D. (1988) *The Gift Economy*. London: Routledge

Child Poverty Action Group (2012) *Child Poverty Facts and Figures*. Available at *http://www.cpag.org. uk/child-poverty-facts-and-figures*

Children's Society (2013) *Hidden from View: The Experiences of Young Carers in England*. London: Children's Society. Available at *http://www.childrenssociety.org.uk/sites/default/files/tcs/report_ hidden-from-view_young-carers_final.pdf*

Chouhan, K. and Lusane, C. (2004) *Black Voluntary and Community Sector Funding: Its Impact on Civic Engagement and Capacity Building*. York: Joseph Rowntree Foundation

Christian, M., Evans, C., Hancock, N., (2013) Family meals can help children reach their 5 a day: a cross-sectional survey of children's dietary intake from London primary schools. *Journal of Epidemiology and Community Health* 64(4): 332–8

Christie, A. (2006) Negotiating the uncomfortable intersections between gender and professional identities in social work. *Critical Social Policy* 26(2): 390–411.

Churchill, H. (2013) Retrenchment and restructuring: family support and children's services reform under the Coalition. *Journal of Children's Services* 8(3): 209–22

Citizens UK (2012) *Citizens' Inquiry into the Tottenham Riots*. Available at *http://www.citizensuk.org/ wp-content/uploads/2012/02/Citizens-Inquiry-into-the-Tottenham-Riots-REPORT.pdf*

Clarke, A. (2001) *The Sociology of Health Care*. London: Prentice Hall.

Clarke, K. (2011) Conservative Party Conference 2011: Ken Clarke says most riders were repeat offenders. *The Telegraph*, 4 October. Available at *http://www.telegraph.co.uk/news/politics/ conservative/8806133/Conservative-Party-Conference-2011-Ken-Clarke-says-most-rioters-were- repeat-offenders.html*

Cleaver, F. (2001) 'Do men matter?' New horizons in gender and development. *Insights* 35(December)

Climens, C. and Combes, H. (2010) (Almost) everything you ever wanted to know about sexuality and learning disability but were always too afraid to ask. In G. Grant, P. Ramcharan, M. Flynn and M. Richardson (eds) *Learning Disability: A Life Cycle Approach*. Buckingham: Open University Press

Close, L. (2009) A positive approach to risk: safeguarding through personalization. *Community Connecting* 20(May/June): 8–12

Cochrane, R. (1977) Mental illness in immigrants to England and Wales: an analysis of mental hospital admissions 1971. *Social Psychiatry* 12: 2–35

Cocker, C. and Hafford-Letchfield, T. (2010) Out and proud? Social work's relationship with lesbian and gay equality. *British Journal of Social Work* 40(6): 1996–2008

Cohen, A. (1954) *Delinquent Boys: The Culture of the Gang*. New York: Free Press

Cohen, A.P. (1985) *The Symbolic Construction of Community*. London: Tavistock

Cohen, R. and Kennedy, P. (2000) *Global Sociology*. Basingstoke: Palgrave

Cohen, S. (1972) *Folk Devils and Moral Panics*. London: Paladin

Coleman, R. (2004) Reclaiming the streets: closed circuit television, neoliberalism and the mystification of social divisions in Liverpool, UK. *Surveillance & Society* 2(2/3): 293–309

College of Social Work (2012a) *The Professional Capabilities Framework*. Available at *http://www. tcsw.org.uk/pcf.aspx*

College of Social Work (2012b) *PCF13 – Advanced and Strategic Level Descriptors*. Available at *http:// www.tcsw.org.uk/uploadedFiles/PCF13NOVAdvancedLevelDescriptors%20(2).pdf*

College of Social Work (2014) *Roles and Functions of Social Workers in England (Advice Note)*. Available at *http://www.tcsw.org.uk/uploadedFiles/TheCollege/_CollegeLibrary/Policy/Roles FunctionsAdviceNote.pdf*

Collins, P.H. (2000). *Black Feminist Thought: Knowledge, Consciousness and the Politics of Empowerment*. 2nd edition. New York: Routledge.

Collins, S. (2008) Statutory social workers: stress, job satisfaction, coping, social support and individual differences. *British Journal of Social Work* 38(6): 1173–93

Commission of the European Communities (1994) *European Social Policy – A Way Forward for the Union*. A White Paper. Part A. Com (94) 333 final, 27 July

Commission for Racial Equality (1997) *The Irish in Britain*. London: CRE

Comstock, G. (1991) *Violence against Lesbians and Gay Men*. New York: Columbia University Press

Connell, R.W. (1987) *Gender and Power: Society, the Person and Sexual Politics*. Cambridge: Polity

Connell, R.W. (1995) *Masculinities*. Cambridge: Polity

Conway, J. (2000) *Housing Policy*. Eastbourne: Gildredge Press

Cooper, J. (2013) Social workers believe Frontline will have a negative impact on practice. *Community Care*, 5 November. Available at *http://www.communitycare.co.uk/2013/11/05/social-workers-believe-frontline-will-have-negative-impact-on-practice/*

Cooper, P. and Bilton, M. (2002) *Attention Deficit/Hyperactivity Disorder*. London: David Fulton

Corker, M. (1998) *Deaf and Disabled, or Deafness Disabled?* Buckingham: Open University Press

Cornwell, E. and Waite, L. (2009) Social disconnectedness, perceived isolation and health among older adults. *Journal of Health and Social Behaviour* 50(1): 31–48

Corsaro, W. (2011) *The Sociology of Childhood*. 3rd edition. London: Pine Forge Press

Cox, A. (2011) Youth gangs in the UK: myth or reality? *Internet Journal of Criminology*. Available at *http://www.internetjournalofcriminology.com/Cox_Youth_Gangs_in_the_UK_Myth_or_Reality_IJC _September_2011.pdf*

Cree, V. (1996) Why do men care? In K. Cavanagh and V. Cree (eds) *Working with Men: Feminism and Social Work*. London: Routledge

Cree, V. (2000) *Sociology for Social Workers and Probation Officers*. London: Routledge.

Cree, W. and O'Corra, S. (2006) *Core Training Standards for Sexual Orientation: Making National Health Services Inclusive for LGB People*. Diverse Identities. Available at *http://www.bipsolutions. com/docstore/pdf/14438.pdf*

Crenshaw, K. (1991). Mapping the margins: intersectionality, identity politics, and violence against women of color. *Stanford Law Review* 43(6): 1241–99

Croisdale-Appelby, D. (2014) *Re-Visioning Social Work Education: An Independent Review*. London: Department of Health

Crompton, R. (1998) *Class and Stratification: An Introduction to Current Debates*. 2nd edition. Cambridge: Polity

Crow, L. (1996) Including all our lives: renewing the social model of disability. In C. Barnes and G. Mercer G (eds) *Exploring the Divide: Illness and Disability*. Leeds: The Disability Press

Cuban, S. (2010) *Advocacy Brief for Unions: The Exploitation of Migrant Care Workers in the Workplace*. London: ESRC

Cumming, E. and Henry, W.E. (1961) *Growing Old*. New York: Basic Books

Dalley, G. (1988) *Ideologies of Caring: Rethinking Community and Collectivism*. Basingstoke: Macmillan

Davies, D. and Neal, C. (eds) (1996) *Pink Therapy: A Guide for Counsellors and Therapists Working with Lesbian, Gay and Bisexual Clients*. Buckingham: Open University Press

Davies, G. (2000) Religion in modern Britain: changing sociological assumptions. *Sociology* 34: 113–28

Davies, Martin (1994) *The Essential Social Worker*. 3rd edition. Aldershot: Arena

Davies, Martin (ed.) (2012) *Social Work with Adults*. London: Palgrave Macmillan

Davies, Matt (2008) *Eradicating Child Poverty: The Role of Key Policy Areas*. Available at *http://www. jrf.org.uk/sites/files/jrf/2271-poverty-exclusion-discrimination.pdf*

Davies, R. (ed.) (1994) *The Kenneth Williams Diaries*. London: HarperCollins

Davis, F. and Lockhart, L. (2010) Introduction. In L. Lockhart and F. Davis (eds) *Domestic Violence: Intersectionality and Culturally Competent Practice*. New York: Columbia University Press

de Beauvoir, S (1997) *The Second Sex*. London: Vintage Classics

Dean, G., Walsh, D., Downing, H. and Shelley, P. (1981) First admission of native-born and immigrants to psychiatric hospitals in South East England 1976. *British Journal of Psychiatry* 139: 506–12

Dearden, C. and Becker, S. (2004) *Young Carers in the UK: The 2004 Report*. London: Carers UK and the Children's Society

Death Penalty Information Center (n.d.) *Deterrence: States Without the Death Penalty Have Had Consistently Lower Murder Rates*. Available at *http://www.deathpenaltyinfo.org/deterrence-states-without-death-penalty-have-had-consistently-lower-murder-rates*

Delgado, R. and Stefancic, J. (2012) *Critical Race Theory: An Introduction*. 2nd edition. New York: New York University Press

Delphy, C. (1993) Rethinking sex and gender. *Women's Studies International Forum* 1(1): 1–9.

Denzin, N.K. (1987) Postmodern children. *Society* 24(3): 32–5

Department for Children, Schools and Family (2009a) *Key Stage 4 Attainment by Pupil Characteristics, in England 2008/09*. London: DCSF

Department for Children, Schools and Family(2009b) *Building a Safe and Confident Future: The Final Report of the Social Work Task Force*. London: HMSO

Department for Communities and Local Government (2012) *Listening to Troubled Families*. London: HMSO

Department for Culture, Media and Sport (2011) *Creative Industries Economic Estimates: Full Statistical Release*. 8 December

Department for Education (2003) *Every Child Matters* (Cm 5860). Available at *https://www.education.gov.uk/consultations/downloadableDocs/EveryChildMatters.pdf*

Department for Education (2011a) *The Munro Report on Child Protection: Interim Report: The Child's Journey*. London: HMSO

Department for Education (2011b) *The Munro Review of Child Protection: Final Report – a Child-Centred System*. London: HMSO

Department for Education (2012a) *National Action Plan to Tackle Child Abuse Linked to Faith or Belief*. Available at *https://www.gov.uk/government/uploads/system/uploads/attachment_data/file/175437/Action_Plan_-_Abuse_linked_to_Faith_or_Belief.pdf*

Department for Education (2012b) *Building a Safe and Confident Future: Maintaining Momentum*. Progress report from the Social Work Reform Board

Department for Education (2013) *Children and Families Bill*. London: HMSO

Department for Education (2014) *Making the Education of Social Workers Consistently Effective – Report of Sir Martin Narey's Independent Review of the Education of Children's Social Workers*. London: HMSO

Department for Education and Skills (2004) *Every Child Matters*. London: HMSO

Department of Health (1989) *Caring for People*. London: HMSO

Department of Health (1999) *National Service Framework for Mental Health*. London: HMSO

Department of Health (2000) *No Secrets: Guidance on Developing and Implementing Multi-Agency Policies and Procedures to Protect Vulnerable Adults from Abuse*. London: HMSO

Department of Health (2001a) *The Expert Patient: A New Approach for Chronic Disease Management for the 21st Century*. London: HMSO

Department of Health (2001b) *Valuing People: A New Strategy for Learning Disability for the 21st Century*. White Paper. London: HMSO

Department of Health (2001c) *National Service Framework for Older People*. London: HMSO

Department of Health (2005) *Independence, Well Being and Choice*. Green Paper. London: HMSO

Department of Health (2006) *Action on Stigma: Promoting Mental Health: Ending Discrimination in Work*. London: SHiFT

Department of Health (2007a) *Putting People First: A Shared Vision and Commitment to the Transformation of Adult Social Care*. London: HMSO

Department of Health (2007b) *Independence, Choice and Risk: A Guide to Best Practice in Supported Decision-Making*. London: HMSO

Department of Health (2007c) *Modernising Adult Social Care – What's Working*. London: HMSO

Department of Health (2007d) *New Ways of Working for Everyone: A Best Practice Implementation Guide*. London: National Institute for Mental Health in England

Department of Health (2009a) *Valuing People Now: A Three Year Strategy for People with Learning Disabilities*. London: HMSO

Department of Health (2009b) *Safeguarding Adults: Report on the Consultation on the Review of 'No Secrets'*. London: HMSO

Department of Health (2010) *Commission on Funding of Care and Support*. Available at *http://www.dilnotcommission.dh.gov.uk*

Department of Health (2011a) *No Health without Mental Health: A Cross-Government Mental Health Outcomes Strategy for People of All Ages*. London: HMSO

Department of Health (2011b) *Healthy Lives, Healthy People: A Call to Action on Obesity in England*. London: HMSO

Department of Health (2011c) *UK Physical Activity Guidelines*. Available at *https://www.gov.uk/government/publications/uk-physical-activity-guidelines*

Department of Health (2012) *Commission on Funding of Care and Support – Next Steps*. Available at *http://www.dilnotcommission.dh.gov.uk/next-steps/*

Department of Health (2013a) *Caring for Our Future*. Available at *http://caringforourfuture.dh.gov.uk*

Department of Health (2013b) *Transforming Care: A National Response to Winterbourne View Hospital*. London: HMSO

Department of Health (2014) *Suicide Prevention Report*. Available at *https://www.gov.uk/government/publications/suicide-prevention-report*

Department of Health and Home Office (2003) *The Victoria Climbié Inquiry: Report of an Inquiry by Lord Laming*. London: HMSO

Department of Health and Social Security (1980) *Inequalities in Health: Report of a Research Working Group*. London: HMSO

Dex, S. (1985) *The Sexual Division of Work: Conceptual Revolutions in the Social Sciences*. Brighton: Harvester Wheatsheaf

Dobash, R. and Dobash, R. (1979) *Violence against Wives*. New York: Free Press

Dobbs, C. and Burholt, V. (2010) Caregiving and carereceiving relationships of older South Asians. *Journal of Gerontopsychology and Geriatric Psychiatry* 23(4): 215–25

Dodd, S. (2013) Personalization, individualism and the politics of disablement. *Disability and Society* 28(2): 260–73

Dominelli, L. (1997) *Sociology for Social Work*. Basingstoke: Macmillan

Dominelli, L. (2002) *Feminist Social Work: Theory and Practice*. Basingstoke: Palgrave Macmillan

Dominelli, L. (2007a) *Revitalising Communities in a Globalising World*. Aldershot: Ashgate

Dominelli, L. (2007b) Contemporary challenges to social work education in the United Kingdom. *Australian Social Work* 60(1): 29–45

Dominelli, L. (2008) *Anti-Racist Social Work*. 3rd edition. Basingstoke: Palgrave Macmillan

Dominelli, L. (2010) *Social Work in a Globalizing World*. Cambridge: Polity

Donald, J. and Rattansi, A. (eds) (1992) *'Race', Culture and Difference*. London: Sage

Donovan, P. (2013) Rochdale serious case reviews find dysfunctional multi-agency working and social care failures. *Community Care*, 20 December. Available at *http://www.communitycare.co.uk/2013/12/20/rochdale-serious-case-reviews-find-dysfunctional-multi-agency-working-social-care-failures/*

Donzelot, J. (1980) *The Policing of Families*. London: Hutchinson

Dorrestein, M. and Hockey, C. (2010) Maximising participation for older people: scoping the occupational therapy role in residential care settings. *New Zealand Journal of Occupational Therapy* 57(2): 49–55

Douglas, R.M. (2002) Anglo-Saxons and the Attacoti: the racialization of Irishness in Britain between the world wars. *Ethnic and Racial Studies* 25: 40–63

Drugscope (n.d.) *How Much Crime is Drug-Related?* Available at *http://www.drugscope.org.uk/resources/faqs/faqpages/how-much-crime-is-drug-related*

Duff, C. (2003) The importance of culture and context: rethinking risk and risk management in the young drug using populations. *Health, Risk and Society* 5(3): 285–99

Duffin, C. (2012) Number of men seeking help for anorexia is increasing. *Mental Health Practice* 16(2): 6–7

Duffy, S. (2010) The citizenship theory of social justice: exploring the meaning of personalization for social work. *Journal of Social Work Practice* 24(3): 253–67

Duffy, S. and Gillespie, J. (2009) *Personalization and Safeguarding*. London: In Control

Duncombe, J. and Marsden, D. (1993) Love and intimacy: the gender division of emotion and 'emotion work': a neglected aspect of sociological discussion of heterosexual relationships. *Sociology* 27(2): 221–41

Dunleavy, P.J. (1986) The growth of sectoral cleavages and the stabilization of state expenditures. *Environment and Planning D: Society and Space* 4(2): 129– 44

Dunning, J. (2011) Social workers losing faith in personalisation. *Community Care*, 23 May. Available at *http://www.communitycare.co.uk/2011/05/23/social-workers-losing-faith-in-personalisation/*

Dworkin, A. (1981) *Pornography: Men Possessing Women*. London: Women's Press

Dwyer, P. and Shaw, S. (2013) *An Introduction to Social Policy*. London: Sage

Edgell, S. (2006) *The Sociology of Work: Continuity and Change in Paid and Unpaid Work*. London: Sage

Ehrenreich, B. and English, D. (1978) *For Her Own Good: 150 Years of the Experts' Advice to Women*. London: Pluto Press

Elias, J. (2003) *Economic Globalisation and Gender Issues*. Cardiff: The Centre for Business Relationship Accountability, Sustainability and Society. Available at *http://www.berlin-divercity.de/diwiki/images/9/98/Economic_globalisation.pdf*

Elliott, F.R. (1996) *Gender, Family and Society*. Basingstoke: Macmillan.

Ellis, H. (1946) *The Psychology of Sex*. 2nd edition. London: Heinemann

Ellis, T. and Boden, I. (2004) Is there a unifying professional culture in Youth Offending Teams? A research note. *British Society of Criminology* 7(6). Available at *http://britsoccrim.org/volume7/006.pdf*

Engels, F. (1902) *The Origin of the Family, Private Property and the State*. Chicago: Charles H. Kerr

Engler, S. (2006) Sweating over sweatshops. *New Internationalist* 395. Available at *http://newint.org/features/2006/11/01/sweatshops/*

Epperson, M., Roberts, L., Ivanoff, A., Tripodi, S. and Gilmer, C. (2013) To what extent is criminal justice content specifically addressed in MSW programs? *Journal of Social Work Education* 49(1): 96–107

Equal Opportunities Commission (2006) *Sex and Power: Who Runs Britain?* Available at *http://www.unece.org/fileadmin/DAM/stats/gender/publications/UK/Sex_and_Power_GB_2006.pdf*

Equality and Human Rights Commission (2009) *Equal Pay Position Paper*. Parliamentary Briefing. London: Equality and Human Rights Commission

Equality and Human Rights Commission (2010) *Stop and Think: A Critical Review of the Use of Stop and Search Powers in England and Wales*. Available at *http://www.equalityhumanrights.com/publication/stop-and-think-critical-review-use-stop-and-search-powers-england-and-wales*

Espeset, E.M., Gulliksen, K.S., Nordbø, R.H., Skårderud, F. and Holte, A. (2011) The link between negative emotions and eating disorder behaviour in patients with anorexia nervosa. *Eating Disorders Review* 20(6): 451–60

Estes, C. (1979) *The Aging Enterprise*. San Francisco: Jossey-Bass

Estes, C. (2001) *Social Policy and Aging*. London: Sage

Evandrou, M. and Glaser, K. (2003) Combining work and family life: the pension penalty of caring. *Ageing and Society* 23(5): 583–603

Evans, G. and Mills, C. (1998) Identifying class structure: a latent class analysis of the criterion-related and construct validity of the Goldthorpe class system. *European Sociological Review* 14(1): 87–106

Evans, T. and Harris, J. (2004) Street-level bureaucracy, social work and the (exaggerated) death of discretion. *British Journal of Social Work* 34(6): 871–95

Evers, A., Pijls, M. and Ungerson, C. (eds) (1994) *Payments for Care: A Comparative Overview.* Aldershot: Avebury

Eysenck, H.J (1971) *Race, Education and Intelligence.* London: Maurice Temple Smith

Fagin, L. and Little, M. (1984) *The Forsaken Families.* Harmondsworth: Penguin

Family and Parenting Institute (2012) *Families in an Age of Austerity.* London: Family and Parenting Institute

Fanon, F. (1952) *Black Skin White Masks.* New York: Grove Press

Farmer, E., Selwyn, J. and Meakings, S. (2013) 'Other children say you're not normal because you don't live with your parents.' Children's views of living with informal kinship carers: social networks, stigma and attachment to carers. *Child and Family Social Work* 15(1): 25–34

Faulks, S. (2006) *Human Traces.* London: Vintage

Fawcett, B. (2000) *Feminist Perspectives on Disability.* Harlow: Prentice Hall

Fawcett Society (2009) *What About Women?* London: The Fawcett Society

Fawcett Society (2012) *The Impact of Austerity on Women.* Fawcett Society Policy Briefing, March. London: The Fawcett Society

Featherstone, M. (1991) *Consumer Culture and Postmodernism.* London: Sage

Featherstone, M. and Hepworth, M. (1991) The mask of ageing and the postmodern life course. In M. Featherstone, M. Hepworth and B.S. Turner (eds) *The Body, Social Process and Cultural Theory.* London: Sage

Felson, M. (1998) *Crime and Everyday Life.* 2nd edition. Thousand Oaks, CA: Pine Forge Press

Fenton, S. (1999) *Ethnicity: Racism, Class and Culture.* Basingstoke: Palgrave Macmillan

Ferguson, C.J. (2013) Moral panic in progress: video games and the media. *The Criminologist* 38(5): 32–5

Ferguson, C.J., Winegard, B. and Winegard, B.M. (2011) Who is the fairest one of all? How evolution guides peer and media influences on female body dissatisfaction. *Review of General Psychology* 15(1): 11–28

Ferguson, I. and Woodward, R. (2009) *Radical Social Work in Practice.* Bristol: Policy Press

Fernando, S. (2010) *Mental Health, Race and Culture.* 3rd edition. Basingstoke: Palgrave Macmillan

Field, J. (1993) Coming out of two closets. *Canadian Woman Studies* 13(4): 18–19

Finch, J. and Groves, D. (1983) *A Labour of Love: Women, Work and Caring.* London: Routledge and Kegan Paul

Finch. J. and Mason, J. (1993) *Negotiating Family Responsibilities.* London: Routledge

Firestone, S. (1971) *The Dialectic of Sex: The Case for Feminist Revolution.* London: Jonathan Cape

Fook, J. (2002) *Social Work: A Critical Introduction.* London: Sage

Fook, J. and Gardner, F. (2007) *Practising Critical Reflection.* Maidenhead: Open University Press

Foucault, M (1979a) *The History of Sexuality, Vol. 1, An Introduction.* London: Allen Lane

Foucault, M. (1979b) *Discipline and Punish.* Harmondsworth: Penguin

Forster, E.M. (1971) *Maurice.* London: Penguin

Francis Report (2012) *The Mid Staffordshire NHS Foundation Trust Public Inquiry.* Available at *http:// www.midstaffspublicinquiry.com*

Fraser, D. (1984) *The Evolution of the British Welfare State.* 2nd edition. London: Macmillan

Fraser, S. and Matthews, S. (2008) *The Critical Practitioner in Social Work and Health Care.* Buckingham: Open University Press

Freire, P. (1972) *Pedagogy of the Oppressed.* Harmondsworth: Penguin

French, S. (1993a) Setting a record straight. In J. Swain, V. Finkelstein, S. French and M. Oliver (eds) *Disabling Barriers – Enabling Environments.* London: Sage

French, S. (1993b) Disability, impairment or something in between? In J. Swain, V. Finkelstein, S. French and M. Oliver (eds) *Disabling Barriers – Enabling Environments.* London: Sage

French, S. and Swain, J. (2012) *Working with Disabled People in Policy and Practice.* London: Palgrave Macmillan

Friedli, L. (2009) *Mental Health, Resilience and Inequalities.* Copenhagen: Mental Health Foundation/ World Health Organization Europe. Available at *http://www.euro.who.int/__data/assets/pdf_ file/0012/100821/E92227.pdf*

Frith, H. and Gleeson, K. (2006) (De)constructing body image. *Journal of Health Psychology* 11(1): 79–90

Frones, I. (1994) Dimensions of childhood. In J. Qvortrup, M. Bardy, G. Sgritta and H. Wintersberger (eds) *Childhood Matters: Social Theory, Practice and Politics*. Aldershot: Avebury

Fruin, D. (2000) *New Directions for Independent Living: Inspection of Independent Living Arrangements for Younger Disabled People*. London: Department of Health

Furedi, F. (2002) *Paranoid Parenting: Why Ignoring the Experts May be Best For Your Child*. Chicago: Chicago Review Press

Furness, S. (2007) An enquiry into students' motivations to train as social workers in England. *Journal of Social Work* 7(2): 239–53

Galilee, J. (2005) *Literature Review on Media Representations of Social Work and Social Workers*. Edinburgh: Scottish Executive

Garland, D. (2002) *The Culture of Control: Crime and Social Order in Contemporary Society*. Chicago: University of Chicago Press

Garrett, P.M. (2002) Social work and the just society: diversity, difference and the sequestration of poverty. *Journal of Social Work* 2(2): 187–210

Garside, R. (2006) Criminality and social justice: challenging the assumptions. In B. Shimshon (ed.) *Social Justice: Criminal Justice*. London: Smith Institute

Gaylard, D. (2008) Policy to practice. In A. Mantell and T. Scragg (eds) *Safeguarding Adults in Social Work*. Exeter: Learning Matters

General Social Care Council (2002) *Codes of Practice for Social Workers and Employers*. London: GSCC

Geyer, R. (2012) Can complexity move UK policy beyond 'evidence-based policy making' and the 'audit culture'? Applying a 'complexity cascade' to education and health policy. *Political Studies* 60(1): 20–43

Ghai, A. (2001) Marginalization and disability: experiences from the Third World. In M. Priestley, (ed.) *Disability and the Life Course: Global Perspectives*. Cambridge: Cambridge University Press

Giddens, A. (1991) *Modernity and Self-Identity: Self and Society in the Late Modern Age*. Cambridge: Polity

Giddens, A. and Sutton, P.W. (2013) *Sociology*. 7th edition. Cambridge: Polity

Gillies, V. (2005) 'Raising the meritocracy': parenting and the individualization of social class. *Sociology* 39(5): 835–53

Gilmore, D. (1990) *Manhood in the Making: Cultural Concepts of Masculinity*. New Haven, CT: Yale University Press

Gilroy, P. (1982) The myth of black criminality. *Socialist Register* 19: 47–56

Gilroy, P. (1997) *There Ain't No Black in the Union Jack*. London: Hutchinson

Ginn, J. and Arber, S. (1993) Ageing and cultural stereotypes of older women. In J. Johnson and R. Slater (eds) *Ageing and Later Life*. London: Sage

Glasby, J. and Littlechild, R. (2009) *Direct Payments and Personal Budgets: Putting Personalization into Practice*. Bristol: Policy Press

Glynn, M. and Addaction (2011) *Dad and Me: Research into the Problems Caused by Absent Fathers*. London: Addaction

Goble, G. (2004) Dependence, independence and normality. In J. Swain, S. French, C. Barnes and C. Thomas (eds) *Disabling Barriers – Enabling Environments*. 2nd edition. London: Sage

Goffman, E. (1961) *Asylums*. Harmondsworth: Penguin

Goffman, E. (1968) *Stigma: Notes on the Management of Spoiled Identity*. Harmondsworth: Penguin

Goffman, E. (1982) The interaction order. *American Sociological Review* 48: 1–17

Goldberg, A. (1999) *Sex, Religion and the Making of Modern Madness*. New York: Open University Press

Golding, J. (1997) *Without Prejudice: MIND Lesbian, Gay and Bisexual Mental Health Awareness Research*. London: MIND Publications

Goldson, B. (1997) Children in trouble: state responses to juvenile crime. In P. Scraton (ed.) *Childhood in Crisis*. London: UCL Press

Golightley, M. (2011) *Social Work and Mental Health*. 4th edition. Exeter: Learning Matters

Goode, E. and Ben-Yehuda, N. (1994) *Moral Panics: The Social Construction of Deviance*. Oxford: Blackwell

Goodey, J. (2004) *Victims and Victimology: Research, Policy and Practice*. London: Longman

Gordon, D., Levitas, R. and Pantazis, C. (eds) (2006) *Poverty and Social Exclusion in Britain: The Millennium Survey*. Bristol: Policy Press

Gould, N. and Martin, D. (2012) Mental health law and social work. In M. Davies (ed.) *Social Work with Adults*. London: Palgrave Macmillan

Goulding, N. and Duggal, A. (2011) *Commissioning Services for Women and Children Who Experience Violence or Abuse: A Guide for Health Commissioners*. London: Department of Health

Gove, W. and Tudor, J. (1973) Adult sex roles and mental illness. *American Journal of Sociology* 78: 812–35

Grady, P. (2004) Social work responses to accompanied asylum-seeking children. In D. Hayes and B. Humphries (eds) *Social Work, Immigration and Asylum*. London: Jessica Kingsley

Graham, H. (1983) Caring: a labour of love. In J. Finch and D. Groves (eds) *A Labour of Love: Women, Work and Caring*. London: Routledge and Kegan Paul

Gramsci, A. (1971) *Selections From the Prison Notebooks*. London: New Left Books

Grant, G., Goward, P., Richardson, M., Flynn, M. and Ramcharan, P. (2010). *Learning Disability: A Life Cycle Approach to Valuing People*. 2nd edition. Buckingham: Open University Press

Gray, M. and Webb, S. (2013) Critical social work. In M. Gray and S. Webb (eds) *Social Work Theories and Methods*. London: Sage

Green, L. (2005) Theorizing sexuality, sexual abuse and residential children's homes: adding gender to the equation. *British Journal of Social Work* 35(4): 453–81

Green, L. (2010) *Understanding the Life Course: Sociological and Psychological Perspectives*. Cambridge: Polity

Griffiths, J. (2010) Is obesity a child protection issue? *Community Care*, 27 August. Available at *http://www.communitycare.co.uk/2010/08/27/is-obesity-a-child-protection-issue/*

Guardian and London School of Economics (2011) *Reading the Riots: Investigating England's Summer of Disorder*. Funded by Joseph Rowntree Foundation.

Habermas, J. (1989) *The Structural Transformation of the Public Sphere: An Inquiry into a Category of Bourgeois Society*. Cambridge: Polity

Hafford-Letchfield, T. (2006) *Management and Organizations in Social Work*. London: Sage

Hakim, C. (1996) *Key Issues in Women's Work: Female Heterogeneity and the Polarization of Women's Employment*. London: Athlone

Hall, Steve (2013) *Theorizing Crime and Deviance: A New Perspective*. London: Sage

Hall, Stuart (1992) New ethnicities. In J. Donald and J. Rattansi, J. (eds) *'Race', Culture and Difference*. London: Sage

Hall, Stuart (1996) *Representation: Cultural Representations and Signifying Practices*. London: Sage/ The Open University

Hall, Stuart and Jefferson, T. (eds) (1976) *Resistance Through Rituals*. London: Hutchinson

Hall, Stuart, Critcher, C., Jefferson, T., Clarke, J. and Roberts, B. (1978) *Policing the Crisis: Mugging, the State and Law and Order*. London: Macmillan

Hallsworth, S. (2005) *Street Crime*. Cullompton: Willan

Halsley, A.H, Heath, A. and Ridge, J. (1980) *Origins and Destinations*. Oxford: Clarendon Press

Hamama, L. (2012) Differences between children's social workers and adults' social workers on sense of burnout, work conditions and organizational social support. *British Journal of Social Work* 42(7): 1333–53

Hanrahan, C. (2012). Critical social theory and the politics of narrative in the mental health professions: the mental health film festival as an emerging postmodern praxis. *British Journal of Social Work* 43(6): 1150–69

Haralambos, M. and Holborn, M. (2004) *Sociology: Themes and Perspectives*. 6th edition. London: Collins

Hari Krishnan, K.S. (2012) No social protection for India's elderly. Inter Press Service. Available at *http://www.globalissues.org/news/2012/11/09/15230*

Harkness, S. (2008) The household division of labour: changes in families' allocation of paid and unpaid work. In J. Scott, S. Dex and H. Joshi (eds), *Women and Employment*. Cheltenham: Edward Elgar

Harris, J. (1998) Scientific management, bureau-professionalism and new managerialism: the labour process of state social work. *British Journal of Social Work* 28(6): 839–62

Harris Interactive (2002) Press release: fewer than half of all lesbian, gay, bisexual and transgender adults surveyed say they have disclosed their sexual orientation to their health care provider. Available at *http://www.thefreelibrary.com/Fewer+than+Half+of+All+Lesbian,+Gay,+Bisexual+and+Transgender+Adults...-a095531283*

Harrison, G. and Melville, R. (2010) *Rethinking Social Work in a Global World*. London: Palgrave Macmillan

Hasenfeld, Y. (2000) Social welfare administration and organizational theory. In R.J. Patti (ed.) *The Handbook of Social Welfare Management*. Newbury Park, CA: Sage

Havighurst, R. (1963) Successful aging. In R.H. Williams, C. Tibbits and W. Donohue (eds) *Processes of Aging: Social and Psychological Perspectives*, Vol. 1. Chicago: University of Chicago Press

Hawkes, A. (2011) UK riots were product of consumerism, and will hit economy, says City broker. *Guardian*, 22 August. Available at *http://www.guardian.co.uk/business/2011/aug/22/uk-riots-economy-consumerism-values*

Hayward, K. and Yar, M. (2006) The 'chav' phenomenon: consumption, media and the construction of a new underclass. *Crime Media Culture* 2(1): 9–28

Hazan, H. (2000) *The Cultural Trap: The Language of Images*. In J. Gubrium and J. Holstein (eds) *Aging and Everyday Life*. Oxford: Blackwell

Heald, O. (2007) Speech of 15 January. Available at *http://www.publications.parliament.uk/pa/cm200607/cmhansrd/cm070111/debtext/70111-0008.htm*

Health Care Professions Council (2012) *Standards of Occupational Proficiency for Social Work*. London: HCPC

Healthcare Commission (2006) *Joint Investigation into Services for People with Learning Difficulties at Cornwall Partnership NHS Trust*. London: Healthcare Commission

Healy, K. (2002) Managing human services in a market environment: what role for social workers? *British Journal of Social Work* 32(5): 527–40

Healy, K. (2005) *Social Work Theories in Context: Creating Frameworks for Practice*. London: Palgrave Macmillan

Healy, K. and Meagher, G. (2004) The reprofessionalization of social work: collaborative approaches for achieving professional recognition. *British Journal of Social Work* 34(2): 243–60

Healy, L.M. (2008) *International Social Work: Professional Action in an Interdependent World*. 2nd edition. New York: Oxford University Press

Heaphy, B. (2011) Critical relational displays. In E. Dermott and J. Seymour (eds) *Displaying Families: A New Concept for the Sociology of Family Life*. London: Palgrave Macmillan

Hearn, J. (1996) Is masculinity dead? A critique of the concept of masculinity/masculinities. In M. Mac an Ghaill (ed.) *Understanding Masculinities*. Buckingham: Open University Press

Hearn, J. and Parkin, W. (2001) *Gender, Sexuality and Violence in Organizations: The Unspoken Forces of Organization Violations*. London: Sage

Heath, H. and Schofield, I. (1999) *Healthy Ageing: Nursing Older People*. London: Mosby

Hehir, B. (2005) Looking for someone to blame. *Nursing Standard* 20(7): 32–3

Heidensohn, F. (1985) *Women and Crime*. London: Macmillan

Hendrick, H. (1992) Children and childhood. *ReFresh* 15. Available at *http://www.ehs.org.uk/dot Asset/fc705ebe-8ed6-412a-8189-404a8c3759c9.pdf*

Hennessy, P. and d'Ancona, M. (2011) David Cameron: It's time for a zero tolerance approach to street crime. *The Telegraph*, 13 August. Available at *http://www.telegraph.co.uk/news/uknews/crime/8700243/David-Cameron-on-UK-riots-Its-time-for-a-zero-tolerance-approach-to-street-crime.html*

Henslin, J. (2010) *Sociology: A Down-to-Earth Approach*. 10th edition. Boston: Pearson

Herbert, H. (1994) Counselling gay men and lesbians with alcohol problems. *Journal of Rehabilitation* 60(2): 2–60

Herdt, G. (1981) *Guardian of the Flutes.* New York: McGraw-Hill

Herrnstein, R.J. and Murray, C. (1994) *The Bell Curve: Intelligence and Class Structure in American Life.* New York: Free Press

Hickman, M. (1995) *Religion, Class and Identity: The State, the Catholic Church and the Education of the Irish in Britain.* Aldershot: Avebury

Hicks, S. (2005) Sexuality: social work theories and practice. In R. Adams, L. Dominelli and M. Payne (eds) *Social Work Futures: Crossing Boundaries, Transforming Practice.* Basingstoke: Palgrave Macmillan

Hicks, S. (2008) Thinking through sexuality. *Journal of Social Work* 8(1): 65–82

Hicks, S. (2009) Sexuality. In R. Adams, L. Dominelli and M. Payne (eds) *Practising Social Work in a Complex World.* London: Palgrave

Hill, Amelia (2003) A lost generation trapped on our forgotten estates. *Observer,* 30 November

Hill, Amelia (2011) Michael Gove relaunches adoption rules with attack on 'ridiculous bureaucracy'. *Guardian,* 22 February. Available at *http://www.theguardian.com/society/2011/feb/22/michael-gove-relaunches-adoption-rules*

Hill, Andrew (2010) *Working in Statutory Contexts.* Cambridge: Polity

Himmelweit, S. (1995) The discovery of 'unpaid work': the social consequences of the expansion of 'work'. *Feminist Economics* 1(2): 1–19

Himmelweit, S., Santos, C., Sevilla, A. and Sofer, C. (2013) Sharing of resources within the family and the economics of household decision-making. *Journal of Marriage and Family* 75(3): 625–39

HM Government (2009) *Work, Recovery & Inclusion.* London: HMSO. Available at *http://www.ndti.org.uk/uploads/files/Work_Recovery_and_Inclusion_PDF.pdf*

HM Government (2010a) *Equality Act.* London: HMSO

HM Government (2010b) *The Coalition: Our Programme for Government.* London: HMSO

HM Government (2011) *Local to Global: Reducing the Risk from Organised Crime.* London: HMSO

HM Government (2014) *Preventing Suicide in England: One Year On.* London: HMSO

Hobcraft, J (1998) *Intergenerational and Life-Course Transmission of Social Exclusion: Influences of Child Poverty, Family Disruption, and Contact with the Police.* CASE paper 15, London School of Economics: ESRC Centre for the Analysis of Social Exclusion

Hochschild, A.R. (1983). *The Managed Heart: Commercialization of Human Feeling.* Berkeley: University of California Press

Hockey, J. (1997) Women in grief: cultural representation and social practice. In D. Field, J. Hockey and N. Small (eds) *Death, Gender and Ethnicity.* London: Routledge

Hockey, J. and James, A. (2003) *Social Identities across the Life Course.* Basingstoke: Palgrave Macmillan

Hogan, R. (1980) Nursing and human sexuality. *Nursing Times* 76: 1299–300

Holland, J., Reynolds, T. and Weller, S. (2007) Transitions, networks and communities: the significance of social capital in the lives of children and young people. *Journal of Youth Studies* 10(1): 97–116

Holloway, M. and Lymbery, M. (2007) Editorial – Caring for people: social work with adults in the next decade and beyond. *British Journal of Social Work* 37(3): 375–86

Holman, R. (1978) *Poverty: Explanation of Social Deprivation.* Oxford: Martin Robertson.

Homan, K. (2010) Athletic-ideal and thin-ideal internalization as prospective predictors of body dissatisfaction, dieting, and compulsive exercise. *Body Image: An International Journal* 7(3): 240–5

Home Office (2002) *Respect and Responsibility: Taking a Stand Against Anti-Social Behaviour.* Cm. 5778. London: HMSO

Home Office (2007) *The Corston Report.* London: HMSO

Home Office (2011) *An Overview of Recorded Crimes and Arrests Resulting from Disorder Events in August 2011.* London: HMSO

Home Office (2012a) *Crime Survey for England and Wales.* London: HMSO. Available at *http://www.crimesurvey.co.uk*

Home Office (2012b) *First Annual Report of the Inter-Departmental Ministerial Group on Human Trafficking.* Available at *https://www.gov.uk/government/uploads/system/uploads/attachment_data/file/118116/human-trafficking-report.pdf*

Home Office (2013a) *Police Workforce, England and Wales*. Available at *http://www.gov.uk/govern ment/publications/police-workforce-england-and-wales-31-march-2013*

Home Office (2013b) *Circular: New Government Domestic Violence and Abuse Definition*. Home Office circular 003

hooks, b. (1991) *Yearning: Race, Gender and Cultural Politics*. New York: Turnaround

Horner, N. (2013) *What is Social Work? Themes and Perspectives*. 3rd edition. London: Sage/Learning Matters

Howe, D. (1992) *An Introduction to Social Work Theory*. 3rd edition. Aldershot: Gower Press

Hughes, M. and Wearing, M. (2007) *Organizations and Management in Social Work*, London: Sage

Hugman, R. (1994) *Ageing and the Care of Older People in Europe*. Basingstoke: Macmillan

Hugman, R. (2010) *Understanding International Social Work*. London: Palgrave Macmillan

Humphries, B. (2004) Refugees, asylum-seekers and social work. In D. Hayes and B. Humphries (eds) *Social Work, Immigration and Asylum*. London: Jessica Kingsley

Hunt, S. (2005) *The Life Course: A Sociological Introduction*. Basingtsoke: Palgrave Macmillan

Hutton, W. (1995) *The State We're In*. London: Jonathan Cape

IMPETUS–PEF (2014) *Make NEETS History in 2014*. Available at *http://impetus-pef.org.uk/ wp-content/uploads/2013/12/Make-NEETS-History-Report_ImpetusPEF_January-2014.pdf*

Independent School Parent Magazine (n.d.) Football: a class act. Available at *http://www.independ entschoolparent.com/extra-curricular/football-a-class-act*

Ingram, R. (2013) Locating emotional intelligence at the heart of social work practice. *British Journal of Social Work* 43(5): 987–1004

Innes, M. (2003) Signal crimes: detective work, mass media and constructing collective memory. In P. Mason (ed.) *Criminal Visions: Media Representations of Crime and Justice*. Cullompton: Willan

International Association of Homes and Services for the Ageing (n.d.) *Global Ageing*. Available at *http://www.iahsa.net/Global_Ageing_Demographics.aspx*

International Federation of Social Work (2012) *Women's Policy Statement*. Available at *http://ifsw. org/policies/women/*

International Labour Organization (2005) *A Global Alliance against Forced Labour: Global Report Under the Follow-Up to the ILO Declaration on Fundamental Principles and Rights at Work. Report of the Director-General*. Geneva: ILO

IOE (2012) *Impact of IOE Research on Higher Education Participation and Funding*. University of London

IPSOS Mori (2012) Two in five Britons don't know when St George's Day is. 28 February. Available at *http://www.ipsos-mori.com/researchpublications/researcharchive/2924/Two-in-five-Britons-dont-know-when-St-Georges-Day-is.aspx*

Isay, R. (1989) *Being Homosexual: Gay Men and Their Development*. London: Penguin

Islam, S. (2005) Sociology of poverty. *Quest for Sociology: Bangladesh eJournal of Sociology* 2(1).

Jackson, C. and Tinkler, P. (2007) 'Ladettes' and 'modern girls': 'troublesome' young femininities. *Sociological Review* 55(2): 251–72

Jackson, S. and Rahman, M. (1997) Up against nature: sociological thoughts on sexuality. In J. Gubbay, C. Middleton and C. Ballard (eds) *The Student's Companion to Sociology*. Oxford: Blackwell

James, A. and James, A. (2012) *Key Concepts in Childhood Studies*. 2nd edition. London: Sage

James, A. and Prout, A. (1997) *Constructing and Reconstructing Childhood: Contemporary Issues in the Sociological Study of Childhood*. 2nd edition. London: Falmer Press

James, I., Mackenzie, L. and Mukaetova-Ladinska, E. (2006) Doll use in care homes for people with dementia. *International Journal of Geriatric Psychiatry* 21(11): 1093–8

Jenks, C. (2005) *Childhood*. 2nd edition. London: Routledge

Jeyasingham, D. (2008) Knowledge/ignorance and the construction of sexuality in social work educa-tion. *Social Work Education: The International Journal* 27(2): 138–51

John, C. (2006) Rise of UK's 'inter-ethnic conflicts'. BBC News, 22 May. Available at *http://news.bbc. co.uk/1/hi/uk/4989202.stm*

Johnson, T. (1972) *Professions and Power*. London: Macmillan.

Jones, C. (2002) Social work and society. In R. Adams, L. Dominelli and M. Payne, M. (eds) *Social Work: Themes, Issues and Critical Debates*. Basingstoke: Palgrave

Jones, Karen, Cooper, B. and Ferguson, H. (2008) *Best Practice in Social Work*. London: Palgrave

Jones, Kathleen (1960) *Mental Health and Social Policy 1845–1959*. London: Routledge and Kegan Paul

Jones, O. (2012) *Chavs: The Demonization of the Working Class*. 2nd edition. London: Verso

Jones, P. (2003) *Introducing Social Theory*. Cambridge: Polity

Jones, S. (1993) *The Language of Genes*. London: Flamingo

Jordan, B. and Drakeford, M. (2012) *Social Work and Social Policy under Austerity*. London: Palgrave

Joseph, I. and Gunter, A. (2011) *Gangs Revisited: What's a Gang and What's Race Got to Do with It?* London: Runnymede Trust

Joseph Rowntree Foundation (2001) *Young Men's Views of Masculinity*. April. Available at *http://www.jrf.org.uk/sites/files/jrf/421.pdf*

Joseph Rowntree Foundation (2008) *Young People and Territoriality in British Cities*. York: Joseph Rowntree Foundation

Kandaswamy, P. (2008) State austerity and the racial politics of same-sex marriage in the US. *Sexualities* 11(6): 706–25

Katz, J., Holland, C., Peace, S. and Taylor, E. (2011) *A Better Life: What Older People with High Support Needs Value*. York: Joseph Rowntree Foundation

Keeling, J. and van Wormer, K. (2012) Social worker interventions in situations of domestic violence: what we can learn from survivors' personal narratives? *British Journal of Social Work* 42(7): 1354–70

Keith, M. (1993) From punishment to discipline? Racism, racialization and social control. In M. Cross and M. Keith (eds) *Racism, the City and the State*. London: Routledge

Kemshall, H. (2010) Risk rationalities in contemporary social work policy and practice. *British Journal of Social Work* 40(4): 1247–62

Kemshall, H., Boeck, T. and Fleming, J. (2009) Risk, youth and moving on. *British Journal of Community Justice* 7(2): 39–52

Kerbo, H.R. (1996) *Social Stratification and Inequality: Class Conflict in Historical and Comparative Perspective*. Boston: WCB/McGraw-Hill

King, M. and McKeown, E. (2003) *Mental Health and Social Wellbeing of Gay Men, Lesbians and Bisexuals in England and Wales*. Joint Project between University College London and MIND

King's Fund Report (2002) *Age Discrimination in Health and Social Care*. London: King's Fund

Kinsella, B. (2011) *Tackling Knife Crime Together – A Review of Local Anti-Knife Crime Projects. Report for the Home Secretary*. London: HMSO

Kinsey, A., Wardell, B.P. and Clyde, M. (1948) *Sexual Behavior in the Human Male*. Philadelphia: W.B. Saunders

Kinsey, A., Wardell, B.P., Clyde, M. and Gebhard, P.H. (1953) *Sexual Behavior in the Human Female*. Philadelphia: W.B. Saunders

Kitwood, T. (1997) *Dementia Reconsidered*. Buckingham: Open University Press

Kleinman, A. (1988) *The Illness Narratives: Suffering, Healing and the Human Condition*. New York: Basic Books

Koutrolikou, P. (2005) *Negotiating 'Common Grounds' through Local Government and Urban Regeneration Policies and Initiatives: The Case of Hackney*. London: Centre for Research on Nationalism, Ethnicity and Multiculturalism (CRONEM), University of Surrey

Laming Report (2009) *The Protection of Children in England: A Progress Report*. London: HMSO

Lansdown, G. (2001) Children's welfare and children's rights. In P. Foley, J. Roche and S. Tucker (eds) *Children in Society: Contemporary Theory, Policy and Practice*. London: Palgrave/The Open University

Laslett, P. (1989) *A Fresh Map of Life: The Emergence of the Third Age*. London: Weidenfeld and Nicolson

Lauder, H., Young, M., Daniels, H., Balarin, M. and Lowe, J. (eds) (2012) *Educating for the Knowledge Economy? Critical Perspectives*. London: Routledge

Laurance, J. (2003) *Pure Madness: How Fear Drives the Mental Health System*. London: Routledge

Laville, S. (2014) Police failures over domestic violence exposed in damning report. *Guardian*, 27 March. Available at *http://www.theguardian.com/society/2014/mar/27/police-failures-domestic-violence-damning-report*

Le Grand, J. (1982) *The Strategy of Equality*. London: Allen & Unwin

Lea, J. and Young, J. (1984) *What is to be Done about Law and Order?* Harmondsworth: Penguin

Leavitt, R. and Power, M. (1989) Emotional socialization in the postmodern era: children in day care. *Social Psychology Quarterly* 52(1): 35–43

Lee, D. and Newby, H. (1983) *The Problem of Sociology*. London: Unwin Hyman

Lee, N. (2001) *Childhood and Society: Growing Up in an Age of Uncertainty*. Buckingham: Open University Press

Leece, J. (2012) The emergence and development of the personalization agenda. In M. Davies (ed.) *Social Work with Adults*. London: Palgrave Macmillan

Lees, S. (1993) Judicial rape. *Women's Studies International Forum* 16(1): 11–36

Levine, R. (2006) *Social Class and Stratification: Classic Statements and Theoretical Debates*. Lanham, MD: Rowman & Littlefield

Levitas, R. (1998) *The Inclusive Society: Social Exclusion and New Labour*. Basingstoke: Macmillan.

Lewin, K. (ed.) (1951) *Field Theory in Social Science*. New York: Harper and Row

Lewis, G. (ed.) (1998) *Forming Nation, Framing Welfare*. London: Routledge in association with Open University Press

Lewis, O. (1998) The culture of poverty. *Society* 35(2): 7–9

Lindsey, L. (2013) *Gender Roles: A Sociological Perspective*. 5th edition. London: Pearson

Lipsky, S. (1987) *Internalized Racism*. Seattle: Rational Island Publishers

Lipton, G. (ed.) (2004) *Gay Men Living with Chronic Illnesses and Disabilities: From Crisis to Crossroads*. Binghampton, NY: Haworth Press

Littlewood, J. and Tinker, A. (1981) *Families in Flats*. London: HMSO

Llewellyn, A. (2009) Sociology and ageing. In A. Kydd, T. Duffy and R. Duffy (eds) *The Care and Wellbeing of Older People: A Textbook for Health Care Students*. Exeter: Reflect Press

Lonsdale, S. (1990) *Women and Disability: The Experience of Physical Disability among Women*. London: Macmillan

Lorant, V., Deliège, D., Eaton, W., Robert, A., Philppot, R. and Ansseau, M. (2003) Socioeconomic inequalities in depression: a meta-analysis. *American Journal of Epidemiology* 157: 98–112.

Lorde, A. (1984) *Sister Outsider*. Berkeley, CA: Crossing Press

Lymbery, M. (2005) *Social Work with Older People: Context, Policy and Practice*. London: Sage

Lymbery, M. (2012) Social work and personalization. *British Journal of Social Work* 42(4): 783–92

Lymbery, M. and Butler, S. (2004) Social work ideals and practice realities: an introduction. In M. Lymbery and S. Butler (eds) *Social Work Ideals and Practice Realities*. Basingstoke: Palgrave Macmillan

Lymbery, M. and Postle, K. (2010) Social work in the context of adult social care in England and the resultant implications for social work education. *British Journal of Social Work* 40(8): 2502–22

Lynch, R. (2014) *Social Work Practice with Older People*. London: Sage

Lyotard, J.-F. (1984) *The Post-Modern Condition*. Manchester: Manchester University Press

Mac an Ghaill, M. (ed.) (1996) *Understanding Masculinities*. Buckingham: Open University Press

McAuley, R. (2007) *Out of Sight: Crime, Youth and Exclusion in Modern Britain*. Cullompton: Willan

McClure, G. (2001) Suicide in children and adolescents in England and Wales 1970–1998. *British Journal of Psychiatry* 198: 469–74

McClymont, M. (1999) Hearing older voices. *Elderly Care* 11(6): 8–12

McDonald, A. (2010) *Social Work with Older People*. Cambridge: Polity

McDonald A. (2006) *Understanding Community Care*. London: Palgrave Macmillan

McDonald, C. (2006) *Challenging Social Work: The Institutional Context of Practice*. London: Palgrave

MacDonald, R. and Marsh, J. (2001) Disconnected youth. *Journal of Youth Studies* 4(4): 373–91

McGovern, D. and Cope, R. (1987) The compulsory detention of males of different ethnic groups with special reference to offender patients. *British Journal of Psychiatry* 150: 505–12

MacInnes, T., Aldridge, H., Bushe, S., Kenway, P. and Tinson, A. (2013) *Monitoring Poverty and Social Exclusion*. York: Joseph Rowntree Foundation

Macionis, J. and Plummer, K. (2012) *Sociology: A Global Introduction*. 5th edition. Harlow: Prentice Hall

McKee, M. and Stuckler, D. (2013) Older people in the UK: under attack from all directions. *Age and Ageing* 42: 11–13

Mackenzie, L., Wood-Mitchell, A. and James, I. 2006. Thinking about dolls. *Journal of Dementia Care* 14(2): 16–17

Mackie, M (1987) *Constructing Women and Men: Gender Socialization*. New York: Holt, Rinehart and Winston

McKinlay, J.B. (1995) The everyday impacts of providing informal care to dependent elders and their consequences for the care recipients. *Journal of Aging and Health* 7(4): 497–528

McLaughlin, E. and Muncie, J. (eds) (2013) *Criminological Perspectives: A Reader*. 3rd edition. London: Sage

MacNicol, J. (1987) In pursuit of the underclass. *Journal of Social Policy* 16(3): 293–318

Macpherson, W. (1999) *The Stephen Lawrence Inquiry: Report of an Inquiry by Sir William Macpherson*. London: Home Office

McRobbie, A (1977) *Jackie: An Ideology of Adolescent Femininity*. Birmingham CCCS Occasional Paper

Malik, K. (1996) *The Meaning of Race: Race, History and Culture in Western Society*. London: Macmillan

Malik, K. (2005) Islamophobia myth. *Prospect*. 20 February

Malpas, S. (2005) *The Postmodern*. New York: Routledge

Mancini, M. (2011) Understanding change in community mental health practices through critical discourse analysis. *British Journal of Social Work* 41(4): 645–67

Mann, K. (1985) The making of a claiming class: the neglect of agency in analyses of the welfare state. *Critical Social Policy* 5(15): 62–74

Mantell, A. (ed.) (2009) *Social Work Skills with Adults*. Exeter: Learning Matters

Manthorpe, J. (2003) Nearest and dearest? The neglect of lesbians in caring relationships. *British Journal of Social Work* 33(6): 753–68

Manthorpe, J. (2009) Review of research on migrant care workers. *Community Care*, 28 August. Available at *http://www.communitycare.co.uk/2009/08/28/review-by-jill-manthorpe-of-research-on-migrant-care-workers/*

Mantle, G. and Backwith, D. (2010) Poverty and social work. *British Journal of Social Work* 40(8): 2380–97

Marsh, I. and Melville, G. (2011) Moral panics and the British media – A look at some contemporary 'folk devils'. *Internet Journal of Criminology* (online). Available at *http://www.internet-journalofcriminology.com/Marsh_Melville_Moral_Panics_and_the_British_Media_March_2011.pdf*

Marsh, J. and Bishop, J. (2014) *Changing Play: Play, Media and Commercial Culture from the 1950s to the Present Day*. Buckingham: Open University Press

Martell, L. (2010) *The Sociology of Globalization*. Cambridge: Polity

Martin, S., Kosberg, J., Sun, F. and Durkin, K. (2012) Social work professions in an aging world: opportunities and perspectives. *Educational Gerontology* 38: 166–78

Martin, T.L. and Doka, K.J. (2000) *Men Don't Cry . . . Women Do: Transcending Gender Stereotypes of Grief*. Philadelphia: Brunner/Mazel

Mason, D. (1995) *Race and Ethnicity in Modern Britain*. Oxford: Oxford University Press

Masters, S. (2003) Long way to go. *BASW Newsletter*, 2 June

Mathews, G., Zeidner, M. and Roberts, R. (2002) *Emotional Intelligence: Science and Myth*. Cambridge, MA: MIT Press

Matter of the Inquiry into the Legality of the Use of Force by the United Kingdom against Iraq (2002) 11 October, chaired by Professor Colin Warbrick, London

Matthews, R. and Young, J. (eds) (1986) *Issues in Realist Criminology*. London: Sage

Matza, D. (1964) *Delinquency and Drift*. New York: Wiley

Meade, M., Florin, J. and Gesler, W. (1988) *Medical Geography*. New York: Guilford Press

Means, R. and Smith, R. (2003) *Community Care: Policy and Practice*. 3rd edition. Bristol: Policy Press

Mencap (n.d.) Advocacy: making choices. Available at *http://www.mencap.org.uk/what-we-do/our-services/advocacy*

Mendes, R. (2013) Active ageing: a right or a duty? *Health Sociology Review* 22(2): 174–85

Mental Health Foundation (2012) Employment is vital for maintaining good health. Available at *http://www.mentalhealth.org.uk/our-news/blog/120629/*

Merton, R. (1938) Social structure and anomie. *American Sociological Review* 3(October): 672–82

Messerschmidt, J. (1993) *Masculinities and Crime*. Lanham, MD: Rowman and Littlefield

Micali, N., Hagberg, K.W., Petersen, I. and Treasure, J.L. (2013) The incidence of eating disorders in the UK in 2000–2009: findings from the General Practitioner Research Database. *BMJ Open* 3. Available at *http://bmjopen.bmj.com/content/3/5/e002646.full?rss=1*

Miles, R. (1989) *Racism*. London: Routledge

Millett, K. (1977) *Sexual Politics*. London: Virago

Mills, C.W. (1959) *The Sociological Imagination*. New York: Oxford University Press

Milmo, C. (2004) The woman on the plinth: the story of Alison Lapper. *Independent*, 17 March

Milner, C., Van Norman, K. and Milner, J. (2011) The media's portrayal of ageing. In J. Beard, S. Biggs, D. Bloom, L. Fried, P. Hogan, A. Kalache and S.J. Olshansky (eds) *Global Population Ageing: Peril or Promise*? Geneva: World Economic Forum

Milner, D. (1975) *Children and Race*. Harmondsworth: Penguin

Milner, J. and Myers, S. (2007) *Working with Violence: Policies and Practices in Risk Assessment and Management*. Basingstoke: Palgrave Macmillan

Ministry of Justice (2011) *Achieving Best Evidence in Criminal Proceedings: Guidance on Interviewing Victims and Witnesses and Guidance on Using Special Measures*. London: HMSO

Ministry of Justice (2012a) *Statistics: Women and the Criminal Justice System*. 22 November. Available at *http://www.justice.gov.uk/statistics/criminal-justice/women*

Ministry of Justice (2012b) *Restorative Justice Action Plan for the Criminal Justice System*. London: HMSO

Ministry of Justice (2012c) *Swift and Sure Justice: The Government's Plans for Reform of the Criminal Justice System*. London: HMSO

Mohanty, C.T. (1992) Feminist encounters: locating the politics of experience. In M. Barrett and A. Phillips (eds) *Destabilizing Theory: Contemporary Feminist Debates*. Cambridge: Polity

Moore, M. (2013) Disability, global conflicts and crises. *Disability and Society* 28(6): 741–3

Moran, N., Arksey, H., Glendinning, C., Jones, K., Netten, A. and Rabiee, P. (2012) Personalisation and carers: Whose rights? Whose benefits? *British Journal of Social Work* 42(3): 461–79

Morgan, C. and Hutchinson, G. (2010) The social determinants of psychosis in migrant and ethnic minority populations: a public health tragedy. *Psychological Medicine* 40: 705–9

Morgan, David (1996) *Family Connections: An Introduction to Family Studies*. Cambridge: Polity

Morgan, Diane (1999) What does a transsexual want? The encounter between psychoanalysis and transsexualism. In K. Moore and S. Whittle (eds) *Reclaiming Genders: Transsexual Grammars at the Fin de Siècle*. London: Cassell

Morgan, T. (2011) *Thinking the Unthinkable: Might There Be No Way Out for Britain? Project Armageddon – the Final Report*. Available from *http://www.tullettprebon.com/Documents/strategyinsights/Tim_Morgan_Report_007.pdf*

Moriarty, J., Manthorpe, J., Stevens, M. and Hussein, S. (2011) Making the transition: comparing research on newly qualified social workers with other professions. *British Journal of Social Work* 41(7): 1340–56

Morley, C. and Dunstan, J. (2013) Critical reflection: a response to neoliberal challenges to field education? *Social Work Education: The International Journal* 32(2): 141–56

Morrell, G., Scott, S., McNeish, D. and Webster, S. (2011). *The August Riots in England: Understanding the Involvement of Young People*. London: National Centre for Social Research

Morris, J. (1989) *Able Lives: Women's Experience of Paralysis*. London: Women's Press

Morris J. (2004) Independent living and community care: a disempowering framework. *Disability and Society* 19(5): 427–43

Morrison, T. (2007) Emotional intelligence, emotion and social work: context, characteristics, complications and contribution. *British Journal of Social Work* 37(2): 245–63

Murdock, G.P. (1949) *Social Structure.* New York: Palgrave Macmillan

Murray, C. (1994) *Underclass: The Crisis Deepens.* London: IEA

Myers, S. (2008) Revisiting Lancaster: more things that every social work student should know. *Social Work Education: The International Journal* 27(2): 203–11

Nathan, J. and Webber, M. (2010) Mental health social work and the bureau-medicalization of mental health care: identity in a changing world. *Journal of Social Work Practice* 24(1), 15–28

National Centre for Social Research (2012) *Smoking, Drinking and Drug Use among Young People in England in 2012.* The Health and Social Care Information Centre

Navarro, V. (1976) *Medicine under Capitalism.* London: Croom Helm

Nelson, A. (2012) *Social Work with Substance Users.* London: Sage

Nettleton, S. (2013) *Sociology of Health and Illness.* 2nd edition. Cambridge: Polity

Nicholson, L. (ed.) (1990) *Feminism/Postmodernism.* London: Routledge

Norfolk, Suffolk and Cambridgeshire Strategic Health Authority (2003) *Independent Inquiry into the Death of David Bennett.* Available at *http://www.irr.org.uk/pdf/bennett_inquiry.pdf*

Norman, A. (1985) *Triple Jeopardy: Growing Old in a Second Homeland.* London: Centre for Policy on Ageing

Norton, R. (1992) *Mother Clap's Molly House: The Gay Subculture in England, 1700–1830.* London: Gay Men's Press

Nott, J. and Gliddon, G. (1854) Types of mankind. In M. Haralambos, R.M. Heald and M. Holborn (eds) *Sociology: Themes and Perspectives.* London: Collins, 2004

NSPCC (2009) *Family Group Conferences in Child Protection* (Factsheet). August. Available at *https://www.nspcc.org.uk/Inform/research/questions/family_group_conferences_in_the_child_protection_process_wda68725.html*

NSPCC (2012) *NSPCC Written Evidence to the Joint Committee on Human Rights Inquiry into the Human Rights of Unaccompanied Migrant Children and Young People in the UK.* October. Available at *http://www.nspcc.org.uk/Inform/research/ctail/evidence-unaccompanied-migrant-children_wdf92733.pdf)*

NSPCC (2014a) *NSPCC Factsheet: Gillick Competency and Fraser Guidelines.* Available at *http://www.nspcc.org.uk/Inform/research/briefings/gillick_wda101615.html*

NSPCC (2014b) *How Safe Are Our Children? NSPCC Research Findings.* March. Available at *http://www.nspcc.org.uk/Inform/research/findings/howsafe/how-safe-2014_wda101852.html*

Nwabuzo, O. (2012) *The Riot Roundtables.* London: Runnymede Trust.

Oak, E. (2009) *Social Work and Social Perspectives.* London: Palgrave Macmillan

Oakley, A. (1974) *The Sociology of Housework.* Oxford: Martin Robertson

O'Byrne, D. (2011) *Introducing Sociological Theory.* Harlow: Pearson Education

Oduaran, A. and Oduaran, C. (2010) Grandparents and HIV and AIDS in sub-Saharan Africa. In M. Izuhara (ed.) *Ageing and Intergenerational Relations: Family Reciprocity from a Global Perspective.* Bristol: Policy Press

OECD (2009) *Health at a Glance 2009: OECD Indicators.* Available at *http://www.oecd.org/health/health-systems/44117530.pdf*

Office of the Deputy Prime Minister (2004) *Mental Health and Social Exclusion: Social Exclusion Unit Report Summary.* London: Social Exclusion Unit

Office for National Statistics (2000) *Social Trends no. 30.* London: HMSO

Office for National Statistics (2001) *The Census 2001.* Available at *http://www.ons.gov.uk*

Office for National Statistics (2005) *Labour Force Survey, Spring 2005 Dataset.* London: HMSO

Office for National Statistics (2006) *Social Trends no. 36.* London: HMSO

Office for National Statistics (2010a) *Social Trends no. 41.* London: HMSO

Office for National Statistics (2010b) *National Population Projections-Based Statistical Bulletin Coverage: UK.* London: HMSO

Office for National Statistics (2011) *The Census 2011*. Available at *http://www.ons.gov.uk*

Office for National Statistics (2012a) *Families and Households, 2012*. Available at *http://www.ons.gov. uk/ons/rel/family-demography/families-and-households/2012/stb-families-households.html*

Office for National Statistics (2012b) *Ethnicity and National Identity in England and Wales 2011*. Available at *http://www.ons.gov.uk/ons/dcp171776_290558.pdf*

Office for National Statistics (2013a) *Detailed Characteristics for England and Wales, March 2011*. Available at *http://www.ons.gov.uk/ons/dcp171778_310514.pdf*

Office for National Statistics (2013b) *Full Story: The Gender Gap in Unpaid Care Provision: Is There an Impact on Health and Economic Position?* London: HMSO

Office for National Statistics (2013c) *Focus on: Violent Crime and Sexual Offences, 2011/12*. London: HMSO

Office for National Statistics (2014) *Stepfamilies in 2011*. London: HMSO. Available at *http://www. ons.gov.uk/ons/rel/family-demography/stepfamilies/2011/stepfamilies-rpt.html?format=print*

O'Keeffe, M., Hills, A., Doyle, M., McCreadie, C., Scholes, S., Constantine, R, Tinker, A., Manthorpe, J., Biggs, S. and Erens, B. (2007) *UK Study of Abuse and Neglect of Older People Prevalence Survey Report*. London: Comic Relief and Department of Health

Oliver, M. (1990) *The Politics of Disablement*. London: Macmillan

Oliver, M. (1993) Disability and dependency: a creation of industrial societies? In J. Swain, V. Finkelstein, S. French and M. Oliver (eds) *Disabling Barrier – Enabling Environments*. London: Sage

Oliver, M. (2004) The social model in action: if I had a hammer. In C. Barnes and G. Mercer (eds) *Implementing the Social Model of Disability: Theory and Research*. Leeds: The Disability Press

Oliver, M. (2013) The social model of disability: thirty years on. *Disability and Society* 28(7): 1024–6

Oliver, M. and Barnes, C. (2012a) Back to the future: the World Report on Disability. *Disability and Society* 27(4): 575–9

Oliver, M. and Barnes, C. (2012b) *The New Politics of Disablement*. London: Palgrave

Oliver, M. and Sapey, B. (2006) *Social Work with Disabled People*. 3rd edition Basingstoke: Palgrave Macmillan

Oliver, M., Sapey, B. and Thomas, P. (2012) *Social Work with Disabled People*. 4th edition. London: Palgrave

Owen, C. and Statham, J. (2009) *Disproportionality in Child Welfare – The Prevalence of Black and Minority Ethnic Children within the 'Looked After' and 'Children in Need' Populations and on Child Protection Registers in England*. Institute of Education, University of London.

Owusu-Bempah, J. (1993) Toeing the white line. In J. Clarke (ed.) *A Crisis in Care? Challenges to Social Work*. London: Sage/The Open University

Pakulski, J. and Waters, M. (1996) *The Death of Class*. London: Sage

Parekh, B. (2000) *The Future of Multi-Ethnic Britain*. London: Profile Books

Parker, J. and Crabtree, S. (2012) Fish need bicycles: an exploration of the perceptions of male social work students on a qualifying course. *British Journal of Social Work* 44(2): 310–27

Parkin, F. (1979) *Marxism and Class Theory: A Bourgeois Critique*. Cambridge: Cambridge University Press

Parsons, T. (1951) *The Social System*. London: Routledge and Kegan Paul

Parsons, T. and Bales, R. (eds) (1955) *Family, Socialization and Interaction Process*. New York: Free Press

Pascall, G. (1997) *Social Policy: A New Feminist Analysis*. London: Routledge

Paul, J. (2002) Suicide attempts among gay and bisexual men: lifetime precedents and antecedents. *American Journal of Public Health* 92(8): 1338–45

Payne, M. (2005) *Modern Social Work Theory: A Critical Introduction*. 2nd edition. London: Palgrave Macmillan

Pearce, J. and Pitts, J.M. (2011) *Youth Gangs, Sexual Violence and Sexual Exploitation: A Scoping Exercise for The Office of the Children's Commissioner for England*. University of Bedfordshire Institute for Applied Social Research.

Pease, R. and Pringle, K. (2001) *A Man's World? Changing Men's Practices in a Globalized World*. London: Zed Books

Peckover, S., Broadhurst, K., White, S., Wastell, D. and Pithouse, A. (2011) The fallacy of formalisation: practice makes process in the assessment of risks to children. In H. Kemshall and B. Wilkinson (eds) *Good Practice in Assessing Risk: Current Knowledge, Issues and Approaches*. London: Jessica Kingsley

Penhale, B. and Parker, J. (2008) *Working with Vulnerable Adults*. London: Routledge

Penna, S. and O'Brien, M. (2013) Neoliberalism. In M. Gray and S. Webb (eds) *Social Work Theories and Methods*. London: Sage

Perrons, D. (2009) *Women and Gender Equity in Employment: Patterns, Progress and Challenges*. Institute for Employment Studies, Working Paper 23.

Perrott, S. (2009) Social work and organizations. In R. Adams, L. Dominelli and M. Payne (eds) *Social Work: Themes, Issues and Critical Debates*. 3rd edition. London: Palgrave

Perry, E. and Francis, B. (2010) *The Social Class Gap for Educational Attainment: A Review of the Literature*. RSA Projects. Available at *http://www.thersa.org/action-research-centre/learning,-cogniton-and-creativity/education/social-justice/the-social-class-gap-for-educational-achievement-a-review-of-the-literature*

Peterson, K. (2004) Looking straight at gay parents. *USA Today*, 9 March. Available at *http://usato day30.usatoday.com/life/lifestyle/2004-03-09-gay-parents_x.htm*

Pew Research Centre (2006) *Europe's Muslims More Moderate: The Great Divide: How Westerners and Muslims View Each Other*. 13-Nation Pew Global Attitudes Survey

Phelan, A. (2010) Socially constructing older people: examining discourses which can shape nurses' understanding and practice. *Journal of Advanced Nursing* 67(4): 893–903

Phillips, J., Ray, M. and Marshall, M. (2006) *Social Work with Older People*. 4th edition. London: Palgrave Macmillan

Phillipson, C. (1998) *Reconstructing Old Age*. London: Sage

Phoenix, A. (1991) *Young Mothers?* Cambridge: Polity

Phoenix, C. and Sparkes, A. C. (2009). Being Fred: big stories, small stories and the accomplishment of a positive ageing identity. *Qualitative Research* 9(2): 83–99

Pickard, S. (1995) *Living on the Front Line*. Aldershot: Avebury

Pilgrim, D. (2009) *Key Concepts in Mental Health*. London: Sage

Pilkington, A. (2003) *Racial Disadvantage and Ethnic Diversity in Britain*. London: Palgrave Macmillan

Pinnock, M. (2004) Rage against the machine. *Community Care*, 15 April. Available at *http://www. communitycare.co.uk/2004/04/15/rage-against-the-machine/*

Playdon, Z. J. (2004) Intersecting oppressions: ending discrimination against lesbians, gay men and trans people in the UK. In B. Brooks-Gordon, L. Gelsthorpe, M. Johnson and A. Bainham (eds) *Sexuality Repositioned: Diversity and the Law*. Oxford: Hart

Pollack, S. (2010) Labelling clients 'risky': social work and the neo-liberal welfare state. *British Journal of Social Work* 40(4): 1263–78

Powell, F. (2001) *The Politics of Social Work*. London: Sage

Powell, J. (2001) Theorizing gerontology: the case of old age, professional power, and social policy in the United Kingdom. *Journal of Aging and Identity* 6(3): 117–35

Power, C. (2004) *Room to Roam: England's Irish Travellers*. Report of Research Funded by the Community Fund. June

Press Association (2012) Witchcraft murder couple jailed for life. *Guardian*, 5 March. Available at *http://www.theguardian.com/uk/2012/mar/05/witchcraft-couple-jailed-for-life*

Prideaux, S.J. (2005) *Not So New Labour: A Sociological Critique of New Labour's Policy and Practice*. Bristol: Policy Press

Priestley, M. (1999) *Disability Politics and Community Care*. London: Jessica Kingsley

Prime Minister's Strategy Unit (2005) *Improving the Life Chances of Disabled People: A Joint Report with Department of Work and Pensions, Department of Health, Department for Education and Skills, Office of the Deputy Prime Minister*. London: Cabinet Office

Prince's Trust (2007) *The Cost of Exclusion: Counting the Cost of Youth Disadvantage in the UK.* London: Prince's Trust

Pringle, K. (1995) *Men, Masculinities and Social Welfare.* London: UCL Press

Prior, P. (1999) *Gender and Mental Health.* Basingstoke: Macmillan

Prison Reform Trust (2013) *Prison: The Facts.* Available at *http://www.prisonreformtrust.org.uk/ Portals/0/Documents/Prisonthefacts.pdf*

Public Health England (2014) *Child Obesity.* London: HMSO

Puhl, R. and Heuer, C. (2009) The stigma of obesity: a review and update. *Obesity,* October: 1–24

Putnam, R.D. (2000) *Bowling Alone: The Collapse and Revival of American Community.* New York: Simon and Schuster

PwC (2013) *Women in Work Index.* Available at *http://www.pwc.co.uk/the-economy/publications/ women-in-work-index.jhtml*

Quam, J.K. (1997) The story of Carrie and Annie. *Journal of Gay and Lesbian Social Services* 6(1): 97–9

Qvortrup, J. (1991) *Childhood as a Social Phenomenon: An Introduction to a Series of National Reports.* 2nd edition. Vienna: European Centre for Social Welfare Policy and Research

Qvortrup, J. (1994) Childhood matters: an introduction. In J. Ovortrup, M. Bardy, G. Sgritta and H. Wintersberger (eds) *Childhood Matters: Social Theory, Practice and Politics.* Aldershot: Avebury

Race, D. (2002) *Learning Disability: A Social Approach.* London: Routledge

Radley, A. (ed.) (1993) *Worlds of Illness: Biographical and Cultural Perspectives on Health and Disease.* London: Routledge

Raleigh, V.S. (1996) Suicide patterns and trends in people of Indian subcontinent and Caribbean origin in England and Wales. *Ethnicity and Health* 1: 55–63

Ralph, R. and Corrigan, P. (eds) (2005) *Recovery in Mental Illness: Broadening Our Understanding of Wellness.* Washington, DC: American Psychological Association

Ramon, S. (2009) Adult mental health in a changing international context: the relevance to social work. *British Journal of Social Work* 39(8): 1615–22

Rattansi, R. (1992) Changing the subject? Racism, culture and education. In J. Donald and A. Rattansi *'Race', Culture and Difference.* London: Sage

Rau, R., Soroko, E., Jasilionis, D. and Vaupel, J.W. (2008) Continued reductions in mortality at advanced ages. *Population and Development Review* 34(4): 747–68

Ray, M., Bernard, M. and Phillips, J. (2009) *Critical Issues in Social Work with Older People.* Basingstoke: Palgrave Macmillan

Ray, S., Sharp, E. and Abrams, D. (2006) *Ageism: A Benchmark of Public Attitudes in Britain.* Age Concern England and University of Kent, Centre for the Study of Group Processes. London: Age Concern; Canterbury: Centre for the Study of Group Processes

Repper, J. and Perkins, R. (2003) *Social Inclusion and Recovery: A Model for Mental Health Practice.* Edinburgh: Bailliere Tindall

Revans, L. (2007) Voice's Blueprint project: children in care have their say. *Looked After Children,* 11 July. Available at *http://www.communitycare.co.uk/2007/07/11/voices-blueprint-project-children-in-care-have-their-say/*

Rex, J. and Tomlinson, S. (1970) *Colonial Immigrants in a British City: A Class Analysis.* London: Routledge and Kegan Paul

Rich, A. (1980) Compulsory heterosexual and lesbian existence. *Signs* 54: 631–60

Richardson, D. (1998) Sexuality and citizenship. *Sociology* 32(1): 83–100

Richardson, D. (2000) *Re-Thinking Sexuality.* London: Sage

Rivers, I. (1995) Mental health issues among young lesbians and gay men bullied in school. *Health and Social Care in the Community* 3(6): 380–8

Roach, S.M. (2004) Sexual behaviour of nursing home residents: staff perceptions and responses. *Journal of Advanced Nursing* 48(4): 371–9

Robinson, K. (2005). Childhood and sexuality: adult constructions and silenced children. In J. Mason and T. Fattore (eds) *Children Taken Seriously: In Theory, Policy and Practice.* London: Jessica Kingsley

Robinson, W. and Harris, J. (2000) Towards a global ruling class? Globalization and the transnational capitalist class. *Science & Society* 64(1): 11–54

Rogers, A. and Pilgrim, D. (2001) *Mental Health Policy in Britain*. 2nd edition. Basingstoke: Palgrave

Rogers, A. and Pilgrim, D. (2010) *A Sociology of Mental Health and Illness*. 4th edition. Buckingham: Open University Press

Rose, H. (1981) Rereading Titmuss: the sexual division of labour. *Journal of Social Policy* 10(4): 477–502

Rosenham, D. (1973) On being sane in insane places. *Science* 179(4070): 250–8

Ross, L. and Waterson, J. (1996) Risk for whom? Social work and people with physical disabilities. In H. Kemshall and J. Pritchard (eds) *Good Practice in Risk Assessment and Risk Management 1*. London: Jessica Kingsley

Roulstone, A. (2012) 'Stuck in the middle with you': towards enabling social work with disabled people. *Social Work Education: The International Journal* 31(2): 142–54

Ruch, G. (2005) Relationship-based practice and reflective practice: holistic approaches to contemporary child care social work. *Child and Family Social Work* 10(2):111–23

Runnymede Trust (1985) *Education for All*. A Summary of the Swann Report on the Education of Minority Children. London: Runnymede Trust.

Runnymede Trust (1997) *Islamophobia: A Challenge for Us All*. Report of the Commission on British Muslims and Islamophobia, chaired by Gordon Conway. London: Runnymede Trust.

Ruth, J.E. and Kenyon, G. (1996) Biography in adult development and aging. In J.E. Birren, G.M. Kenyon, J.E. Ruth, J.J.F. Schroots and T. Svensson (eds) *Aging and Biography: Explorations in Adult Development.* New York: Springer

Rutherford, T. (2012) *Population Ageing: Statistics*. London: House of Commons Library

Said, E. (1997) *Orientalism*. London: Harmondsworth

Sainsbury Centre for Mental Health (2002) *Breaking the Circles of Fear: A Review of the Relationship between Mental Health Services and African and Caribbean Communities*. London: Sainsbury Centre for Mental Health

Saltiel, D. (2013) Understanding complexity in families' lives: the usefulness of 'family practices' as an aid to decision-making. *Child and Family Social Work* 18: 15–24

Samuel, M. (2011) The rise of non-qualified social care staff under personalisation. *Community Care*, 20 May. Available at *http://www.communitycare.co.uk/2011/05/20/the-rise-of-non-qualified-social-care-staff-under-personalisation/*

Sandman, D., Simantov, E. and An, C. (2000) *Out of Touch: American Men and the Health Care System*. New York: The Commonwealth Fund

Sarup, D. (1996) *Identity, Culture and the Postmodern World*. Edinburgh/Edinburgh University Press

Sashidharan, S.P. (2003) *Inside Outside: Improving Mental Health Services for Black and Minority Ethnic Communities in England*. Department of Health. Available at *http://webarchive.national archives.gov.uk/+/www.dh.gov.uk/en/Publicationsandstatistics/Publications/PublicationsPolicy AndGuidance/DH_4084558*

Savage, M. and Warde, A. (1993) *Urban Sociology, Capitalism and Modernity*. Basingstoke: Macmillan

Save the Children (2007) *Child Trafficking in Manchester: A Report on the Evidence and Agency Responses to Child Trafficking*. London: Save the Children

Scambler, G. (1997) *Sociology as Applied to Medicine*. 4th edition. London: Bailliere Tindall

Scarman Report (1982) *The Brixton Disorders, April 10–12, 1981: Report of an Inquiry by the Rt. Hon. The Lord Scarman, OBE*. London: HMSO

Scharf, T. and Keating, N. (eds) (2012) *From Exclusion to Inclusion in Old Age: A Global Challenge*. Bristol: Policy Press

Scharf, T., Phillipson, C. and Kingston, A.E. (2003) *Older People in Deprived Neighbourhoods: Social Exclusion and Quality of Life in Old Age*. ESRC Project.

Scheff, T. (1966) *Being Mentally Ill: A Sociological Theory*. Chicago: Aldine

Schizophrenia Commission (2012) *The Abandoned Illness: A Report from the Schizophrenia Commission*. London: Rethink Mental Illness

Schneider, J. (2000) Effects of cybersex addiction on the family: results of a survey. *Sexual Addiction and Compulsivity* 7: 31–58

Schon, D.A. (1983) *Educating the Reflective Practitioner: Towards a New Design for Teaching and Learning in the Professions*. San Francisco: Jossey-Bass

Scott, H. (1984) *Working Your Way to the Bottom: The Feminization of Poverty*. London: Pandora Press

Scott-Hill, M. (2004) Impairment, difference and 'identity'. In J. Swain, S. French, C. Barnes and J. Thomas (eds) *Disabling Barriers – Enabling Environments*. 2nd edition. London: Sage

Scraton, P. (ed.) (1987) *Law, Order and the Authoritarian State*. Milton Keynes: Open University Press

Scull, A. (1979) *Museums of Madness*. Harmondsworth: Penguin

Selwyn, J., Frazer, L. and Fitzgerald, A. (2004) *Finding Adoptive Families for Black, Asian and Black Mixed-Parentage Children: Agency Policy and Practice*. Executive summary and best practice guide. London: NCH

Shah, A. (2010) *Poverty Facts and Stats*. Global Issues, 20 September. Available at *http://www.globalissues.org/*

Shah, R., McNiece, N. and Majeed, A. (2001) Socio-demographic differences in general practice consultation rates for psychiatric disorders among patients aged 16–64. *Health Statistics Quarterly* 11: 5–10

Shakespeare, T. (1998) Choices and rights: eugenics, genetics and disability equality. *Disability & Society* 13(5): 665–81

Shakespeare, T. and Watson, N. (2001) The social model of disability: an outdated ideology? *Research and Social Sciences and Disability* 2: 9–28

Shakespeare, T., Gillespie-Sells, K. and Davies, D. (1996) The sexual politics of disability: untold desires. *Journal of the Royal College of General Practitioners* 26: 746–50

Sharkey, P. (2007) *The Essentials of Community Care*. London: Palgrave

Sheldon, A. (2004) Women and disability. In J. Swain, S. French, C. Barnes and C. Thomas (eds) *Disabling Barriers – Enabling Environments*. 2nd edition. London: Sage

Sheldon, B. and MacDonald, G. (2009) *A Textbook for Social Work*. London: Routledge

Shelter (n.d.) *The Impact of Domestic Violence and Abuse on a Family's Housing Situation and Their Emotional and Physical Wellbeing*. Bristol Keys To The Future (KTTF). Available at *http://england.shelter.org.uk/__data/assets/pdf_file/0017/273500/Case_study_domestic_abuse_Bristol.pdf*

Sherry, M.J. (1973) *The Nature and Evolution of Female Sex*. New York: Random House

Shilling, C. (1993) *The Body and Social Theory*. London: Sage

Showalter, E. (1987) *The Female Malady: Women, Madness and English Culture 1830–1980*. Harmondsworth: Penguin

Sigman, A. (2012) Children 'spend more time watching TV than at school'. *The Telegraph*, 9 October 2012. Available at *http://www.telegraph.co.uk/education/educationnews/9595317/Children-spend-more-time-watching-TV-than-at-school.html*

Simon, A., Owen, C., Moss, P. and Cameron, C. (2003) *Mapping the Care Workforce: Supporting Joined-Up Thinking*. London: Institute of Education

Sinfield, A. (1978) Analyses in the social division of welfare. *Journal of Social Policy* 7(2): 129–56

Singh, G. (1992) *Race and Social Work: From Black Pathology to Black Perspectives*. Race Relations Unit, University of Bradford

Sissay, L. (2012) On inter-racial adoption, Cameron is wrong. Colour blindness is a disability. *Guardian*, 13 March. Available at *http://www.theguardian.com/commentisfree/2012/mar/13/inter-racial-adoption-cameron-wrong*

Sivanandan, A. (2004) *Racism in the Age of Globalization*. London: Institute of Race Relations

Sloan, P. (2011) *Housing and Regeneration Research*. Communities Analytical Services, Scottish Government.

Smaje, C. (1995) *Health, 'Race' and Ethnicity: Making Sense of the Evidence*. London: King's Fund Institute

Smart, C. (1977) *Women, Crime and Criminology*. London: Routledge and Kegan Paul

Smith, A. (1986) *The Ethnic Origins of Nations*. Oxford: Blackwell

Smith, R. (2008) *Social Work and Power*. London: Palgrave

Smith-Battle, L. (2000) The vulnerabilities of teenage mothers. *Advances in Nursing Science*, September: 29–40

Social Care Institute for Excellence (2005a) *Being a Father to a Child with Disabilities: Issues and What Helps*. Research Briefing. 18 October. London: SCIE

Social Care Institute for Excellence (2005b) *Managing Risk and Minimising Mistakes in Services to Children and Families*. London: SCIE

Social Care Institute for Excellence (2007) *A Common Purpose: Recovery in Future Mental Health Services*. London: SCIE

Social Care Institute for Excellence (2010) *Dignity in Care*. Available at *http://www.scie.org.uk/publications/guides/guide15/*

Social Care Institute for Excellence (2011a) *Child Protection with BME Families: A Conference Report*. May. London: SCIE

Social Care Institute for Excellence (2011b) *Mental Health, Employment and the Social Care Workforce*. London: SCIE

Social Services Inspectorate Wales (2000) *In Safe Hands*. Cardiff: HMSO

Social Work Reform Board (2010) *Building a Safe and Confident Future: One Year On*. Progress Report from the Social Work Reform Board. Available at *http://www.education.gov.uk/swrb*

Spicker, P. (2011) *Social Policy: Theory and Practice*. 3rd edition. Bristol: Policy Press

Stainton, T. and Boyce, S. (2004) 'I have got my life back': users' experience of direct payments. *Disability and Society* 19(5): 443–54

Stalker, K. (2003) Managing risk and uncertainty in social work: a literature review. *Journal of Social Work* 3(2): 211–33

Stanford, S. (2010) 'Speaking back' to fear: responding to the moral dilemmas of risk in social work practice. *British Journal of Social Work* 40(4): 1065–80

Stanford, S. (2011) Constructing moral responses to risk: a framework for hopeful social work practice. *British Journal of Social Work* 41(8): 1514–31

Statham, J. (2011) *Grandparents Providing Child Care*. Loughborough: Childhood Wellbeing Research Centre

Stice, E. (2002) Risk and maintenance factors for eating pathology: a meta-analytic review. *Psychological Bulletin* 128(5): 825–48

Stoller, E. and Gibson, R.C. (1994) *Worlds of Difference: Inequality and the Aging Experience*. Thousand Oaks, CA: Pine Forge Press

Stonewall (2012) *The School Report: The Experience of Gay Young People in Britain*. Stonewall/Centre of Family Research, University of Cambridge

Strickland, P. (2013) *Domestic Violence: House of Commons Library*. London: HMSO

Swain, J. and French, S. (2014) International perspectives on disability. In J. Swain, S. French, C. Barnes and C. Thomas (eds) *Disabling Barriers – Enabling Environments*. 3rd edition. London: Sage

Taylor, D. and Field, S. (2007) *Sociology of Health and Health Care*. 4th edition. Oxford: Blackwell

Taylor, F.W. (1911) *Principles of Scientific Management*. New York: Harper

Taylor, G. (1989) Challenges from the margins. In J. Clarke (ed.) *A Crisis in Care? Challenges to Social Work*. London: Sage/The Open University

Taylor, I., Walton, P. and Young, J. (1973) *The New Criminology: For a Social Theory of Deviance*. London: Routledge and Kegan Paul

Tew, J. (2011) *Social Approaches to Mental Distress*. London: Palgrave

Tew, J., Ramon, S., Slade, M., Bird, V., Melton, J. and Boutillier, C. (2012) Social factors and recovery from mental health difficulties: a review of the evidence. *British Journal of Social Work* 42(3): 443–60

Thoits, P.A. (1985) Self-labelling process in mental illness: the role of emotional deviance. *American Journal of Sociology* 91: 221–49

Thomas, C. (1999) *Female Forms: Experiencing and Understanding Disability*. Buckingham: Open University Press

Thomas, C. (2004) How is disability understood? An examination of sociological approaches. *Disability and Society* 19(6): 569–83

Thomas, D. and Woods, H. (2003) *Working with People with Learning Disabilities: Theory to Practice*. London: Jessica Kingsley

Thomas, N. (2005) *Social Work with Young People in Care*. London: Palgrave Macmillan

Thompson, N. (1998) *Promoting Equality: Challenging Discrimination and Oppression in the Human Services*. Basingstoke: Macmillan

Thompson, N. (2005) *Understanding Social Work: Preparing for Practice*. 2nd edition. Basingstoke: Palgrave

Thompson, P. (1989) *The Nature of Work*. 2nd edition. Basingstoke: Macmillan

Thorogood, N. (1987) Race, class and gender: the politics of housework. In J. Brannen and G. Wilson (eds) *Give and Take in Families*. London: Allen & Unwin

Tinker, A. (1992) *Elderly People in Modern Society*. London: Longman

Titmuss, R.M. (1958) *Essays on 'the Welfare State'*. London: Allen & Unwin

Titmuss, R.M. (1967) The relationship between income maintenance and social service benefits: an overview. *International Social Security Review* 20(1): 57–66

Titterton, M. (2011) Positive risk taking with people at risk of harm. In H. Kemshall and B. Wilkinson (eds) *Good Practice in Assessing Risk: Current Knowledge, Issues and Approaches*. London: Jessica Kingsley

Tocqueville, A. de (1994) *Democracy in America*. London: Fontana

Toennies, F. (1963) *Community and Society*. New York: Harper and Row

Townsend, P. (1979) *Poverty in the United Kingdom: A Survey of Household Resources and Standards of Living*. Harmondsworth: Penguin

Townsend, P. (1981) The structured dependency of the elderly: a creation of social policy in the twentieth century. *Ageing and Society* 1(1): 5–28

Trotter, J. (2000) Lesbian and gay issues in social work with young people: resilience and success through confronting, conforming and escaping. *British Journal of Social Work* 30(1): 115–23

Tsui, M. (2005) *Social Work Supervision*. London: Sage

Tumin, M. (1953) Some principles of stratification: a critical analysis. *American Sociological Review* 18(4): 387–93

Tumin, M. (2010) 'Some principles of stratification' by Kingsley Davis and Wilbert Moore, with a response by Melvin Tumin. In J. Macionis and N. Benokraitis (eds) *Seeing Ourselves: Classic, Contemporary, and Cross-Cultural Readings in Sociology*. 4th edition. London: Pearson

Turner, B.S. (1992) *Regulating Bodies: Essays in Medical Sociology*, London: Routledge

Twigg, J. (1993) *Informal Care in Europe*. University of York Social Policy Research Unit

UK Border Agency (2013) *Processing an Asylum Application from a Child*. Available at *https://www.gov.uk/government/uploads/system/uploads/attachment_data/file/257469/processingasylumapplication1.pdf*

UK Cards Association (2011) *A Decade of Cards - 2000-2010 and Beyond*. London: UK Cards Association

UK Parliament (2010) *The Ageing Population*. Briefing Paper. Available at *http://www.parliament.uk*

UNAIDS (2006) *UNAIDS Report on the Global AIDS Epidemic*. Available at *http://www.unaids.org.globalreport/Global_report.htm*

Ungerson, C. (1997) Social politics and the commodification of care. *Social Politics* 4: 362–81

UNICEF (2006) *Child Protection Information Sheet: What is Child Protection?* Available at *http://www.unicef.org/publications/index_34146.html*

United Nations (1985) *Standard Minimum Rules for the Administration of Juvenile Justice (the Beijing Rules)*. New York: UN

United Nations (1989) *Convention on the Rights of the Child*. Resolution 44/25, 20 November. New York: UN

United Nations Office on Drugs and Crime (2012) *Global Report on Trafficking in Persons*. Available at *http://www.unodc.org/documents/data-and-analysis/glotip/Trafficking_in_Persons_2012_web.pdf*

United Nations Office on Drugs and Crime (2013). *World Drug Report*. Available at *http://www.unodc.org/unodc/secured/wdr/wdr2013/World_Drug_Report_2013.pdf*

US Department of State (2007) *Trafficking in Persons Report*. Available at *http://www.state.gov/j/tip/rls/tiprpt/2007/*

Van Gennep, A. (1960) *The Rites of Passage*. London: Routledge and Kegan Paul

van Wormer, K., Roberts, A.R., Springer, D.W. and Brownell, P. (2008) Forensic social work: current and emerging developments. In K.M. Sowers and B. White (eds) *Comprehensive Handbook of Social Work and Social Welfare: The Profession of Social Work*, Vol. 1. Hoboken, NJ: John Wiley & Sons

Victor, C. (2005) *The Social Context of Ageing: A Textbook of Gerontology*. London: Routledge

Victor C. and Bowling, A. (2012) A longitudinal analysis of loneliness among older people in Great Britain. *Journal of Psychology* 146(3): 313–31

Victor, C., Burholt, V. and Martin, W. (2012) Loneliness and ethnic minority elders in Great Britain: an exploratory study. *Journal of Cross-Cultural Gerontology* 27(1): 65–78

Vincent, J., Tulle, E. and Bond, J. (2008) The anti-ageing enterprise: science, knowledge, expertise, rhetoric and values. *Journal of Aging Studies* 22: 291–4

Vogel, E. and Bell, N. (1968) The emotionally disturbed child as the family scapegoat. In N. Bell and E. Vogel (eds) *A Modern Introduction to the Family*. New York: Free Press

Vosler, N.R. (1996) *New Approaches to Family Practice: Confronting Economic Stress*. Thousand Oaks, CA: Sage

Walby, S (1990) *Theorizing Patriarchy*. London: Basil Blackwell

Walker, A. (1994) Poverty and inequality in old age. In J. Bond, P. Coleman and S.M. Peace (eds) *Ageing in Society: An Introduction to Social Gerontology*. London: Sage

Walklate, S. (1995) *Gender and Crime*. Hemel Hempstead: Harvester Wheatsheaf

Walter, T., Littlewood, J. and Pickering, M. (1995) Death in the news: the public invigilation of private emotion. *Sociology* 3(4): 579–96

Warner, M. (1993) *Fear of a Queer Planet: Queer Politics and Social Theory*. Minneapolis: University of Minnesota Press

Warren, J. (2007) *Service User and Carer Participation in Social Work*. Exeter: Learning Matters

Webb, S.A. (2006) *Social Work in a Risk Society*. London: Palgrave Macmillan

Webber, M. (2012) AMHP survey analysis: 'a depressingly familiar picture of an undervalued workforce'. *Community Care*, 2 October. Available at *http://www.communitycare.co.uk/2012/10/02/amhp-survey-analysis-a-depressingly-familiar-picture-of-an-undervalued-workforce/*

Webber, M. and Nathan, J. (2012) Social policy and mental health social work. In M. Davies (ed.) *Social Work with Adults*. London: Palgrave Macmillan

Weber, M. (1976) *The Protestant Ethic and the Spirit of Capitalism*. London: Allen & Unwin

Weeks, J. (2007) *The World We Have Won: The Remaking of Erotic and Intimate Life*. London: Routledge

Weeks, J. (2010) *Sexuality*. 3rd edition. London: Routledge

Weiss, I. (2005) Is there a global common core to social work? A cross-national comparative study of BSW graduate students. *Social Work* 50(2): 101–10

Wenger, G.C. (1991) A network typology: from theory to practice. *Journal of Aging Studies* 5: 147–62

West, C. and Zimmerman, D. (1987) Doing gender. *Gender and Society* 1(2): 125–51

White, B. (2008) *Comprehensive Handbook of Social Work and Social Welfare: The Profession of Social Work*. Hoboken, NJ: John Wiley and Sons

White, K. (2009) *An Introduction to the Sociology of Health and Illness*. 2nd edition. London: Sage

Whittington, C. (2003) *Learning for Collaborative Practice with Other Professions and Agencies: A Study to Inform the Development of the Degree in Social Work (Summary Report)*. London: Department of Health

Wigfall, V. (2006) Bringing back community: family support from the bottom up. *Children and Society* 20: 17–29

Wikström, P.-O. H., Oberwittler, D., Treiber, K. and Hardie, B. (2012) *Breaking Rules: The Social and Situational Dynamics of Young People's Urban Crime*. Oxford: Oxford University Press

Wilkins, D. and Boahen, G. (2013) *Critical Analysis Skills for Social Workers*. Maidenhead: Open University Press/McGraw-Hill Education

Williams, F. (1996) Postmodernism, feminism and the question of difference. In N. Parton (ed.) *Social Theory, Social Change and Social Work*. London: Routledge

Williams, L. and Germov, J. (1999) The thin ideal: women, food and dieting. In J. Germov and L. Williams (eds) *A Sociology of Food and Nutrition: The Social Appetite*. Oxford: Oxford University Press

Williams, M. (2013) 40% of fathers do not take paternity leave. *Guardian*, 7 January. Available at *http://careers.theguardian.com/fathers-choose-not-to-take-paternity-leave*

Williams, P. (2009) *Social Work with People with Learning Difficulties*. 2nd edition. Exeter: Learning Matters

Williams, Simon (1987) Goffman, interactionism and the management of stigma in everyday life. In G. Scambler (ed.) *Sociological Theory and Medical Sociology*. London: Tavistock

Williams, Simon Johnson (2000) *Medicine and the Body*. London: Sage

Williams-Findlay, R. (2014) The representation of disabled people in the news media. In J. Swain, S. French, C. Barnes and J. Thomas (eds) *Disabling Barriers – Enabling Environments*. 3rd edition. London: Sage

Wilson, A.N. (2006) *After the Victorians*. London: Arrow

Wilson, Gail (2000) *Understanding Old Age*. London: Sage

Wilson, George (2013) Evidencing reflective practice in social work education: theoretical uncertainties and practical challenges. *British Journal of Social Work* 43(1): 154–72

Wilson, J.Q. and Kelling, G. (1982) Broken windows. *Atlantic Monthly*, March: 29–38

Wilton, T. (2000) *Sexualities in Health and Social Care*. Buckingham: Open University Press

Windle, K., Francis, J. and Coomber, C. (2011) *Preventing Loneliness and Social Isolation: Interventions and Outcomes. Social Care Institute for Excellence (SCIE) Research Briefing 39*. Available at *http://www.scie.org.uk/publications/briefings/briefing39/*

Wolfensberger, W. (1972) *The Principle of Normalization in Human Services*. Toronto: National Institute on Mental Retardation

Wood, P. (1980) *International Classifications of Impairments, Disabilities and Handicaps*. Geneva: World Health Organization

Woodin, S. (2014) Care: controlling and personalising services. In J. Swain, S. French, C. Barnes and J. Thomas (eds) *Disabling Barriers – Enabling Environments*. 3rd edition. London: Sage

Woods, B., Spector, A., Jones, C., Orrell, M. and Davies, S. (2009) *Reminiscence Therapy for Dementia (Review)*. London: Cochrane Library

World Health Organization (n.d.a) Definition of an older or elderly person. Available at *http://www.who.int/healthinfo/survey/ageingdefnolder/en/*

World Health Organization (n.d.b) *Are You Ready? What You Need to Know About Ageing*. Available at *http://www.who.int/world-health-day/2012/toolkit/background/en/*

World Health Organizationt (2001) *World Health Report 2001: Mental Health: New Understanding, New Hope*. Available at *http://www.who.int/whr/2001/en/*

World Health Organization (2011) *World Report on Disability*. Available at *http://www.who.int/disabilities/world_report/2011/en/*

Wright, E.O. (1978) *Class, Crisis and the State*. London: New Left Books

Wright, E.O. (1997) *Class Counts: Comparative Studies in Class Analysis*. Cambridge: Cambridge University Press

Wright, F. (2012) Social work practice with unaccompanied asylum-seeking young people facing removal. *British Journal of Social Work*. Advanced Access. doi: 10.1093/bjsw/bcs175

Wurm, S., Warner, L., Ziegelmann, J., Wolff, J. and Schuz, B. (2013) How do negative self-perceptions of aging become a self-fulfilling prophecy? *Psychology and Aging* 28(4): 1088–97

Wyness, M. (2011) *Childhood and Society: An Introduction to the Sociology of Childhood*. Basingstoke: Palgrave

Young, J. (1971) *The Drug Takers*. London: Paladin

Young, J. (1986) Ten points of realism. In R. Matthews and J. Young (eds) *Issues in Realist Criminology.* London: Sage

Young, J. (1999) *The Exclusive Society: Social Exclusion, Crime and Difference in Late Modernity.* London: Sage

Young, M. (1962) *The Rise of the Meritocracy.* Harmondsworth: Penguin

Young, M. and Wilmott, P. (1973) *The Symmetrical Family: A Study of Work and Leisure in the London Region.* London: Routledge and Kegan Paul

Index